Republic of Capital

Republic of Capital

BUENOS AIRES AND
THE LEGAL TRANSFORMATION
OF THE ATLANTIC WORLD

Jeremy Adelman

STANFORD UNIVERSITY PRESS
STANFORD, CALIFORNIA

Stanford University Press
Stanford, California
© 1999 by the Board of Trustees of the
Leland Stanford Junior University
Printed in the United States of America

CIP data appear at the end of the book

To Eric, Nicole, and Jacob

⌒ Acknowledgments

This book is an effort to address several constituencies of readers who, like continents, live in almost separate intellectual worlds. Argentines, Latin Americans, North Americans, and students of the Atlantic world; historians, social scientists, and scholars of political literature—each tends to treat the other with a healthy dose of skepticism, sometimes with good reason. Other times, unwitting neglect prevails. An effort to navigate these wide expanses between the continents in our overly professionalized world runs the risk of being an unwelcome intrusion, irritating more than inspiring, bothering more than provoking. Certainly, in the course of writing *Republic of Capital* I have often lost sight of my audiences, and confused the story—or stories—I was trying to tell. I was, for very long periods of time, at sea. While aware that I could reach land eventually by taking any tack and sticking to it, I preferred to float, not wanting to lose a potential relationship with any shore.

To keep my head straight, I have needed good navigational aides. To support me when I feared that this venture was pointless, I relied on many friends and colleagues. In England, the late D. C. M. Platt, Patrick O'Brien, Colin Lewis, Brian Hamnett, and Simon Collier (before he left for Vanderbilt University) were all early supporters of this project. Conversations with Lucy Riall, Cathy Crawford, and Steve Smith (who reminded me that I was not *not* tackling the stormy issue of class-formation), as well as other colleagues at the University of Essex, were most helpful. Early presentations at Essex, Cambridge, and the Institute of Latin American Studies in London helped clear my thoughts. At my dissertation defense in Oxford in 1989, Malcolm Deas suggested that I unpack the role of the state in the comparative development of the Argentine and Canadian economies. Little did I know that I was already on a path that might lead to some partial answers to his queries. A decade later: this book.

Peter Blanchard of the University of Toronto, who introduced me to Latin American history, was always ready to come to my financial assistance with what turned out to be compelling letters of support. I only hope I can do the same for my own students.

The move to the United States in 1992 stimulated some rethinking—as well as befuddlement. More time at sea. New friends here were important in revising my thoughts and updating my charts. Conversations with Steve Aron, Dirk Hartog, Bill Jordan, Phil Nord, Ted Rabb, and Dan Rodgers in Princeton's History Department were important, especially as my mooring with political economy began to loosen. Ongoing conversations with Arcadio Díaz-Quiñones prompted me to reread foundational texts that I had read with the over-surgical eye of the social scientific historian searching the skies for "data." Many others commented on parts of this text and helped me over rough waters: Sheri Berman, Katherine Bliss, Miguel Centeno, John Coatsworth, Ariel de la Fuente, Richard Graham, Donna Guy, Charlie Hale, Michael Jiménez, Jessica Korn, Roberto Madero, Karl Monsma, Gustavo Paz, David Rock, and Nina Tanenwald. Presentations at the University of Michigan, Harvard University, New York University, Stanford University, the University of Pittsburgh, and the University of Iowa proved enormously useful. I am grateful to students and friends at these institutions for their time and comments. Katrina Roberts reacquainted me with Borges.

Roberto Pitalucca, Fabian and Alejandro Herrero, and Karen Caplan were all incredibly helpful research assistants when I hit land.

Porteño shores are where I racked up my biggest intellectual debts. Colleagues in Buenos Aires offered unflinching friendship and support. Hilda Sabato opened the doors of PEHESA at the Universidad de Buenos Aires *twice*. Victor Tau Anzoátegui did the same at the Instituto de Historia del Derecho "Ricardo Levene," also *twice*. All four occasions allowed me to ventilate some ideas and steered me away from some treacherous currents. I am grateful to the participants for the good humor with which they received this frighteningly ambitious project. Many other friends helped along the way: José Carlos Chiaramonte, Gaston Doucet, Juan Carlos Garavaglia, Jorge Gelman, Noemí Goldman, Gabriela Gresores, Juan Carlos Korol, Carlos Mayo, Zacarías Moutoukias, Jorge Myers, Ricardo Salvatore, Pepe Nun, and Beatríz Sarlo. Pilar González shared her pearls of wisdom. Elizabet Cipoletta was a true friend and stalwart supporter when working at the Archivo General de la Nación was so difficult that it made many of us believe that official destructive neglect was deliberate. Susana Giambiagi and her family were, and continue to be, closest of friends, and few of these chapters were composed without my recalling moments with them in Buenos Aires. These were the friends who allowed me to look at Buenos Aires from offshore in the first place. I am aware that many foreign scholars study Argentina and Latin America to partake in academic debate at home, often willfully or carelessly (I don't know which is worse) overlooking research and historiographies within the region—indeed often passing over their own dependence on Latin American scholarship. I hope I have not done that here. Indeed, it is my appreciation for Argentina's travails and its scholars that has compelled me to try to project these histories to audiences who may not be aware of their complexity or importance.

Four people read this book in earlier drafts from cover to cover: Stanley Stein, my friend and colleague at Princeton, has inspired me with his peerless ability to find the smallest of shoals while keeping his eye on the global map; Samuel Amaral spotted a list of errors and misunderstandings; Tulio Halperín Donghi offered a long reflection on the first draft of this work, and nearly inspired me to take to the seas again, not out of despair, but realizing that there was so much more to discover; and my mother, Margaret Adelman, my favorite writer of the Atlantic world, spent hours, days, and I fear weeks going over my log and picking out its inconsistencies and infelicities.

Books, like expeditions at sea, especially when they take so long, cost money. The British Academy and the Nuffield Foundation covered several summer trips to Buenos Aires while I taught at the University of Essex. The History Department, the Program in Latin American Studies, and the University Committee for Research in the Humanities and the Social Sciences at Princeton University financed return trips to the archives. But this project would never have survived without the initial help of the Social Sciences and Humanities Research Council of Canada, whose post-doctoral fellowship enabled me to spend two years in Buenos Aires from 1989 to 1991. Let me express by deepest gratitude to Canadian taxpayers whose support of research and the arts provide a model of cosmopolitan enlightenment. The Philip and Beulah Rollins Preceptorship at Princeton enabled me to take a year's leave to finish the manuscript. I am thankful, finally to John and Pat Coatsworth for their companionship, and the staff of the David Rockefeller Center for Latin American Studies while I was a visiting fellow at Harvard in 1996–97. It was there that the fragmented pieces for the mosaic of audiences finally began to fall into place.

This book is dedicated to Eric, Nicole, and Jacob. More than anyone, they have provided me with a shore on which to land, where I might unpack, dry out, and recover before setting sail again. Any man would thank the stars for just one day of their friendship and love. No words can express my gratitude for the years of their company.

J.A.

☞ Contents

Republic of Capital

1 ☞ Toward a Political History of Economic Life

In September 1815, a heavily indebted Buenos Aires merchant appealed to local courts for succor. He owed his fortune to a panoply of creditors. In normal circumstances, commerce big and small relied on credit. But 1815 was a tough year for capitalists, and a decisive one in Atlantic history as the beam of time tilted from one century to the next. Around him, a war raged over the fate of Spain's South American possessions, a war that was devastating age-old commerce. In Europe 1815 was a culminating point, bringing peace after decades of revolution and warfare; in Spanish America it was an initial turning point in what was to become a century of turmoil. Facing incarceration, this merchant pleaded to the Commercial Tribunal to rescue him from the "hurried and imprudent abuses that creditors are inflicting on this poor merchant," steeping his defense in the language of proper entitlements and immunities of upstanding property-owning subjects. These arguments persuaded the magistrates: the court postponed an embargo on the family's possessions and offered clemency even while it recognized the merchant's failure to honor his contracts. But in the end, the merchant could not recover from the economic ruin of war. The debts piled up; eventually bailiffs dragged the pleading merchant to jail.[1]

Our victim, Santiago Esperon, exemplified the fate of many merchants occupying a strategic location in one of the central entrepôts of the Atlantic commercial system. Proud, prosperous, and powerful, the Buenos Aires mercantile class fueled the trade routes between Europe and South America, only to be engulfed in the crisis of mercantilism and sucked into the vortex of revolution. The saga of Esperon, his colleagues, and his class tells us much about how merchant capital coped with massive collective violence over the shape of the political community, how their strategies and actions transformed the meaning of law and justice, and how state-formation shaped the reconstruction of commercial capitalism in the nineteenth century. Esperon and the merchants of empire flourished under the umbrella of mercantilism, a politically constituted regime of wealth-seeking in which capitalists relied upon legal favors and privileges percolating down from the sovereign. As warfare and revolution shredded the legal ligaments of mercantile fortunes, capitalists struggled to create an alternative juridical world to define and uphold their property rights. They would eventually do so by shifting legal sovereignty to the possessor and codifying the instrumental logic of markets. Esperon's agony came at one of the inflection points of this transformation and exemplifies convulsions of the trans-Atlantic shift from controlled to free markets, and from political to private property.

In the colonial era, Buenos Aires connected European markets with one of the world's largest sources of specie: Andean silver. A century later, Buenos Aires reemerged as the hub of the world's fastest growing export economy based on agrarian staples. In this transformation, merchants played a crucial role, the sequence and consequence of which were unforeseeable to protagonists. Over the course of almost a century, capitalists and rulers experimented with and rearranged the balance between private interests and public power to pull the region out of the maelstrom that eviscerated Santiago Esperon's once-prosperous colonial enterprise.

This book describes the collapse, beginning in the late eighteenth century, of the Spanish Empire in the River Plate region of South America, followed by pendular swings between state-building and civil war, and a culminating triumph of liberal constitutionalism in the 1860's; it traces the transition from colonial Natural Law to instrumental legal understandings of property. As such, the developments of constitutionalism and property law were more than coincidences: the agony of the polity shaped the rituals and practices arbitrating economic justice, while the crisis of property animated the support for a centralized and executive-dominated state. In dialectical fashion, politics shaped private law while the effort to formalize the domain of property directed the course of political struggles.

A Political History of Economics

Republic of Capital is a political history of economics. This book treats the institutional fabric of everyday life, over the long run, as both the setting for social interaction, and thus a determinant of macro-social change, as well as an effect of conflict and bargaining, an unanticipated outcome of collective action. The causality runs deliberately in both directions. Politics shaped the rules of economic activity; economic forces contoured political possibilities and improbabilities.[2] However, if pressed to give an ultimate "cause," *Republic of Capital* places great emphasis on the political struggle for supremacy in the Atlantic world as the detonator of republican transformations on both sides of the ocean, struggles that culminated in the collapse of European empires in the Americas. But if imperial competition precipitated a crisis and collapse of the ancien régime, explaining the patterns of republican successors requires a broad analytic framework to steer us away from simple nomothetic reasoning.

This book does not suggest that the narrative of long-term transformation is nothing but a sequence of unstructured contingencies, accidents, or mere happenings. There existed, to borrow Marshall Sahlins's term, a "structure of the conjuncture" of state-building and class-formation.[3] People—rulers, capitalists, peasants—understood and advanced their interests in identifiable historic and strategic contexts. These contexts shaped the spectrum of possibilities of public arrangements of power and private claims on property.

To make sense of this structure of the conjuncture, this book braids several narrative approaches. First, it explores the evolution of political ideas. From late imperial champions of Enlightened reform, to the rise of Romanticism, and the final emergence of an instrumental political theory that emphasized order over liberty, the ideological peregrinations of liberalism framed republican projects and promises. In particular, political nostra informed perceived ideal balances between social autonomy and public power. Ideas framed imagined possibilities and animated peoples' political choices.

These ideas, however, emerged and changed in institutional contexts. Thus, the book traces the political-economic downfall of a mercantile colony, a half-century of civil war over disparate visions for the republic, and internecine battles within liberal rulership. The failed effort to nurture public institutions in the wake of colonial collapse provided the setting for intellectuals to reappraise secular faiths. Institutions conditioned available political and economic resources and patterned rules governing their possession. Accordingly, a central concern of this book is to depict the ebb and flow of constitutionalist efforts—failed and triumphant alike. What constitutionalists sought were durable rules to govern the process of rule-making, to give institutional girding to politics and public power.

What public rulers could and could not do depended in turn on proprietary transformations—especially the concerns of possessors of capital able and willing (or neither) to back some political projects over others. Capital interests themselves were anything but static, especially considering Buenos Aires' aperture to the Atlantic economy from the days of its founding. Consequently, this book follows the travails of merchant capitalists' efforts to stabilize market relations through daily management of conflicts over debts, failed contracts, and the status of money. Private claims over valuable assets—and the ability to enforce them—animated personal interests and shaped what capitalists wanted and expected from public rulers.

In other words, *Republic of Capital* weaves back and forth between disparate *ideas* shaping republican visions, conflict over *institutions* representing citizens in public and private matters, and daily practices of arbitrating *interests* to account for the long-term reordering of the global political economy from colonial mercantilism to commercial capitalism. This conceptual threnody conveys a sense of the mutually constituting fields of social life. For instance, *Republic of Capital* insists that interests not be treated as given, pre-constituted preferences, as the current vogue of "positive political economy" maintains.[4] Rather, they are located and shaped in ideational and institutional contexts. Yet, at the same time, capitalists' interests are not purely reducible to other spheres, but enjoy a measure of autonomy and even, in the last instance, partial determining powers over the shape of evolving political economies. The same balancing act applies to institutional and ideational levels. None are reducible to the other, but each is patterned by other fields of social life.

Braiding ideas, institutions, and interests into a narrative of long-term transformation implies a looser form of causality. Each field is mutually constitutive and indeterminate at the same time. At particular moments and faced with specific problems (like how did the collapse of public institutions and warfare alter the interests of capital and reshape political ideology), the causal lines run one way and are thin and sharply defined. But seen from a greater distance, the larger transformations described in *Republic of Capital* give way to broader, blurred and curving lines of causation. This may dissatisfy many social scientists looking for unambiguous nomothetic explanations. On the other hand, many historians may object to causal claims altogether, preferring more interpretevist, unstructured observations. This book represents an effort to transcend this divide between explanatory and interpretive accounts of modern life.

Bourdieu

Buenos Aires and the Atlantic World

The structure of the conjuncture was an Atlantic setting. Buenos Aires' transformation from ancien régime colonialism to modern constitutionalism was not unique. It was a trans-Atlantic phenomenon with a con- *Colonial* stellation of variations around a familiar theme. As such, the River Plate was one corner of an Atlantic world adapting to the fallout of the American, French, and Spanish American revolutions. *Republic of Capital* places Argentina (and Buenos Aires in particular) in a comparative con- *comparative* text. No less than other republics, Argentina was a theater for liberal ex- *theater* perimentation and consolidation. In particular, inhabitants of the region wrestled with divergent projects for the political community. If the state-form was a shared ideal, its shape and attributes were not the source of consensus.[5] For much of the nineteenth century, Argentines, like Mexi- *Liberal* can, American, and French citizens struggled to reconcile a liberal ten- *tension on* sion between public representation and private property, between for- *Public* malizing the powers of a political capital with the unimpeachable rights *v.* of personal capital. *Private*

Buenos Aires did more than just express a trans-Atlantic problem- *trans-Atlantic* atic. Citizens of the city felt *part* of an Atlantic world. *Porteños*, as they are called, saw themselves as participants in a saga unfolding on both sides of the ocean. Intra-European struggles and the spread of revolutionary pulses sundered the colonial-metropolitan system. *Porteños* read and reflected upon the principal tracts of the Enlightenment and post-Enlightenment, and never desisted from understanding their place in the universe in regional as well as trans-Atlantic terms, and accordingly grappled with the turmoil of the age of revolution in languages familiar to citizens elsewhere. Ultimately, the transformation of Atlantic trade and capital flows induced state-builders and investors to nurture a po- *exports* litical community oriented to the promise of European demand for commodities, and a magnet for Europe's capital and migrants. From start to finish, the story of state-formation and economic reconstruction was a cosmopolitan process. The Atlantic world was a historical setting in two senses. It was a theater for homologous, though not identical, transformations from ancien régimes to modern ones, incomplete and faltering

Homologous

though they may be. It was also a world of commonly shared convictions and aspirations in which an emerging citizenry looked as much afar as locally for inspiration, illustration, and incentives for their private and public enterprises.

But being part of the Atlantic world did not mean that international workings unfolded according to universal rules. This book treats the Argentine experience as a distinctive expression of larger processes—as an example of difference within unity. Two political variables marked the postcolonial and republican transformations in the River Plate: first, the collapse of the Spanish empire left a profound political vacuum; second, revolution and civil war mobilized society into deeply antagonistic camps whose wars destroyed the foundations of property and social hierarchy. Together, these unintended bequests of the viceregal overthrow in 1810 meant that constitutional architects had to juggle the following seemingly incompatible goals: stabilize property rights through the rule of law and integrate the polity under the shelter of legitimate institutions whose rules were themselves constantly contested by rival forces. Argentina speaks to the conflicts and complexities of creating institutional ligaments of capitalism when the political channels for dealing with collective conflict were themselves disputed branches of public power.

Comparisons help the *Republic of Capital* address ways in which nineteenth-century liberalism has been idealized. This book contrasts Buenos Aires with other Atlantic societies to explore both unity (relations of connection) of the Atlantic, as well as differences (relations of comparison)—to separate unique, and therefore contingent, dimensions, from universal and therefore more structural causal forces driving the liberal experience.[6] The American and French Revolutions are often seen as markers of a new era in social, political, and economic relations. The crisis of Old World mercantilism and the implosion of absolutist states gave way to democratizing polities and burgeoning market relations. It is generally accepted that what made this era unique was the uncoupling of polity and economy. Whereas ancien régimes meddled in economic activities as much as they preserved the rule of the privileged, post-revolutionary states unfettered entrepreneurial activity while enfranchising at least part of their citizenry. The state's withdrawal from the economic realm even as it claimed to represent a broader social base comprised two simultaneous components of the drive toward "liberty."

Over the long run, the structure of the conjuncture can be broken into separate moments. *Republic of Capital* suggests a succession of three conjunctures. (1) Revolution seized the Atlantic world during the years 1776 to the 1820's. Beginning with North American secession and culminating in the separation of Latin American colonies from their Iberian cores, the dynastic bridge between metropoles and peripheries went up in flames that engulfed the entire hemisphere. (2) From the rubble of war emerged new efforts to stabilize political communities and social relations from the 1820's to the 1850's. Fledgling republics grappled with highly mobilized societies and deep fissures among political camps. In the case of the United States, the carnage of the frontier, wars with Mexico, and finally the Civil War comprised a set of violent episodes and processes that transformed state powers and redrafted North American property rights. In Spanish America, analogous struggles had similar effects, although republics south of the Río Grande could not fall back on the accepted constitutional frameworks that lent the United States a patina of political stability. (3) Dismayed by the extended effects of revolution by mobilization, Spanish American statesmen aimed to wind down the fractious effects of conflict over the shape of the political community; elites settled for a framework of state that shifted the premium to top-down integration. Spanish America (soon to be joined by Brazil) came to resemble less the aspirational republicanism of the United States and more the constructivist purpose of *Risorgimento* Italy or unified Germany. The River Plate passed through a sequence of conjunctures, from revolution, to anarchy, to order. Each moment left its mark on public power and private rights. Putting the conjunctures together reveals a long-term process of structural change, from the demise of ancien régime dynasties and private privilege to orderly republican models of equality of legal subjects and the rights of private property holders. In this fashion, *Republic of Capital* is a contextual account of short-term events while examining the conjunctural forces contouring dramatic change over time. While attentive to the structure of the conjuncture, this book seeks to tell a tale of how the structure itself—in this case the public and private legal fabrics of Atlantic capitalism—transformed.

Economics and Law

Realizing the rights of citizens and realizing the rights of property are often treated as separate phenomena. State-formation and economic development until the late eighteenth century were seen as interlaced processes, thereafter coming apart in the wake of democratic revolutions to obey divergent story-lines. In narratives of state-formation, the ensuing century is treated as one of increasing "incorporation" of popular sectors and gradual, if fitful, democratization of modern states.[7] For students of the market, the nineteenth century has come to represent its purest, most competitive moment. Accordingly, economic historians have come to see here evidence of resource-allocation and distribution free of statist control or interference.[8]

The nineteenth century's apparent uniqueness rests not only on an initial climacteric (democratic revolutions). It also implies closure. Secular political enfranchisement and waning market competition ushered in a new era in modern social relations by 1900. Thus the late nineteenth century has come to embody the twilight of an image of society bequeathed by the struggles against absolutism and mercantilism. Railroads, increasing concentration of asset-ownership, and the rising costs of warfare and military preparedness invited new patterns of state regulation and management of the economy. Likewise, new social demands eclipsed earlier notions of citizenship, evolving—in T. H. Marshall's classic formulation—from civil, to political, to social claimsmaking.[9] Now, popular demands included rights at the workplace and guarantees of family incomes. Faced with pressures to regulate market relations and involve themselves in economic redistribution, states reunited that which had been uncoupled a century earlier: polity and economy.

Historiographically speaking, by the turn of the nineteenth century the separated narratives of state-formation and market-driven development once again converged to fuse in the inter-war years in a panoply of new isms: welfarism, fascism, populism, and corporatism. It was not by chance that Friedrich Hayek chose to title his 1944 classic Jeremiad *The Road to Serfdom*—as if reuniting polity and economy in the twentieth century would restore the status quo before the democratic revolutions.[10]

Hayek was not a loner. Much contemporary theory in the social sciences, from neo-classical to Marxist, rests on such a view of the nineteenth century. It was, we have come to believe, the glorious century of liberalism: rational and instrumental agents disposed of their property rights with minimal, if any, state interference, while these same peoples asked only that governments dismantle old privileges and immunities, and to uphold the interests of the nation as a whole. Recent theory cannot proclaim its originality in this matter: John Stuart Mill and Karl Marx agreed that what made their epoch unique was the freeing of the economy from political forces. For Marx, the great breakthrough of capitalism was to develop a system of production in which (unlike feudalism) property owners did not rely on *political* power to preserve their supremacy, precisely because, as he noted in *Grundrisse*, the abstraction of market relations became universal to all social relations.[11] Modern states could proclaim blind defense of the rule of law and universal political representation of a "people" while letting the economy obey entirely different sets of laws of motion.

There was something unique, indeed remarkable, about the era spanning the late eighteenth and late nineteenth centuries, from the age of revolution to the age of order. But the received view leaves the historian in something of a muddle. Short of embracing notions of predestination or sedulous pursuits of liberty—which, not always without merit, became common frames for textbooks of the New World's republican histories (in Argentina no less than the United States)—it becomes more difficult to fit the narratives of market- and state-formation into separable plots following a common trajectory. Indeed, much recent historical work questions the neat and tidy divisions of polity and economy altogether, especially in moments of economic duress or convulsion. Seen over the long run, neither of the story-lines were free from backsliding, contestation, and in some cases, full-blown counter-revolution. Historians (and I would include myself in this group) have more often come to treat the triumph of liberalism as both contingent and an unintended consequence of collective struggles, whether for national independence or social recognition.

For the historian of Latin America, the received view of the nineteenth century has been especially problematic. No less than the United States, the Latin American republics were the by-products of a crumbling mercantilist and absolutist order, informed, from their inception, by discourses of popular sovereignty and the freedom to own and dispose of property. But if North Americans could invoke triumphalist master-narratives for their republic, Spanish Americans had no such choice. For them, the quest for liberty seemed to have faltered from the moment it erupted onto the historical stage. Conflict with Spain in the 1810's and 1820's gave way to decades of civil war and turmoil. There was no linear path, no secular unfolding, not even a great political catharsis. Even the abolition of slavery was presented as an afterthought with little meaning for people of color in the region. Instead, scenes of territorial loss, fragmentation, and economic retrogression dominate the writing on the nineteenth century. In Spanish America, narratives of market- and state-formation could only be disentangled with great difficulty, perhaps because neither story-line ended in triumph.

As a result, however, the rise of the market came to be causally related to the failure of political liberalism—as if disenfranchisement were the cost to be paid for market-driven economic development. By the end of the nineteenth century, market forces had finally come to prevail, but in the face of decades of popular resistance and unrest, so that liberal champions of the rights of property had to forsake democratic rights in order to stabilize market relations. From this view has flowed a long historiographic tradition that sees Spanish America as a region where liberalism either "failed" or achieved only partial and tenuous success. For *dependentistas* and neo-liberals (in the Latin American sense) alike, Spanish America underwent no truly full-blooded liberal experience.[12] (Indeed, the current apostles of *neo-liberalismo* in the region quite openly present themselves as the proponents of a liberalism that Latin America—purportedly—never enjoyed.)[13]

Spanish America has come to represent a continental exception to a trans-Atlantic rule about the diffusion of liberalism in the nineteenth century. In this respect, Argentina was paradigmatic. Argentina has come to embody "failure," like the rest of the region, because it deviated from a path blazoned by other republics before it—especially the United States. The culprits in the story have varied: from personalistic and over-ambitious state-builders, chiliastic *caudillos*, and unreconciled peasants refusing to expose themselves to the manifold bounty of the market—at least this is how they are portrayed. In the way historians of Spanish America have come to plot national narratives, these personalities and the political effects of their actions redirected the fates of their countries *in the course of* persistently breaking down the proper boundaries between the autonomous realms of the market and the state.

The upshot—and here we come to the core of the problem at hand—was to reinforce Marx's and Hayek's visions of the state-economy split under classical liberalism. Latin Americans, and Argentines in particular, were the exceptions that proved the rule about the benevolent effects of separating polity from market. What is more, historians and social scientists of Latin America attributed the tortuous nature of market and "not so fficiently separated"

state-formation in their countries to the fact that these realms were not sufficiently separated: the market became either over-politicized or the state was "captured" and made to service the interests of propertied classes. Either way, the dual but autonomous components of liberty remained the cornerstone of what successful liberalism was supposed to accomplish. The problem was: Argentines and Spanish Americans kept conflating the two and, in so doing, undermined or postponed the triumph of either.

Q   This book will not question the uniqueness of the nineteenth century. But it does recast the split narratives of market- and state-formation— for at issue was a political process consolidating the rule of law. Specifically, this book asks one large question: how did the Argentine state balance the need to create a legal order that would be legitimately recognized as the patrimony of a citizenry while at the same time upholding a system that would protect the rights of property? Achieving this—and I would contend that by the 1860's, this is precisely what liberals had succeeded in creating—was a political proposition because it struck at the heart of generations of rancor and war over the makeup of the country. As long as the constitutional foundations of the republic remained contested, challenged, and repeatedly overthrown, the status of property and contracts themselves was imperiled. In other words, the market, in order to function, required as a precondition a political arrangement that would settle and preserve a legal order to legitimate private property and contractarian culture as a whole.   Legal

Consolidation
rule of
law

Seen from the vantage point of artisans, landowners, and especially merchants, Argentines were all too aware of this problem. In the end, it was especially merchant capital that provided the crucial social "agency" behind Argentine state-formation. Merchants needed defensible contracts and fiduciary for their businesses—and they recognized that only public authorities could uphold their proprietary claims. Over the long run this book explores changing notions of property and entitlement among merchants, from a humanist tradition (in which property was treated as a condition for virtuous personhood, and therefore good citizenship—Santiago Esperon's cant), to a more modern language of jurisprudence (in which property was seen as a relationship with things, over which merchants acquired rights to use and dispose). This transition was anything but smooth or complete. Indeed, political exigencies and persistent legal uncertainty prolonged the lifespan of humanist no-

capital

Property

humanist

tions precisely because it offered to merchants a compass by which to organize and legitimate their pursuits and to arbitrate conflicts within their own embattled community.

Endemic civil war, the breakdown of the Viceroyalty, and clashes with neighboring republics wreaked havoc in the larger political economy. The search for fungible resources in order to address unremitting fiscal and monetary disorder sent state leaders to merchants in search of credit and financial support. The ensuing dalliance between capitalists and rulers defies easy or reductive analysis—the state did not emerge as the functional tool for merchant capital, nor did the state operate according to endogenous rules oblivious of civil society. Public deliberation and more secluded negotiation over law and constitution-making shed light on the outlook and behavior of economic agents as well as the desperate and not always purposive activities of political leaders. This process also says a great deal about liberal ideology and juridical practice at work in the day-to-day management of public and private finances—aspects that demonstrate just how far Argentines' own sense of a liberal promise did *not* rest on a separation of the state from the market, the public from the private.

In the end, this book argues that Argentina was not an exception to a liberal norm derived from an idealized view of a North Atlantic model (and to which few historians would subscribe, but which nonetheless dogs the literature—hence the shibboleth of "exceptionalism"). Rather, it exemplifies a more extreme and openly conflictual process of legal construction of market relations, because the political machinery to consolidate a liberal regime was itself so contested. Accordingly, Argentina was (and is) no less liberal than other republics; it is not a case of persistent liberal failure. Such a formulation has always struck me as ahistorical, and indeed silly, and would not be so important to address were it not so pandemic. This version of Argentine (and for that matter the rest of Latin American) history rests as much on an indigenous sense of failure or exceptionalism as it does on an idealized vision of how liberalism triumphed in other corners of the Atlantic world. Cast in a comparative context, the Argentine example invites students of market- and state-formation in the nineteenth century to query whether it is useful to rely on the stark dichotomies of polity and economy at all. In this light, can alternative meanings be retrieved from the democratic revolutions and their progeny that paved the way for liberalism's first century?

In what follows

What follows, then, is a political history of economic life, an exploration of the embeddedness of property and exchange relations within social and political contexts.

Law and Economics

Much of my thinking about the relationship between public authority and private rights, and their mediation by the rule of law, has evolved in a dialogue with what is called the "new institutionalism" in economic history or "public choice" theories of macrosocial change more broadly.[14] Both my reliance upon the insights of this field of work, and ultimately my discomforts, are sprinkled liberally—perhaps overly so for historians looking for uncontaminated narratives—throughout the text. Two general contributions merit emphasis here. First, this turn in the social sciences and social scientific history place great attention on the micro-foundations of macro-social or political developments. This draws greater attention to the "agency" behind faceless institutions and asks students to consider motivations and rationality animating collective action. Second, especially at the hands of Douglass North, market and property-rights evolution are embedded in broader social and political matrices.[15] Indeed, new institutionalists are very explicit about their concern for the institutional settings of economic and social activity. In both these respects, this book adds to the literature, although remarkably little has been written from this standpoint on Latin America.[16] Whereas legality and rules have often been seen negatively as repressive, "controlling" devices, the new institutional turn prefers to see them as enabling and conductive.

There are, however, troubles, some of greater, others of lesser, significance. Since my reservations appear frequently through the narrative, especially as the text unfolds, let me just say at the outset that this book challenges the presumptions of the new institutionalism in three ways.

First, peoples' interests are not presumed to be self-evident and continuous; agents are not just wealth maximizers under constraint. Even the most opportunistic market participants—merchant capitalists—evinced shifting and troubled notions of their rights and entitlements, and thus altered their strategies to make the best of what they possessed. Interests were, to use a hackneyed phrase, socially constructed. This does not mean that people invented notions of the good life out of thin

air (or by reading rarefied signifiers as some "theorists" would argue).
Rather, this book treats material interests as the by-product of the legal
cultures of communities—in this case the community of merchants in
the city of Buenos Aires. By exploring the conflicts and mutations of the
interests of capital, this book offers an account of how capitalist classes
come into being through intra-mercantile strife and engagement with
the broader social and political power, especially the public guardians of
the legal rights of capital. Interests and preferences were not revealed
points of departure, but contextually situated and therefore problematic.

Second, this book tackles institutions as settings where individuals,
groups, and classes reconciled their disputes. Institutions provided
mechanisms to resolve collective dilemmas, and under optimal circumstances enabled people to negotiate, make deals, and strike contracts
with some measure of confidence that these arrangements would be enforceable. This is the role of institutions. But the function of institutions
is not the same as an account of what nurtures institutional settings into
being, what causes rules in the first place.[17] Broadly speaking, *Republic of
Capital* casts the problem in constitutional terms because the institutional
fabric of public life was such a highly contested issue in nineteenth-
century Latin America. Constitutional framing of institutional life had to
perform a double task: give public organization to the political community and inscribe legal norms governing social relations. All too often
these objectives clashed, and therefore defy straightforward causal accounts of institutional development. This book offers no covering law
explaining public rule-making precisely because institutional rules were
the outcomes of deep conflict. Conflict of this nature and scale simply
presents too many indeterminacies and contingencies to flatten into a
monochromatic functionalist narrative.

Finally, over the long run, political ideas clearly mattered. The language of politics framed what was permissible and stigmatized the illegitimate. One simply cannot understand the depth of rancor and the degree to which people were willing to sacrifice the lives and livelihoods
of families and neighbors through much of Argentina's nineteenth century, without an appreciation of the political visions that animated their
struggles. Such convictions emerged out of shared practical experiences
as well as the consumption of a diet of liberal literature. The political architects of statehood and the juridical establishment in Buenos Aires
wrestled with evident tensions between liberty and property, turning to
experience elsewhere for potential guidance. If nothing else, the re-

peated failure of constitutional blueprints compelled jurists and intellectuals to re-examine their faiths, ultimately devising a formula for public life that they thought would transcend old enmities. This self-reflective intellectual process shaped meanings of property and the terms for encoding them into law.

Interests, institutions, and ideas shaped each other in the course of state- and market-formation. *Republic of Capital* balances separation and connection, independence and interaction of these fields. None was necessarily reducible to the other, operating instead as discrete spheres of activity. In this effort to depict the political history of economic development over a long period of change and upheaval, *Republic of Capital* seeks to respect the relative autonomy of each domain. But autonomous domains do not imply disconnection. While this book does not advance universal, never mind parsimonious, claims about the causal lines between market development and political change, it emphasizes the interaction between these spheres of social life, the conflict between interests, institutions, and ideas as the motor of transformation from ancien régimes to liberal republics.

☞ The Age of Revolution, 1780's–1820's

2 ⫷ Imperial Reconstitution and the Limits of Political Property

Las colonias, como las vírgenes, vivían para su claustro.
Juan Bautista Alberdi

Buenos Aires in Atlantic Context

Buenos Aires was the progeny of a trans-Atlantic struggle over trade and silver. By the middle of the eighteenth century, Spain's competitors homed in on the silver-producing provinces for their specie and chipped away at vulnerable corners of the realm, especially in the Caribbean and southern South America. To remedy centuries of decay, the Bourbon monarchy modulated centuries of commercial and political practices in order to integrate their New World possessions more effectively into the empire. In the guise of reform, Madrid struggled to shore up an old model.

In this ambiguous effort to reform, and not transform, the early modern structures of empire, Buenos Aires operated as a fulcrum. The city's importance was rooted less in its dominion over new resources than its place as gateway to the oldest of New World staples, Andean silver, and especially the silver veins of Potosí. The Imperial City of Potosí was one of the greatest sources of silver in world history. According to doctrines whose life spans lasted well into the nineteenth century, *19th h* precious metal meant wealth: the greater the accumulation of specie, the more affluent the society. To realize this maxim, Spain forced Andean Indians to carry sacks of silver from the mines of the Cerro Rico mountain, to load caravans of mules with the bounty, and to lead the treasure of the Spanish empire to port, where the silver was dispatched to the peninsula. From there, as generations of historians have noted, colonial specie entered the sinews of European finance and commerce, contributing to the Old World's transformation and upheaval.[1]

Buenos
Aires

Andes

Silver mining

Bourbon
Reform

If Potosí was the heartland of Spain's South American possessions, Buenos Aires was its hinterland, for two centuries a backwater, minor dusty town at the mouth of the River Plate. As the entrepôt for contraband, a way station for Jesuits en route to Paraguay or Córdoba, Buenos Aires was often more an irritant than an asset. To foreigners, the River Plate was a convenient back-door to the Andes, and neighboring Brazil was more than willing to play the accomplice in the game of draining Spain of its much-needed silver. Thus, while Buenos Aires was but a periphery to the Andean economy, Spanish officials could ill-afford to neglect its mounting notoriety.

The crown decided to shake up its South American possessions to seal off the silver-hemorrhaging. Bourbon reforms revived silver mining and minting in Potosí. Between 1720 and 1740, Potosí recovered average annual production levels of the 1580's (when the Cerro Rico yielded 43 percent of the world silver supply), and by 1790, silver output had doubled once again to 28 million fine ounces. To stop the drainage to competitors, the Bourbons overhauled the channels of trade and shipment. In 1776, with the creation of the new Viceroyalty of the River Plate, Buenos Aires dislodged Lima as the exclusive port of call for Alto Peru, becoming one of the primary hubs of the Spanish realm and shedding its reputation as a habitat for denizen traders and commercial brigands. But it was still a port to service the highlands. Buenos Aires, until 1810, mediated between Andean production of specie and its European consumers. As such, it was one of an archipelago of ports along the eastern shores of the New World facing its counterparts of the Old—a nodal point in what R. R. Palmer has called, in his classic study of democratic revolutions, the "Atlantic civilization."[2]

That Buenos Aires should become a viceregal capital at the same time that Britain's thirteen colonies erupted in revolt is not just a coincidence. Over the course of the eighteenth century, the British, French, Portuguese, and Spanish were caught in the ever-tightening noose of imperial rivalry abroad and turmoil within. Measures to revive imperial fortunes were part of a set—often called the Bourbon Reforms—designed specifically to give the Spanish crown the means to defend itself in Europe and fend off its rivals in the colonies. Buenos Aires, unlike Boston, was the beneficiary of imperial reform intended to thwart disintegration and to reverse Spain's decadence. Herein lay a central feature of colonial Buenos Aires: its commercial and administrative existence depended on the preservation of the flow of silver from Potosí to

Cádiz. The city's social complexion and fealty to empire rested on the preservation of colonial commerce and specie flow. Consequently, for creole elites, the spectacle of events in the British and French empires, their loss of the thirteen colonies and Saint Domingue respectively, bordered on anathema.

As the child of imperial reform, Buenos Aires flourished. For four decades, the capital of the sprawling Viceroyalty (including present-day Argentina, Uruguay, Paraguay, and Bolivia) took its mandate seriously—sending goods to and from Spain and her subjects in South America. And yet Buenos Aires could not escape the whirlpool into which Spain—along with the rest of the Atlantic world—was being sucked. There is a fundamental paradox here: Buenos Aires, the port that benefited most from empire, became the primary locus of revolution after 1810. How did this corner of Bourbon authority come to spurn its own political handmaiden? For the moment, we will have to leave this question open-ended, for we should not presuppose, as many have done, that the revolution of 1810 was latent in Buenos Aires' condition a generation earlier. There was nothing inevitable about the fragmentation of the Hispanic world. The collapse of Spain's empire was due more to hammer-blows inflicted at its core—the peninsula itself—and less to the failure of any test of loyalty on the part of colonial subjects. The creoles of Buenos Aires remained faithful to the end, as much out of conviction as from necessity.[3]

Does this mean that secular transformations within the River Plate colonies played no role at all in the Spanish empire's implosion? Not quite. Spain's power in the New World always rested on a delicate equipoise of interests and regions. In a multilayered matrix of sovereignties, Hispanic subjects owed their allegiance to local political identities (especially their province or city), corporate interests (especially the guild or juridically constituted group to which most subjects belonged, voluntarily or otherwise), and the crown and its representatives.[4] All these loyalties overlapped, and it is misleading to portray Spain's realm as an undiluted absolutism in which the monarch acted out some Bodinian ideal-type.[5] Ruling the realm was a juggling act of heroic proportion. But over the centuries, weakness at home and difficulties sustaining the colonies' flow of surpluses to the metropole eventually required some recalibrating of the imperial order. The reforms that flowed from Bourbon plumes were meant to stir the empire from its own torpor. Reforms, however, yielded unintended—and perilous—effects. By unleashing a sequence of structural transformations, Bourbon reforms upset the delicate equipoise of the realm. Imperial reconstitution had double-edged consequences that could scarcely have been anticipated.

Nor was structural change the only source of disequilibrium in colonial River Plate society. If imperial reform aimed to shore up the realm against Atlantic rivals—and the jury is still out on whether Spain succeeded in this effort—no amount of tinkering could rescue Spain from the effects this rivalry had on its competitors' heartlands. While war-making cost Britain its prize possessions in the Americas, this had only remote consequences for South America. More troublesome was Spain's neighbor, France. Bellicosity eventually also took its toll on Europe's super-power, for whom Atlantic rivalries despoiled a once-rich public treasury. Fiscal and governmental mismanagement in the ancien régime soon plunged France into revolution and opened a political chasm within Europe. The mercantilist wars of Europe's periphery gave way to continental carnage, sucking Spain into the vortex. The costs of mounting conflict and the effects on the commercial apparatus upon which the Spanish colonies based their welfare intensified and accelerated the hammer-blows. The Spanish Bourbons made constant short-term adjustments to colonial, and increasingly, continental war-making. In meeting emergency needs, the crown compounded the underlying disequilibrium unleashed by secular change. We can describe developments—long- and short-term alike—in Buenos Aires from 1776 to 1810 as creating the conditions for a potential revolution, a context for revolutionary possibilities rather than its proximate causes.[6]

Decline and Reconstitution of Empire

According to Louis XIV of France, writing in the thick of the War of Spanish Succession, "the principal objective of this war is commerce with the Indies and the riches they produce."[7] In 1713, the Treaty of Utrecht brought peace to Spain but did not stifle the conflagration's causes. This peace merely delayed the moment of reckoning for European imperial powers' struggle for mastery within Europe and domination of Atlantic trade. But peace came with a cost: Spain lost its main European possessions to its rivals, and in the New World ceded the rights to sell slaves in colonial ports (the *asiento*) to the British for 30 years, and gave up the tiny fortress of Sacramento across the River Plate from Buenos Aires, to Britain's own ward, Portugal. For Spain these were troublesome losses; with the loss of its European dominions, Spain's greatness now depended exclusively on the management of American possessions. The last two concessions were to prove especially costly to Bourbon efforts to revitalize their realm—and pushed Buenos Aires increasingly to the fore of imperial concern. Over the long run, the settlement of Utrecht helped galvanize the British-Portuguese alliance and transferred the lucrative sale of Africans to British hands. Utrecht eventually compelled Spanish monarchs to fix their sights on the River Plate.

Smuggling eclipsed piracy as a means to drain Spain's crucial source of treasure, silver. The arrival of British slave ships to colonial ports immediately became occasions for colonial subjects to partake in illicit— *Illicit* and endemic—contraband, using New World specie to pay for the cargo. The *asiento* was a perpetual source of complaint for Spanish officials. Buenos Aires in particular festered with outlaw commerce: British *Outlaw commerce* ships and Portuguese corsairs entered the River Plate unimpeded, introducing merchandise with impunity and siphoning silver from the *Silver* Andes, often with the open complicity of local merchants and officials.[8]

As the mercantilist wars among European empires intensified over the eighteenth century, the cost of postponing serious policy changes mounted. Finally, the combination of Ferdinand's death, the ascension of the more robust Carlos III, the devastation of the Seven Years' War (including Britain's occupation of Havana and Manila in 1762), and the glaring effects Spain's economic entropy provoked a new spirit of governance at home, and especially abroad. Calls for reform date well back to seventeenth-century pamphleteers, the *arbitristas*. Aware of the surrounding Hispanic decadence, and fearing the consequences of further neglect, they promoted remedies to restore imperial splendor. The *arbitristas'* successors a century later were in many ways no different, though they were willing to embrace more daring reforms. For writers such as Gerónimo de Ustáriz and José Campillo, or officials like José de Patiño and the Marquis of Ensenada, Spain could ill-afford to put off its medicine.[9]

From the time he took power in 1759 until his death in 1788, Carlos III issued a sweeping array of royal decrees and orders—all designed to reconstitute the empire by recombining its component parts. Many of the measures revived Hapsburg practices, such as the *visita general* (tours by high-level officials with mandates to recommend reforms), some simply scrubbed clean old policies that had suffered from neglect,

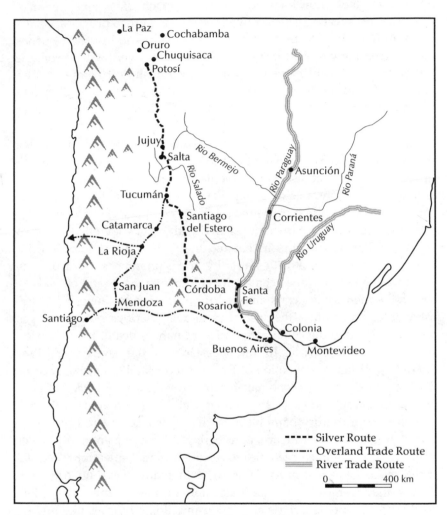

La Paz
Cochabamba
Oruro
Chuquisaca
Potosí

Jujuy
Salta
Rio Bermejo
Rio Salado
Rio Paraguay
Asunción
Rio Paraná

Tucumán
Santiago
del Estero
Corrientes
Rio Uruguay

Catamarca
La Rioja

San Juan
Córdoba
Santa
Fe
Mendoza
Rosario
Santiago
Colonia
Buenos Aires
Montevideo

- - - - Silver Route
- · - · - Overland Trade Route
≡≡≡≡ River Trade Route

0   400 km

Map 1. Silver and Trade Routes in the Eighteenth Century

+ax

such as the reorganization of *alcabala* (excise) tax collection. Other steps were more innovative. But none introduced a decisive rupture with past practices—hence the preference to describe this effort as a reconstitution of empire rather than full-blooded renovation.[10] As far as the River Plate was concerned, two sets of measures transformed Buenos Aires' colonial political economy by making the city a privileged linchpin in the archipelago of American ports facing Europe: administration and trade. Both aspects of imperial reconstitution aimed to incorporate Buenos Aires and the River Plate more effectively into the imperial order.

In 1776, the Viceroyalty of the River Plate came into being. For centuries, the southern Andes—and hence the main silver mines—faced west, toward the old viceregal capital of Lima. The overland journey to the *Topography* Pacific, shipment up the coast, and conveyance over the Central American Isthmus to the Caribbean was a long, expensive, and inefficient route. Moreover, Buenos Aires to the east—much the closer port to the mines and metropolitan markets—drained the region with illicit trade. *Illicit trade* By making Buenos Aires the new hub of commerce, officials sought to staunch the smuggling and promote traffic to the metropole. Hereafter, the trade route went south from Potosí, at a height of 3,500 meters, through the gorge of the Quebrada de Humahuaca, to the fertile valleys of Jujuy, Salta, and San Miguel to Tucumán, whose rivers gave way finally to the flat pampas, and eventually debouched into the River Plate and the sea (Map 1). Carts trundled out of Buenos Aires and reached as far as Jujuy, beyond which the topography permitted only muletrains. The round-trip overland took up to one blistering year.[11]

A proliferation of administrative measures reinforced the new viceregal axis to the Atlantic. Hoping to improve official efficacy, the monarch clamped down on the sales of offices for fiscal purposes. He also cleansed the judiciary *de haut en bas*. The executive also came in for refurbishing. To help the new Viceroy and his Governors, though seldom with comity, Carlos III designated the River Plate as his testing ground for the Intendancy system in 1782 to bolster executive accountability. All this tightened and restructured the colonial bureaucracy, to incorporate the once-wayward River Plate region into the broader matrix of colonial institutions, with the ultimate purpose of harnessing more effectively the flow of specie and revenue that had hitherto disappeared into the deep pockets of venal officials or shrewd merchants.[12]

These reforms were more a boon to Buenos Aires than to Spain. First consider the fiscal effects of these changes. The River Plate hosted 14

(remittances)

separate fiscal districts sending remittances to Buenos Aires and thence to Spain. Overwhelmingly, revenues came from Potosí and Buenos Aires districts, reflecting the importance of the Viceroyalty's poles: the mines and the port. Most revenue, it must be said, was earmarked for local-level needs such as the payment of officials, support of missions, mints, jails, churches, and, most of all, defense. What surplus remained went to the crown in Spain.[13]

The Viceroyalty more than paid for itself, though seldom by much. In no year did spending exceed revenues, though occasionally the surfeit nearly disappeared. Overall, from 1791 to 1805, the Buenos Aires treasury received 34 million pesos in revenue, and remitted 8.6 million to Spain.[14] To be sure, the royal system of double-entry bookkeeping is a labyrinth of traps for historians, not least the habit of shuffling funds to and from accounts within the same capacious ledgers. This became a convenient system for disguising shortfalls and later, especially during wars, a more than convenient regime for deficit-financing. The overall long-term trends of income and spending nonetheless reveal a precarious imbalance: a very modest surplus for Spain, but one that might easily disappear under duress.

Silver — The strength—and potential weakness—of the fiscal system was the reliance on silver-mining revenues. Revenues rose in response to administrative changes, the opening of new collection agencies, and more effective implementation. But reforms only embellished an old archaic fiscal structure descended from the sixteenth century. The largest revenue-contributor was Potosí, which, according to the pioneering work of John J. TePaske and Herbert S. Klein, never proffered less than one-third of all the region's collections, followed by Oruro—both being the principal mining centers of the Viceroyalty. Roughly 60 percent of all Buenos Aires receipts from 1791 to 1805 came from the Potosí *caja* alone.[15] The highlands were net surplus producers: the area regularly collected more than it needed for local needs, and thus was a reliable remitter to the central Treasury.

Buenos Aires, the fulcrum of a modernizing empire, thrived in this archaic exploitation of the Andes. Before shipment to Spain, all collections passed through the viceregal capital. To be sure, the Buenos Aires *caja* did boast its own rising revenues, especially from burgeoning overland and overseas trading. The capital, however, gobbled up these commercial receipts. Local returns seldom matched local spending, and the city dipped into highland remittances (which theoretically were bound for Spain) to cover its own local needs. If the highlands were a surplus and saving region, Buenos Aires emerged as a net spender living off highland surpluses and sending a trickle on to Spain.[16] For Spain, this was a revenue disappointment; for Buenos Aires, Bourbon reforms were a fiscal bonanza.

The second field of reform was commercial policy. For centuries, the guidelines of Spanish trade obeyed a double logic stemming from a single source: mercantilist conviction. A loose body of principles frequently lacking the systematic rigor of subsequent economic thinking, mercantilism was nonetheless the first semi-coherent economic doctrine of state-building. In the words of Thomas Hobbes, "wealth is power and power is wealth." This maxim hinged on the notion of a favorable balance of trade—the surplus of which would theoretically wind up in the coffers of the crown. While private economic activity was by no means proscribed, some of the profits were supposed to aggregate into public state wealth. This was measured in the store of specie resting in national—imperial—treasuries. In the last instance, the goal was accumulation of specie, and hence the store of money, realized through systematic surpluses in trade and revenue flows from colonies to metropoles, all destined to state coffers.[17]

In Spain, officials enforced policies to ensure that the shipment of goods and specie from the Americas to the metropole exceeded the reverse-flow. Thus the first parameter of Hispanic mercantilism aimed to thwart competition from foreign powers in the peninsula and colonies. In practice, however, especially with the *asiento* and rampant smuggling, these barriers were more porous than impenetrable. Second, the crown granted privileges and exclusive rights to major metropolitan mercantile houses to ply wares in the colonies. All goods had to flow between selected colonial ports (at first Lima and Veracrúz) and Seville. Theory proscribed all other ports of call. A royal ordinance created the Casa de Contratación in 1503 (as of 1717 based in Cádiz) as the first administrative body to deal with Spain's new possessions and to operate as the custodian of peninsular mercantilism. The Casa functioned as the clearinghouse for merchandise trade with the Indies, with a special mandate to monitor the market, buying and selling produce when most advantageous to the crown. The agents for this giant monopoly were the port's merchants. Seville and later Cádiz magnates sent their minions out to the hinterland with special licenses to peddle peninsular goods. If Spain tried to monopolize trade with its American colonies, merchants used their privileged positions in the selected ports to exercise oligopolistic privileges to thwart rivals from other ports. To take an example, merchants from Veracrúz enjoyed legal powers to control the trade through Campeche. Effectively, this entitled the merchants to enjoy exclusive prerogatives over a determined market. To reinforce regional commercial hegemony, merchants erected guilds, *consulados* (final completion in Mexico came in 1604 and Lima in 1613). Guilds performed two roles: to act as the collective face of merchant interests before public authorities in the colonies; and to be the home for a court to settle commercial disputes. Membership and participation in the guild reinforced internal hierarchies within the merchant community and redoubled their regional hegemony. The Cádiz licensing system and monopoly, combined with colonial guilds' political and legal functions, conferred immense puissance to the city's merchants. Accordingly, they zealously protected their right to control the freight on convoys or register ships, restricted the number of licenses, and controlled economic justice within the guild's court to ensure that merchants could reap oligopolistic rents.[18]

The Spanish system made commercial property into a politically allocated right. Rent-seeking merchants, protected from foreign interlopers and enjoying special charters, themselves had an interest in protecting Spain's monopoly. Big merchants, alongside royal officials, thereby became the wardens of an economic system designed not so much to impoverish outlying colonies as to enrich the metropole—in effect, the State dispensed rights to trade under the protection of regulated guilds, and in return, merchants reciprocated with what Hilton Root has called "loyalty rights."[19] In practice, however, merchants' entrepreneurial style calcified official trade. Collusion and oligopoly among the main metropolitan merchants dampened any upstart entrepreneur's incentive to play by official rules. Moreover, even the most loyal merchants could scarcely suppress the temptation to handle illicit goods, which, because they were cheaper, offered the promise of even more personal profits. As the eighteenth century wore on, rigid mercantilism became a set of cracked and leaky dams protecting an increasingly flooded plain.

The barricades of Spanish mercantilism, the symbiotic relationship between sovereign revenues and private merchant rents, could not withstand the tidal flows of European industrialization. Spain's competitors, especially Britain and France, became effective at selling their wares to colonial consumers—their goods were cheaper, better, and often unavailable. Nor could Spain hold back the effects of diversification within the Americas. Many colonies had become staple producers for markets outside the Peninsula itself: the River Plate in particular produced goods like hides and jerked beef for consumption across the Americas. Cádiz's monopoly over the entire structure of colonial trade forced merchants to conduct their business outside conventional legal channels. Even the famous fleet system (in which Spanish vessels had to sail in large convoys to thwart attackers and curb illicit trade temptations) that had for so long preserved the grip of Seville and Cádiz could not possibly handle the scale and variety of cargoes. Carlos III's so-called commercial reforms were in fact designed to claw back the realm's control of intra-imperial trade—shares of which had been eroding for over a century. The King wanted to recalibrate (and not dismantle) the symbiosis of politically allocated property rights and private rents.[20]

The mercantilist dams gave way. In 1721, Spanish regulators freed Buenos Aires from exclusive dependence on convoys sailing to Lima; thereafter independent galleons (the *navío de registro*) were permitted to sail from Cádiz to Buenos Aires. More dramatically, a series of decrees began to lower duties on the shipment of goods between the metropole and colonies—especially affecting wine from the west and raw cotton from the east. In 1768, trade between Peru and Nueva Granada opened. This became the first of a series of decrees opening channels of commerce within the empire. The Cádiz monopoly lapsed. One by one ports in Spain and the colonies embraced newfound rights to trade with other legal ports of call. In 1778, Carlos III issued a capstone ordinance removing barriers to a whole host of ports—in all, 14 in Spain and 35 in the Americas, including Buenos Aires—declaring that "only a *free and protected commerce* between European and American Spaniards can restore Agriculture, Industry, and Population in my Dominions to their former vigor."[21] Finally, after almost three centuries as guardian of colonial trade, the Casa de Contratación closed in 1790.

It is important to note that these reforms did not attack the core principles of mercantilism. For one, merchant guilds retained their legal powers in all corners of the realm: courts dispensed commercial justice; consulado members continued to exercise regional control in the colonies at the expense of rival ports. Merchants in the colonies retained their privileges even if Cádiz (unhappily) relinquished its metropolitan

monopoly. If anything, Carlos III's commercial decrees simply spread
political trading rights more widely across the realm. In so doing, reform made rent-seeking merchants in the colonies ever more responsible
for upholding mercantilist precepts and defending their political property. Moreover, "*comercio libre*" should not be interpreted anachronisti-
cally. It did not mean free trade as we now know it—or as it came to be
understood after the 1830's, as unrestricted rights to ply wares within or
across boundaries. Rather, *comercio libre* meant rights to trade among the
legalized Spanish archipelago of ports, fomenting trade within the empire to enhance the flow of specie to royal coffers. Foreigners were still
prohibited; duties remained high; vessels had to be Spanish and crewed
mainly by nationals. Above all, there was no vision of a new trading regime, composed of new markets or new products. In this respect, commercial reform meant to reconstitute the relationship between mining,
trade, and specie flow to Spain—it opened up new arteries, cleansed old
ones, and recognized *de jure* what was already happening *de facto*.[22] To
José de Gálvez, Carlos III's oracular Minister of the Indies (1776–87) and
more than anyone responsible for Buenos Aires' new status in the empire, one large impulse patterned reform: "As mining is the origin and
source of the metals that enliven and stimulate all the human occupations and universal trade in this world, justice requires that it merit special attention from the government."[23]

Trade figures confirm a sudden surge of commerce following "lib-
eralization." It is likely that trade was already flourishing, but much of it
in *sub rosa* channels. The new decrees simply allowed merchants to declare what they had been previously hiding from authorities. But there
can be little doubt that fewer restrictions did lower barriers to entry for
poorer producers and merchants and that this stimulated new economic
activity, which translated into rising trade. Either way, the decrees had
the effect of registering a licit commercial boom—and thus more revenue for the crown. The export index from Spain increased six-fold, while
the import index struck an even more stunning fifteen-fold rise from
1778 to 1785. Over the years 1782 to 1796, the River Plate accounted for
12 percent of all Spain's colonial imports—only Veracrúz and Havana
handled more. The bulk of this trade, not surprisingly, was silver—and
the years 1776 to 1783 yielded a stunning leap in specie shipments out of
Buenos Aires—accounting for over 80 percent of the port's exports.[24]

Comercio libre intended to do more than foster trade between colonial and metropolitan ports; it also aimed to foment exchange among all ports of the realm—even between colonial nodes. To date, we lack data for trade among the colonies themselves, but given the profile of pampean production, it is likely that pastoral products such as hides and jerked beef found vibrant markets elsewhere in the New World—especially slave colonies of the Caribbean. In 1785, Buenos Aires sent its first shipment of jerked beef to Cuba for slave consumption, and as the island's sugar economy flourished in the wake of the Saint Domingue uprising, the River Plate became an important provender of foodstuffs. More significant was the export of hides, which until 1778 were destined mainly for highland mining needs. Declaring *comercio libre* enabled hides to be exported legally: between 1779 and 1784, average hide shipments overseas reached 446,757, rising after the Treaty of Versailles to an average of 758,117 between 1792 and 1796. Still, the products of ranching represented a fraction of the port's handlings—a share, however, that rose almost without interruption, and which became ever more prominent as silver mining slid into decline after 1790.[25] But this shift to hides and pastoral products can easily be exaggerated: specie flows continued to dominate; hide exports grew only gradually after 1778: the real expansion came in the 1790's, despite the appearance of greater freedom of trade, Buenos Aires' relationship to the Atlantic economy resembled more its seventeenth-century lineage than a future incarnation of nineteenth-century free trade.

As the main South American conduit for specie and trade flows to Spain, Buenos Aires moved from troublesome outpost to Archimedean point in a recalibrated empire. Though Bourbon reform never quite measured up to Madrid's hopes of restored grandeur, it utterly transformed Buenos Aires. The viceregal capital thrived off fiscal remittances flowing from the highlands; the renaissance of silver mining nourished a vibrant local market; and new commercial opportunities stimulated regional diversification of products and opened a truly pan-Atlantic horizon of trade. Thus, for *porteños*, local prosperity was more than inseparable from imperial might. For Buenos Aires, reconstituting the empire enabled the city to exploit its privileged place as crucial mediator in the trans-Atlantic axis of Old World hunger for silver and its dwindling Andean supply. The crown revised the institutional fabric of imperial commerce, but it did not transform merchants' interests as purveyors of loyalty rights in return for privileged rents.

A Commercial Empire of the River Plate

If Buenos Aires was a hub for a reconstituted early modern empire, it also became the core of a more modern political economy. Between port and mine lay thousands of miles of territory, much of it flat grasslands known as the pampas—now a region transformed by Buenos Aires' new status as nodal point in a commercial archipelago. In the eighteenth century, Buenos Aires developed its own hinterland in the pampas, and by 1810 could be said to rule over a commercial dominion in the making. In this fashion Buenos Aires and Potosí flourished symbiotically— both found thriving external markets for their staples while exports monetized the provincial economies around these axes.

The silver economy's effects spread well beyond the mineshaft. In a series of classic studies, Carlos Sempat Assadourian described the emergence of an economic "space" whose rhythms and boundaries followed the pulse of highland mining. Silver production in Potosí had slumped for over a century before reviving in the 1720's. Exemptions from royalties, access to finance, improved techniques, falling prices of mercury, coupled with the redoubling of the forced labor drafts (the *mita*), helped spur recovery. From 1720 to 1780, silver output tripled in Potosí, generating demand for goods produced in neighboring provinces, yielding a relative degree of regional self-sufficiency. As provendors for the mining complex, scattered corners of Potosí's economic "space" oriented themselves toward the internal market. The circulation of mining capital primed a region whose fortunes rose and fell with silver output.[26] Thus, a broad radius around Cerro Rico felt the pull of mines; the "space" was alive with new energy just as Buenos Aires was emerging as its mediator with Europe.

Potosí's commercial riptides reached as far as the pampas. Córdoba produced textiles for the highlands as early as the 1580's, and while the clothing *obrajes* eventually waned, the region soon supplied the mines with wheat, mules, and especially cattle. As silver picked up in the eighteenth century, so did local woolen manufacturing. Other local beneficiaries included Santiago del Estero and Catamarca—also textile sources. Paraguay sent its tea (*yerba mate*), cotton, and sugar to the highlands. But the real legatees were the way stations en route: Salta (cattle, wheat, grease, and wine) and Tucumán (a great purveyor and fattener of mules from its own environs and the Littoral, beasts of burden for the refineries, and especially endless transportation caravans). Even the

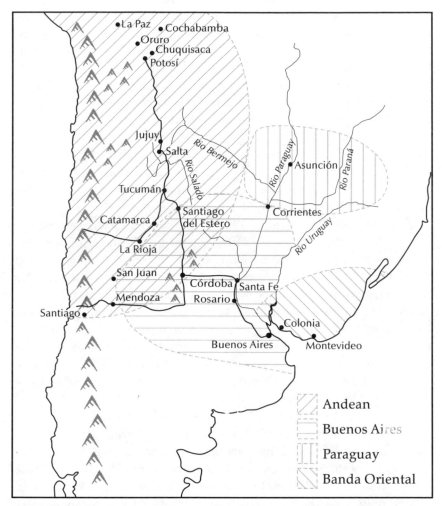

La Paz • Cochabamba
Oruro
Chuquisaca
Potosí

Jujuy
Salta
Río Bermejo
Río Paraguay
Asunción
Río Paraná

Tucumán
Río Salado
Santiago
del Estero
Corrientes
Catamarca
Río Uruguay
La Rioja
San Juan
Córdoba
Santa Fe
Mendoza
Rosario
Santiago
Colonia
Buenos Aires
Montevideo

Andean
Buenos Aires
Paraguay
Banda Oriental

Map 2. Primary Economic Spaces in the Viceroyalty of the River Plate in the Late Eighteenth Century

Littoral (the riverine districts of the River Plate drainage basin) sent increasing numbers of hides for leather use in mining (see Map 2).[27]

As the eighteenth century came to a close, Buenos Aires began to tug at Potosí's economic "space." Consumer demand in the port soon lured provinces that once faced only the highland market. Local producers as far as the piedmont began selling their merchandise to the *porteño* market. Some of the livestock raised in the lowland valleys for highland mining was diverted to Littoral outlets. Córdoba's trading radius shifted as wheat, and even woolen and some cotton textiles, flowed from west to east rather than the other way around. By the 1790's, the province was more enmeshed in Buenos Aires' orbit than Potosí's. Much the same can be said of wine and aguardiente of San Juan and Mendoza.[28] Some provinces enjoyed the benefits of two commercial poles, their earlier highland spatial orientation and the new magnet of the port.

Regional monetization stoked the lure of telluric fortunes in the territories surrounding the mouth of the River Plate. In the centuries after the explorer Garay introduced cattle to the region in the 1570's, feral herds of *ganado cimarrón* roamed throughout the Littoral. By the middle of the eighteenth century the Jesuits conducted a booming business slaughtering in the Upper Mesopotamia; Indians had long since abandoned arable agriculture and gathering, and, having adopted the horse as a primary means of transport (and warfare), found rustling a lucrative venture—in 1751 one raid reached as far as the town of Pergamino. Indeed, so bountiful was the pillage of hoofed beasts, that feral herds were fast depleting by mid century.[29]

As a result, the eighteenth century witnessed a secular conversion in property rights in the Littoral: the combination of expanding commercial outlets and scarcity of livestock induced ranchers to invest more in herds of domesticated beasts. For the *estancieros* (ranchers) of the River Plate cattle, not land, was the principal destination for investment. Landed units had to be held in such large extensions for grazing to yield profits. Without fencing and public enforcement, enclosures were impracticable. Besides, Spain's legal system treated these lands under an array of rubrics of possession, few of which could be called outright absolute private property. Besides, the sheer abundance of land, and therefore low prices or barriers to entry, thwarted most temptations to fix prices or claim exclusive domains.[30]

This generalization needs some spatial nuancing. The relative absence of full-blooded private property in land was more characteristic of frontier districts. Within the frontier, closer to urban centers, land was more systematically parceled and privatized. Indeed, plot sizes and insecurity of tenure tended to shrink in direct proportion to their distance from the market. Consequently, as Garavaglia and Gelman have noted, it is important to distinguish between landownership and access to land.[31] Access was almost limitless; but ownership was not. Titles came in a myriad of forms and spanned the spectrum from unconditional domains to highly contingent use-rights, in general obeying the rule that proximity to markets led to greater individual security of title.

Combined, the existence of a spectrum of rights (from relative to absolute property) with commercial incentives yielded concentric bands of land use radiating out of market centers like Buenos Aires, Montevideo, and other Littoral towns. Market gardening on small *chacras* flourished in zones contiguous to urban sites, and indeed the boundary between town and country frequently blurred in these sub-urban belts. Farther afield, farmers raised cash crops, mainly grain and especially wheat for local consumption, and combined arable agriculture with husbandry. Stretching into the pampa itself, arable agriculture gave way to ranching. But even here, as historians are increasingly discovering, the workers on estates frequently sowed crops on their plots, for both domestic and local market consumption, and outback squatting was rampant. In the words of one contemporary "people are bored with formalities, costs, and visits to the notary, and have discovered a way of coming to hold land arbitrarily."[32] Thus, great heterogeneity in land uses complemented, and indeed reinforced, the juridical complexity of land titles. To confuse matters, land use did not necessarily imply, to say nothing of cause, legal evolution—that would have to await the effects of the revolution of 1810. Agriculturalists were not necessarily landowners, nor for that matter were ranchers—within any different group, the gamut of squatters, cash tenants, share-croppers, and outright owners coexisted.

Simplistic portrayals of the emerging landed regime of the Littoral do not capture the region's deep ambiguities and the fullness of its contradictions. The long-standing image of a binary society polarized between an enriched and oligarchical landed elite and an exploited mass of semi-coerced *conchabados*—in short, the notion of "feudalism" in the River Plate has not stood the test of empirical verification.[33] Very few *estancieros* boasted herds of more than 1,000 head of cattle; most possessed several hundred. Moreover, it is easy, given the jural form of landholding, to exaggerate the prominence of large units. Use-rights were frequently conditional; the average value of land was extremely low. Education was poor; Indians frequently decimated stocks; and, bereft of a system of entailment (legal fetters on the partition of properties among heirs), estates often splintered into micro-units upon the death of their owners. Carlos Mayo's thorough survey of estate probates discloses a very rustic life-style among the *estancieros*: many died without even shoes and socks in their wardrobes.[34]

Moving down the social ladder does not reveal dramatic impoverishment. Urban growth stimulated a market-attuned peasantry who rented or owned land and fetched rising prices—albeit highly unstable—for their output. In the coastal districts from San Isidro and Las Conchas and in the areas of Colonia and Soriano (these being among the oldest colonized counties in the River Plate), inland to more recently settled counties of Matanzas and Luján, wheat cultivation flourished among yeoman producers. Aggregated, these petty transactions sufficed to produce a thriving market. Balancing wheat and growing population suggests sustained and significant productivity and consumption growth.[35] And finally, while the threat of coercion was a specter haunting propertyless sectors, the open frontier, a less than perfect invigilation system, and with relatively easy plebeian access to the means of subsistence, enabled Indians, *gauchos*, and marginal casual workers to float in and out of the labor market on their own terms. As Félix de Azara noted in his famous survey of 1801, workers preferred seasonal employment on estates over full-time contracts in agriculture precisely because it allowed them to combine high seasonal wages with the autonomy of subsisting outside the market nexus.[36] As long as the frontier remained open, control of land and labor markets rested well beyond the reach of any social class. Conflict was endemic, not as a cosmic clash of diametrically opposed social classes, but rather as everyday forms of litigation and negotiation over disputed terms of property rights, violations of barely enforceable contracts, and even plebeian defense of customary access to open lands.[37]

The picture presented so far best portrays the belt of land in the countryside around Buenos Aires where elites on the whole stayed in the city, where produce went to local market consumption, and where the openness of the frontier created a porous society. In other Littoral provinces, frontier dynamics created different, and much tenser, social milieus. In Corrientes, after constant legal battling with Jesuits protecting the autonomy of Guaraní Indians culminating in the ouster of the Order in 1767, *estancieros* dragooned Indians from the north to work on estates. Absentee ranchers staked dubious exclusive claims to land, abusing an ineffective legal system to enforce their unilateral domains. In the waning days of the colony, crime and social stress were on the rise.[38]

Tenser still was the Banda Oriental across the River Plate from Buenos Aires. There, the balance of city and country skewed the other way: bereft of special commercial concessions, the Montevideo elite took a greater interest in landed rather than mercantile investments. Accordingly, the hinterland became the domain for large *latifundios* exporting its produce to foreign markets. In 1780, Francisco Medina, having studied whale-salting techniques in the south Atlantic, introduced the first *saladero*, or factory for processing beef (for sale mainly to slave colonies in Havana and neighboring Brazil) just outside Colonia. The need for higher quality cattle induced ranchers to herd their livestock in *rodeos* and even to begin breeding finer stocks.[39] Transformations in production in turn compelled changes in property relations. Bigger producers avidly began claim-staking "open" *baldío* lands in the 1760's, and their *denuncias*, or cases before land officers, introduced a sharper, more dramatic rupture with the prevailing system of open-access resource use. By 1810, most of the land of current-day Uruguay was in private hands. Moreover, many of the big landowners were also prominent merchants in Montevideo—using their financial and commercial networks to promote the refining, sale, and export of the Banda Oriental's staples. The elite also relied on a mobile, mounted labor force. Estate workers came from the ranks of *gauchos* and Indians from the northern Mission districts, and lived in notorious penury—their avenues to subsistence cut off by the exhaustion of feral cattle and the parceling of land.[40] In contrast to Buenos Aires, the rural Banda Oriental was thus more modern and dynamic and tapped into a wider array of markets, but it was also more deeply divided and dichotomized in property relations. Thus by 1810, the Banda Oriental was already seething with rural social conflict. However, in none of these more polarized rural societies did development obliterate vast numbers of interstitial groups—especially small- and medium-sized agriculturalists, a decisive swing group, as we shall see, when the revolution militarized the countryside.[41]

Imperial reconstitution, the recovery of mining, and wider commercial outlets transformed the countryside of the Littoral. By the 1790's, the area was in the throes of an ambiguous and far from complete capitalist transformation. This was, nonetheless, a capitalist transformation from above: mercantilist revamping by the state, coupled with privileges afforded to merchant capital after the Seven Years' War, set the parameters of economic expansion. Thus, if there were an elite prospering with imperial reconstitution, it was nestled in the viceregal capital and identified more with the circulation of money and goods than their production. In short, political property rights endured as the mainstay for dynastic wealth.

If Buenos Aires' dominion over the River Plate rested in part on its constitutional authority, its other pillar of strength came from the city's merchants, great and small. In the balance between urban merchants and country producers, the former milked the latter. Merchants obeyed a licensing system that restricted competition—they carved out semi-exclusive markets for themselves and sold their wares at inflated prices. Moreover, the generic dearth of cash allowed merchants to use advances—short-term loans—to pad their earnings. One Italian-born merchant of Buenos Aires, Domingo Belgrano Pérez, controlled a broad tapestry of commercial affairs from France to Brazil, stitched together by the ornate threading of finance, especially the practice of sale on credit. Many merchants established ties with rural taverns and general stores (the *pulperías*) to sell goods on consignment. More commonly, each January, as the harvest drew to a close, the city's most prominent dealers gathered their itinerant sales force (the platoons of *mercachifles* who loaded their carts, mules, or backs with consumer items and hocked their loads along rural byways) and sent them out into the hinterland just as the supply of rural staples was especially abundant. Some wealthy rural-dwellers already contracted their own salesmen and adopted this commercial strategy within their estate or locale. Modest producers had less recourse to defense against mercantile oligopsony and collaboration. In general, merchants sold their goods at collusively inflated prices and bought rural produce at seasonally depressed prices—a neat system of unequal exchange between the country and city.[42]

This network transcended the Littoral. The most powerful *porteño* merchants extended their network into the heart of the mining economy. Some Spanish merchants ventured from the peninsula to Potosí—such as Antonio Zabalet, Luis de Oruate, and Pedro Antonio Azcárate—leaving behind agents in the port. More commonly, European dealers based themselves in Buenos Aires and operated through a network of regional satraps. José Martínez de Hoz, peninsular *doyen* of a regional commercial dynasty, forged ties with the Tagle family of Jujuy, a town that functioned as the gateway from the lowland valleys to the highlands. The Tagles commanded a web of contacts from Córdoba, Salta, and throughout the *altiplano*, through which they retailed merchandise (mainly clothing, hats and silk scarves—modest epicures for isolated elites) sent from de Hoz's Buenos Aires warehouses. All along the line, each intermediary socked high markups on European commodities.[43]

Politically defended collusive habits reduced merchants' risks and yielded handsome rents, but the mercantile fabric was spun as much out of informal thread as formal marketing methods. If unequal exchange was the weave of merchant power, kinship and marriage among scions was its woof. The patriarchs of merchant families kept a keen eye out for eligible nuptial partners for their children, rigorously screening circles of sociability for convenience. Marriage into the families of partners or even commercial rivals ensured that the business of buying and selling remained within the same circle. Kinship maneuvering along these lines was all the more important to retain a merchant house's status since, without an effective system of primogeniture (where inheritance fell to a single heir, thereby preserving the entity of family property) dynasties could quickly splinter. Nor did Spanish law yet foster the formation of private joint-stock firms. Fictive kinship ties among merchant families provided an alternative means to uphold dynastic continuity. But it was not necessarily a hermetically closed circle—for as the regional economy boomed and trade grew and diversified, new merchants constantly entered the field. The tapestry of the merchants elite incorporated *parvenus* traders—especially if their commercial dexterity quickly pushed them up the social order—by taking sons and daughters as eligible grooms and brides. To the unfortunate offspring, love and romance were secondary considerations in marital choice. But big merchants, in the end, could not always control the variables: fertility rates among the wealthy remained high, creating heirs who could not always be conveniently placed, some children effectively resisted the unilateral dictates of their parents (sons in particular, often opted for prestigious professions like law rather than stay in the family business), and the constant in-migration of new merchants unspun any potential fabric of oligarchy.[44] To be sure, merchants constituted a local elite, but, much as they tried, they could not form an aristocracy.

Estancieros, especially the larger ones, were hardly absent from this thickening matrix of power. Indeed, colonial development and diversification presented the possibility of establishing alternative, and not necessarily subversive, arenas to express common concerns. From the 1770's, ranchers lobbied to secure exclusive rights to a protected local market for their produce and struggled to gain some control over the commercial system, to little avail. In effect, their efforts to replicate the merchants' delicate but nonetheless effective system to stabilize prices could not transcend some obvious collective action problems. In light of the numbers and variety of rural producers, ensuring compliance with any collusive regime—to become a true corporate guild—was a tall order, to say the least. Ranchers did keep up their verbal battles in petitions and claims to the Cabildo (municipal council) and Consulado (merchant guild), which grew with intensity in the 1790's. In their demands for more liberal slave-importing policies and greater access to foreign markets of neutral powers to sell their staples, they soon found allies among some merchants who were already chafing under the Consulado's strict reign. But any latent conflict was quickly doused. On the whole, ranchers were much the junior partners in the alliance with merchants.[45] Institutions helped nurture the emergence of new interests but did not fundamentally alter social hierarchies or allegiances. How did this society fare under duress?

Tradewinds of War

It is tempting to conclude that the Bourbons succeeded in reconstituting their realm and making Buenos Aires into an effective outpost for royal mercantilism. In renewing mercantilism, Spanish authorities created a regional commercial empire in the River Plate. But they could not insulate this creation from the effects of the French Revolution and European war. In 1793, allies dragged a reluctant Spain into a war against revolutionary France. Then, in a desperate about-face to avoid an invasion by Jacobin armies, Spain sided with France and declared war against Britain in 1796, only to have her fleet smashed at the hands of Admiral Horatio Nelson at the Battle of Cape St. Vincent in February 1797, whereupon the British naval commander began a stiff blockade of Cádiz. Less than a decade later, in 1805, Nelson reenacted the damage to the Armada at Trafalgar. Save the brief respite following the Peace of Amiens (1802–4), Spain was at war with the Atlantic commercial might of the

British from 1796 to 1808. On average, between 1797 and 1820 (thus, considering also the effects of the wars for independence in parts of South America), Spain's exports to her colonies were scarcely more than the value of 1778, on the eve of *comercio libre.*[46] Spain's alignment, the escalation of conflict and the effects of the continental blockade issued powerful hammer-blows against the reconstituted dams of Spanish mercantilism.

War intensified the crown's thirst for revenues. Marshaling a fighting force in Europe was daunting enough, but rebuilding a crushed Armada to defend beleaguered sea-lanes was another. To make matters worse, Carlos IV (1788–1808) was less than up to the job, and let his shady Minister Godoy control policy. The crown turned to the dominions for financial help. Unfortunately, this round of war embroiled colonies in their own urgent need to defend borders against interlopers. Napoleon coaxed Spain into a declaration of war against Portugal in February of 1801, and while this was inconsequential in the European theater, it opened the way for Brazilian forces to invade the Banda Oriental. Known as the "Guerra de las Naranjas," the conflict for supremacy in the River Plate soaked up Buenos Aires' remittances to Spain. The Brazilian invasion destroyed *estancias* as far as the River Ibicuy, and pampean Indians exploited Spain's threadbare defenses and stepped up their plunder of livestock in daring *charrúa* strikes as deep as the River Negro. Local authorities created new garrisons to fend off invaders, most famously the mounted Blandengues, from whose ranks would rise a generation of creole officers, the most famous being José de Artigas. Urban militias, such as the Patricios, kept order closer to home. In sum, from 1797 Buenos Aires' spending soared—more than doubling the 1787 level—only to abate, and then rise again after the turn of the century.[47] The collapse in trade eviscerated customs returns. In 1798, revenues from port traffic dropped to one-third of the previous year's income. For the next four years, until the Peace of Amiens, customs were nil. Local authorities made up for the deficits by absorbing Spanish remittances and systematized borrowing through the legerdemain of accounting transfers.[48]

War also hammered trade and crippled colonial political economies. Mercury, for instance, ever the crucial input for extracting silver from highland ores, had to come from Europe. Blockades that attended the naval war interrupted mercury imports. Silver output began a plunge downward—a decline from which the southern Andes would never again rise. Potosí's recovery under the Bourbons was probably waning even without the shock of mercury shortages. Either way, mining slumped continuously after the turn of the century, sapping a source of revenue just at a time when both Madrid and Buenos Aires coveted liquidity.[49]

The entire highland's economic "space"—a society already rife with tension—felt the blows. Since the Tupac Amaru and Tupac Catari rebellions of the 1780's, civil and military officials kept a close eye on the Andes.[50] At the same time, pressures on the mining sector compelled local officials to rely ever more on forced labor drafts, the *mita*, to prop output—which is to say, sustain profits to rentier owners and operators. The need to supply (and support) *mitayos* only aggravated the burden on communities.[51] Increased vigilance was more than matched by rising tension.

The highland mining districts exploded in revolt in 1805. For years, the region was plagued by drought: food supplies dwindled; the lagoons feeding the silver refineries of Potosí began to dry up, throwing thousands out of work. Fiscal pressure forced Intendants and *corregidores* to reap taxes and collect tribute from an immizerated indigenous population. The new chapter of upheaval was a shadow of the 1780's insurrection, but was not easy for local civil and military authorities to suppress. Coerced Andean *mitayos* fled the mines in droves, and it took several years of vicious enforcement to restore work in the shafts and slag heaps. One alarmed Potosí merchant moaned that the city "is an epidemic of disease, hunger and poverty, as anyone who descends from there will tell you, and all of Peru has fallen behind as a result of the generalized drought. I will go there and see, but I hope my God spares me from this enterprise and brings me no more, for everything I see is overturned and in ruins."[52] On the heels of the rural revolt came an urban insurrection of 1809 in Chuquisaca. Rebels, mainly creoles angry at the despotic pretensions of the Junta of Seville's envoy, José Manuel Goyeneche, and his alignment with the arch-reactionary Governor of Potosí, Francisco de Paula Sanz, seized the town and within days the insurrection spread to La Paz. Goyeneche fled to Cuzco where he appealed to Lima's Viceroy Abascal to lend him an army to crush the rebels. Goyeneche and Paula Sanz marched a royal army to Chuquisaca and proceeded to pummel the city into submission. The insurrection's leaders faced public executions and their bodies were left dangling in the town square.[53]

If the riptides of European wars and revolution upset the uneasy balance in the archaic world of highland silver, they also dislocated the expectations of uninterrupted prosperity in colonial ports—including Buenos Aires. How did Buenos Aires' merchants adjust to short-run shocks? Did upheaval shake mercantilist convictions? For several years before the continental conflagration erupted, the city's largest wholesalers, Manuel Rodríguez, Bernardo Sancho Larrea, and Martín de Sarratea had been pushing for a Consulado—a guardian for commercial interests before public authorities and a regulatory agent to monitor the behavior of merchants themselves. In the end, to cope with the effects of war and manage business uncertainties in the Viceroyalty, a royal decree created a merchant guild in 1794. In effect, the guild enabled local merchants to make policy on the spot with greater acuity—and effectiveness—in protecting political property and mercantile rents.[54]

Upholding the institutional girders of merchants' rents—preserving Buenos Aires' commercial command over the entire region and dispensing rights to ply new trade routes—was a thorny problem. Scarcely had the guild opened its doors than it faced two immediate issues that drove a wedge within the seeming like-mindedness of the city's economic elite. Both issues poised the merchant class against itself: some (especially the more privileged networks) wanted to deal with the crisis by redoubling the enforcement of mercantilist rules, while others (often smaller, involved more in exporting) wanted to open up the hermetic circle of guild privileges to cope with shortages and market-blows caused by war. The former considered themselves loyal custodians of an ancient and naturalized hierarchy of property; the latter presented themselves as entrepreneurs capable of adapting the colonial system to trans-Atlantic exigencies, and therefore able to rescue the ancien régime of property from myopic misrule.

Blockades created serious shortages of imported goods. The crisis of mercantilism began to reveal the contradictory interests within the port's guilds. To cope with sudden shortages, authorities turned a blind eye to merchants reaching out to unconventional (especially British) suppliers, many of whom had already begun to invade Spanish American ports. But for some merchants, relaxation led to brigandry. Accordingly, the Buenos Aires Consulado issued a battery of punitive decrees to crack down on illegal traders. In December 1795, the Potosí branch of the Consulado arrested one merchant on his way from Jujuy to the mining center with a load of forbidden goods.[55]

Warfare also led to a stockpile of staples for export. For years, producers and merchants had been calling for more imports of Africans to help alleviate the high cost of labor until finally the crown abolished the *asiento* in 1791, leaving the right to import slaves to individual merchants licensed by the Consulado. As it was, most slaves came not from Africa, but from Brazil. Opening the gateway to slave vessels from Rio de Janeiro offered the opportunity to export stockpiled staples to new, illegal markets. Some merchants pounced on this opportunity. But this implied throwing their weight around in the Consulado, upsetting the delicate balance of rent-seeking merchants, each enjoying their take of trade. Tomás Antonio Romero, one of the city's most powerful magnates running the trade routes from Potosí, a seasoned provider for the Royal Navy, and in control of the port's slave shipments from 1784, battled to fend off other merchants' demands for a cut in the slave trade business. In 1793, he convinced authorities to allow him to increase his annual quota to 1,000 slaves (to be bought in Brazil) and permission to ship 250,000 pesos' worth of staples on English ships. This provoked a stir among competitors, who charged that so many exports would create scarcities and drive up the price of locally consumed staples, and worse, that Romero's imports would flood the local market. Others accused the local Superintendant Francisco de Paula Sanz of corruption (which would eventually lead to his dispatch to Potosí where he would rule with an iron fist).[56] To heal the rifts, the new Consulado reduced Romero's deal to 100,000 pesos' worth of exports. When the French merchant the Count of Liniers appealed for a similar concession (slave imports and export quotas for hides in particular), the Consulado denied the appeal on the grounds that hides were technically not *frutos del país* (staples) and were meant for local consumption.[57] The question of slave imports was the less divisive issue; at the heart of the controversy was the threat of uncontrolled cargoes and thus the menace to mercantilist rents upheld through allocated trading rights. The compression on the Bourbon system began to shatter merchants' consensus over the mechanisms to dispense property rights.

This did not prevent some rural producers and merchants from intensifying the campaign to allow trade with allies. One petition of producers even called for the creation of a public joint-stock company to promote exports of the region's meat.[58] Another noted that the countryside "produced immense harvests of grains capable of supporting not only Spain in case of shortages, but also the rest of Europe."[59] In his application to export staples to "foreign colonies" in 1796, Manuel Aguirre explicitly argued that bending the old mercantilist rules would not deprive Spain of scarce goods, for locals were stockpiling hides and meat that Spain did not need. But he reintroduced the chimera of foreign cargoes. Ships leaving with hides and other staples, he argued, could return with goods such as sugar, cotton, coffee, and slaves, none of which were available in Spain anyway, and therefore did not constitute a threat to entrenched legal privileges. He was, perhaps, too sanguine about big merchants' ability to tolerate even the specter of interloping. Aguirre's presentation detonated a heated debate between old oligopolists determined to maintain their grip over imports, against merchants (backed by rural producers) looking for new commercial networks. One of his detractors fiercely opposed the concession, maintaining that "return cargoes are not supposed to exceed the value of the sale of extracted goods to foreign colonies, because otherwise they would easily open the free route to fraud and indirect commerce by foreigners to the detriment of our provinces." He added that such "infractions and palpable damage due to the return cargoes on these ships" were already taking their toll.[60] Thereafter, the Consulado struggled to balance contradictory interests of exporters and merchants who felt that any traffic of vessels to carry staples would widen the possibility of illicit trade and erode the power of large oligopolists.

Matters grew more complicated once Spain declared war on Britain in 1797. Now that Britain need not respect the trading formalities of its turncoat ally, British merchants looked upon Spain's isolation from her colonies as an invitation to flood prohibited markets. Shipments to Spain's colonies soared during the war years 1796 to 1802—almost all of them illegal. Even with the return of peace after Amiens, trade continued. By the time war resumed in 1805, the British established solid toeholds in the most important ports, and Buenos Aires most of all.[61] Desperate to seem as if he were in control of matters and as a sop to colonial consumers—but to the chagrin of the Cádiz Consulado—Carlos IV legalized colonies' rights to trade with "neutral" powers in 1797. He added the unenforceable condition that ships unloading foreign merchandise return to Spanish ports with colonial produce. This was a decisive turn because it forsook the old principle of excluding foreigners from colonial trade. One by one, Consulado branches in the Americas reluctantly embraced the measure. In Buenos Aires, a furious debate erupted in the guild's meeting hall. The combination of merchant grumbling in Cádiz and uproar among oligopolists in the colonies prompted a new royal order revoking the 1797 decree on trade with neutrals, restoring the *status quo ante* in April 1799—a move applauded by some of the Consulado's directors, the Spanish oligopolists Martín de Alzaga, José Martínez de Hoz, and Diego Agüero. Their triumph was pyrrhic.

By now, not a few merchants, creole and peninsular alike, many of whom like Tomás Fernández and Francisco Antonio de Escalada were also Consulado members, had come to profit from handling foreign merchandise and dispatching staple exports. Manuel Aguirre proclaimed their position openly in the Consulado. Exports were good for everyone: "when we comprehend this promise . . . it will facilitate and multiply the extraction of staples and products from Buenos Aires that is the whole purpose and objective of the policies of Our Sovereign." In the meantime, a prostrate Spain was hardly able to furnish the Viceroyalty with needed goods. At stake was the whole principle of oligopoly powers and protection of mercantile privileges. Aguirre, again: "although there are some who, by establishment and connection, can trade with Cádiz, Lima, or Havana, etc., they have a particular interest in sustaining these links to fix monopolies and in this fashion undermining at their birth all reciprocal trade of our staples with foreign colonies, and in so doing sacrifice the common good to their own particular interests."[62] From the viewpoint of Littoral producers and their merchant allies, as Aguirre decried, Cádiz had declared commercial war against Buenos Aires.

For all intents and purposes, the contradictory swings in peninsular policy only confirmed what officials were accepting in practice: the crown's hold over policy lay in shambles. Management of the commercial and fiscal crisis fell to authorities and Consulados in the Americas— but it was becoming clear to all members of the merchant guild of Buenos Aires that harmonious self-management was an empty hope.[63] For the time being, oligopolists maintained the upper hand, even though their grip on the trading system of the Viceroyalty was beginning to slip.

Several aspects of this debate deserve emphasis. First, oligopolists' opponents were not arguing for creole rights over peninsulars; local and Spanish-born merchants and *estancieros* could be found in both camps. Defense of local commercial interests at no point translated into a challenge to crown authority—quite the opposite, for many merchants complained that oligopolists were betraying the monarch's benevolent disposition to his subjects. Second, they were not the champions of any "free-trade" dogma *avant la lettre*. While they wanted to open trade arteries within the empire and with neutrals, they still clung to the fundamental conviction that the empire must realize trade surpluses as a whole. Their concern was that such a tight circle of mercantile privilege choked overall commerce and, by depriving exporters of outlets, weakened the realm's ability to export more than it imported in aggregate. The result, as Aguirre and his followers had warned, was that oligopoly merchants (again, mainly importers who wanted firm control over the traffic of vessels into and out of the ports of empire) with links to Cádiz placed their own particular interests ahead of the concerns of the empire. They exploited the nostrums and practices of rent-seeking mercantilism to undermine its own survival. The new merchants began to express the notion that commerce was a right, and not a privilege, not because they believed in an entirely different proprietary order, but because the old system was being strangled by abuse.

Conclusion

Unwittingly, Buenos Aires cultivated within itself a latent schism between two different kinds of colonial economies: one, a traditional but not yet waning concern to handle precious metals, and another embarking on a whole new generation of primary staples from land. By the late eighteenth century, South America was in the throes of a deep transformation from one export orientation to another, from a sixteenth-century obsession with precious metals to the nineteenth-century hunger for foodstuffs and raw materials for an industrial age. In a last ditch effort to prolong the life span of that earlier "Hapsburg paradigm" (to use the *bon mots* of Stanley and Barbara Stein), the Bourbons conceived the city of Buenos Aires as a gateway to the Andes via the River Plate. Their framework for such an operation was to reconstitute the empire with a renovated bureaucracy and commercial reform, making Buenos Aires the privileged and effective outpost for mercantilism. But the very nature of imperial reconstitution unleashed the unintended consequence of economic diversification, husbanding an incipient agrarian transformation.

This latent schism had a spatial expression: mining was a highland business based on an archaic system of forced and semi-coerced labor; agrarian production thrived in the Littoral, predicated on more modern practices of labor recruitment. These two regions, two logics of extraction and oriented to different consumers, harbored two wholly distinguishable regimes of property relations. These two regions coexisted within the same polity, indeed, they lived symbiotically. Rural staples flowed to the highlands as inputs and foodstuffs; and so long as silver flowed back down, the highlands injected liquidity that helped nourish the emerging pampean economy. The Potosí-Cádiz axis did not inhibit the development of the new hinterland; quite the opposite.

What combined these two systems, or "articulated" their disparities—to use the fighting word of structuralism—was merchant capital. Merchants bought staples (silver or hides) and sold merchandise from and to whoever offered the prospect of personal gain. They could bridge diverse logics of enterprise in large measure because their services did not subvert relations of production, whether highland-archaic or lowland-modern. Merchants and the extended web of commerce gave the Viceroyalty of the River Plate a thick patina of coherence. This system rested on a symbiotic relationship with a state that defended merchants' rights to exclude interlopers (and thus earn rents) in return for the loyalty of merchant capital to the monarch.

So long as silver flowed, the reconstituted mercantilist system and the world of officially protected property rights and privileges thrived. But as the silver economy plunged into crisis and warfare engulfed the Atlantic world after the French Revolution, the viceregal equipoise was doomed. The true irony was the following: if there was a deep problem simmering in the heart of the Viceroyalty, it came from the merchants themselves, the primary beneficiaries of colonial mercantilism. Responding to the short-term exigencies of war, commercial turmoil, and the gyrations of increasingly incompetent authorities in Madrid, merchants and their guild had to manage the attacks on imperial trading arteries. Faced with these challenges, they could not reconcile the impulse to defend individual merchant property and privileges with concessions to shore up the system as a whole. Imperial reconstitution ran up against its central dilemma: personal property depended on political allocation, but as the empire began to crack, merchant capitalists quite rationally redoubled their rent-seeking opportunism. As the Atlantic world slid into revolution, the ancien régime link between Bourbon dynastic power and the property of merchant capital was put to its definitive test.

3 ⌒ The Quest for Equipoise in the Shadow of Revolution

> En cualquier especie de gobierno todos aman especulativamente la libertad, y practicamente el despotismo; y que me contento con un sistema durable y pacífico, aunque con algunos debilidades, mejor que con otro uniforme, perfecto y grandioso, expuesto continuamente á vicisitudes y desasiegos.
>
> Victorián de Villaba, "Apuntes para una reforma de España"

> A state without the means of some change is without the means of its conservation.
>
> Edmund Burke, *Reflections on the Revolution in France*

Reform Without Rupture

In retrospect, Bourbon efforts to reconstitute their empire on more diversified and dynamic grounds had all the makings of a Sisyphean project. Madrid's institutional reforms, falling well short of dismantling and reassembling its operation, seem doomed to failure—at least to our eyes. Entrenched interests, sycophantish bureaucrats, uncompetitive merchants, and a disgruntled mass of indigenous peasantry made for a particularly noxious mix for any well-intentioned imperial rebuilder. Seen in this light, imperial collapse was foreordained.

This formulation of the past—especially when we are dealing with the prelude to and causes of major upheaval—can, despite its attractions, mislead. Even if the institutions and interests of empire appeared doomed for destruction, this did not mean that imperial subjects wanted or foresaw such a fate. What role did ideas play in the twilight of the Spanish domain? Faced with mounting trans-Atlantic conflict, Spain's worrying political torpor under the hapless hand of Charles IV, and the stubbornness of Buenos Aires' merchants, how did local creole thinkers apprehend, interpret, and issue remedies for the River Plate's plight?

For many creole leaders, the demise of their colonial world was not in sight, though its health was cause for deep concern. This chapter explores how creoles in Buenos Aires grappled with the turbulence surrounding them during the waning days of the empire, which, through their eyes, was more menaced than doomed. By 1789, the fateful year that brought the fatal blow to Bourbon power in Paris, the architects of imperial reconstitution, José de Gálvez and Carlos III, had only recently died (the former in 1787, the latter in 1788). Hitherto, Spanish policies revived revenues and commerce for the empire and brought new provinces such as the River Plate into juridical being. To creoles and colonial officials, imperial reconstitution to shore up the realm was working.

The conjuncture around 1789–90 gave altogether new meaning to the reformist purpose. Until then, reform aimed to reverse what seemed to be terminal decline from the seventeenth century. After 1789, reform became an urgent necessity to cope not so much with longer-term structural problems, but with the shorter-term specter of spreading revolution. Creole cries to save their provinces from the threat of wholesale social explosion grafted onto the restorationist motives behind earlier reforms.

There is a long historiographic tradition of investing in creole writers prescient powers to diagnose their present and anticipate their future; intellectual pioneers become framers of their own fate. In the world of ideas, creoles translated the perception of a troubled empire into a rising sense of national independence. José Ingenieros offers precisely this sort of interpretation in his landmark *La evolución de las ideas argentinas* (1918), where he explored democratic aspirations chafing under the weakening absolutist hand of the Spanish monarchs. The eighteenth-century Enlightenment infused young creoles with "the formation of an increasingly marked American spirit, until it became a revolutionary anxiety. . . . A freedom in economic and intellectual matters sparked a desire for progress among native whites; and when the metropolis could not condone such dangerous notions, they began, logically, to think of liberty."[1] Upon reaching New World shores, the Enlightenment eroded the sense of identity between colonials and metropolitans.

If the Enlightenment was the ideological and cultural backdrop for new concepts of political community, it was also linked to its late eighteenth-century correlate: revolution. In these imaginings, creole intellectuals converted the emerging sense of selfhood into radicalism, to champion a full rejection of the ancien régime through a praxis of vio-

Voilence

lent upheaval. New identities merged, seamlessly—and perhaps more important, intentionally—into a new form of politics infused by the example of other revolutionary societies of the Atlantic world, especially the United States and France. The Enlightenment not only revealed truisms about despotism (it is a venal thing); it offered a radically different understanding of political virtue, one that could only be realized through a decisive and willful rupture with the past. *ruption / change*

despotism

This is, more or less, Benedict Anderson's understanding of the process of national self-determination. In his sweeping and rightly celebrated book, *Imagined Communities: Reflections on the Origins and Spread of Nationalism*, Anderson sees in colonial subjectivity the making of a creole identity, one that serves as a sort of prototype for the formation of "national" consciousness. Intellectuals and writers created, invented, national communities out of new images of collective boundaries and notions of sovereignty. Combined, the long-term effects of the Enlightenment and print capitalism created the conditions for a distinct, new image of political community on the periphery—one that might serve as a template for subsequent nationalisms. If Spanish American–wide nationalism (along the lines of the thirteen colonies) failed to cohere, it was due to its comparative sprawl and economic backwardness. Creoles soon differentiated themselves from Europeans, but could not identify with themselves across their provincial boundaries. Accordingly, creole yearnings for separation from the metropole created the ideological preconditions for revolution, while separation from each other sowed the seeds for endemic civil war on the heels of independence.

ouch!

When the Enlightenment is cast across the Atlantic in this way, Buenos Aires should appear as a thriving milieu for surging ideas of the political community. By exploring creole reflections and concerns, this chapter assesses this causal relationship between the Enlightenment and creole identity, and how notions of property and political membership recast creoles' sense of place in empire. It also provides a glimpse into the mindsets of men who would soon become principal protagonists of the revolution. What comes clear from the writings of these reformers is just how unconcerned they were about separation from the metropole, how obsessed they became with continuing reform precisely to bolster the connection between the periphery and the core of Spain's trans-Atlantic realm—all of this animated by a profound desire to avoid revolution.

In the Shadow of Revolution

Print capitalism [handwritten margin note]

One important facet of Bourbon imperial reconstitution was the opportunity it created for more public intellectual debate and advocacy of
change [handwritten margin note] recipes for change. By the end of the eighteenth century, Spanish cities
like Madrid, Barcelona, and Seville—not to mention the academic cen-
ters of Valladolid and Salamanca—hosted dozens of associations and
social clubs dedicated to contemplating the fate of the realm. Printers
made a brisk business out of the steady flow of pamphlets, broadsheets,
and circulars for at least a limited "public" readership.

This was no less true of the colonies. The Bourbon reforms acted as a
tonic for creoles themselves to voice, legitimately, concerns about the
future. Buenos Aires, to complement its belated but growing centrality
to the empire, also emerged as an important city championing the cause
of reform within empire. In the late eighteenth and early nineteenth
centuries, especially as trans-Atlantic war plunged Spain into deep fiscal
Political Economy [handwritten margin note] and political crisis, creole reformers of Buenos Aires offered a series of
meditations on political economy and sketches of policies to serve as
lettered city [handwritten margin note] elixirs of empire. Buenos Aires became, in Angel Rama's words, a "lettered city," an urban center within the empire, whose learned energies
flourished with unprecedented autonomy.[2] If Buenos Aires' interests
and institutions were recognizable birthrights of Bourbon reform, the
same held for the city's intellectuals.

Yet Atlantic war and revolution inspired mounting concern. By the
late eighteenth century, the River Plate had become a siphon for European and North American publications and a vibrant flow of broadsheets and *pasquines*. Locals were well apprised of distant events, in
particular the fallout of revolutions within Spain's competitors, Britain
and France. Peninsulars and creoles alike followed the separation of
both of Spain's main rivals' colonial jewels: for Britain the thirteen colo-
Haiti. [handwritten margin note] nies; for France, Saint Domingue. By 1791, Caribbean slave revolts ignited fears that folded into preexisting apprehensions in the highlands
of River Plate Viceroyalty. The quick succession of news arriving in
Buenos Aires, first of the execution of the French monarchy and then the
shocking declaration of war against France in 1793, accentuated official
alarm. This spectacle prompted Madrid to send secret instructions to
squelch any secessionist talk, especially targeting French intellectual influences. Authorities outlawed the dissemination of subversive tracts
and commanded that all stamps, plates, and manuscripts relating to

France be embargoed and shipped to Spain, to little effect. Yet the classic books of the Enlightenment, the works of Raynal, Rousseau, Montesquieu, and Voltaire continued to adorn the personal libraries of the Buenos Aires establishment. Rumors of plots circulated in the streets of Buenos Aires, especially after the captain and crew of the French vessel *Le Dragon* faced charges of cavorting with the local populace. Troops patrolled the streets of Buenos Aires and Montevideo, and the paranoia hit a high-water mark in early 1795 with a wave of unrest of Frenchmen and some creoles.[3]

France, however, was not the only source of Enlightenment inspiration and reflection. Spain too had a long tradition of semi-public debate over reform. The works of Italian and French political economists were common intellectual staples in the metropolis as well as far-flung colonies. Adam Smith's *Wealth of Nations*, already available in French, was translated to Spanish at Valladolid in 1794. Perhaps of equal weight were the "Memorias" and "Informes" of Campomanes and Jovellanos, tracts (written by, and to, ministers of the Bourbon courts in Madrid) that called for the relaxation of restrictions on trade, the modernization of education, and most trenchantly, support to agriculture and landed interests.[4]

These writings flowed from the pens of physiocrats, and by the 1770's they constituted a loose but coherent body of thought concerned with growing signs of social malaise and their economic causes. In Paris, where much of the new political economy was born, physiocratic economists issued a series of tracts that began shifting foundational notions of virtue, society, and prosperity. François Quesnay—the royal physician and Adam Smith's inspiration—offered a profound prescription for reform. The cornerstone of this vision was a transformed approach to nature: if European dynasts had treated their possessions as the monarch's property to be allocated among loyal followers, now— following Locke's *Second Treatise*—property emerged out of the application of labor to land, not *a priori* universal claims. Nature's role was not so much to honor great men or furnish royal wealth, but rather to be the source of prosperity for society as a whole. The well-being of all members reflected the power and sagacity of leaders. Accordingly, the heroes of Quesnay's new political economy were not warriors but farmers, the producers of a society's crucial bounty: food. Thus, material and, for perhaps the first time deductively, spiritual health shifted from the direct grip of the State to the behavior and incentives facing proprietors

who had earned their titles through private application of effort and labor.

To the revalorization of nature went, almost as a direct consequence,
a revision of the State. Quesnay's contemporary Turgot (briefly Louis
XVI's Controleur Général) pushed the consequences of physiocracy one
step further. Heretofore, the monarch allocated property as a privilege.
Corporate guilds acted as the custodians of politically derived rights, re-
ciprocating their gratitude with suppliant payments. In turn, corporate
guilds managed their internal affairs, controlling conflict and distributing rewards among constituent members. For Turgot, this political form
of property stifled creativity and enterprise. Coddled and protected
guild members served their own interests, inflating prices of their merchandise and services, limiting competition, and depressing returns to
direct producers, farmers, and manufacturers. For Turgot, the State
should be less interested in managing its allocative powers than in defending private property owners and their just rewards. What is more,
taxes on producers had become illegitimate incursions on the natural
rights of men—as they were coming to be imaged in pre-revolutionary
France—to enhance their personhood through exclusive enjoyment of
their property.[5]

If this emerging notion of capitalist property discharged economic
and moral images of man as proprietor and political *before* the State (and
thus governed by worldly and material drives to self- and community
betterment), it was firmly rooted in a changing notion of commerce.
Trading rights were traditionally treated as the purvey of dynasts and
the means to thwart imperial rival ambitions. To some commentators,
however, warfare was the *result* of these artificial barriers to trade: merchants and warriors fought to protect their domains because they did
not enjoy rights to trade freely with each other. Montesquieu in particular argued that free exchange between people curbed any temptation to
bellicosity. Freer commerce would allow merchants to trade the benefits
of these resources rather than fight over them. In this image of *doux
commerce*, trading exercised a civilizing influence on social relations; the
market, in these circumstances, tamed its participants. Exchange, for
Montesquieu, can "make custom gentle."[6]

Together, trading and rights to enjoy property free from unjust State
tampering altered the vision of a balance between private interests and
public concerns—making the former, once the scourge of political theorists, the bedrock of a new image of society, one in which economic

forces would play an increasing role as passion-tamer and tonic for civic virtue.[7] It also had a secondary role—and one that enjoyed an especially powerful appeal in the less advanced areas of Europe and their overseas possessions. In Naples and Madrid, emerging notions of capitalist property served also as remedies for the agonizing concern about how to reverse imperial decadence. In many ways, Spain was the European power that most sought to translate the new nostrums into policy under the Bourbons. Not surprisingly, the works of José del Campillo, Campomanes, and Jovellanos all echoed French thought, but inflected it with urgency. The monarch would have to embrace these new notions of property and commerce or suffer the same fate as Rome—a disturbing exemplar to which the Spanish were repeatedly compared: collapse as a result of external pounding on an internally decaying realm. This made the colonies all the more important for security of boundaries and the trading health of the empire. Thus physiocratic reform, to complement its peaceable and virtuous effects, also solved problems of social and economic backwardness.

Perhaps the most widely read of champions of reform-to-reverse-decay were the Neapolitan political economists Gaetano Filangeri, Ferdinando Galiani, and especially Antonio Genovesi, the Professor of Moral Philosophy and later Political Economy at the University of Naples. For decades, Neapolitan writers shaped the terms of discussion and policy in Spain, so that when Carlos III assumed the throne after his sojourn in Naples, he only intensified the links between Madrid and the Kingdom of Naples—a link forged out a deep but expedient anxiety to cope with backwardness, and increasingly, shortages and famines.[8] Genovesi, whose three-volume *Lezioni di commercio* provided lengthy passages to be translated, transcribed, and imported—plagiarized if you will—into the tracts of some local writers in the River Plate, was perhaps the most commonly read political economist in the Viceroyalty.[9] What little we know of the private libraries in the River Plate testify to the importance of Italian writers: aside from the legal codes, manuals, and commentaries (the obligatory bibliographic accoutrements for any jurist or theologian), only Aquinas and Augustine, Cervantes, and the Inca Garcilaso de la Vega's *Historia de Florida* and *Comentarios reales* eclipsed French and especially Italian physiocrats.[10] All around them, Neapolitans, and their readers throughout the Spanish realm, saw unnecessary idleness. Educational, agrarian, and commercial reform could enliven and stimulate dormant or suppressed interests to use resources productively.

The Neapolitan Enlightenment, already well versed in the entreaties to modify policies to enable Southern Italy to catch up with other surging corners of Europe, gave political economy a stronger "growth" orientation. This was especially appealing to subjects in the River Plate who were likewise conscious of the mis- and under-use of local capabilities. For Manuel Belgrano, Genovesi's translator into Spanish (actually he translated from the French a version of *Principios de la ciencia económico-política* in 1796 and dedicated it to the Viceroy in Buenos Aires Melo de Portugal in a futile effort to bring him on side), the lesson was unambiguous: "The more the state approximates absolute liberty in the universe of foreign and internal commerce, the more it ensures its own eternal prosperity: if it preserves obstacles, all steps to prosperity are belated and slow."[11] Another Buenos Aires lawyer, asked to opine on appropriate sentencing for cattle thefts, intoned that the region's economic troubles owed themselves to the insecurity of property rights and thus the overkill of cattle stocks, which in turn depresses the "good of the Province" and violates "the authority of Magistrates who must always be responsible for the happiness or decadence of the Peoples he governs" in the name of the King.[12]

In political terms, these were hardly fighting words. This decay-reversing and growth-oriented approach to society and policy did not necessarily upset canonical views of the State as an ethical and teleological entity ruled by a royal power whose "office" gave voice to a general *res publica* for the realization of a shared good. Indeed, it would be a profound mistake to conflate the spread of emerging capitalist theories of property with a revolutionary State-theory. To be sure, the critique of absolutist foibles and excesses destabilized visions of an all-knowing and necessarily benevolent sovereign. But more often than not, physiocracy and the valorization of private interests blended into underlying notions of a Catholic Monarchy concerned in essence with the well-being of subject peoples. The King was, when all was said and done, subject to Natural Law no less than his subjects, even if he were free from the specific laws and customs that governed the social fabric. In this view of a sovereign beholden to his subjects' material and spiritual "common weal," new political economy meshed with an older scholastic framework. Indeed, the reforms championed in Paris, Madrid, and Naples, and echoed in Buenos Aires and Alto Peru, could be said to rescue the monarch from his venal and stifling entourage. Attention to the possibilities of agrarian and commercial revival could restore the greatness of the crown. To be sure, there were frictions in all this. Were property rights pre-political? Were the contractual foundations of society rooted in a natural submission to authority or to a pact among persons? For the moment, however, reformist writers struggled to assimilate new currents of thought with highly instrumental purposes and within the capacious, even self-contradictory umbrella of the Catholic Enlightenment.[13] Even if the epistemic worlds to which authors referred seem so clearly antagonistic to us now, the problem of backwardness of the empire and concern about challenges to authority meant that Enlightenment voices in the colonies could champion deep reform while maintaining their fervent regalism—precisely because they could rhetorically present their designs as measures to rescue the monarch and his realm from the specter of collapse and, increasingly, revolution.

The Quest for Equipoise

The mental world of creole writers appealed to an eclectic assortment of registers, from modern images of exchange and production to baroque notions of divine rulers. The most important writings or manifestos animating "public" debate (owing to ink and paper shortages, especially in days of war, or even logistical mishaps, some of these texts reached only limited circulation) came from the hands of political economists, men concerned with the state of trade and production in the colony and empire. Many, such as Belgrano, were organic intellectuals of the merchant class itself—most were merchants themselves, or the progeny of mercantile families, and thus directed their writings from very self-conscious social locations with direct interests at stake. They nonetheless attest to prevailing anxieties and meanings of the Enlightenment (even if this had a somewhat materialist hue) in the River Plate.

One of the primary theaters for discussion and reflection was the newly created (in 1794) merchant guild (Consulado de Comercio) in Buenos Aires. Its royal mandate of "promoting that which most enhances the good and prosperity of Commerce" almost by definition made its officers and members critical actors in the ensuing controversy over how to confront external threats with alterations to the local political economy.[14] The guild's secretary, the young lawyer Belgrano, son of an Italian merchant and trained in law in Spain, plotted out, in a series of "Memorias" and newspaper articles, the concerns and ambitions for the guild and its constituency. His *cursus vitae* has him fighting to drive

back the British expeditionary forces in 1806–7, and in 1810 becoming
one of the leaders of the creole patriot cause, leading armies against
royal regiments in Paraguay in 1811 and in Upper Peru in 1812. Both
campaigns ended in disaster and paved the way for the splintering of
the Viceroyalty. Yet, as the chief exponent of constitutional monarchy in
the region, Belgrano struggled, dispairingly, until his early death in
1820, to keep Argentina from imploding into civil war.[15]

Belgrano's cue came from Italian political economists—though he
seems to have read most of their works in French. As Genovesi's translator, he preached apostolic truths about wealth and commercial policy
and used his tiny plot of land near the Recoleta to experiment with
crops. Nature, in the River Plate, gave the monarch enviable opportunities: "Among all ancient peoples, agriculture was the *delicia* of great
men, and nature itself appears available and pleased to let men destine
themselves to it; for if not, why do the seasons change? Why does cold
follow heat so that land might rest to conserve the nutrients that feed it?
Rain, wind, gusts, in a word, this marvelous and immutable order that
God has prescribed to nature, has no other objective than the successive
renewal of the necessary fruits for our existence."[16] In Belgrano's
schema, it behooved the monarch to revive this natural balance and dependency, to restore an ancient link to land.

Belgrano enjoyed a privileged place from which to spread his message. The Consulado entrusted him with the job—among others—of delivering an annual address on the state of the colony and proposals for
acceptable fine-tuning. In his first "Memoria" in 1796, Belgrano proclaimed that "Agriculture is the real destiny of man."[17] With this, he
sought to reframe the way in which merchants understood the origins of
their welfare, shifting the emphasis from specie (the illusion of wealth)
to land (its fount). At first blush, the call for agrarian and commercial reform appears to fly in the face of the Consulado's mercantilist girding.
Specie and silver flow had long been the commanding *raison d'etre* of the
port, acting as monopolizing entrepôt between highland Andean precious metals and European consumers. The trade both was lucrative and
fit the overall mercantilist design for Spanish imperial wealth. If Buenos
Aires was doing so well by this system, the call for an agrarian and not
precious-metals–oriented theory of wealth made Belgrano's *memorias* a
conceptual breakthrough—a breakthrough, however, that recoiled from
challenging some principles of Spanish colonialism.

Belgrano's efforts to shift attention away from silver to agriculture

without disrupting imperial precepts hinged on a particular understanding of trade itself. Often regarded as a herald of free trade in the
Spanish empire, Belgrano did not consider free trade on its own as a
motor of revival. The guild's lawyer, therefore, did not strike at the heart
of mercantilism's insistence that trade within the empire should aggregate into metropolitan surpluses. This is clear in his discrepancy with
Adam Smith's embrace of freer trade. Belgrano's notion of wealth rested
on a division of labor, but one that should not be confused with Smith's.
The latter's image of open and competitive trading among people with
different aptitudes and endowments envisioned a division of labor con-
ducive to specialization. For Smith, societies should concentrate on activities reflecting their distinct abilities. In this schema trade flowed from
social difference. Accordingly, there was no primary source of wealth
creation; rising incomes stemmed from market exchange. Belgrano, a
close reader of Smith, disagreed. "Everything depends on and results
from the cultivation of land. Without it, there are no primary materials
for the arts, and therefore industry is unable to operate, and there are no
goods for commerce to distribute. Whatever other wealth exists in an
agrarian state will be a precarious wealth, and depending on others has
no means of its own."[18] In this vein, the lawyer called for a closer alignment with the doctrines of Quesnay and Turgot in France, and the
Spanish technocrats surrounding Jovellanos. The argument was: foster
agricultural development; trade will follow. Social difference across nations was the result of economic growth and not the basis of trade that
created growth. This formulation enabled Belgrano to query components of mercantilism without overturning the architecture of highly
controlled and regulated commerce.

Belgrano was no loner. The founder of one of the River Plate's first
newspapers in 1802, the *Semanario*, Juan Hipólito Vieytes extolled the
unfulfilled promise of agriculture. "Now we know," Vieytes wrote in
the paper's prospectus, "that agriculture is the first, the noblest, and
the most indispensable occupation of man; it is the base of all societies,
that which supports the state, and makes men simple, faithful, and
honorable. To agriculture alone people owe their wealth and opulence, and without it they would find themselves forever trapped in
oppression and misery." The owner of a soap factory and some land
outside Buenos Aires, Vieytes soon took a leading role alongside Belgrano in the events of 1810. In the long essay that followed this prologue, Vieytes concluded that "without the cultivation of land, all

commerce is precarious, for it would lack the funds that themselves are the product of nature."[19]

Other authors were clearer about what required dismantling. Many felt that royal obsession with specie was the main obstacle to a sound agrarian economy. Manuel José Lavardén, the son of a colonial official, educated in Chuquisaca and Spain, and later founder of the Sociedad Patriótica, Literaria y Económica (one of the many associations proliferating across the empire), lamented the windfall of the Spanish conquest, identifying it as the ultimate source of the empire's problems. Having discovered the natural wealth of America's metals, Spain built a magnificent empire on ephemeral foundations. With time, "her agriculture and industry were degenerating while the abundance of gold was increasingly prejudicial, and rather than animate the arts, it raised the cost of labor."[20] Lavardén, more than Belgrano, practiced what he preached. Having made a modest fortune from ranching and slaughtering, he joined with one of Buenos Aires most powerful merchants, Tomás Antonio Romero, and together they launched a project in 1798 to erect a massive slaughterhouse outside the capital. In his widespread essays (and somewhat mediocre poetry) Lavardén hammered away at an idée fixe: the colony needed to open its trading avenues and allow landed producers to sell their output in markets abroad to tap its brilliant potential.

Lavardén and Belgrano, however, had first to dislodge convictions that silver was the fount of all wealth. They and others repeatedly called on merchants and the crown to pay attention to land as the origin of wealth and to treat specie as the mere means by which landed products are transacted. By 1810, on the eve of the revolution, Belgrano was growing impatient: "From the moment that conventional stamps were established on silver and gold, they have served as the instrument of commerce and as a measure of value, and so it is not strange that they have been confused with the real and only source of wealth, and that the opulence of the people should be assessed according to the proportion of coin they treasure . . ."[21] In this anti-bullion spirit, Mariano Moreno was perhaps the most pointed of critics. A lawyer trained in Chuquisaca, adviser to High Court (the Audiencia), and translator into Spanish of Rousseau's *Contrat Social*—and we will revisit this latter work in the next chapter—he issued a blistering appeal to the Viceroy: "Money is not wealth, but it is compatible with all the ills and pressures of an extreme misery; she is nothing more than a conventional sign with which all exchangeable products are represented, and thus subject to all the vi-

Monuy ~ Circulation

cissitudes of circulation, rising and falling in price in the market according to abundance or scarcity . . ."[22]

If Belgrano, Vieytes, and Lavardén exemplified the interests of forward-looking merchants and landowners, Moreno was made of different cloth, and best testifies to the assimilation of the new political economy into an older naturalistic view of the world. The eldest son of a minor official in the Spanish treasury, he never dipped into the world of trade or enterprise. Upon graduation from Buenos Aires' Colegio de San Carlos, he went to Chuquisaca in Alto Peru to study theology, changing partway through to law, though preserving his concern for the divine in his notion of justice. The academic ambience of Chuquisaca fostered a bridge between the Enlightenment and Thomas Aquinas's Natural Law doctrines, and like many of his predecessors (Bernardo Monteagudo, Juan José Paso, and others), Moreno wove a deeply moral sensibility into his disquisitions on property and exchange.[23]

In large measure this anxiety reflected his lessons from Victorián de Villaba. Villaba, like Belgrano, looked to Antonio Genovesi for guidance on how to free market forces while avoiding social upheaval, and indeed also translated *Lezioni* into Spanish, using his prologue to present a paradigm of modest reform while preserving fealty to crown and clergy. A charismatic Aragonese theologian and jurist—in 1789 he was named *Fiscal* to the High Court of Charcas, a title that made him the "Natural Protector" of Indians—Villaba squared off in a confrontation with Francisco de Paula Sanz, who used his presidency in nearby Potosí to defend the interests of miners and enforce the *mita*. The exchange prompted the jurist to write, in 1793, his "Discurso sobre la mita de Potosí." This stirring moral diatribe denounced the *mita* as neither public, nor just, concluding that the economic function of money is universal and not meant to service those under whose control it has fallen.[24] In general, however, Villaba's appeal had conservative roots, for he was preoccupied with the danger that abuse and excess would sow the seeds of revolution. In a widely circulated tract, he later argued that "in an epoch in which the spirit of liberty is making such progress and the enthusiasm that supports it creates upheaval, all good citizens should dedicate their meditations to avoid a revolution, which such abuses [referring to the liberty of miners to exploit Indians] prepare and which the example of other peoples foretells, and which must be feared more than any of the misfortunes we suffer and so much wish to remedy."[25] To his dying day (1802), Villaba championed the cause of justice and the rights of men precisely because he feared that left to their own devices, men of privilege would abuse their powers and imperil the divine order.

This message resonated through the legal training at Chuquisaca, a South American outpost of the Catholic Enlightenment. After graduation from the law faculty (where rote learning of canonic, Roman and Castilian legislation was the fare), the students were sent by the University on a two-year apprenticeship to the Academia Carolina, where they were housed and supported by the Archbishopric, though formally supervised by the magistrates of the High Court.[26] Here Villaba dedicated his special attentions to shaping aspiring lawyers. In the private libraries of Villaba and the magnate Secretary of the Archbishopric, Matías Terrazas, who boasted one of the Viceroyalty's finest collections, Moreno and other students ingested an eclectic diet of books, from Aquinas and Augustine, to Abbé Raynal and perhaps most important, Rousseau. How these texts were taught will never be entirely clear, and it is probable that idiosyncratic interpretations circulated freely.[27] It was here that Moreno wrote his first tract in 1802, his thesis "Sobre el servicio personal de los indios en general y sobre el particular de Yanaconas y Mitarios," echoing much of what Villaba had denounced a decade earlier, but with a more enthusiastic embrace of notions of liberty he had learned in the libraries of his tutors. "Freedom," he wrote, "is a natural faculty of man to make of himself what he wishes without any coercion." From this principle, Moreno reproved not just the abuses of miners, but the entire mercantilist obsession with specie, arguing that, from the start, the conquest of the Indians sowed the seeds of moral decrepitude and menaced the empire with eventual destruction.[28]

The problem, as far as Belgrano, Vieytes, Lavardén, and Moreno were concerned—each with their own shading—was comparatively simple, but very deeply entrenched. To channel surpluses into royal coffers, centuries of mercantilism had generated tomes of legal impediments to new sorts of enterprises: monopoly trading companies, the protection of feudal landowners in the peninsula by keeping out "American" produce, and disincentives to settling newcomers on the land. In Europe, the monarchies were belatedly coming to recognize the folly of neglecting agrarian production, even in Spain. But when it came to the colonies, Madrid continued to see the region not as one capable of growing, but as one aimed solely at absorbing the metropolis's products in return for staples Spain lacked. The crown stifled colonies "because it did not see agriculture as an art in need of study, reflection, and regulation." For Lavardén, "the extraction of silver will continue to impoverish the nation [by which he meant the empire as a whole] and drive it to ruin . . ."[29]

Reform without revolution required, first, a change in the definition of wealth. If Belgrano did not share Adam Smith's incipient doctrine of comparative advantage, he followed the broad Enlightenment shift in understanding about the origins of value. Determining values in classical political economy had a direct link with notions of property. Hitherto, property under the anciens régimes implied something belonging to one person to the exclusion of others; in practice it meant property in public office, a whole host of privileges (to trade, given by the Casa de Contratación for instance), prerogatives (to enjoy monopoly retail rights among Indians—i.e. the *repartimiento*), and hereditary distinctions.[30] Such a proprietary regime presumed that wealth was politically constituted, the natural monopoly of monarchs, and measurable by the amount of specie hoarded in the treasury. The system of channeling silver from Potosí to Madrid via Buenos Aires required forcible unequal exchange between colony and metropolis. It also fundamentally confused the measure of value with source of wealth. For Belgrano, "money is in reality a commodity (*fruto*) identical to others; and for the same reason it flows to markets to exchange for the goods it seeks to acquire by its means. A country without mines, says Smith, should by necessity derive silver and gold from foreign countries in the same way that a country without vines acquires the wine it wishes to consume."[31] Money is a commodity like others, except that it serves as a medium of exchange for other commodities. It is a measure and not source of value. Accordingly, the mercantilist apparatus founded on the notion that royal stores of specie determined a society's wealth naturally inclined its followers to believe that their own welfare depended on gaining access to royal property through stations, privileges, and prerogatives.

As a result, soil was the unexploited patrimony of the colony; a truer source of wealth. It was also seen as the basis of an alternative view of property—one that aligned itself with spreading Enlightenment discourses in Europe. For Locke, value was determined by the application of human labor to nature as a private activity, prior to the emergence of the state. Accordingly, property was pre-political and emerged from a naturalistic world, and the faculties applied to nature established a broad measure by which to derive values, values that in turn would be recognized in the course of exchange. With property, passions could be channeled in productive enterprises: "The course of man's passions," argued Lavardén, "though it may exceed the limits of necessity, when it does not reach extremes, brings thousands of benefits to society, and without it there can be no opulence. The extremes are well known: public scandal, insubordination against authority, damage to honor, health, and herein lies everything that must be impeded. This is the charge of public men of respectable authority."[32] As it was, Spanish absolutism generated odious and corrupt forms of property that not only stood in the way of an enlightened, rational world but depleted the regime of its natural source of legitimacy.[33] Once again Moreno: "Sir, the farmers of our land are not enjoying the fruits of their hard work with the honors our benign monarch dispenses; the sweat of their brow yields a bread that does not excite the gratitude of those whom it feeds; and in their forgotten dignity and importance, they are condemned to live in obscurity during the moments they rest from their burdensome labors."[34]

By imagining a spreading agrarian system in the River Plate, reformers did not imply a yeomanry producing first for household subsistence. Rather, in Belgrano's view agriculturalists were to be market producers. Without incentives to produce for pecuniary reward, rural surpluses "would be unknown, that spring of opulence of all peoples."[35] The problem was, Spanish regulators protected urban interests by controlling (and depressing) consumer prices of rural produce. This practice had to end: "The farmer must enjoy complete freedom in the sale and extraction of his produce." What is more, the practice of granting monopolies on the sale of particular commodities intensified agrarian torpor: "I hope," said Belgrano to the merchants of the Consulado, "that by acclamation this thinking is adopted to avoid the great monopolies that currently flourish in this city, because these men [the monopolists] are deprived of all affection for their peers and only aspire to their *particular* interest, and it does not matter to them that the most useful class of the state, as economists say about society's productive class, lives in misery and nakedness."[36] This did not mean he was averse to monopoly; far from it. Monopoly should not be a private but a public enterprise, so that the government should buy the produce of the land, pay a fair and just price to farmers, and export the surplus to Europe. In this fashion, "as the famous Quesnay says, . . . an agrarian State must be populated with rich farmers." Agrarian surpluses thereby became the linchpin binding rural wealth and commercial fortune. Both were mutually dependent, farmers to provide surpluses for sale and export, merchants to ensure the outlets for farmers' produce.[37] "To support agriculture," claimed Lavardén, "this means finding middlemen to foment their produce through all means possible and allow farmers to prosper; it means finding the means for farmers to be opulent."[38]

The symbiotic relationship between commerce and agriculture not only implied new meanings to the concept of property, but it was to provide the social bases for an organic self-sustained prosperity within Empire. For Manuel José de Lavardén, agrarian reforms would promote "the goods and projects of proprietors, and these would be favorable to the KING, to his subjects and the Patria."[39] Agrarianism, in turn, identified the historical particularity of America. The New World had ample land; Europe did not. It made sense then to imagine colonies yielding rural surpluses for European consumers who were clustered increasingly in industrializing cities. "By good fortune, we have a country whose resources exceed necessity. The old commerce hurt Spanish agriculture, industry, and navigation. Now we will shift to an entirely inverse order. In a new spirit we will view these sectors, beginning with agriculture as the prime engine of our circulation."[40] Like Jefferson writing at more or less the same time, River Plate physiocrats argued that wealth had its origins in agriculture and was measured by rural output (and not stocks of precious metals). This accounted for a more perfect and benevolent balance between, if not metropolis and colony, then Europe and America.[41]

The failure of agriculture and the weakness of absolute private property plagued all of society. "Oh Sirs," complained Belgrano in his first *Memoria*, "it is necessary to confess that poverty has been and is rooted in our own selves, and that the powerful have done nothing more than trade with Europe . . . and thus they decide that any wealth or indigence is not only among agriculturalists, but among all classes . . ."[42] In his second *Memoria*, Belgrano castigated the system even further, noting the deleterious effect on public morals—upbraiding female lapses in particular: "Here you see a resource by which the wretched earn their livings, and principally the female sex, a sex that in this country lives in disgrace, exposed to misery and nudity, to the horrors of hunger and attacks of disease, . . . exposed to prostitution, from which so many of society's ills result, so much so that it serves as an impediment to matrimony, one of the disgraces that accompanies the nature of this vice . . ."[43] In this gendered specter of moral degradation Belgrano presented to his audience the fear of both poverty and the atrophy of masculinity.

"There is no doubt sirs," he said in his last address to the Consulado, "honor and reward are the two foundations most appropriate to avoid the slumber of the spirit of Man, for whatever his State may be, nature is never as covetous when it concedes a great collective spirit to the inhabitant of a cabin [i.e. the farmer]."[44] For Vieytes, this system reduced people to immaturity and vice. "Such a sad situation will keep our America in its infancy for unlimited time unless we arrive at a common agreement to inflame the farmer's heart and shake him from the lethargy to which his inaction has condemned him."[45] Obstacles to wealth and property were also then inextricably matters concerning the moral fabric of the society. Calibrating material freedoms could revive personal virtues and reverse social decadence.

Supporting agriculture did something else in the New World: it addressed the fear of racial tension, an especially gruesome menace in the wake of the revolution of Saint Domingue in 1791. Indeed, much of the discussion of property was inextricably bound up with the problem of slavery—even in a society like the River Plate, which did not base itself on plantation production but in which a third of Buenos Aires' population on the eve of revolution was enslaved. Agriculture gave good employment for races of inferior breed, Belgrano felt, because "the races with particularity [by which he meant colored] will always be prejudicial to the arts." Giving land to people of African descent was not only a way of bonding them to more productive occupations, it would help preserve social hierarchies between blacks and whites. "People with Spanish names," warned Belgrano, "that is without black or mulatto blood, these unfortunate people view with horror the prospect of confusing themselves with blacks and mulattos, and would rather live in misery and infelicity than to take side with one of those [i.e. people of color], and without recourse to work, these people deliver themselves to idleness, the fecund mother of all vices."[46]

More often, the concern for racial peace—if not harmony—blurred into a general anxiety about plebeian disorder, especially perpetrated by unruly gauchos who insisted on rustling cattle and wantonly slaughtering herds. One appeal to the crown from proprietors of the Banda Oriental called for martial discipline in the countryside to curb "a lineage of people who has never known fear, whose occupation is to lead with fierce spears and to mock authority with ease, and who barely value their lives, and who kill their brethren with the same serenity with which they kill a cow."[47] The option and security of ownership would foster racial and social harmony by keeping freed slaves, slave descendants, and plebeian sectors in line as they discovered the promise of social mobility. Furthermore, stabilizing rural property would sow the seeds of a prosperous rural world and thus present to plebeians attractions of purposive occupations. In general, the promise of rural wealth to the unpropertied was the only true and durable solution to economic stagnation and social tension. As another petition concluded, this time by farmers, "The profits that those who work the land earn are the springs that bring them alive, and this desire allows agriculture to flourish; all work hard for their interest and utility; and he who is persuaded that there is a man who labors for a different motive is a puerile thinker, for this way nations are ruined, inclined to vice and fanaticism."[48] Vice was an affliction not only of the propertyless poor. The rich, obsessed with their politically derived monopolies and silver, also learned bad habits and an aversion to work. Vieytes in particular, excoriated "the other professions dedicated to luxuries" and the "deprivation to which they reduce societies."[49]

Physiocratic doctrines and proposals for agrarian exports were assembled on the backs of Locke's labor theory of value. This model distinguished between productive and unproductive labor and identified classes and sectors affiliated with each camp. The problem with the Spanish empire was its overpopulation with unproductive agents. The New World, properly exploited, offered a way out. Without the proper incentives to rural production, the share of labor apportioned to agriculture, and thereby productive value, would shrink. These incentives included fair and just prices for rural produce, access to markets, access to funds for investment, and better education for rural folk. In Europe, each farmer had to support five "individuals in inaction and abandonment." Once again, America was different, and could thereby avoid the Malthusian threat of subsistence crises. God blessed the New World with great land, proclaimed the Banda Oriental ranchers, "though despite so much potential, we must confess that its inhabitants are the world's poorest."[50] Repeatedly, authors dwelt on the colonies' untapped potential and thus complementary relationship with Europe—one that might indeed spare the New World the threats of proletarianization and impoverishment. Referring to the situation in Europe, Belgrano observed: "We do not believe that this deplorable situation applies to our happy province; but we cannot avoid confessing that she has a very high portion of entirely unapplied hands, both as a consequence of the abundance of our limitless territory, and also for lack of a powerful stimulus to animate, vivify, and give energy to inert arms."[51] The charge of unproductive labor was levied especially against elites, many of whom squandered resources in public offices or rents rather than fostering production. Poor administration led to wasted land, either lying fallow in crown hands or held in enormous estates. Lavardén in particular excoriated large landowners for depressing production by holding back land from potential use by smallholders. Boasting a blueprint for colonization that would privatize land and transfer holdings from monopolists, Lavardén promoted an elaborate vision for concentric circles of farmers producing different staples depending on their proximity to the market. "For this reason," he claimed, "there is no other solution than to divide up land among proprietors, enlarging the size of units in geometric proportion to the distance from the center [Buenos Aires]."[52]

The obstacles to wealth, rural production, social harmony, and public morals were to be found in antiquated understandings and practices of property. Only by abandoning the absolutist notion of political property, embracing the idea of effective private property, and applying the concept to land in particular would the colony rescue itself, and thereby save the empire from the venality that was smothering it. "The lack of property brings with it abandonment," warned Moreno. "It brings an aversion to work, because he who cannot call that which is his possession and in consequence cannot dispose of it, he who is exposed to losing beforehand all his goods, and who cannot console himself by leaving a fixed establishment for his dear family when he closes his eyes will look with tedium toward the alien place that should be the indispensable necessity giving him life, but is now only a source of indifference."[53] These champions of reform saw in their solutions, not just the key to prosperity and stability, but a way out of the growing sense of misrule, if not illegitimacy that was slowly encircling the throne in Madrid.

Conclusion

Late-colonial intellectuals drew on an eclectic range of sources to create a "mobile rhetoric" of reform.[54] A shifting blend of Adam Smith, physiocracy, Lockean liberalism, and Natural Law doctrines provided elements with which to articulate a new balance between colony and empire—all within the generous embrace of the Enlightenment. Rather than being enmeshed in a chain that was by necessity exploitative and extractive, colonies and metropolis could grow through a set of organic links. Indeed, some would argue that this was the only way to rescue colonies *for* the empire—and avoid potential insurrection, the modal nightmare after 1791 being as much Haitian violence as French Terror. Reform was necessary for colony and metropolis alike.

With the discourse of reform within empire came a new brand of property-talk, one that did not square easily with centuries of imperial practice and doctrine. Since the Conquest, authorities treated a society's patrimony not as a bequest to individuals to realize private productive activities, but as a source of State-allocated political property for those it considered worthy and loyal. This kind of property, by the late eighteenth century, was a recipe for disaster. New property-talk came from men aware that obsession with specie flow from the highlands overshadowed regional and agrarian interests in the pampas. It may be reductive to depict Belgrano, Vieytes, Moreno, or Lavardén as the mouthpieces or organic intellectuals of an agrarian bourgeoisie. For one thing, such a class was much more latent than it was puissant. But they certainly viewed European-colonized grasslands, and not highlands dominated demographically by Indians, as a new pole of growth deserving of its own attention and policies. Their immediate concern, however, was with reordering property, from its political construction through royal privilege and grants, to absolute private property. Such property-talk was the point of entry to appraise and denounce the corruption and venality gripping public administration—sowing the seeds not only for poor government, but for relaxed morality at home, indigence, and vice. Accordingly, the critique of imperial policy and the conceptual novelty of proprietary discourse aimed to cleanse royal subjects of the bad habits they were acquiring, and in this fashion rebuild the natural pristine bond between subjects of the realm and royal power.

All told, this growing sophistication in the conception of property rights introduced a new way to think about politics. Rather than relying on some divine rhetoric and elaborate map of obligations and trust, creole understandings invoked a political economy in which a commonwealth's subjects realized their potential through ownership and exchange. Agrarian production yielded independence and virtue, yet at the same time created a fabric for sociability through trade—within a local society, and across a realm that spanned the Atlantic ocean. Society came to be represented as an economic mechanism—and creoles implored the emperor to appreciate this new reality and embrace, without

in any way disturbing the ties of loyalty, this new "sociology of liberty."[55] This new model of interdependence tapped into human abilities
Labor to reason, created a framework for a division of labor, and thus elaborated a civic spirit that would reanimate the bonds of legitimacy between the King and his subjects in the colonies. In this fashion, a new
way of imagining politics and debating reform were reconcilable with a
long tradition of natural jurisprudence. After all, if the world were in essence God's property, and the King its worldly custodian, individuation
of rights and respect for the privatized personality of commercial men
simply enhanced productive and responsible use of God's estate.[56]

So, it would seem, the writings of these creole *penseurs* aimed to preserve empire, defuse social tension, and abort the threat of any revolution. Does this mean that these writings had no effect on a revolution in
which their authors took such protagonistic roles in 1810? The immediate causes and consequences of Buenos Aires' revolution will be treated
in detail in the next chapter, but we may still speculate about whether
physiocratic and more generally Enlightenment notions contributed to a
malaise in the colonies. To echo Roger Chartier's words on the French
Revolution, did new ideas contribute to the "conditions of possibility"
for revolution?[57]

My answer would be, Yes. First, they channeled concerns about misguided policy into a coherent set of alternatives. To be sure, late-colonial
intellectuals struggled to formulate solutions to the vexing—and growing—dilemmas of empire, and imagined a reconfigured balance between new and old worlds precisely to preserve the imperial equipoise.
But these solutions created a grid against which to judge imperial policy
and its own well-being. As events in Europe worsened with Napoleon's
invasion of the peninsula, creole intellectuals struggled to come to terms
with the new conjuncture. But they found missives from Spanish
authority downright counterproductive and retrograde. Under threat,
imperial decision-makers resorted to old instincts: protecting powerful
merchants and taxing colonial producers. Such measures, seen as pan-
dering to the proclivities of unproductive elites, stuck sharply in the
craw of Buenos Aires' publicists of reform. In the eyes of many, imperial
authorities were destroying the empire and creating the conditions for
catastrophe.

Second, the concern with property reflected positive and negative
anxieties. In positive terms, creoles valorized the potential of this
emerging hinterland closer to the port—a potential that could be real-

ized by security of title and generous incentives to invest. In negative terms, authorities had to curb what was seen as licentiousness among its plebeian population, which at best cost productive proprietors their rightful due, and at worst threatened insurrection. As imperial authority began to shudder, creoles feared backsliding on positive proprietary gestures and aggravation of negative forces in the countryside. In short, the specter of catastrophe looked increasingly like uncontrollable plebeian encroachment.

On both scores, the Enlightenment corpus—widely defined— enabled creoles to understand their place in the imperial world with some degree of appreciation for their own colonial specificity. They were destined as primary producers for external markets and thus depended on a stable trans-Atlantic structure of commerce and royal power. Moreover, temporally, they saw themselves as part of a trans-Atlantic world in the throes of a transition from bullionist mercantilism to commercial liberty, whose culmination would place societies on a forward-moving path to harmonious development. Yet, even under duress, creole intellectuals did not presuppose an inevitable revolutionary outcome; from their inception, new ideas did not harbor the triumph of a new society. In their meaning was simply a prophecy, not a prediction, of what might come to pass. No one knew there would be, much less wanted, a revolution in Buenos Aires in the waning days of the empire. But emerging critiques and programs for reform enabled people to imagine an alternative order within, at least for the time being, imperial equipoise. They did not call for revolution, but imperial restoration.

If creole words added up to prophecies, they were meant more as a collective Jeremiad: warnings to the crown, its ministers, and officials of the potential calamity of neglecting the fortunes of their colonies. Prior to 1810 there was no demand for a different social hierarchy, nothing resembling the egalitarian spirit of North American or French republicanism. In attacking the notion of political property and vices generated by centuries of mercantilist regulation, River Plate Enlightenment reformers decried abuses of authority, inefficiencies of the landed system, and withering legitimacy of royal officers. If they called for an invigorated rural order, it did not necessarily imply any social realignment from top to bottom. Quite the obverse: reform was meant to improve the social welfare of the colony and thus eliminate potential sources of instability or insurrection.

Nor was there any vindication of a revolutionary representative or-

der—one we normally associate with new concepts of property. Elsewhere, Lockean cant discharged the notion of natural rights to representation for the defense of property itself—defense, that is, against absolutist despotism. In the twilight of the Spanish Empire, Enlightenment
creoles, having followed events in Europe and Haiti, stopped short of
advocating a fuller emancipatory agenda. In this sense they stepped
back from a battle unfolding in other corners of the Atlantic world: the
struggle over the meaning of the good life—was it to be found in a natural hierarchical order or in a universe of leveled individual producers?
In other revolutionary regimes, opinion was swinging in favor of the
latter. But in Buenos Aires, thinkers still struggled to incorporate their
concern for prosperity, social harmony, and legitimate rule within a
framework of empire, because, as Mariano Moreno made abundantly
clear in his reflections on the 1787 Constitutional Assembly in Philadelphia, monarchy still seemed to be the only viable means to reconcile the
Viceroyalty's increasingly tense and volatile collective sovereignties.[58]
The crown, for all its laments, was still the only agent capable of defending "the interest and security of all." Any other agent would serve
only its particular cause at the expense of others.

This indeed was what animated the River Plate Enlightenment critique of colonial policy: it had fallen prey to the interests of particular
political-property holders at the expense of the rest of society. It was
time to restore the powers of a transcendent authority like the monarch,
to recognize the good of the whole, and especially to foster the proprietary conditions for a healthy, stable society. Although the critique was
not quite "revolutionary," it contained a kernel of novelty, suggesting at
least a relocation of the source of sovereignty away from the crown to
society. Moreno explicitly, and his colleagues more implicitly, argued
that the "pact" between crown and society had to be revived in defense,
not of public privilege, but of private property. Herein lurked a notion
of socially oriented, property-owning rational actors endowed with
rights to representation before the crown in the interest of common production and the enjoyment of economic and social values. This neither
subverted monarchical authority nor vindicated any universal image of
rights-possessing individuals. In the quest for a new equipoise within
empire, however, *this* was the pervading call for government among
creole reformers.[59]

By the time Napoleon invaded and occupied Spain in 1808, leading
to the constitutional crisis of 1810, River Plate intellectuals were calling

for a different order, one in which wealth came from the land, and was enhanced through trade; one in which subjects were property-owning agents prior to their political constitution. And though the notion was still inchoate in 1810, they were nearing the proposition that political rights would flow from private property, and not vice versa. But this still implied deep social hierarchy and a determined aversion to broad political representation. Caught between their dreams for a new natural order and its decaying predecessor, creoles struggled to navigate the transition guided by the stars of empire. While hardly revolutionary in themselves, such aspirations helped create the conditions, however unintended they might be, for a great rupture with the past.

4 ☽ From Revolution to Civil War

> Escribí: Somos oradores sin fieles, ideólogos sin discípulos, predi-
> cadores en el desierto. No hay nada detrás de nosotros; nada,
> debajo de nosotros, que nos sostenga. Revolucionarios sin
> revolución: eso somos. Para decirlo todo: muertos con permiso.
> Aun así, elijamos las palabras que el desierto recibirá: no hay
> revolución sin revolucionarios.
>
> Andrés Rivera, *La revolución es un sueño eterno*

The Problem of Buenos Aires' Revolution

Revolutions usually lead the revolutionaries; new regimes seldom reflect their original proponents' vision. The late eighteenth-century upheaval that shattered the Atlantic empires was no exception. England,
France, and soon Spain and Portugal would lose their main possessions.
In the age of democratic revolutions, to borrow R. R. Palmer's coinage,
the ancien régime of restricted property rights and limited representation gave way to new paradigms of personal entitlements and public
powers. Seldom, however, did the architects of the new regime share a
strong sense of what their achievements would resemble when they
embarked on their struggles. New republican systems were, for the most
part, more unintended results of imperial collapse than products of willful, intended change.

This was especially true of mainland Spanish America. As the twilight of Europe's presence in mainland America approached, Spanish
creoles were only beginning to sort out the intellectual principles of an
alternative political community. They envisioned a world in which the
rights of private property would prevail over political prerogatives,
where virtue would flow from purposive activity applied to nature and
not from colonial offices and special corporate prerogatives. In their
mind's eye, rights should eclipse privileges and profit-making should
displace rent-seeking; interests should obey market, not political rules.

This shifting vision of a new society still lacked a robust notion of an alternative representative system. What kinds of institutions would realize the emerging ideas of community and enable interests to flourish? Creoles did not share a political theodicy comparable to the power and popularity of convictions that had so mobilized people in France in 1789 and the United States in 1776 (however pockmarked these convictions were on the ground). As one of the military commanders of Buenos Aires' armies noted in 1829, as he watched his patriotic cause degenerate into civil war, "we proceeded through a revolution but without any plan or coordination."[1] Indeed, more than for either of the other two revolutionary theaters of France and the United States, the catalyst for the institutional breakup of the Spanish empire was external. Madrid got sucked into the maelstrom of the French Revolution and upheaval of European power-balances—culminating in the occupation of the Peninsula by Napoleonic forces. Shorn of the supreme authority of the monarch, the colonies undertook a degree of self-determination they were both unfamiliar with and scarcely beginning to imagine. In short, creoles struggled to forge a stable and legitimate institutional order only after the complete collapse of the ancien régime.

The South American challenge of institution-making after revolution differed in other important respects from the United States and France. As a post-colonial phenomenon, the struggle was to achieve self-rule. And as a reaction against entrenched mercantilist political awards, the struggle was also to destroy the power of estates in favor of the universal rights to proprietorship under the mantle of republicanism. This compounded the problem. For not only did creoles not share a common outlook, not only were they prompted by external events to embrace a shared cause, but the forms of collective representation emerged at a moment when the state was very weak or did not exist at all. This made it exceedingly difficult for revolutionary leaders to conduct the course of the dual struggle for self-rule and republicanism. New actors appeared on the political scene at the very same time that the rules of collective decision-making lacked even a semblance of legitimacy.[2]

Imperial Collapse

Buenos Aires' revolution erupted overseas. When the European powers went to war after dashing the peace of Amiens, Spain buckled to Napoleon's hermetic Continental System and withdrew its fleet to the shelter

of the Cádiz harbor (and when it did try to escape, Lord Nelson pound-
ed the Armada at Cape Trafalgar). Having severed the sea-lanes, European war cut off Spanish colonies from their metropolis.[3]

England now enjoyed unobstructed access to Spanish colonies and
their coveted silver. The only impediment was the threadbare defenses
within the viceroyalties themselves. These were hardly up to the task of
defending the remaining Bourbon possessions in the New World. English adventurers turned their sights on the River Plate. Upon learning of
Napoleon's decisive triumph over the Third Coalition at Austerlitz (December 1805) and informed that a large shipment of silver had just arrived in Buenos Aires from Potosí, Sir Home Popham organized an expedition to take the capital of the Viceroyalty. For their part, British merchants, having lost their markets in the Continent, were desperately
happy to rally behind the adventure. "Buenos Aires" noted Mariano
Moreno, "centralizes the hopes of many who dedicate themselves to
commerce in these thriving regions."[4]

From start to finish, it was a comedic escapade. Buenos Aires creoles
greeted the English troops with inscrutable ambivalence, but Viceroy
Sobremonte fled with his retinue and the colonial Treasury. According
to Major Alexander Gillespie, "we entered the capital in the afternoon,
in a wide order of column, to give a more imposing shew to our little
band, amidst a downpour of water, and a very slippery ascent to it. The
balconies of the houses were lined with the fair sex, who smiled a wel-
come, and seemed by no means displeased with the change."[5] This wel-
come soon vanished. Spanish importers feared the flood of cheap British
wares and the competition of new merchants. Led by Martín de Alzaga,
a major power-broker in the Consulado and Cabildo, and fervent defender of Cádiz's grip on trade, they plotted resistance and soon fielded
a force of some 2,500 loyalists. Export merchants also grew disen-
chanted. Hopes of booming British demand for staples were exaggerated. Disillusioned with the British occupants, Buenos Aires turned
against the invaders. Creole militias under Juan Martín de Pueyrredón
and Cornelio de Saavedra, and especially the French-born officer Santiago de Liniers who rallied forces from Montevideo, defeated and im-
prisoned the band of invaders. A second, larger British invasion fared
no better. Eventually, hungry and battered British troops withdrew from
the estuary of the River Plate.[6]

In a proper sense, Buenos Aires' revolution began here, for the effects of this episode were as profound as they were multiple. First, the

balance of political power swung from the Viceroy and the Audiencia to the Cabildo and the local militias—where creoles played a much more active role. Even while the sermons and discourses that flowed in the aftermath of the reconquest of Buenos Aires proclaimed fealty to crown, church, and fatherland, in the eyes of creoles and peninsulars alike, the Viceroy's ability to command and therefore rule a fractious society waned.[7]

Second, few believed that Spain was in any position to defend her colonies. This applied to both external threats as well as internal ones. Externally, Brazil—always a rival for regional supremacy—made its presence increasingly felt. Fleeing Napoleon, the Braganza dynasty moved from Lisbon to Rio de Janeiro, bringing a lust for recovering greatness in tow. *Porteños* worried about the spread of eager Portuguese and British traders and the return of armed marauders.[8] The internal threat came from local creoles who refused to abide by the dictates of peninsular potentates arrogantly enforcing their licensed prerogatives.[9]

News from Europe only aggravated the power vacuum. Bourbon authority in Madrid collapsed. French troops occupied the Peninsula on their way to Portugal, and in May of 1808 Napoleon incarcerated both Charles IV and his son Ferdinand VII at Bayonne—all of which sparked massive revolt. This deluge of news shocked *porteño* authorities and enlivened the discord in the city's Consulado over trade policy and debate in the Cabildo over the source of political sovereignty. Creoles argued for a greater measure of autonomy in response to the fragmentation of authority in the peninsula.[10]

Events irrevocably tilted the balance in favor of creole forces. Within the Consulado, monopolists were losing the debate over whether to maintain barriers to the entry of foreign goods and uphold the licensing system. In the Cabildo, peninsulars resented the Viceroy's willingness to discuss public affairs with locals. Creoles compelled the lame-duck Viceroy Beltasar Cisneros to declare free trade in November 1809 and then began hatching their plot for self-rule.[11] From the crumbling detritus of imperial authority was emerging a loose coalition of creole reformers, open-trade merchants, and military power.

This was, however, a marriage of convenience among partners who were being pushed into union by the pressure of external events. They still did not boast a common cause and lacked an affirmative purpose. If they harbored an incipient principle of identity—they were "American Spaniards" with no fewer rights than "Peninsular Spaniards"—they did not share a principle of alternative, a project for the future. Their fusion was forged by what they did not like more than by what they did like. As such, it was an alliance vulnerable to shocks that disturbed the basis of convenience. The very logic of winning self-rule within the empire shifted the terms of debate from *who* would rule to *how* they would rule.

The Sovereignty Question

If revolutions topple systems of political power, overthrowing rulers is only part of the story. Creating a new regime requires generating a sense that the new is more legitimate than the old. In Buenos Aires, the quest for legitimacy rested on some identification of the sources of sovereignty—with the King going, or gone, the people, a citizenry, had to take his place. Who would be "the people" and how they would be represented became much more intractable issues than creole revolutionaries could ever have imagined.[12] Their first efforts to reconcile these issues rested on the preservation of traditional public venues of authority—the Cabildo and the Consulado—to tease an incipient political subject out of colonial modes of representation.

There was little discussion of these issues prior to the events of May 1810. Creoles backed the Viceroy against ultra-monarchists and monopolistic merchants, squelching debate among creoles about an alternative representative order.[13] Creoles also recoiled from widespread discussion of a new form of politics for fear of civil discord. In the *Correo de Comercio*, a new broadsheet representing the interests of Buenos Aires' creoles and especially the export merchants of the city, Manuel Belgrano raised the specter of a natural propensity of people to fractious disunion. He may have had some of his own more radical friends in mind when he warned that he could "imagine the most horrible disasters of a society, whatever type of government rules: just let disunion lead to civil wars, and our enemies, no matter how weak they might be, will enter to ruin the most florescent of empires." "Union," he insisted, "is the only way of rescuing nations from a state of oppression by their enemies."[14] Even the firebrand Bernardo Monteagudo, a former law student from the University of San Francisco Xavier in Chuquisaca, warned that countries that pass so suddenly from servitude to liberty run the risk of slipping into anarchy, civil strife, and thus an even worse form of bondage.[15]

In May of 1810, news of the fall of Andalusia to the French intensified contradictory pressures on the Viceroy. Creole leaders began to accept the inevitable: they could no longer hide behind the dwindling authority of the Viceroy and had to take matters into their own hands and square off directly against reactionary forces of Spanish oligopolist merchants led by Martín de Alzaga and the ultra-monarchist governor of Montevideo, Francisco Elío. Creoles (and even some Spaniards) rallied to an Open Cabildo, a general call to all the city's "neighbors" to gather at the municipal headquarters to deliberate the capital's fate. On May 22, a small crowd gathered in the central square of the city in front of the Cabildo, while 251 notables met inside. The orator of the moment was Juan José Castelli, a lawyer, like Moreno and Monteagudo, trained in theology and jurisprudence in Chuquisaca, and fervent defender of creole rights. He insisted that the revolution did not begin in Buenos Aires; *porteños* wanted peaceable and lawful coexistence; the revolution, in fact, had begun in Spain; Buenos Aires simply had to respond to necessity with a new form of collective rulership. "No one can cast the entire nation as delinquent, nor its individuals who have shared their opinions publicly in these most critical circumstances of the State," intoned Castelli, "but we are threatened with mortal convulsions from all sides, and thus embrace a representative government based on a most legitimate and proper sovereignty." Accordingly, he called for the resignation of the Viceroy and magistrates of the High Court, and for the Cabildo to name a Junta to assume executive functions until a constitution could be drafted.[16] The men of the Cabildo accepted that the constitutional crisis of the Spanish empire shifted the foundations of sovereignty to the colonies themselves, and began speaking, henceforth, of a "nation" and "fatherland" distinct from the metropolis. On a gray and rainy May 25, with a small band of patriots and militiamen huddled in the square, the Cabildo proclaimed its Junta the center of political authority in the Viceroyalty. The Viceroy and Audiencia magistrates boarded a British ship and left the capital.[17]

This was a reluctant revolution, and so far bloodless. Creoles did not articulate a new social order, promised nothing commercially that had not already been ratified by the Viceroy, and shied away from universalist vocabularies of a "citizenry" endowed with inalienable rights to representation. Indeed, fear was the order of the day—and nothing was so terrifying as reenacting the carnage of France and Saint Domingue. If the French Revolution let partisanship take sway over tolerance and unleashed "bloody fanaticism" (in the words of *El Censor*), creole leaders must preserve unity and amity among their peoples in order for their own revolution to survive.[18]

To solve the riddle of how to alter the polity but avoid destabilizing the delicate equipoise of power in the region, the Cabildo members hoped to foment the requisite patriotism and create a public spirit of united purpose. The main tool was a projected constitution. Like the United States patriots, Buenos Aires creoles accepted that the members of this new political community did not yet share deep ties of common identity, and thus relied on the carapace of a constitution to create the foundations for this community. But unlike the United States, creoles did not envision a diffused and decentralized polity, but one that replicated the Spanish (and for that matter French) institutional and ideological centralism.[19]

Above all, continuity with ancien régime constitutionalism avoided the peril of inducting new social actors onto the political stage prematurely. The problem for "emerging peoples" deprived of experience with self-rule, as Monteagudo argued in a long essay entitled "Passions," was that "their hearts are still in a state of indifference and thus are susceptible to any impression that a deft hand might suggest to them."[20] This concern about the unbridled powers of untutored men echoed most forcefully through one of the most famous tracts written in the heat of the Viceroy's overthrow, and exemplifies the political spirit of the creoles assembled in the Cabildo. A few months after the Viceroy left Buenos Aires, Moreno put the final touches to a translation of Rousseau's *Du Contrat Social*. His prologue celebrated the "glorious installation of Buenos Aires' provisional government," but warned that Spain had deprived colonists of an experience in community and self-rule, and let erode the pact that bound the people to a sovereign. This pact or contract "is the root and only origin of obedience," and it required rebuilding. Herein lay "the aspirations for a judicious and enduring constitution that might restore rights to the people, and protect them against future usurpers."[21]

The problem, as far as Moreno and his colleagues were concerned, was how to create a people out of an inorganic mass, how to legitimate the revolution without destabilizing authority. To run this gauntlet, Article 9 of the Cabildo Acts on May 25 called people to elect delegates to an assembly to select "the form of government they consider most convenient." And it was the job of Cabildos to convoke these "people"— more specifically "the principal and sanest part of the *vecindario* [urban neighbors]."[22] Some conceptual breakthroughs are nestled in here—and they would discharge messages with unintended revolutionary implications. The first was a shifting notion of sovereignty. With the monarch in confinement and with his representative toppled from office, legitimacy required displacing the source of support from divine lineage to popular consent—and this required some notion of a "people." Moreno, now the Secretary of the First Junta and the intellectual leader of the revolutionary movement, spelled this out in a manuscript circulated among his peers to outline the principles of the new regime. "The links uniting the people to the King," he wrote, "differ from those that unite man with man: a people is a people before submitting to the King." If the people of the empire existed prior to its emperor, the problem was that centuries of misrule had corroded the links of sociability. Moreno believed the job of revolutionaries was to restore the fabric of this ancient social bonding prior to the existence of the state. "There is no need to create a people, because they already exist; all we need is to give it a head so that it may rule itself according to the diverse forms with which a moral body can be integrated."[23] The Secretary called for a new contract binding a sovereign people to new rulers. One of his peers, Monteagudo, echoed this message of a resurrected people downtrodden by centuries of "tyranny." "Sovereignty," he proclaimed at the inauguration of the Patriotic Society in January of 1812, "resides only in the people and authority in laws."[24]

But this was not yet a people prepared to rule themselves. If the people, and not the crown, were now sovereign, revolutionaries had to confront the dual issues of popular liberties and rights—the twin pillars of citizenship. In the United States and France, citizens could reclaim their natural entitlements; Buenos Aires posed a more vexing problem. The historical experience of deprivation and tyranny in Spanish America had not prepared people for responsible liberty. Whether they knew it or not, the people needed coaching; they required guidance. Echoing Rousseau, Monteagudo noted that "people are born free, which is to say independent, and thus at the discretion of their own will and absolute arbiter of whatever they wish, according to the capacity of their energies and their reason or instinct."[25] But premature concession of freedoms would lead to the domain of license and not liberty.

Faced with a sovereign, potentially free, but unprepared people, how did creole revolutionaries reconcile a historical experience of malign Spanish rule with the universal Enlightenment promise that all men

should be normatively free even if they were positively incapable of enjoying their freedom? For this purpose Moreno designed a hierarchy of
citizenship, with an autonomous revolutionary political elite at the top.
Like Madison before him, he distrusted the republican political subject,
but accepted its protagonism to build a new legitimacy.[26] Moreno's conviction rested less on what *class* of men should dominate politics than
what *kind* of men should rule.[27] Class was not an irrelevant matter, but
as far as government was concerned, men of property could be as misguided as the propertyless—especially if these men had been schooled
in monopolistic and rent-seeking practices. Spanish mercantilism had
done just that, and thus sagacious rulership required even an autonomy
from the economic elite. The enlightened elite should be endowed with
powers to govern and impose a new rule of law, but needed popular
ratification lest their right to rule be questioned and thus the legitimacy
of the project be cast in doubt.

To negotiate this delicate transition, creole leaders experimented
with hybrid representative institutions. At best, the rupture paved the
way for suffrage rights in principle, with restrictions in practice. During
the early phase of the revolution, few formal requisites encumbered entitlements to voting. *Vecinos*, neighbors of the city, met in open municipal assemblies who then in turn elected men to Cabildo or Junta (and
later Triumvirate and Directorial positions as creoles experimented with
types of regimes) offices. But the *vecindario* was not a boundless cate-
gory, and implied a traditional notion of the propertied *pater familias*.
There was little need to elaborate who could and who could not meet at
the Cabildo since most people—at least at this early stage—accepted the
decorum of political discrimination. The first full electoral law came in
1815, when the vocabulary of citizens began to displace neighbors. Accompanying this law was a trend to tie suffrage to property requirements. While in the abstract all "free men" could vote, citizenship could
lapse under certain circumstances, like "falling" into a salaried unpropertied state. Riddled with exceptions and left deliberately vague, the
new suffrage allowed officials on the ground to uphold a traditional
sense of who deserved, and to what extent they would be represented.
This pattern of representation did not break with conventions of local
assembly, but rather built on them as a means of sustaining rituals of legitimation.[28]

Making representation flexible and evolving did not necessarily insulate the emerging regime from abuse or attack. Faced with these sorts

of threats, Moreno noted in the most notorious revolutionary tract, the state had to take measures that violated civil liberties to ensure the long - run survival of political liberties. The Secretary issued his infamous "Plan of Operations" to the First Junta in August of 1810, sketching out a list of drastic measures to control and invigilate society, to monitor ene- mies and eliminate any menace to the creole project. Revolutions are not for the soft, warned Moreno: a new republic "is never cemented without rigor or punishment, mixed with the spilled blood of anyone who im- pedes its progress." The report oozed with gruesome prescriptions of "cutting heads, spilling blood, and sacrificing at all costs, even when they resemble the customs of cannibals and Caribs." The report has rightfully gone down in history as an extreme example of enlightened vanguardism. But all the imagery of severed heads and rivers of blood obfuscates Moreno's central message: the Junta, ruled by men of reason, must take drastic action if necessary because an inorganic people en- dowed with rights will too easily let the good of the community fall prey to the ambitions of opportunistic individuals' "intrigue, ambition, and egotism." The public welfare must be immunized from private pur- suits—even among the capitalists. "If private interests gain over the general good, the noble shock to a nation is the most powerful source of all the excesses and upheaval of the social order."[29]

In the eyes of the revolutionary leadership, people were sovereign, but their individual passions threatened to overwhelm the communal concerns. Accordingly, emerging public institutions had to remain vigi- lant: while defending widespread suffrage rights in principle in the name of a popular sovereign, in the breach they upheld traditional rep- resentative bodies and practices of political exclusion. In the new con- stitution, Moreno promised his followers, a primitive social pact would be revived on modern terms, to reconcile more virtuously the tension between new collective sovereignty and individual claims to personal property. There was, as the Secretary argued, a homology between sta- bilizing the new public contract between the state and the people and the ability of people to contract privately among themselves.[30] The con- stitution served a dual purpose: integrating the political community and providing the means for gradually tutoring people out of their bad hab- its. In this fashion, the constitution would help dismantle the old system without destabilizing private entitlements—at least not yet.

The Revolution: Phase I

For all the pragmatism of the revolutionaries, the revolution imploded into a power vacuum. Few outside Buenos Aires liked what they heard, even if they shared the distaste for peninsular arrogance, especially once Ferdinand restored Bourbon authority in Madrid in 1814 and threatened to restore revanchist absolutism. Moreover, even within Buenos Aires, the creoles quickly collapsed into disunion. The result was the dismemberment of the Viceroyalty into four separate republics and endemic civil war.

One of the Junta's first moves was an attempt to preserve the integrity of the River Plate Viceroyalty. The key was Alto Peru, for without access to Potosí silver and the preservation of the commercial axis from the highlands to European consumers, Buenos Aires would lose its reason for being. The brutal nature of mining production and taxation on communities created a tenser social ambience, and thus greater fear among the wealthy propertied sectors, than in the more modern commercial regions like the Pampas. Thus from the start, convincing a cross-class alliance of forces in the highlands to join in Buenos Aires' revolutionary venture was a difficult proposition. Indeed, the revolutionaries dropped broad appeals altogether. Moreno's instructions to one of his envoys warned that "Potosí is the most delicate *pueblo* of the Viceroyalty, and it is imperative to use the toughest of tones. . . . You must appreciate that all Europeans in this moment of convulsion will be our enemies; everything must be done to place all means possible in the hands of the natives."[31]

The Junta recruited its first army, and in June of 1810 it began the march to Córdoba and thence into the silver heartland, where eventually imperial forces crushed the Junta's revolutionary legions. The patriotic army began triumphantly and allowed Juan José Castelli, the Junta's envoy, to capture the bastions of peninsular authority around Potosí—including the President of the Audiencia Vicente Nieto and the despised loyalist Governor Paula Sanz. After a summary trial, Castelli ordered their execution for the good of the revolution—an act that did not win him any popularity among other royal officers and invigorated their will to resist. When Castelli released Indians from tribute and the *mita*, adding that Andean peoples were "equal to all other classes before the law," he horrified the local European patriciate.[32] Eventually, at the Desaguadero River, the superior imperial armies shredded the Buenos Aires columns, who, routed, withdrew in tatters to Jujuy.[33] Buenos Aires never gave up on its dreams of reuniting the highlands with the port, and Manuel Belgrano led a second expedition to Potosí in late 1812. A better political economist than general, Belgrano was no match for the military cunning of Joaquín de la Pezuela; again the royalists drove the *porteño* armies out of the silver district for good, leaving the battle against Ferdinand to local guerrilla forces—who if anything were a more daunting foe for royalists. Pezuela himself would lament that "we are only the owners of the soil on which we trod."[34]

The carnage at Desaguadero, known as the Battle of Huaqui, was a decisive moment in the long course of the revolution. Buenos Aires lost access to the silver regions. The entire northern flank from Salta to Tucumán, even Córdoba, lay open to royal assault. The royalists ensconced in Montevideo revived their determination to stand against Buenos Aires. And of course, Brazilian legions could not help but see in the ruins of the Army of the North an opportunity to carve out some territory from their borderlands with the Viceroyalty. In short, it was a disaster, and completely unraveled what little existed of Buenos Aires' blueprint for the Viceroyalty. The Junta dissolved, only to be replaced by the first of a series of triumvirates.

Less decisive, but almost as demoralizing, was the expedition to free Paraguay. Asunción was another loyalist redoubt, but Buenos Aires was determined to rid the Viceroyalty of peninsular armies. Manuel Belgrano, now a general, led an army to Paraguay, convinced that "there awaited a great party for the revolution." But his cause went down to defeat in September 1811 to a tough enemy. Never liking Buenos Aires' presumed control of riverine traffic, Paraguayan creoles turned against their "liberators." But, having driven out Belgrano's forces, creoles turned their weapons on royalists and proclaimed independence from Madrid in mid-1811, thereby separating Paraguay permanently from the fractious polity downstream.[35]

The loss of Alto Peru was decisive, the loss of Paraguay demoralizing, but over the long run, the war over Montevideo would be the most draining (see Map 3). Deprived of its access to silver, Buenos Aires struggled with the soaring economic and political costs of the campaigns. The Montevideo elite balked at the *porteño* Cabildo's repudiation of Spanish authority. In February of 1811, Francisco Elío, who had promoted himself from Governor to Viceroy, declared war on Buenos Aires. His revanchist style, however, alienated the countryside, a world

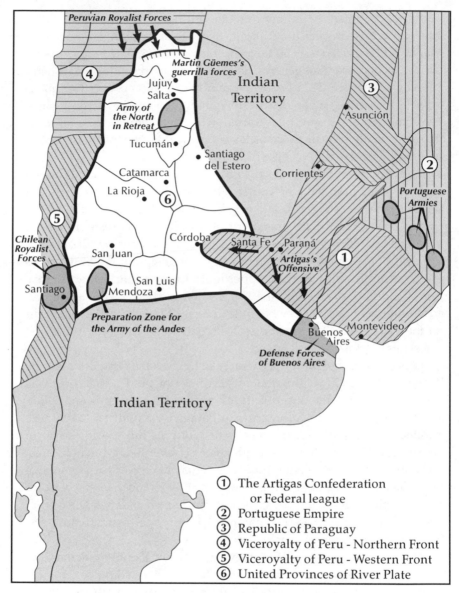

Map 3. The United Provinces of the River Plate, June 1816

The following text appears within the map image:

Peruvian Royalist Forces

Martín Güemes's guerrilla forces

Indian Territory

④

Jujuy
Salta

Army of
the North
in Retreat

③

Asunción

Tucumán

Santiago
del Estero

②

Catamarca

Corrientes

Portuguese
Armies

La Rioja

⑥

Chilean
Royalist
Forces

Córdoba

Santa Fe

Paraná

①

San Juan

Artigas's
Offensive

Santiago

San Luis
Mendoza

Preparation Zone for
the Army of the Andes

Montevideo

Buenos
Aires

Defense Forces
of Buenos Aires

Indian Territory

① The Artigas Confederation
   or Federal league
② Portuguese Empire
③ Republic of Paraguay
④ Viceroyalty of Peru - Northern Front
⑤ Viceroyalty of Peru - Western Front
⑥ United Provinces of River Plate

seething with unsettled scores between a plebeian peasantry, rural proletariat, and a despised urban patriciate. The rural population rose up
against the urban "tyrants" to wage a full-scale social revolution against
the landed and mercantile elites on the north shore of the river. In the
course of the war, the Banda Oriental and its neighboring provinces,
Entre Ríos, Corrientes, and Santa Fe, emerged as the heartland of River
Plate federalism. Thus, the popular appeal of an alternative agrarian order posed the most potent challenge to Buenos Aires' domination of the
region.[36]

The federalist cause was incarnate in the erstwhile frontier officer
José Gervasio Artigas.[37] Artigas had a vision of a countryside populated
less by large absentee-owned *estancias* than by single-family home-
steads. Especially as the pamphlet literature on the meanings of the
North American revolution circulated throughout the region, Artigas
began to champion an explicitly rural redistributionist program to un-
wind the deleterious effects of Spanish proprietary habits. Moreover, the
talk of popular sovereignty, so widespread in the latter half of 1810, informed Artigas's sense of a "sovereign will" amenable to and capable of
self-determination—and, crucially, whose political form was a loosely
autonomous province. The provinces could ally to defend themselves
against outside forces, but otherwise rural communities would govern
themselves in local assemblies. Artigas raised the banner, not just of political revolution, but of a social one as well.[38]

The specter of social revolution redoubled loyalist determination.
Elío, locked into the starving city, appealed to the court in Rio de Janeiro
for help. The Braganza dynasty was happy to oblige and dispatched an
army southward, driving Artigas back as far as Entre Ríos. Montevideo
joined Asunción and Potosí as bastions of opposition to Buenos Aires.

So long as Buenos Aires and the popular forces of the Banda Oriental
shared a common enemy in the person of Elío and absolutist restoration,
they combined forces. But otherwise Buenos Aires distrusted any program for social revolution. Political leaders in the capital were disposed
to help the patriotic cause when it suited their own self-defense, but they
were also willing to martyr their allies when the city's fortunes turned
for the worst. Buenos Aires shifted from support to disinterest, to open
hostility to the social revolution across the river, converting Artigas from
ally to enemy. Especially as Artigas's appeal to the rural folk of other
Littoral provinces began to spread, the Buenos Aires patriciate reacted
with horror. One Santa Fe estate-owner warned his friend in Buenos Ai-

res that "the insurrection of the Orientals is a general sentiment among the locals, who, lamentably, do not dissent from the hatred of the capital. We are now swept in the Oriental and Entre Ríos territory and are menaced as far as the Paraná River with an imminent invasion. . . . We should not fool ourselves, these people [the Santafesinos] will deliver themselves to the bloodbath, pillage, and war, and will take an enormous force to reduce them to order."[39] As this model of revolution electrified the other provinces of the Littoral and began to spread into the backyard of Buenos Aires itself, *porteño* authorities committed the desperate act of inviting the Portuguese to occupy and stabilize the unruly borderlands. In the ensuring war, the Banda Oriental was destroyed, depopulated, and despoiled.

A decade of warfare in the Banda Oriental was a decisive formative experience for federalists. With time, the power balance shifted from the urban patriciate to a new generation of rural leaders.[40] In the carnage, a generation of fighting men rose through the ranks of revolutionary forces to become leaders of the Littoral provinces. Thus if the Banda Oriental became the revolution's bleeding grounds, the area also became the breeding grounds for agrarian federalism echoed across the region— and through the decades. Indeed, as part of his defense against Buenos Aires and Brazil, Artigas negotiated an alliance among provinces of the Littoral, the Provincial or Federal League in 1815, from whose ranks, local rural leaders like José Francisco Rodríguez in Entre Ríos, and Estanislao López and Mariano Vera from Santa Fe emerged as regional chieftains. The League provided a prototype alliance for later interprovincial dealings arbitrated among military strongmen.[41]

As the Viceroyalty cracked into local warring theaters, *porteño* revolutionaries modified their original aim from preserving the capital's domain over the region to maintaining stability at home. They were not even successful at this. Factionalism erupted within the First Junta. Conservatives worried about Moreno, Castelli, and others' more aggressive agenda. In the struggle, the conservatives stripped Moreno of his helmsmanship and sent him on a mission to Europe. In early 1811, the former Secretary set sail for London, and while at sea perished in obscure circumstances.[42] But as the news of setbacks in Paraguay, Alto Peru, and the Banda Oriental flooded into the capital, the conservatives lost their grip. Subsequent forms of government (the Junta gave way to Triumvirates that gave way to a Directorship) relied increasingly on authoritarian means to maintain control. The only political force to maintain any prestige in the eyes of Buenos Aires society was the military—whose repeated failures were ascribed to hapless politicians. In particular, Generals José de San Martín and Carlos María Alvear—two young, charismatic, and seasoned warriors—struggled to professionalize the fighting forces.[43]

The revolution unraveled in its own bailiwick, and accelerated the dismantling of old regime institutions. Exhausted and hungry troops rebelled in December 1811, only to be suppressed by troops recalled from the Banda Oriental front. The city's peninsulars seized upon the chaos to lead an uprising to topple the crumbling creole regime—but like other power rivals, they had an exaggerated sense of their own appeal. This tolled the death knell of the oligopolist merchants, literally. By now, the one thing creoles could agree upon was that peninsulars presented the worst of a menu of disagreeable options. In July 1812, creole police snuffed out the plotting rebels, and as a warning to other reactionary intrigues, strung up two symbols of Spanish power, a priest and a Spanish merchant, leaving their bodies to dangle in the central square. The second victim was none other than the despised Martín de Alzaga, the former defender of Buenos Aires against the British, ally of Elío, and exemplar of Spanish mercantile power in the city. As his body swung, one happy artisan embraced the trunk of the gallows, and in a gesture of gratitude for the execution of his creditor, tossed coins in the air—provoking a mêlée among the jeering onlookers who scrambled to gather up the coins. Gangs of young men prowled the streets attacking symbols of wealth and authority, smashing the windows of their political leaders.[44] The revolution reached its nadir in October of the same year when furious soldiers marched out of their barracks, surrounded the central square, and trained their artillery on the Cabildo where the First Triumvirate gathered. Meanwhile, the depressed orator of the revolution Castelli languished in jail, where cancer metastasized from his mouth through the rest of his body. The revolution opened up a power vacuum: no party, faction, or political force could control its trajectory, but each was strong enough to neutralize its rivals.

With the Viceroyalty splintering into autonomous provinces, or bolting from the Buenos Aires project altogether, and with the city's revolutionary leaders incapable of mounting a common front, it is a wonder that deputies continued to meet to deliberate an enduring framework for the new state. They still shared Moreno's initial belief that the constitution must serve as the carapace of political integration.

This spirit animated a series of congresses and assemblies held over the first decade of the revolution.

The first major Constitutional Assembly, held in 1813, opened the debate over the form of political community to succeed the ancien régime. Deputies wrangled over a mélange of principles drawn from the examples of the French Revolution, the American Constitution, and the Spanish Constitution of 1812, including the idea of inalienable rights of man that the First Triumvirate had proclaimed in November of 1811. In the lead was Bernardo Monteagudo and the Sociedad Patriótica, who borrowed the French 1795 Constitution's Declaration of Rights. The most lasting institutional innovation, however, was the debate of provincial sovereignty, for the Assembly convoked representatives of "confederated provinces" to generate "a reciprocal confidence between people and the government." Accordingly, the Assembly gave federalism constitutional legitimacy, even though delegates tumbled into a bitter dispute over the degree of federalist decentralizing. In the end, internal discord, coupled with the misfortunes of war in Alto Peru and the Banda Oriental, deprived the Assembly of any ability to draft an enduring charter of statehood. The next effort came in 1816, in the city of Tucumán. By then, Europe and the rest of Latin America were shifting from revolutionary fervor to restoration. Buenos Aires stood very much alone, caught between rural and social revolution across the Littoral, royalist power in the northwest, and Brazilian armies crossing the borderlands. But even at Tucumán, internal feuding prevailed. Belgrano, fearing that the struggle would end in complete collapse, proposed that the River Plate fashion itself as a constitutional monarchy along British lines, with an Inca descendant ruling from the top. This went nowhere.[45] Instead, the deputies declared full independence from Spain and embraced in principle what was already transpiring in fact, the notion of republican self-rule. On July 9, 1816, the Congress of Tucumán declared the United Provinces of the River Plate to be sovereign. The Viceroyalty became a republic by default.

Once again, agreeing on what kind of state to build was much harder than agreeing on what to overthrow. The Tucumán Congress mandated a drafting committee to come up with an acceptable blueprint. After almost two years of wrangling, the commission submitted a plan to the Assembly. It called for a division of powers, but nestled a good deal of power in the Senate as a force of caution. It proclaimed provincial autonomy in a national union.[46] But the timing could not have been worse. By this point the provinces had become fully fledged actors. In the spirit of the Articles of Confederation in the United States—which themselves narrowly escaped being scotched by state assemblies—the River Plate provinces reserved the right to join the union. When news spread of Buenos Aires' invitation to Brazilians to do the dirty work of smashing up the Artigas alliance in the borderlands, many provinces rejected the plan in a wave of ire against the capital's intrigues. The country was independent, but its first blueprint for republican integration was a non-starter.

Meanwhile, the Littoral provinces, fed up with Buenos Aires' machinations, directed their not-insignificant forces against the capital. If until 1820, Buenos Aires had managed to escape outside attack, it could no longer fend off its neighbors. Federalist cavalry led by Artigas's erstwhile allies Francisco Ramírez from Entre Ríos and Estanislao López from Santa Fe, wiped out the Buenos Aires army at Cepeda on February 1, 1820, leaving the city defenseless. *Porteños* quaked at the fear of an invading "mob." The invaders sacked the capital. Satisfied, the federal cavalrymen withdrew, leaving behind a city in turmoil. On June 20, one of the last remaining dispirited revolutionary leaders, Manuel Belgrano, died.

Matters finally stabilized by the end of 1820. The new heroes were military men: Coronel Manuel Dorrego and General Martín Rodríguez, federal army leaders who helped settle the internecine squabbling and drove back belligerent Indians. Then they faced the remnants of Buenos Aires' civilian authority: the Cabildo, where the last urban centralist forces took refuge. Eventually, the urban patriciate of Buenos Aires reconciled itself to an alliance with the new military power of the federal troops.[47] Rodríguez took final aim at the old colonial assemblies and corporations, abolished the discredited Cabildos of Luján and Buenos Aires, and then dismantled the Consulado. Hereafter, public authority would be woven out of altogether new institutional fabric.

The Fiscal Crisis of the Revolution

If 1820 was a watershed for revolutionary representation and constitution-making, it also signified the ruin of the old colonial fiscal patterns. Just as the city's creoles initially saw the Cabildo and a reconstituted centralized Viceroyalty ruled from Buenos Aires as the framework of post-colonial rule, so too did they rely on the conventions of colonial finance. Consequently, as the institutional fabric of colonialism unraveled into revolutionary civil strife, the financial costs of endemic warfare sundered the basis of merchant property.[48]

The eruption in 1810 inflicted powerful blows to the fortunes of Buenos Aires' mercantile class. First, with the loss of Alto Peru, the silver supply plummeted, wiping out a crucial fiscal source for the city's treasury and cutting off liquidity circulation through the region's commercial sinews. When Belgrano's legions marched upon Alto Peru to restore the union between Potosí and Buenos Aires, Manuel José García prayed for victory. "We cannot possibly begin to think about the importance of public finance without relying on the mining branch, for in this country mining wealth is our common resource."[49] As it was, silver output from Potosí was falling even without the effects of revolution.[50] Warfare simply converted a secular probability into a dramatic rupture.

Moreover, *porteño* merchants, coddled on mercantilist protection, faced the world market on radically new terms. It is important, however, to distinguish among the sectors affected by free trade. Liberating trade markets affected above all an emerging group of export merchants, some of whom had extended their investments into land beyond the capital. This group had been chafing since the 1790's under the rigid controls of merchants who zealously protected their fiefdoms, and would only emerge as an important economic player with the flourishing of the export sector once the revolutionary wars ended. Then there was the class of powerful wholesale import merchants, most of them peninsulars or identified with the interests and power of Cádiz, whose own Consulado lobbied Madrid persistently to retain the barriers to entry against any *arriviste* traders. The combined effects of the British invasions and flood of cheap manufactures, Viceroy Cisneros's declaration of open trade in November 1809, and then the turn against all symbolic and material icons of peninsular power in Buenos Aires devastated the legal foundations of mercantilist accumulation. But it took a decade of warfare finally to eviscerate their political power.

First, oligopolist merchants faced a flood of manufactures. When the British invaders withdrew, they left behind stockpiles of cheap goods they hoped would serve as a lure for creole fealty to the British crown. The merchants who accompanied the expedition—many of whom remained in the city—introduced a system of public auctions to retailers willing to handle their imported wares, thereby allowing them to select according to price and quantity and by-passing the mark-ups of the guild traders. To worsen matters, if the old import houses insisted on cash payments in Buenos Aires and fixed-term payments in Interior outpost retailers, the British offered credit, or at least payment upon sale of the good. This altogether simpler and less encumbered merchandising also introduced cheaper Lancashire calicoes and muslins.[51]

Throughout the Viceroyalty, the cost of cotton textiles dropped. José Antonio de Saracívar in Jujuy, a local plier for a Buenos Aires merchant house, informed his boss that "even here goods are selling cheaply," adding that he lamented the devastation it was causing to their business, "I am sorry for the bankruptcy you must be suffering."[52] The Consulado entertained the fury of oligopolists who denounced the English as corrupting contrabandists. The Consulado's chief trustee, and bitter enemy of the Secretary Belgrano, took aim at "the abuses and excesses that some merchants commit in the distribution of goods in return for textiles," and denounced the violation "of ancient customs" at the hands of the Viceroy's leniency and refusal to impose the force of law. From the point of view of creoles who had long since been venting their anger at short-sighted merchants of the Consulado, this was a turn of events to celebrate.[53]

When the Viceroy opened the port in November of 1809, he incurred the eternal wrath of peninsular import merchants. The decibel level of complaints in the Consulado echoed the arguments over sovereignty in the Cabildo. The big merchants of the guild denounced the Viceroy, not for his intolerance of creole interests. Quite the opposite: he was not tough enough in upholding the corporate traditions of Spanish imperialism. The Consulado's trustee, Manuel Gregorio Yaniz, grew hysterical. He called for the expulsion of all foreign merchants and anyone found violating commercial "custom."[54] Porteño agents' reports from Córdoba warned of troubles recovering credits because the market was awash in a glut of commodities.[55] From the open port decree onward, the oligopoly merchants began plotting their viceregal putsch.

If the commercial opening after 1806 foreshadowed larger scale processes, so too did the mounting fiscal pressure on the viceregal treasury. As remittances from Potosí stabilized and then sagged after 1800, eroding Buenos Aires' cut on transfers to Spain, and as the military costs of defending frontiers mounted, merchants faced ad hoc official requests for funds. In late 1801, the Viceroy appealed to the Consulado to help pay for urban militias, and when he threatened to arrest uncooperative merchants, the Consulado balked.[56] The British invasions intensified public requests for private charity. In June 1806, anticipating the arrival of the interlopers, Viceroy Sobremonte called for an "open loan" in return for bonds yielding 6 percent. This time, the Consulado was more cooperative—not surprising since the prospect of a British occupation threatened merchants' livelihoods altogether. The guild issued injunctions to its members, "the powerful subjects," to help meet "the urgencies of the Monarchy when they can, and they must do so without damage or risk, for they are guaranteed complete repayment of their capital and the most solid mode of realizing interests."[57] As militias battled British troops, requests for funding came with greater frequency and compliance.

From a financial standpoint, 1810 was a disaster. The conflict intensified public authorities' appeals to private potentates.[58] And as public dependence degenerated into desperation, requests for funds evolved into forced loans. At first, the Juntas called for emergency loans in the same manner as funds raised during the British invasions. In early July, Moreno met with Consulado members to outline the revolutionary program and enlist financial support.[59] In the following years, some loans were earmarked for specific costs—these were normally small amounts recruited from one or two merchants—and the government promised to repay its debts very quickly.[60] On other occasions, the Consulado offered the government funds from its own accounts—from 1811 to 1815, Buenos Aires corporations, the Consulado above all, loaned 670,726 pesos to the revolutionary regimes.[61] Revolutionary finance, shorn of colonial revenues, drove the succession of regimes to live near the frontier of public sector subsistence.

In due course, subsistence led to penury, and thus a blizzard of requests for increasingly larger loans. The dilemma was that the ability to repay loans sank just as the need to enlist them rose. The revolutionary treasury fell quickly into arrears and forced 1.2 million pesos out of the pockets of local merchants between 1810 and 1819.[62] This pattern of involuntary lending was not lost upon merchants, who protested repeatedly before the Consulado, which in turn sent a steady flow of messages to the government to honor its debts to the guild's members. By May 1812, the Consulado asked the government to earmark a regular portion of its import tax revenues to begin bringing down its accumulated obligations to merchants. Two years later, the Consulado warned the government that in the quest for commercial golden eggs, it was strangling the goose of the merchant class. "The time has arrived," argued the guild, "for commerce is in complete decay owing to the obstructions of your issues, especially in the Interior, in the other provinces, which need, now more than ever, Supreme protection to repair the damage."[63] Peninsular merchants fared worst. Attacked by zealous revolutionaries, they soon became the targets for direct expropriation. One modest retailer, Juan Turnet, pleaded to be released from the exaction of 375 pesos, so that he might support his five children "and numerous family." Citing his willingness to contribute to earlier loans, he was now completely broke.[64]

Ad hoc loans soon evolved into formal systems of scrip. The succession of governments issued "bonds" yielding usually between 6 and 8 percent interest in amounts around 150 pesos. The turning point was July 1813, with the issue of *pagarés sellados*. Merchants accepted this paper hoping that the fiscal house would become solvent in the future. With time, these bonds evolved into media of exchange. As the flow of silver evaporated, merchants had to make up for the liquidity shortage. They did so with revolutionary bonds that, far from being legal tender, at least served the fiduciary purpose of alleviating the absence of cash. While not intended as such, loans became forms of monetary emissions—and as arrears rose, these emissions soared. Where silver had supported monetary circulation, now paper was taking its place.[65] And this paper quickly depreciated. Revolutionary finance stumbled on to inflation as a means to finance collective violence.

1810 also threw open local trade to world markets for good. For the next half-century, the River Plate may qualify as one of the world's most market-driven societies. If it was a troubled region, this was not because market forces did not percolate through the economy enough, but rather because the market's legal and political foundations were still matters of violent contention. Merchants did not necessarily greet world market forces happily. For many, global integration spelled ruin. Rising competition and greater instability shattered the girding system of protection and prerogatives. In 1814, the Consulado observed that "the political convulsions that simultaneously and successively descend upon this country have caused considerable losses to our capitalists throughout the diverse corners in which they conduct their trade; and this hampers the regular operation of their businesses at the very time we need to fructify commercial activity . . ."[66] Faced with new competition, many called for a return to the old protectionist order. It is worth citing the complaints of Manuel Aguirre. The same merchant who served as the standard-bearer for freer trade in the 1790's, now chastened, lamented the competitive turn. "These abuses inflicted on our inexperienced citizens have brought deep and ruinous consequences to the country," he told the Consulado; "you have to be possessed of the most apathetic indolence and humiliating egotism not to be touched by the sad picture presented by the commerce of our country, and what awaits its future."[67]

Such laments accomplished little. The government went deaf on merchant appeals for the same reason they turned to the very same merchants for support: money. The only way out of the fiscal bind, now that silver flows had evaporated, was through the promotion of international trade and the invitation to foreign, especially British merchants. Over the long run, customs revenues had to replace remittances from Potosí as the main source of public sector funding.[68] Import taxes replaced rents from silver; Buenos Aires converted its monopoly over outbound highland silver and revenue shipments to a control of inbound commodities flooding into a post-mercantilist open market, and could not afford to deprive itself of a new source of revenue—even if it meant exposing local merchants to the powerful winds of Atlantic free trade.

In total, by October 1821, the revolutionary governments of Buenos Aires owed a debt of 1.6 million pesos. One third came from shares issued against state assets, one third were amortization bills and paper notes, and a quarter stemmed from 16 ad hoc forced loans raised from 1813 to 1821.[69] Indeed, by the time Buenos Aires was besieged and occupied by federal cavalrymen in 1820, the city's governments were in the business of printing 100-peso notes (in the winter of 1820, they issued fully 40,000 pesos in new scrip) to distribute among merchants to repay loans. Governments had long since given up on paying their own meager officials and could barely field an army. Inflation was careening—indeed, inflation was emerging as the most decisive tax of all. In the absence of any means to borrow voluntarily or muster revenues by conventional means, inflation was the last desperate resort. The result was profoundly paradoxical: government debt monetized an economy crippled by the loss of its fiduciary mainstay, silver. And yet, by virtue of the government's being the primary issuer of money, governmental inability to maintain fiscal order was also the primary source of monetary instability. In effect, the state enjoyed a monopoly over a power it could not yet wield.[70]

Combined, revolutionary finance and free trade sundered the old rentier pact between merchants and the sovereign. Market forces, albeit unstable and bereft of legal procedure and stable means of exchange, now dominated. Merchants, once the elite of the Viceroyalty and functioning hand-in-glove with political power, could no longer command unrivaled authority. With the *dénouement* of colonial merchant capital, the closure of the Consulado was for all intents and purposes an afterthought. The private corporate world of the guild gave way to a new regime in which merchants would operate as one of a set of actors vying for control of state institutions. Now, deprived of political property, merchants elected to support public institutions, not out of conviction, but out of desperation to create any sort of proprietary regime to stabilize market relations.

The first decade of the revolution saw Buenos Aires creoles trying to create a new political community out of the shell of the institutions of its colonial predecessor. By 1820, coaxing a new order out of the old became an impossible strategy for a simple reason: the old colonial institutions, Cabildos, Consulados, and the image of a reincarnated Viceroyalty in a republican form, lay in ruins. Cabildos, tight nuclei of well-to-do neighbors in Buenos Aires, had clearly exhausted their ability to speak for any general will. The Consulado, in turn, ceased allocating rights to earn oligopoly rents, spoke no longer for a merchant class, and failed to perform the function as the vehicle for harnessing private funds for public ventures. If the old colonial and corporate framework of power collapsed, a new model still awaited emergence.

The Revolution: Phase II

In this crisis, provinces were born, including that of Buenos Aires.[71] By 1820, this offered a group of *porteños* the chance to redirect the course of the revolution. Rather than rely on the crumbling pillars of the old order, they sought to erect new walls out of emerging provinces. The guiding principle of this effort was the formation of a "public." Whereas prior institutions still reflected colonial corporate ways, the new image of the republic imagined a people gathered in spaces open to all citizens, and perhaps most important, rulers accountable to state authority for their legal being—and not vice versa. The Buenos Aires governments of the 1820's sought to build new public institutions to legitimate their claims to speak for the community and more effectively to penetrate society in search of fungible assets with which to support state activities.[72] No less than its predecessor, this was a revolution from above, now bent on subjecting rulers to representative, public institutions.

The shift to creating "public" institutions was largely the work of the enlightened, portly diplomat Bernardino Rivadavia. A former associate of Belgrano's, Rivadavia played a secondary role in the revolution's first phase, winding up in Paris and London for most of the 1810's. In Europe, Rivadavia brushed shoulders with the liberals of the day, especially Jeremy Bentham and James Mill in London.[73] Both Bentham and Mill supported Latin American independence, and the former was especially keen to see the area implement many of his utilitarian political principles. Bentham, unhappy with the haphazard and arbitrary features of common law, believed in the idea of a great foundational code to embody a complete and systematic model of public and private law. He found in Rivadavia a more than willing collaborator and showered the Argentine statesman with encouraging letters and recommendations. Rivadavia was Bentham's most devout follower and calibrated much of his legislative agenda to the rationalist precepts of his tutor— including a deep faith in the unilateral power of law to shape society, an aversion to United States–style federalism, and a preference for representative institutions. In August 1822, Rivadavia sent his blueprint legislative package to Bentham, adding that it is "entirely based on your unimpeachable and indisputable truths contained in your work." Bentham praised his disciple for placing the River Plate on a "firm and happy footing." Colonial habits and institutions rested on privileges and immunities from a universal law blindly applying to all political subjects. For Benthamite epigones, "unitarians," the new model trumpeted general covering laws for all public affairs.[74]

The construction of a more generalized "public" was more than an intellectual concern. Unitarian ideas grafted onto a process of political incorporation already under way in the first decade of the revolution. From 1815 onwards, creole leaders spoke increasingly in the universalist cant of a citizenry with natural rights to self-representation—and this meant extending the franchise into the countryside. Moreover, warfare and mobilization shifted the gravity of power away from the city toward the countryside. With the abolition of the Cabildos and the creation of a provincial assembly, the rural political world joined urban Buenos Aires. The new assembly, comprised of 49 members, included 24 from the city and 24 from the country and one from Patagonia—half of whom faced election every year. The executive was to be elected from the assembly every three years. Furthermore, the new assembly then passed an electoral law that extended the vote to all adult men of the province, without property or literacy requirements. To be sure, aspects of ancien régime representation persisted, especially in the selection of candidates and the mobilization of constituencies (which still left many voters *de facto* out of the picture), and it was still a political world in which the city loomed over its countryside. Still, the demise of Cabildos and expansion of suffrage aimed to restore legitimacy to hobbled state authority by making institutions more public.[75]

Unitarians took this process of incorporation one step further. They yearned to enshrine all this in a constitutional framework and to reunite the Viceroyalty with the approval of provincial assemblies and not in spite of them.[76] In 1824, feeling that the representative institutions of the republic could bear the weight of reopening the divisive matter of what kind of national state to create, the Rodríguez government convoked a National Constitutional Congress in late 1824. By early 1826, the assembly began discussing a blueprint for the state, drafted in large part by Rivadavia's associate, Julián Segundo de Agüero, and defended according to the high principles of utilitarian rationalism. Years of rancor, it seems, had still not chastened Buenos Aires' ambition to be the capital of a centralized republic, and to the anguish of many of the provincial deputies, the *porteño* unitarians presented a version of earlier centralist plans. To hasten the reintegration of the provinces of the defunct Viceroyalty, the Congress widened the powers of the Buenos Aires executive, conferring transitional authority over economic matters, security, and foreign affairs. Thus from early 1825, Buenos Aires recovered its place as the executive center.[77]

A crucial aspect of constructing a new set of public institutions was to put revolutionary finances on sounder foundations, to create what contemporaries called "Public Finance." According to one prominent legislator, "no institution deserves more attention than *crédito público*."[78] By the 1820's, the River Plate was quickly adapting to the world market, extending its landed frontier outward, and beginning to enclose territories for cattle grazing. Despite these secular changes, it was still a region recovering from the loss of silver, and as Raúl Prebisch observed in one of his first essays, a region dependent on paper money. Paper money relied on revenues, and revenues depended on trade and the domain over natural resources. Buenos Aires abounded in the latter and had the virtual monopoly over the former.[79] To date, finance had been raised through traditional levies and the will of private merchants through the Consulado. The unitarian architects sought to replace the old method of finance with the institutions of state—to create "public credit" in place of private lending. Indeed, "public credit" was seen as the cornerstone for private fortune: "*Crédito público*, this instrument of wealth, far from being contrary to liberty, is its firmest support, and is destined to become its incontrovertible base."[80]

The new administration of Martín Rodriguez—for whom Rivadavia served as Minister of Government—commissioned a British accountant, Santiago Wilde, to report on the extent of the province's debt and propose a blueprint for financial reform. While only a fraction of Wilde's recommendations evolved into legislation, the new government overhauled the Finance Ministry into proper collection, treasury, and accounting departments and systematized customs into scales of tariffs by commodity and value (making customs, by 1822, the source of 80 percent of provincial revenues). The objective, as the Minister of Finance, Manuel José García, declared, was to dispense with "the horrendous plague of forced loans."[81]

Full-blown public credit, however, required other antecedent amendments apart from administrative reform. The state's assets needed to be identified and valorized in order to harness their potential as security for public borrowing. This brings us to the use of land and mining to secure public ventures. A decree of July 1822 forbade the sale of all public lands and made them available to occupants through long-term (ten-year) renewable and inheritable leases. The idea was: the government retained nominal ownership of the land to use as collateral against its loans, while at the same time fomenting agrarian settlement on the frontier because the entry cost of access to the resource was so low. Moreover, legislators felt, land speculators should not corner the land market. For Rivadavia, this enabled Buenos Aires to create the sound conditions for capitalist development, avoid rural proletarianization, and attract entrepreneurial European farmers.[82] In May 1826, Rivadavia promulgated an *enfiteusis* decree that formalized the leasing system. Under the *enfiteusis* system, Buenos Aires' patrimony in land could perform the double task of supporting public credit and animating private fortunes.[83]

The other mainstay was mining. Once again, legislators could not help but revive the image of a region shot through with silver lodes whose exploitation would furnish rents for the government. Perhaps even more than land, the unitarians expected mining wealth to support the new public credit scheme. Having lost Potosí, they turned their sight on the mirage of deposits in the province of La Rioja and the mines of Famatina. Compared to Mexico, wrote Rivadavia to intrigued British investors, the provinces of the interior sheltered "an undoubted abundance" of silver and gold deposits, which "with the weakest and most imperfect of efforts are easily extracted in quantity . . ." Mining companies scrambled for money to begin digging. Combining mining revenues and the influx of foreign capital, unitarians hoped, would restore Buenos Aires' place as one of the Atlantic world's great specie entrepôts. Not surprisingly, the promise of telluric fortunes turned out to be more fantastic than feasible. Disgruntled investors concluded their ventures in a storm of accusations of conniving and duplicity.[84]

MX

To reinforce the promise of land and mining as a means to consolidate the government's public credit, Rivadavia's final component was foreign capital. In the wake of the Napoleonic Wars, London emerged as the leading international supplier of investible funds and home to an emerging cluster of prestigious and well-connected financiers. Among the most powerful was the firm of Baring Brothers who, by the 1820's, was in the business of channeling funds to capital-starved independent Latin American countries. From the British angle, this was more than a felicitous chance. According to the Tory *The Quarterly Review*, "South America presents a market for the skill and expertise of our merchants, which we hope and believe will not long be witholden from them."[85] Unitarians wanted to mount this financial bandwagon. In 1824 the governments arranged with Baring Brothers to raise a nominal loan of one million pounds on the London money market. Like many financial dealings at this conjuncture, the operation had all the makings of a speculative stock-job and yielded handsome rewards to Baring Brothers. Buenos Aires was soon awash in money, much of it soon to be squandered on warfare.[86]

Credit

Baring Brothers

If land, mining, and foreign investment were to support the project of constructing a public financial world, it still required state institutions to realign private interests with the public good. Indeed, most unitarian energies were directed at consolidating the public debt and putting state finance on a sustainable diet. Their job improved as Buenos Aires began to enjoy a brief peaceful respite. With five years of peace from 1821 to 1825, demilitarization slashed spending, and attention shifted to im-

public finance

proving revenues and consolidating the groaning public debt. Exports boosted customs revenues and thus took care of much of the revenue anxiety (though they did not necessarily keep pace with imports).[87]

To solve the debt problem, Wilde had urged the creation of a funding system to begin repaying old debt, hold a store of capital to cover short-term dips, and serve as a general symbol of state creditworthiness. The funding system would be backed in part by a sinking fund generated out of customs returns, portions of which were earmarked for direct deposit, and managed by a government-appointed Commissioner. Above all, the fund would issue a new generation of bonds yielding 6 percent interest (4 percent on old viceregal debt), which, now resting on firmer fiscal grounds, would displace the old, worthless paper. New bond issues immediately confronted wary investors. Merchants, the primary consumer of these instruments and burnt so often in the past, were so disinterested that in short order the bonds were selling at less than 30 percent of their face value. But the first interest payment due on January 1, 1822 was honored promptly—as were all other quarterly payments for the next few years. In short order, a combination of upbeat government talk and palpable signs of recovery restored merchants' confidence: within months of their issue, bonds were selling at 85 percent.[88] In effect, the government was well on the way to converting its worthless short-term obligations to more stable, publicly acceptable, and manageable longer-term debt. This did not mean that the unitarians *reduced* their debt-load. They merely *converted* it, hoping that future foreign investment, and an export boom in mining and agrarian staples, would yield customs returns to make the long-term debt more manageable. Indeed, total debt, long and short, rose dramatically in a few short years. From 1.8 million pesos in 1821, Buenos Aires' outstanding obligations rose to 6.5 million pesos by 1825.[89] Some gambles work out; this one did not—largely for political reasons.

Liquidity—private money and credit—was still a chronic problem. To build a public market for funds and commodities, unitarians sought to solve the shortages by creating a bank that would manage emissions carefully, and thus provide merchants with a viable instrument of exchange. This would also curb the use of short-term public scrip as media of exchange. Merchants could use private money to buy long-term public bonds. In 1822, Finance Minister García sponsored the creation of the Banco de Buenos Aires—a private bank based on shareholder capital with an exclusive monopoly to receive deposits and issue notes for twenty years. It won swift approval in the Assembly (despite some grumbling about the monopoly clause) and among its shareholders.[90] The capital base of the Bank was weak and never built up hard reserves, and the managers gradually overextended credit (especially by discounting bills).[91] The hope was, nonetheless, to create public rules to enable private money to circulate and invest in state finance—to recouple public institutions of rulership with private interests of capital. Here was the making of a republic for capital and with capital.

This was not necessarily, however, a regime constructed *by* capital. To be sure, a capitalist's dream-rules do not necessarily make for successful blueprints for institutionalizing market relations. Political arrangements are required to enable market rules to rule. In Buenos Aires, republic foundations were anything but stable. A solvent state emerged as the premise for the entire public and private financial structure. Constitutional turmoil soon destabilized this precarious foundation. First, the government tried to use banking legislation, not just to create a public market for money, but to reinforce the goal of regional reintegration. If the new bankers always worried about the government's pressure to issue more liquidity to revive the economy, nothing could have prepared them for Congress's enthusiasm for a new National Bank. Once Buenos Aires became the seat of the new national executive, and as the Constitutional Congress neared approving a blueprint for provincial union, *porteño* leaders quickly introduced the idea of creating yet another bank—this time with a pan-provincial scope, and with deeper ties with the emerging national regime. The National Bank would attend to the needs of the region's periphery and reintegrate the provinces into the Buenos Aires monetary orbit. Yet the Provincial Bank was supposed to enjoy a twenty-year exclusive charter as a condition for its role in creating a public market for money. In January 1825, the alarmed bankers warned the minister about the loss of their "prerogatives and privileges" and reminded him of "the instability of public guarantees, which are still not strengthened by confidence or the irresistible power of time, [and] . . . the risks this proposal lends to accumulated property that is only beginning to emerge for the first time in a public form."[92]

Then bankers faced a dramatic reversal in financial climate. London financiers went bust and forced Buenos Aires to intensify reliance on domestic sources. At the same time, Brazil and Buenos Aires went to war. In December 1825, the Imperial navy blockaded the port of Buenos Aires and choked trade—in turn slashing customs receipts. In January,

Buenos Aires marched its armies to square off with imperial troops. After a thousand days of grinding indecisive warfare, a British-brokered
armistice finally created the state of Uruguay as a buffer between the
republic in Buenos Aires and its imperial neighbor.[93] An acute shortage
of liquidity swept the region. The provinces howled in penury.

As renewed warfare gutted public credit, the unitarians tried to print
their way out of the mayhem. Desperate to have the Congress and local
assemblies approve the new constitution, the government grasped for a
means to alleviate provincial malaise. Their short-term solution was to
ratify the new National Bank, which opened its doors and immediately
began flooding the River Plate with banknotes in early 1826.[94] Bereft of
any confidence, without support from the merchant class, Bank money
quickly plummeted in value. Even the new, more supine "National"
bankers balked at the government's direct request for 300,000 pesos to
pay for war in July 1827, and warned of an imminent "paralysis" of the
"social machinery." Undaunted, the government recklessly exploited
the Bank's lending powers to finance its war. By the time an armistice
was signed, the government owed fully 13.4 million pesos to the Bank,
which had, for all intents and purposes, ceased its public operations,
and had become a bankrupt extension of a bankrupt polity.[95]

War, then provincial rejection of the constitutional blueprint, eviscerated the unitarian experiment and sent the political economy into an
inflationary tailspin. Local opposition finally brought the unitarians
down. Scarcely a week after approving the National Bank, the Congress
elected Rivadavia the first President of the United Provinces of the River
Plate. At his inauguration, Rivadavia delivered a short speech of utilitarian vintage, promising to use "the state to organize the social elements it has, in this way to produce in less and less time more and more
results." But his legislative agenda, starting with a plan to split the
province of Buenos Aires in two, and then a centralist constitution for
the whole republic, went down in flames. Furious provincials—
especially representing rural Buenos Aires—blasted the fledgling government.[96] Finally, the news that Rivadavia was willing to let Brazil have
the Banda Oriental in order to restore peace sent *porteños* to the streets to
vent their opposition. In disgrace, after little more than a year as President of the Republic, Rivadavia resigned on June 27, 1827, and set sail
for exile, never to return to Buenos Aires.

The unitarian experiment collapsed amid crippling internal and international war. With Buenos Aires severed from Andean sources of sil-

ver, the city had to find a new niche in the Atlantic economy. The pampean export sector, however, was still too incipient to sustain a wave of imports, and most years recorded trade deficits; mining in the Interior was never more than a shadow of its Alto Peruvian predecessor; foreign capital turned into a one-shot deal that could not forestall balance-of-payments problems. Thus, just as Buenos Aires struggled to adapt to the post-mercantilist Atlantic economy, its underlying export sector was still too weak to sustain the fiscal and financial apparatus upon which state-builders sought to build their new public institutions and around which to reintegrate the dispersed—and warring—parts of the republic.

Conclusion

This chapter has explored the dilemmas of institution-making in a revolutionary context, where no common idea governed the political community, and where no dominant class of interests was positioned to impose its will. If the revolution had shattered the tottering equipoise upon which Buenos Aires merchants balanced their fortunes, they were soon forced to play by new political rules to defend their property. The old corporate world of commercial regulation and self-defense gave way to open-market competition and reliance on the state to protect the rights of capital. The fungible nature of commercial capital had made merchants unavoidable targets for expropriation through forced loans and inflationary taxation. Herein lay a basic political quandary: the state had to uphold the rights of capital to foster a more robust and modern capitalist economy, yet the new revolutionary and increasingly representative state's own foundations were anything but solid. In the drive to legitimate the revolution by opening the state to more regional and social pluralist accommodation, collective decision-making faced mounting internal rivalry. When no single class, region, or city could exert authority over the crumbling remains of the Viceroyalty, the capital's power and the rights of merchant capital began to unravel.

The efforts to create new public institutions to reconsolidate the capital's power and the girding of merchant capital only intensified the drift to civil discord. In the 1820's, the turn to financial institution-formation meshed with the emerging publicness of the revolutionary state. The funding and banking institutions designed by merchants and unitarians were supposed to sustain a public world of money—to secure property, not through the exercise of private power, but through publicly respected authority. So, on the one hand, the state created new public institutions to foster a notion of credit, and create the possibility for an ever denser network of exchange relations through the use of money. On the other, the state used this power to fund its own integrative objectives, in so doing destabilizing the institutions that were supposed to stabilize new property relations.

Contingent and structural factors foiled creole revolutionary efforts to cobble together a new political community in the wake of imperial collapse. By contrast, patriots in the United States succeeded, albeit barely. Contingencies were enormously important. North American Federalists counted on good fortune: counter-revolutionary loyalists were hobbled; no neighbor supported the English; and French support helped tilt the balance in favor of patriots. Even then, it had taken some deft financial footwork by Alexander Hamilton to put the new regime on sounder foundations. Shrewd leadership scraped the Articles of Confederation through state assemblies. But structural factors were no less important. The underlying social tension in the Viceroyalty, especially in the Andes and Banda Oriental, intensified the rancor and inflated the costs of liberation. Then the recrudescence of rivalry with Brazil gutted efforts to follow Hamilton's model of public credit. The revolution shattered old regime institutions legitimating authority and buttressing the legal foundations of private fortunes. But the revolution was less successful in positively creating successor institutions for public rule and private property.

Once the revolution collapsed into civil war, restoration was impossible. Buenos Aires was unlike France: the River Plate had simply gone too far down the revolutionary road to restore the fabric of state legitimacy by rekindling monarchy. Why? Because this was a war for self-rule; restoration of an ancien régime in Buenos Aires would have meant returning to the imperial mold. Nor could Buenos Aires emulate the United States' softer restorationist spirit by reviving a Whig tradition. Why? Because this was also a war involving proprietary transformation; returning to pre-1810 local arrangements implied restoring the power of political property and estates of rent-seeking merchants. Revolutionary war destroyed the old institutional world for good. It condemned Buenos Aires to face a republican future without a bridge backwards. The bridge ahead leaned into a dark precipice.

☞ The Age of "Anarchy," 1820's –1850's

5 ⌐ Rosas Agonistes, or the Political Economy of Cronyism

Famosamente infame
su nombre fue desolación en la casa,
idolátrico amor en el gauchaje
y horror del tajo en la garganta.
Hoy el olvido borra su censo de muertes,
porque son venales las muertes
si las pensamos como parte del Tiempo,
esa inmortalidad infatigable
que anonada con silenciosa culpa las razas
y en cuya herida siempre abierta
que el último dios habrá de restañar el último día,
cabe toda la sangre derramada.
No sé si Rosas
fue sólo un ávido puñal como los abuelos decían;
creo que fue como tú y yo
un hecho entre los hechos
que vivió en la zozobra cotidiana
y dirigió para exaltaciones y penas
la incertidumbre de otros.

Jorge Luís Borges

Explaining Caudillos   *182O*

The demise of the unitarian experiments of the 1820's dashed the last hopes of institutional change guided by enlightened revolutionaries. The reality of civil war supplanted the promise of a constitution as the political compass for Buenos Aires and the River Plate provinces. No region, class, or sector's interests could marshal the resources to impose its will on rivals or generate consensus among them, but each rival possessed sufficient power to check the projects of adversaries. The sun of the colonial order had set, but the components of a new order still lingered predawn, below the horizon. To those accustomed to colonial security or yearning for the stable rule of capital, this was anarchy.

Buenos Aires expressed a variation on an Atlantic theme. The Age of Revolution permanently changed the status of monarchs and shook the privileged world of rentier classes. Legal equality of political subjects and the autonomy of private agents—the twin pillars of liberalism—could be disruptive as well as liberating. At least until the 1850's, European and New World leaders struggled to preserve some continuity in the seismic ruptures provoked by revolution. By the 1850's, new models of public law were to provide a framework for stability. What bridged revolutionary constitutionalism of the early nineteenth century and the new spirit of the second half of the century?

In post-revolutionary Spanish America, revolutionary efforts to consolidate stable public law ceded to a new form of rule: the regime of caudillos. In the River Plate, the dominant caudillo was the longtime Governor of the province of Buenos Aires, Juan Manuel de Rosas (1829–32, 1835–52). The fragmentation of the viceregal space gave way to shaky provincial sovereignties riddled with internal ferment and jostling constantly with equally insecure neighbors. Accordingly, governors, most of whom had cut their military teeth in two decades of revolutionary warfare, emerged as the poles of dispersed political power. But just as Buenos Aires was the most powerful province in the mosaic, Rosas was the most powerful governor—the *primus inter pares*—in the faltering movement from colonialism to statehood, from mercantilism to free trade, from a regime of contingent political property to absolute private property. In this long transition, the River Plate, and most of Spanish America, had suffered in a condition of almost permanent flux in which caudillos began to emerge as the impermanent icons of political authority.[1]

Historians have not treated caudillos kindly. They emerge as obstacles to state-formation in Latin America and help account for the setbacks in the long march to democratic liberalism.[2] As a throwback to a feudal pattern or recidivist flotsam from the independence wars, they champion that which is seen as the most corrosive force in negotiating the transition from colonial to post-colonial authority: lawlessness. In ruling with an iron fist and not a coda, caudillos stymied the benign efforts of constitutionalists to reconsolidate the state on new legal foundations. To make matters worse, their power base in provincial polities presented an alternative legitimating framework to the nation-state. Not

surprisingly, to many historians federalism and the belief in a less centralized state resting on provincial autonomy comes across as an intractable hindrance to the unity of the successor states to Spanish power.
Caudillismo became a political framework for disunion.[3]

This view presents us with two difficulties. First, such a characteri-
zation associates state-formation with the consolidation of unitary polities, and regards public law regimes resting on multiple sovereignties as
weak and predisposed to fragmentation. With the end of the Napoleonic
era, however, new statesmen uncoupled liberalism from centralism.[4]
Other structures could frame the political community, including multilayered polities. Second, the concern with the caudillos' sanguinary behavior obscures their source of social power; lost to view is any understanding of the constituencies that buttressed caudillo longevity. The
image of Rosas as an all-powerful personalist tyrant, while colorful and
entertaining, stresses his person rather than the fullness of his powers—
especially command over public powers to create private rights. These
powers, in turn, emanated from deep-seated change as the Atlantic
world shifted from one structure of the conjuncture to the next.

Buenos Aires was in the throes of a trans-Atlantic transformation
from anciens régimes to new representative orders, and from political
claims to privileges and entitlements to private stakes in property. If
late-colonial officials and reformers dreamed of Buenos Aires as a capital in a reconstituted imperial system, revolution thrust the city's capitalists into an entirely transformed financial and commercial Atlantic
order. With free trade and representative polities sweeping the Old and
New Worlds, merchants and monarchs could no longer nourish each
other's source of rents.

While transformations differ from reconstitutions, they do not un-
couple politics from economics. Enabling competitive forces to thrive
did not remove the power of public authority over private interests,
while emerging interests remapped potential constituencies for political
brokers. This chapter argues that Rosas was both a by-product and a
custodian of an interaction among self-interested parties who found in
the Governor a means to distribute and enforce property rights through
a particular kind of legal practice. Rosas used the state to confer rights to
social actors. Such gestures were not meant to immunize or shelter them
from competition and thus coddle their oligopoly rents. Unlike the colonial era, the new conjuncture required that merchants compete among
themselves for market shares. What Rosas could do was give Buenos

Aires and the capital's merchants competitive advantages over other ports and merchants. In exchange, he insisted that his social constituents bankroll his political maneuvering, especially the financing of low-intensity warfare. At the same time, social actors turned to the power of the Governor to create the possibility for the existence of these rights. Propertied sectors urged the Governor to restore order, even if it lacked sound legal foundations. Rosas's survival depended on his ability to meet these needs. In this *quid pro quo* between the caudillo and new property holders, a kind of cronyism emerged, one that provided a crucial mediating process between the destruction of the ancien régime and the triumph of its successor.[5]

Rosas's regime was a contingent response to a specific kind of opportunity structure. Rapid commercialization had transformed the bedrock of property rights—hiking the returns to absolute private dominions, and intensifying claims for the protection of property. At the same time, public authority was weak. The deals struck between public power and private claimants reflect this tentative condition. Once a proprietary elite was to command more strength, and public authority was to display an ability to provide public goods (like law or stable money), the balance of private and public interests shifted, eventually reconverging around a constitutional arrangement in the 1850's. But in the wake of revolution and civil war, cronyism was the order of the day.

Cronyism, it should be stressed, was a highly unstable arrangement. In the first place, Rosas's social alliance lacked cohesion, and without cohesion, the alignment tended to evict as many parties as it included. More important, Rosas and his filial type ruled through an incomplete (not absent) legal order. Rosas preferred to issue and enforce executive decrees rather than champion a constitutional order *tout cour*. In so doing, he balked at the precommitment powers of a constitution—the ability to integrate social actors into a series of meta rules and regulations that would provide stability, accountability, and credibility to public and private rights.[6] His power rested on the rule of quasi-law: sanctions and dictates of an unstable state bereft of deep legitimacy and lacking an accepted covering law for public affairs, even while the state enforced particular laws governing the concerns of civil society. In short, without a stable constitutional order, the means to resolve disputes over the highest of all political stakes remained contestable. Rosas helped confer rights to private agents, and they requited his favor with support. But in the end, the state could not uphold and enforce these rights absolutely.

If the caudillo personified anything, it was this transitional incomplete-ness. Accordingly, Rosas's very success in distilling a new order from the revolutionary aftermath set the stage for his downfall.

Rosas's Genesis

Rosas's authority emerged out of widespread social fatigue born of the fracturing of the Platine political universe. Coming to power as a mili-tary man, he promised the people of Buenos Aires that he would un-wind the tensions wrought by revolutionary militarization. It took one last tragic episode of civil war, now involving an armed clash between *porteño* factions themselves, to create the possibility for his rise.

When Colonel Manuel Dorrego took over from the unitarians in August 1827, he tried to navigate the province out of the unitarian storm by promising to restore powers to the province.[7] Federalists took control of the government of Buenos Aires. They believed that the core of politi-cal sovereignty lay in the provincial and not in the national government, and distrusted the proclamations of the city's big merchants and their overextended financial institutions. Dorrego promised to dismantle the teetering citadels of merchant power and began negotiating pacts with neighboring provinces. Merchants, and especially those invested in the National Bank, cried foul and insisted on the sanctity of the "legitimate-ly acquired property rights." Another merchant denounced the Gover-nor: "This man who today presides over the country is ruining it. . . . He is diabolical and will bring an end to the country if he stays in power."[8] In response, Dorrego's Minister of Finance pilloried big money interests as the malefactors of the republic's troubles: "It is important to consider that the country cannot be subjected to an aristocracy, no matter what type, and even less a mercantile aristocracy, which is the most damaging and dangerous of all . . ."[9]

The unitarians and their financial backers mounted their last stand. When the humiliated and dispirited national army under General Juan Lavalle returned from the Oriental front, it besieged the city. Refusing to kneel to federalists, Lavalle led his troops into Buenos Aires on Decem-ber 1 and toppled Dorrego. Lavalle's coup provoked a massive rural up-rising across the province in late 1828 and early 1829. Popular *montonero* forces crushed the legions of the national army, as General Rauch dis-covered, fatally, at the Battle of Puente de Márquez. The *levée* horrified the province's propertied patriciate. Indeed, ranchers' fear that rebels would attack their property prompted them to embrace the insurrection and direct popular forces against the unitarians in the city. With time, *montonero* bands rallied behind the Indian-fighting caudillo, Colonel Rosas, who offered to back their grievances against urban moneyed interests and their centralizing designs. Rosas's role was crucial: he presented himself to popular and landed sides as both a symbol of unity and the voice of anti-unitarian opposition.[10]

In the meantime, Governor Dorrego, having escaped the capital, joined these rural militias under Rosas's helm. In a bloody showdown at Navarro outside Buenos Aires, Lavalle triumphed. Dorrego fled, only to be captured at the border and returned to Navarro in chains. Lavalle personally ordered Dorrego shot. This act of sangfroid issued a riptide of revulsion across the region; warfare engulfed the province. Lavalle's control of the city degenerated into a reign of terror. Eventually, Rosas's militia, with the backing of Santa Fe's army, drove Lavalle from the city and he retreated to Montevideo, leaving Buenos Aires exhausted.[11]

This gruesome episode was the closing chapter in the constitutional revolution from above. Henceforth, public leaders ceased championing their cause from the commanding heights of a hobbled state. Furthermore, the *decembrista* revolt and Dorrego's execution inspired an aversion to constitutional-talk altogether. Both unitarian and federalist calls for a supreme law of the land fell on deaf ears. Citizens across the region recognized that the constitution had failed to provide the carapace for a new political community.

If Dorrego's death suspended constitutional-talk, his funeral marked the beginning of a new era of quasi-law. A triumphant Rosas entered the city in November 1829, greeted by the police band and cheering crowds. As a capstone to the rituals of civil war, provincial militias escorted Dorrego's corpse back to the city, where it was treated to an elaborate funeral service. Rosas, though he was never a devotee of the fallen federalist, did not let the moment of mourning pass without some political theatrics. His mien and words were meant to dispel Buenos Aires' fear of civil war and anarchy; he arrogated to himself and personified the symbols of power. After an elaborate mass at the Cathedral, the cortege wound its way through the streets of Buenos Aires to the cemetery. The city's population was drummed out to witness the spectacle of a mounted General Rosas (he had been promoted to Brigadier in January 1829) in full military regalia and bearing Dorrego's own sword, leading a somber parade in his wake. Beneath the impassive visage, Rosas presented himself as the avenger of the fallen federalist, and affirmed, in consecrating Dorrego's death, his style of rule: "Dorrego! Enlightened victim of civil dissent! Rest in peace. . . . The fatherland, honor, and religion are today satisfied in paying the ultimate tribute to the first magistrate of the Republic sentenced to die in the silence of its own laws."[12] In early December 1829, the Provincial Assembly proclaimed Rosas the new governor. Several weeks later the Assembly approved sweeping legislation against libel, and defamation of public morals and authority, and declared that Rosas was "the Restorer of the Laws."

The Domain of Quasi-Law

Rosas aimed to wind down the effects of revolution while nurturing a new social bloc to support political authority. For what must have seemed a political eternity to the citizens of Buenos Aires, he occupied the office of Governor from 1829 to 1832 and 1835 to 1852 (and in the interim years he was in effect the poltergeist of power). To many, the vaunted but turbulent revolutionary cause had been unsupportable. Yet the revolution itself had inducted new social actors into a political arena governed by new modes of legitimation. In a society seething with conflict, the political and economic elites were determined to avoid direct class confrontation, especially after this specter had raised its frightening head during the 1828–29 *montonero* uprising.[13] Rosas had to juggle the need to provide a semblance of legitimacy with the powers to defuse class antagonisms, especially now that he had to contend with a politicized and agitated countryside. The issue was: how to stabilize property and inculcate respect for authority without reinitiating divisive deliberation over the meta laws of the land?

One solution was to rely on laws the revolutionaries had authored that had reshaped the ways in which citizens conducted politics. New political practices, especially elections and the rituals of new public assemblies, effected this purpose. Every few years the province underwent noisy but not highly contested races for the seats in the Legislature, which in turn, invoked great acts of fanfare and official decorum to "elect" the Governor—replete with sententious discourses on the Assembly's place as the cipher for a public will. A delicate process of intra-elite negotiating selected the roster of candidates before the election. Once the real jostling behind closed doors was over, the citizenry voted for their choice of notables. When Rosas presented himself as a candidate to the Executive, he was always elected. He never seized power by force of arms, even though military might was his single most important political asset. Indeed, the rites of civilian command soon subordinated military power to the provincial governments—especially once the national army was disbanded and its remnants retreated into Lavalle's roving forces. Backroom brokerage and the rituals of representation enabled the occupants of political offices to present themselves collectively as the voices transcending class, sectoral, and regional interests. The machinery of representation helped generate a sense that the Governor ruled beyond particular interests and in favor of a general will.[14]

If the organs of politics helped transcend dangerous enmities, the convergence within and between social classes over the terms of public rulership was hardly frictionless. Rosas governed for a shaky, but untrammeled term until 1832. In the following three years, Buenos Aires began to slip back into old antagonisms under Governors Balcarce and Viamonte. And when the people of Buenos Aires learned in February of 1835 that an armed band of men linked to the Governor of Córdoba, who in turn allied with Santa Fé's Estanislao López, had ambushed Facundo Quiroga while he was on a mission from Buenos Aires, fear of a civil war gripped the province. Panic at the prospect of a relapse into old ways drove the Legislature to plead to Rosas to return to the governorship. Deputies promised him an extended term of five years and the "sum of public powers" to use extraordinary measures to deal with people who threatened to undermine the system. Rosas insisted on a popular plebiscite: at the end of March, almost 10,000 men voted on Rosas's extraordinary powers. Only eight voted to deny him new authorities. In April 1835, Rosas reassumed the mantle of the Executive with unsurpassed, but formally sanctioned, powers over legislative and judicial matters. It was only henceforth that Rosas's regime took on the trappings of a soft dictatorship. In subsequent "elections" Rosas would play the part of the reluctant ruler, the Legislature would grovel and then approve the bundle of articles of the March 1835 Law, and finally it would give the caudillo another five years' mandate with extraordinary powers to pursue his mission as the "Restorer of the Laws."[15]

Thus, over time the state metamorphosed into a more authoritarian expression of the political will of the elite, even as it struggled to preserve a semblance of legitimacy in the eyes of the citizenry. Especially after 1837, Rosas ruled with an increasingly merciless bent. Not surprisingly, the decorum of elections became ever more ornate and trium-

phalist as their significance waned. This ambiguity was resolved in Rosas's own political convictions: as far as the Governor was concerned,
law and constitution-talk were the causes of division and not unity, discord and not stability. Echoing de Maistre and Bonald, Rosas preferred
an image of a society guided by organic metaphors in which people
would relate to public life through their functional roles and corporate
places—and not as freestanding individuals endowed with eternal unimpeachable rights. Rights were relative, depending on the needs of the
whole and the location of the person in question. In this understanding
of the political community, people had public lives, making contracts,
discussing the merits or demerits of their elected representatives. But,
they did not query the political principles underlying the regime as a
whole—something Rosas felt that revolutionary constitutionalists did
with reckless abandon. Indeed, the very notion of a formal constitution
only elicited Rosas's bile. In a famous 1834 letter to his caudillo confrere
Facundo Quiroga, Rosas spelled out his aversions to more constitution-
talk in no uncertain terms. Revolutionary constitutionalists had "aggravated the public mind, misled opinion, placed in opposition private interest, propagated immorality and intrigue, and divided society into
bands, which have scarcely left a vestige of former ties." He was not
averse to an assembly to debate the terms of meta laws, but this could
only follow social and economic rebuilding, attending to the private
concerns of the citizenry. "[I]f every State does not possess in itself the
elements for maintaining their respective order, the creation of a General
Representative Government is of no use but to agitate the whole Republic in every partial disorder that takes place, and cause the conflagration
of any one of the States to be spread over all the rest."[16] In this fashion,
Rosas could defend the principles of natural hierarchy, order, and republicanism, and indeed specific laws in practice, while at the same time
balking at the concept of a covering law for the state as a whole.

The principle of upholding quasi-law to restore particular laws echoed through many of the newspapers of the Rosas era—most of which
acted as filterless conduits of Rosista pieties. The Governor's intellectual
mouthpiece, the Neapolitan Pedro de Angelis, edited the *Gaceta Mercantil*, published the *Archivo Americano* for a wider audience (400 copies of a
1,500 print run were sent abroad), and played a direct role in *The British
Packet*, which served the merchant community. In the pages of these
newspapers—the only ones to circulate in Buenos Aires with any regu-
larity—Rosas's legal ideas found expression and deliberation. In re-

sponse to pamphlets calling for a constitution for the Confederation, the
Archivo Americano warned of the risks of reopening old antagonisms,
championing instead a loose pact among provinces. A confederation
without a constitution allowed provinces to join in common defense
without interfering in local autonomy, provided stability, and allowed
order to percolate through society. This kind of inter-provincial "pact,"
the editors argued, "is a national pact: and General Rosas saved it from
degenerating into a coactive alliance against the free will and rights of
each of the Confederated Provinces." The challenge was to sediment order and respect for law first, and perhaps, in the long run, create constitutions: "That [Rosas] has been wise in the selection of means is demonstrated by the power of opinion with which he has overcome the most
severe conflicts, organizing the State whilst conducting it to the termi-
nation of a long but just and necessary struggle. . . . [T]he sentiment of
public duty and legal obedience rooted in the majority of the country are
not the fictions of partiality. A definitive constitution without these
bases would always be chimerical and impossible."[17] This had been precisely the mistake of revolutionaries and unitarians: using the constitution *first* as the carapace of integration, to *create* that which did not already exist. Rosas and his followers sought to invert the causal order, to
create the social conditions for the possibility of a constitution.[18]

This political bricolage justified quasi-legal means to consolidate legal ends, but faced its supreme test in handling inter-provincial affairs.
Rosas came to power thanks to the work of provincial armies from Santa
Fe, and at least from the outset, could not rule without the tacit support
of his Littoral neighbors. Caudillo allies were necessary because the
unitarian enemy was still alive and well—ensconced in Montevideo under Lavalle, and under General José María Paz in Córdoba. Paz waged a
scorched-earth campaign against rebel *montoneros*, and denied the Interior to Rosas. Quiroga, Rosas's main ally in the Interior, straggled to
Buenos Aires, where he was received with official exuberance. To check
unitarian spread and to control rivalries unleashed within provinces,
Rosas approved of other governors' plans to forge a League of the Littoral Provinces. Unity was necessary for defensive reasons, as the
League's architects, Buenos Aires' Rosas, Santa Fe's López, and Corrientes's Pedro Ferré proclaimed: "If the four Littoral provinces now appear more powerful and better financed, it is because circumstances require a system that will rescue the governments from instability and
other dangers presented by an isolated existence."[19] On January 4, 1831,

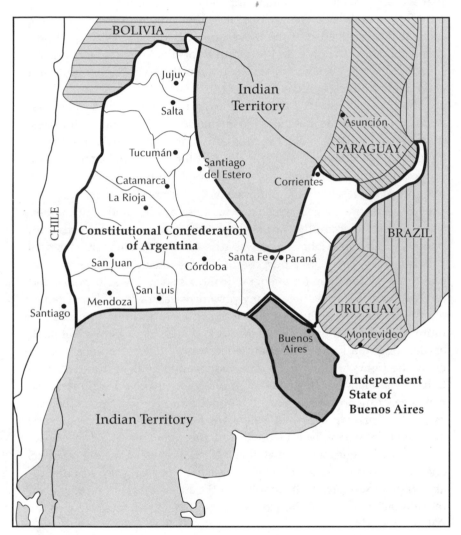

BOLIVIA

Jujuy

Salta

Indian
Territory

Asunción

PARAGUAY

Tucumán

Santiago
del Estero

Corrientes

Catamarca

La Rioja

CHILE

BRAZIL

**Constitutional Confederation
of Argentina**

San Juan

Córdoba

Santa Fe   Paraná

San Luis

Mendoza

URUGUAY

Santiago

Buenos
Aires

Montevideo

**Independent
State of
Buenos Aires**

Indian Territory

Map 4. The River Plate in the Era of Juan Manuel de Rosas

the governors of Entre Ríos, Santa Fe, and Buenos Aires approved a Pact that would provide a membrane for the conduct of interprovincial affairs for twenty years. One by one, the other provinces joined, and the Littoral Pact evolved into the Governors' League (see Map 4). Rosas called the Pact "the base and foundation of the Argentine Confederation, which, if it ever falters, will condemn the Republic to profound chaos and appalling anarchy."[20]

The 1831 Pact reflected the principles and dilemmas of quasi-law. As a means to thwart the ambitions of constitution-makers and centralizers, it was meant more as a defense mechanism against the exhausted principles of earlier dogmas. While it did call for some future congress to create a federal government, this was never consummated. Moreover, a temporary Representative Committee of the Littoral Provinces was supposed to exercise powers to make war, raise armies, and sign treaties. The Committee promptly entrusted the Governor of Buenos Aires with matters of foreign relations and was dissolved within a year. This deal proclaimed no affirmative purpose of a more integrated state; the Pact was not a handmaiden for a federal order. As such, it was unstable and required constant brokerage. Many provinces yearned for a truer federalism, especially Corrientes, which was still a power in its own right. A more enduring and equitable framework would, many provincial leaders felt, imply a form of riparian federalism: Littoral provinces would enjoy the rights to trade freely and independently along the river systems of the Platine region, and no province or city could command the privilege of monopolizing trans-Atlantic traffic. The Pact presumed an association of sovereign and truly equal provinces. Old physiocratic anti-monopolist language blended into the remnants of Artigas's decentralized League, and animated an alternative vision for the republic, one in which provinces and their propertied citizenry enjoyed unmediated rights to partake in the bounty of the market. Riparian federalism meant that Buenos Aires had to forfeit its place as the gatekeeper to the Atlantic world.[21]

Riparian federalism threatened Rosas's power. His cronyism rested on his ability to guarantee the *porteño* patriciate's control over riverine trade in return for its loyalty. Consequently, his need to deal with his internal constituents threw him into a constant struggle with his neighbors. Appreciating this problem requires an understanding of the effects of the reincorporation of Buenos Aires into the trans-Atlantic economy in the wake of revolution.

The New Export Staples

Colonial merchants and institutional reformers had earlier touted change within a reconstituted mercantilist empire. The revolution, however, shattered all hopes of restoring the *status quo ante*. It opened the way for Buenos Aires' full immersion into the transforming Atlantic system, held together by freer flows of capital, people, and commodities. The nineteenth century would become the century of "free trade."

The transforming Atlantic system redefined local commercial networks, creating room for a new generation of capital interests. The revolution dismantled mercantilism's bulwarks; merchants could ply their wares irrespective of the Merchant Guild's sensibilities. The River Plate was suddenly now a market-driven economy. The prospect of social mobility—upward as well as downward—was both an inducement and a fear for the city's merchant class. Wealth was as precarious as it was alluring. Indeed, from the very start, *porteños* sometimes harbored misgivings about unbridled competition, but the promise of making fortunes from the new staple trades and the deluge of cheap British manufactures overwhelmed any incipient debate over trade policy.

To the extent that Buenos Aires promulgated commercial guidelines, it was for revenue purposes: levies on exports and tariffs on imports were the great source of income for the state. Rivadavia modulated customs to make money, not to protect native industries. Most import duties charged 15 percent ad valorem, some as low as 5 percent with a minor protectionist levy of 30 percent, on commodities like furniture, carts, footwear, and alcoholic beverages, goods for which there were accessible local substitutes. All goods shipped out of Buenos Aires faced a 4 percent ad valorem levy, except cow hides (which paid a simple *real* each), and jerked beef, grains, wool and finished leather, and manufactured goods, which flowed free of exactions. In 1836, Rosas recalibrated the schedules, offering minor protectionist concessions to matters of light consumable artisanal goods (like 35 percent on furniture, footwear, and finished textiles) and farmers (prohibiting imported flour and wheat when prices dropped below 50 pesos per *fanega* [22.5 liters]). In 1850, the British envoy to Buenos Aires, Henry Southern, informed Lord Palmerston that Buenos Aires' commercial duties far eclipsed Britain's in their liberality.[22] Buenos Aires became one of the world's first great free-trade ports. To the editors of *El Regulador* (the ironic name was surely unintended), Buenos Aires promised to be the Atlantic world's reincarnation of Carthage, Venice, and Amsterdam.[23] Customs reforms exposed the River Plate to the forces of comparative advantage; they also consolidated the city's hold over indirect revenues from trans-Atlantic trade.

Shipping boomed. Despite all the interruptions of wars, blockades, and volatile credit supply, the trend of ships entering and leaving the port of Buenos Aires was systematically upward. In the 1840's, cargo handling soared. In 1844 alone, 620 foreign ships visited the port; in 1849, 801 ships cast their anchors in the delta of the River Plate.[24]

Finally, European markets eased restrictions on staple imports. A new generation of staples joined hides as the mainstays the pampean export sector. The Continent in particular was a hungry market for Buenos Aires' wool. Antwerp and other Low Country ports' demand was almost insatiable. In turn, the British repeal of the Navigation Acts and the Corn Laws threw local markets open to agrarian staples (though it would take several more decades to exploit fully this new bonanza). And the booming slave economies of Brazil, the Caribbean, and the United States sucked up the region's production of jerked beef. As far as Buenos Aires was concerned, the River Plate was trailblazing the new Atlantic order, proving that the capital was the first true disciple of Adam Smith's free-trade doctrines—thereby giving a patina of intellectual weight to what had been embraced without much deliberation.[25]

Prices of Buenos Aires exportables soared. In this era of volatile monetary values and shifting exchange rates, price data are notoriously imperfect. Some trends, however, can be gleaned. Before the revolution, prices on the whole moved in accordance with local supply, which was in turn most often affected by drought, pestilence, or disturbances. With the British invasions of 1806–7, prices of rural exportables began to rise in the local market—but only reached the Bourbon high-water mark of 1760–62 in 1815. Suddenly, prices jumped in 1816. By 1819, according to Juan Carlos Garavaglia's calculations, rural staples fetched three times their 1815 prices. The trend continued into the 1820's, when after a brief dip in 1820–21, prices climbed, thanks especially to a plummeting paper peso. In the Rosas years, the peso continued to sag and world market prices rose—supporting the handsome prices of rural staples, though returns could be extremely volatile.[26]

The combination of lower barriers to entry and rising exportable prices induced a rapid shift in attention to the rural sector and away from domestic consumables, and even away from merchandise handling of imports—a sector many creole entrepreneurs preferred to leave to their *arriviste* competitors from Europe. Producers for the local market soon began to feel the competitive effects of manufactured imports.[27] River Plate producers for the local market, however, were mainly located in the Interior provinces, where high transport costs (and the effects of war and depreciating currencies) still sheltered them somewhat from the deluge; Buenos Aires, however, all but dismantled its local industries except for the most rustic products or export-refining.

The more remarkable transformation took place in the export sector as Buenos Aires shifted from handling silver and modest exports of hides, to the shipment of a spectrum of new staples to a variety of markets. The figures from local sources must be treated with great caution. Woodbine Parish, the British envoy to Buenos Aires, however, aggregated his findings—though he would urge caution, and may have underestimated his calculations.[28] From 1822 to 1837, the value of exports of "native produce" (excluding precious metals) rose modestly from £1 million to £1,127,427 (scarcely a 10 percent increase), but by 1849 had reached £2,537,821, though it dropped a little bit thereafter, once the accumulated stocks from the port were cleared in the wake of a prolonged blockade. Not only did exports rise, but there was a significant recomposition within the city's shipments. If in the 1820's, hides had accounted for over two thirds the total value of shipments, by 1849, they accounted for half. Indeed, in absolute terms, hide exports fell. The global increase in the value of exports is attributable to tallow, jerked beef, and increasingly, wool shipments. By mid-century, Buenos Aires exports were more diversified and less rustic, and found consumers in a broader range of markets. This suggests not just an expansion of processes latent in the late-colonial years, but a wholesale transformation of the exports sector in response to easier access to markets for new staples and rising prices for all staples.

The degree of market volatility merits emphasis. Before the drift to trans-Atlantic free trade, foreign consumption of South American staples had always been precarious. In general, the system of bills of exchange and lading (the primary means to sustain long-distance trade in the absence of stable foreign exchange markets) bordered on cumbersome. If it worked, this was thanks to the good reputation and caution of the main merchant houses in European cities and the ability of merchants in the American trading ports to discount these instruments without too much hesitation. Indeed, as we shall see in the next chapter, a plethora of merchant moneys lubricated the system—but they were far from secure and often unenforceable. But the most troublesome source of volatility was political turbulence within the River Plate. Endemic low-level civil warfare among provinces aggravated chronic inflation and a wavering paper peso, and on occasion, Buenos Aires was subjected to blockades: Brazil prowled the River Plate for almost three years from 1826 to 1828; France tried to impose its will on an unbending Buenos Aires for almost as long (from 1838 to 1840), the stiffest blockade of all lasting from September 1845 to mid 1847. Reinsertion into the flow of Atlantic commerce may have restored Buenos Aires' growth, but it did not immunize merchants and producers from risk, as the mercantilist system did by dispensing property rights to earn oligopoly rents.[29]

This sort of turbulence shaped business strategies. Producers and merchants adapted to these hazards by preferring non-perishable goods that could be unloaded once the crisis passed, eschewed dependence on credit, and generally minimized liquidity requirements. In technical terms, they opted for illiquid investments to reduce the asset specificity of their holdings as a hedge against non-credible commitments. Furthermore, they substituted, where possible, short-term contracts for longer-term ones to maximize their responsiveness to price and monetary changes. Under such uncertain circumstances and faced with great volatility in markets, Buenos Aires capitalists adopted a decidedly risk-averse approach to economic affairs, while at the same time being opportunistic.[30]

So much for micro-level adaptation to a difficult economic environment. Merchants wielded an additional option: they could lobby political authorities. If the restoration of the guild system to immunize merchants against competition was out of the question, porteño merchants were not without means to earn other sources of rent: they could try to shut out other ports from handling the traffic between the Atlantic and the vast hinterland of the River Plate's burgeoning commerce. Buenos Aires could control regional trade at the expense of provincial ports, and the city's merchants could thwart regional competition (even if they could not alleviate competition among themselves). This Rosas was prepared to do, not because he had any affection for merchants (he boasted a distaste for the urban dandyism of the salon and money-handling). Rather, controlling river trade meant that Buenos Aires could monopolize the most lucrative source of revenues: the customhouse. The public purse would win its fiscal bounty while private merchants could dominate the commanding heights of trans-Atlantic trade. Just as the transformation of the staples trade buoyed Buenos Aires' prosperity, it also provided the substructure for Rosas's cronyism. The Governor and the merchants swapped opportunistic loyalties; the interest of merchant capital dovetailed with the aspirations of the regional capital.[31]

The way to justify commercial centralism in the age of oceanic freer trade was to argue that the systems of the Plata, Uruguay, and especially the Paraná rivers constituted "interior rivers" of Argentine territory. In this fashion, barriers to international trade dropped without eroding Buenos Aires' authority over regional commerce.[32] The problem was that some provinces did not see the confederation in the same terms, in particular the Littoral. But Buenos Aires' claim to sovereign control over "national" and international trade helped Rosas justify the closure or harassment of other ports of call along the River Plate system. Once Pedro Ferré, the resilient Governor of Corrientes, was driven from office in late 1842 and this Littoral province readmitted to the Confederation under the terms of the 1831 Pact, Rosas clamped down on its ports, arguing that these were necessary measures to end "the desolating war that [the unitarians] still carry on with desperate tenacity, and by their depredations upon the property of the inhabitants of the confederated Provinces."[33] In due course, even foreign powers would accept this doctrine since it rearranged the mosaic of regional power and had little net effect on the ability to sell or buy from the River Plate as a whole.[34]

Buenos Aires' commercial hegemony inspired merchants' support for Governor Rosas. According to one observer, the government was "the best paymaster, and transactions with it are sought by the merchant and dealer with no preference to any other."[35] Indeed, merchants in Buenos Aires berated the French and British authorities when they sided with riparian federalists by throwing up a blockade in 1845, arguing that support for Rosas was the best guarantee of stable exchange, and enhanced the interests of the merchants most inclined to support trans-Atlantic trade.[36] London and Manchester merchants castigated Palmerston for his betrayal of what should be Britain's natural support for Buenos Aires' supremacy. A petition bearing signatures of Britain's financial and merchant potentates, including Baring and Rothschild, noted that "we consider it self-evident that a country which stands in relation to us of customer and debtor, as Buenos Ayres does, cannot be made to suffer in its trade and finances, without the effects recoiling upon ourselves."[37] Foreign confidence in the power of the capital to ab-

sorb the Atlantic's commodities prompted foreign merchants to flood to
Buenos Aires once the Anglo-French blockade was lifted in 1848. Within
a year, the market was awash with European manufactures and many
merchants saw the prices of their wares drop. The glut prompted some
to sound the alarms of a "mercantile crisis," while others appealed to the
government for relief. Not surprisingly, Rosas balked.[38] Yet this did not
prevent merchants from appealing to Rosas to withdraw his retirement
notice in late 1849: "The liberty we enjoy in the possession of our property, and in the transaction of our business; and the uniform kindness
with which our proper requests have been always attended to, are reasons that (apart from others of a high political order, but which we do
not consider ourselves entitled to discuss) draw forth our warmest ex-
pressions of gratitude."[39] To creole and foreign merchants alike, cronyism was still a lucrative business. Accordingly, they draped the caudillo
in the garb of munificence.

Buenos Aires' symbiotic cronyism presented something of a dilemma for other provinces. So long as customs flowed to *porteño* coffers,
other provinces were deprived of a source of revenue. They tinkered, to
be sure, with direct taxes on land, levies on overland trans-provincial
commerce, stamp duties, and so on. But in the context of the nineteenth
century, when customs were the key to fiscal solvency in the rapidly
commercializing societies of the Atlantic basin (unlike, say, the aristocratic absolutisms of the ancien régime or the agrarian despotisms of the
Ottoman or Ming dynasties), the River Plate provinces outside Buenos
Aires faced constant penury.[40] During the long reign of Manuel López in
Córdoba—of all provincial regimes his was one of the least spendthrift
and most innovative in shifting to new types of direct taxes—balancing
the books was a Herculean effort. From 1830 to 1855, the public debt
rose by 60 percent (while fully 63 percent of spending was earmarked
for the military). In Mendoza, the provincial treasury wallowed in a
perpetual mess: when the local government tried to create its own coinage to free itself from chronic liquidity shortage, its *cuño* immediately
plummeted in value. Only trans-Andean trade with Chile or Bolivia res-
cued the Cuyo region from absolute fiscal poverty. Tucumán, the old
colonial entrepôt between Buenos Aires and Potosí silver, lost its traditional commercial role and quickly went the way of its neighbors. This
did not prevent the provinces of Tucumán, Salta, Jujuy, and Catamarca
from forming the Coalición del Norte and creating their own Mortgage
Bank with powers to issue "credit notes" (in large part to finance pro-

vincial operations). By the 1840's, the Interior was entirely awash in bo-
gus money. The sturdiest money came from neighboring Bolivia.[41]

If landlocked Interior finances produced little more than misery for
treasurers and local merchants alike, the situation differed—and was
more explosive—for the Littoral provinces. For the riverine districts, the
dilemma was even graver, because they *could* open ports and divert
some of the traffic from Buenos Aires, thereby creating customhouses
and autonomous revenue machines for themselves. Doing so, moreover,
pried open opportunities for provincial merchants who otherwise had to
operate through houses in Buenos Aires.[42] This is precisely what made
these provinces, and Corrientes above all, especially before 1838, the
base for much anti-*rosismo*. Indeed, Governor Pedro Ferré and his associates could boast an impressive fiscal record until Buenos Aires orches-
trated the destruction of *correntino* federalism. Entre Ríos and Santa Fe,
more obedient to the will of Buenos Aires, and lacking robust trading
economies of their own, fared less well.[43] Ironically, it was the relative
peace afforded to Entre Ríos in the 1840's that allowed its economy to
blossom, and local traders and administrators to nurse hopes of moving
out of Buenos Aires' shadow. By 1849 Entre Ríos was beginning to rum-
ble. The erstwhile Rosas ally, General Justo José de Urquiza, began to in-
sist that his province enjoyed autonomous rights to trade directly with
the outside world. Henry Southern, the British envoy to Buenos Aires,
warned Lord Palmerston that this simmering demand for riparian federalism would drive Urquiza to reject the "commercial thralldom" to
Buenos Aires, and hinted of a looming clash between Buenos Aires and
the other Littoral provinces.[44] Thus, just as the center of gravity of the
River Plate's political economy shifted from the Interior to the Littoral, it
befell the Littoral provinces to present a credible case for their own
brand of riparian federalism. To do so, they also had to topple Rosas.

The Expanding Frontier

The transformation of the Atlantic trading system presented Rosas with
another means with which to enlist the loyalty of his cronies. Booming
exports meant expanded production in the countryside, and this entailed a very rapid occupation of frontier lands—which, as in all other
American societies blessed with open-access resources, presented the
state with a priceless (literally) resource to create societies in the mind's
eye of its elite. If in North America, land speculators saw in frontier

lands an opportunity to divvy the territory among a commercial yeomanry, in Buenos Aires, no such opportunity presented itself. Lack of
cash, a shortage of land-seeking migrants, and especially a bewildering
and insecure system of land titles undermined the types of ventures so
common to the North American frontier. If a landed elite emerged in the
River Plate, it was to a very large extent the result of Rosista policies, fueled by mounting external demand for staples.

What made this massive transfer possible was a series of campaigns
against pampean Indian peoples, whose occupancy of the land was less
troublesome than their habit of cattle rustling. In early 1832, the Governor led an expedition from his estate of Los Cerrillos, and drove the Indians as far as the Negro River. This did not end Indian marauding, but
for a time it did eliminate attacks north of the Salado River and reduced
the menace of cattle rustling south of the River.[45]

Rosas converted the murkiness of the legal regime governing property rights into a political and economic resource. Nicolás Avellaneda's
1865 study of land law illustrated how Rosas mutated early settlement-
promotion into a basis for cronyism and promotion of cattle production.
The *enfiteusis* laws of the 1820's were an attempt to put some uniformity
to the frontier, enabling the state to dispense access to large lots for
twenty years (later this was reduced to ten years) with the hope that
new holders would attract pioneers for agrarian production and set
aside some land for grazing on estates. Land, however, remained public
patrimony, and served as security on public credit. In an effort to induce
rural investment, Dorrego relaxed stipulations on maximum size of
plots, and in 1829 the provincial government restored the system of
granting freeholds as *mercedes* to compensate citizens for public service
or to liquidate their credits. The government suspended new leaseholds
in 1832, and then legalized sales of 1,500 square leagues in 1836. And,
then, in 1839, Rosas issued a sweeping decree allocating *premio* land—
rewards to military men for their campaigns beyond the fort line. Some
officers kept their windfall to build personal dynasties, while others sold
the concessions to landowners seeking frontier domains.

The problem remained, how to deal with all the land dispensed as
leaseholds, especially when their contracts came up for renewal around
1838? The government distinguished between lands within and beyond
the line of forts (Map 4)—and permitted contracts to lapse into outright
freeholds for territory within the defended frontier (where most of the

coveted land was anyway). The new legal regime favoring privatization opened the floodgates for appropriation of very large units.[46]

The emergence of the large estate in these years is incontrovertible.[47] But *who* benefited? Even before Rosas began to privatize, much of the frontier land was taken up by the *porteño* patriciate, who under Rosas converted leases or tenuous freeholds into absolute estates. A close examination of 203 members of the urban dominant class's ownership of rural land reveals that import and export merchants were the largest benefactors from privatization. They took up the largest extensions and consumed a significant proportion of all privatized land.[48] The most legendary appropriator of public lands was the Anchorena family, whose occupational migration from *porteño* merchant potentates weary of supporting the costs of warfare, to rural dynasts, represented a common change for the old urban elite: they ruralized their wealth by taking up Rosas's generous offer of cheap (or free) land. By 1864, the three Anchorena brothers owned 23 different properties spanning 1.6 million acres and constituting probably the largest single landholding family in the region. Their estate-holding around the Fuerte Azul became one the country's greatest estates, though only in the second half of the century, with the advent of the railway and barbed wire, did it begin to exhibit all the aristocratic pretensions of its owners. Throughout his reign, Rosas could count on the fealty of the Anchorenas, for financial support, as loyal mouthpieces in the Legislative Assembly, and as political brokers for votes among the Anchorenas's vast subaltern dependencies.[49] The effect of Rosas's cronyist approach to property generated, in a few short years, a small class of large landowners, mainly comprised of merchants looking for less fungible and specific assets, as well as military officers and administrators whose loyalty to the caudillo was a passport to vast rural wealth.

The spread of *estancia* landholding did not obliterate smaller units of land. Especially closer to the city, garden plots owned by modest producers not only survived but encroached on hitherto estate lands in the belts outside Buenos Aires—especially as urban growth fueled demand for foodstuffs. Moreover, as is increasingly clear from land surveys over time, large estates quickly broke up over generations. Without primogeniture, and since the first decade of the revolution abolished legal entails, estates fragmented among heirs, most of whom sold their bequest rather than reconsolidate estates through real or fictive kin networks.

One sample of landowners in 1864 reveals that fewer than 18 percent of them had owned land in 1836. What we know of inheritance patterns is that Argentine property was partible in the extreme, and that rich families—barring some notorious and legendary exceptions—tended to abandon the countryside in favor of urban assets in the course of transgenerational gentrification. In short, there was a vibrant land market that permitted relatively easy access until the turn of the century.[50]

The power of time to splinter *estanciero* wealth should force us to be cautious about posturing any "Junkerist" road to capitalism in the River Plate.[51] So too does the growing evidence of hybrid forms of occupancy. A distinction between maldistribution of ownership of land and restrictions on access to it may help. The dispersal of formal titles reflects the prominence of large units, but this may exaggerate their real weight. Many producers avoided ownership altogether. At least until 1890, many rural producers did not immediately avail themselves of freehold options, and preferred to lease from public authorities, and increasingly absentee landlords. This applied to large and small producers alike. What they shared was an aversion to locking up their capital in titles— as a means both to reduce risk and to invest in other types of property. Property rights in cattle were frequently more secure than land— especially as branding took hold. As Samuel Amaral has shown in his exhaustive study of estate probate records, many *estancieros* sank more in mobile and fungible quadrupeds than in land. And as Hilda Sabato has shown in her research on the wool frontier, some producers leased estate land in order to build up their flocks.[52] Nor should we ignore evidence of widespread spontaneous occupancy or squatting, especially on frontier lands. Throughout the Pampas, modest plots survived, indeed flourished, in the interstices of legal loopholes.[53]

Leasing and squatting on land in small, medium, and large units presented a fluid means of entry and exit for modest and large entrepreneurs alike, and its prevalence undermines the image of a rural aristocracy in the making. Yet the overall effects of parceling "open" frontier land altered the structure of rural property relations to enable new owners to lay claim to the substantial rents flowing from production of staples for the Atlantic market.

In combining protection of Buenos Aires' effective monopoly of riverine traffic with allocation of land to a handful of loyal *estancieros*, Rosas bonded a following among the city's merchants and the emerging landed class. One crucial but unintended effect of this process was the political reconsolidation of *porteño* capital itself *through* cronyism. After the collapse of mercantilist rent-seeking, merchants intensified a process that had begun in the midst of the revolution itself: shifting their asset-holding to rural production. If this gave them better hedges against the insecurity of commercial contracts, it also laid the basis for overcoming the old dichotomy that had so bothered physiocrats in the final decades of the empire: the division between the interests of merchants bent on protecting their privileges, and the interests of competitive agrarian producers. By the 1840's, merchants and large rural landowners saw themselves as the bulwarks of a common regime of absolute private property. Landowners oversaw the production of the new generation of staples while merchants handled shipments through Buenos Aires and provided necessary credit—all of which was negotiated privately through contracts.

In many cases, not only did merchant and landed forms of property converge functionally, but they fused within households. Families, such as the Anchorenas, the Unzués, the Pereyras, or the Caseys would straddle these sectors: sons, brothers, and cousins would divide tasks among themselves to handle diversified operations, and daughters were encouraged to marry sons of potential proprietary allies. Even webs of fictive kinship emerged to allow business to occur among producing and trading "relatives." Restricted to the upper echelon of Buenos Aires society, this applied to creole as well as foreign proprietors in their effort to cope with uncertainty: the fluctuations in the value of money (and its frequent scarcity) and difficulties enforcing contracts with a state apparatus whose judiciary was ineffective at best. Moral suasion within the family, whether fictive or real, was one way to conduct stable business when a truly "public" system of legal enforcement of contracts did not yet exist.[54]

In the colonial era, the business of merchant capital combined archaic forms of accumulation in the Andes with more modern commerce near the coast, and ultimately linked New World producers with Old World consumers—all under the protective mantle of mercantilism. Freer trade and privatized resources compelled and enabled merchants to adapt their enterprises to new structures of the conjuncture. But they still straddled producing and consuming regions; they remained the mediators of a transforming Atlantic economy. Furthermore, they still relied on politics as a mainstay for their interests.

Herein lay the ambiguity of Rosas's cronyism for the Buenos Aires elite. On the one hand he was the handmaiden for a reconstituted elite that identified with private property holding and market competition whose business relied increasingly on *private* contracts. Merchants and their landed cousins thrived off Rosas's preservation of Buenos Aires' grip on Atlantic trade; private capital needed to preserve the political power of the regional capital. On the other hand, by ruling through quasi-law, he did not create *public* institutions of governance to allow property owners to contract under stable and credible conditions. This was a transition, but under Rosas, one that would remain by definition incomplete. In the end, it was the internal contradictions of his quasi-legal regime that prevented the new capitalists of Buenos Aires from fully identifying with his brand of rulership. But they were not the social agents behind the realignment of private and public power. The job of deposing the quasi-law system fell to the Littoral provinces.

The Caudillo's Discontents

The Littoral provinces objected to Rosas's practice of keeping customs revenues and mercantile business to Buenos Aires. This struggle brought Montevideo back into the picture, in part because the Banda Oriental also wanted to rid Buenos Aires' hegemony from the River Plate, and because much of the opposition had ensconced itself on that side of the river. Feuding meant constant warfare, though always outside the boundaries of the province of Buenos Aires, occasional blockades, a perpetual fiscal shortfall, and consequently recurrence to monetary emissions to cover the province's military expenses.

The most immediate umbrage came from riparian federalists who wanted to keep their provinces open to trans-Atlantic trade. Throughout the region, tension and confrontation were endemic.[55] In the Interior, Rosas lost his crucial ally, Facundo Quiroga, who had managed to sow together a brief (if unhappy) pause in the violence (some, indeed, speculate that Rosas had Quiroga assassinated to restore Interior havoc and prevent any rival from emerging—though this has yet to be proven definitively). On the whole, however, the disturbances in the Interior did not involve Buenos Aires troops or financial resources. Rosas let the Interior governors hammer out their disputes on their own, interjecting in intrigues only when his own acolytes and his coalition of the League of Governors were in peril. In the Littoral, however, war engulfed the region in two major episodes. In both, Montevideo and the Banda Oriental, where many of Rosas's *porteño* opponents had escaped his wrath and whose merchants chafed under the weight of Buenos Aires' control of Atlantic traffic, offered a base for the anti-Rosas alliances. In both cases, Rosas's primary advantage was the internal weakness of his opponents. The *mésalliance* of riparian federalists in the Littoral provinces and old unitarians in the Banda Oriental invited constant squabbling and open defections.

The first confrontation revolved around the province of Corrientes, which had long since been the champion of riparian federalism. Pedro Ferré objected to Rosas's refusal to enact some of the provisions of the 1831 Pact, most especially the convocation of a constitutional assembly to draft a federalist constitution, and to a lesser degree because *correntinos* wanted more protection for native industries.[56] The clash finally erupted in 1838. The timing could not have been worse for Corrientes. Rosas's biggest military threat, in fact, had come from the aging Santa Fe caudillo Estanislao López, and together with Corrientes (and backed by Uruguay and implicitly by Brazil) they might have been able to mount a respectable force against Buenos Aires. But López's death in 1838, and the succession of Domingo Cullen and Juan Pablo López as Santa Fe's governors, drew this neighboring province more directly into the orbit of Rosas's control, depriving riparian federalists of a crucial ally. Yet they went to war, with disastrous consequences for the anti-Rosistas.

Riparian federalists aligned themselves with Montevideo merchants (many of whom were foreigners, especially French), hoping they had a crucial resource in the promise of French naval support. The French admiralty—following the requests of the Montevideo merchant community—erected an ineffective blockade of Buenos Aires shipping in March 1838, bringing hardship to *porteños*, but scarcely crippled the province's power. The Corrientes cause immediately retreated and was soon defeated at the battle of Pago Largo (March 31, 1839). In the bloodletting, the victorious General Urquiza ordered hundreds (some put the figure as high as 1,900) of *correntino* prisoners shot, including the sons of prominent merchants and ranchers. A savage war over the province ensued for four years, leaving Corrientes a practical wasteland.[57] Thereafter, the fighting shifted to Uruguay, where Lavalle and General Fructuoso Rivera upheld the struggle. They managed to drive Rosas's henchman General Oribe from the Banda Oriental, whereupon Lavalle invaded Entre Ríos, only to let Governor Echague's superior artillery shred his cavalry. Having temporarily given up on Entre Ríos,

Lavalle decided to tackle Buenos Aires directly. But instead of invading Buenos Aires immediately (while the Interior was temporarily under the helm of Paz's Liga del Interior and landowners in the south of Buenos Aires were revolting against the punitive levies Rosas was extracting to pay for his campaigns), he withdrew to Santa Fe in August 1840 to regain his breath. In the meantime, the French blockade began to waver, the Liga del Norte unraveled, Rosas savagely subdued the opponents in Buenos Aires, and General Oribe mounted a come-back operation, attacking Lavalle's rear flank and defeating the unitarian army at Quebracho Herrado on November 28, 1840. Lavalle gathered the remains of the old national army and beat a retreat to Bolivia (there was nowhere else to find refuge as the region fell to Rosista governors). Oribe gave chase, defeating unitarian troops in Tucumán, and slaughtering all the captured officers "in ordinary form," except for the young Governor of the province, Marcos Avellaneda (Nicolás's father), whose "head was . . . struck off in order to be exposed to public view in the plaza of the city of Tucumán."[58] Lavalle made it to Jujuy, but as he was about to cross into the erstwhile silver territory, federalist marksmen pumped bullets through his body on October 8, 1841. In a gesture of undying loyalty, Lavalle's troops strapped his corpse to the back of a horse and continued their straggling and not unheroic withdrawal to an Andean safe-haven, burying their leader in a Potosí cathedral—a fitting repose for a seasoned unitarian.[59]

Not all was lost, however, for Rosas's provincial opposition. General Paz, for one, still harassed the Littoral front. Montevideo still remained a redoubt for exiles and the base for anti-Rosas plotting, even though Oribe's encampment at El Cerrito bled Montevideo's resources. The big difference in this second episode was the role of the British. Once again, the French admiralty succumbed to the siren calls of Montevideo's French merchants. Now, so did the British. Together they sealed off the port of Buenos Aires in early 1845 in the name of upholding "free river" trade—the idea that all riparian ports enjoyed rights to unmediated access to trans-Atlantic commerce. As far as the British were concerned this was "what North Americans call 'State Rights.'"[60] Especially with the prowling of the Royal Navy under Commander Purvis, this blockade was far more damaging to the province's war-making capacity than earlier ones, sapping the city of customs revenues, and taking its toll on producers who saw prices for their staples plummet. In an effort to rally the Littoral provinces to the cause, the British and French fleets sent a convoy up the River Paraná, destined ultimately for Asunción. The mission ran into trouble at the Vuelta de Obligado (where Rosas's forces ran a chain across the river and then floated burning barges against the choked intruders). Still, the flotilla managed to break through, selling most of the wares upstream. But the British Foreign Office was livid at the naked use of naval force to promote the interests of private merchants—and soon began to dismantle the blockade, leaving the French and their writhing allies to their own devices.[61]

For a second time, the cause of riparian federalism collapsed, this time because it was so much weaker, and relied more on the caprice of European backing and hapless leadership from Montevideo under General Rivera. This time Rosista forces were indomitable on land. Oribe hemmed Rivera into Montevideo while the newest of the Littoral caudillos, Justo José de Urquiza, now governor of the ever more prosperous Entre Ríos, proved the most effective of Rosas's weapons, wreaking havoc among the unitarian armies. Fighting was not without its heroics. Guiseppe Garibaldi, whose own Italian cause seemed lost, joined the unitarians and saw substantial action throughout the region. He watched in amazement as gaucho *montoneros* on both sides rode fearlessly into battle, often facing improbable odds (he would deploy this theatrical ferocity to great effect in his Sicilian campaign, especially in the liberation of Palermo), and learned the art of guerrilla fighting on horseback.[62] In the end, however, the organized cavalry and artillery of Urquiza was overwhelming, and he decisively trounced General Paz at the battle of Vences on November 27, 1847.[63]

Rosas emerged from his victories over Littoral adversaries stronger than ever. In few cases, however, is Gibbon's pithy observation on Emperor Maximus that "his success was the immediate cause of his destruction" truer than of Buenos Aires' cronyism. Rosas could wage war because he had the financial wherewithal—deep pockets replenished with customshouse earnings, something his Littoral rivals craved and for which they were nevertheless prepared to martyr their provinces. But if his finances allowed him to win a war, it took its toll on cronyism. War-making cost money. Faced with shortfalls, Rosas printed more paper pesos. As the value of pesos rocked between highs and lows, oscillations exacerbated the contractual uncertainty that beleaguered the Governor's clientele. In the arithmetic of endemic collective violence, the Buenos Aires government controlled the money-printing racket but was also the single most damaging threat to the efficacy of the racket.[64]

Spending patterns moved in lock-step with warfare. From 1830, once Rosas was in power, expenditures rose mildly at first, and then subsided as an unstable "peace" settled in. When Pedro de Angelis reported to the Governor on the state of public finances in late 1833, he observed that unrest in the provinces had drained the treasury, forcing officials to reduce spending in other areas, such as hospitals, the University of Buenos Aires (which ceased paying its faculty), and police. The combination of Rosas's pacification of the Indian frontier and potentially stable affairs among the provinces augured well.[65] Warfare in 1838–42 and 1846–49, however, dashed these hopes. If aggregate spending hovered between 10 and 13 million pesos from 1830 to 1834, by 1840, spending reached 48.5 million pesos, subsiding back to 31 million in 1846, but leaping to 48 million by 1849. From 50 to 70 percent of total spending was earmarked for the costs of warfare.[66] For the emissary of the British bondholders of the lapsed 1824 loan, endemic war inspired pessimism: "The war in the Provinces and with the Banda Oriental absorbs all the means which are at the disposal of the Government. . . ."[67]

If warfare took its toll on efforts to stabilize expenditures, it was even more debilitating to revenues. From 1829 to 1833, revenues began to climb out of the deep well left by the abolition of old colonial levies. Taxes on exports and especially imports constituted about three quarters of Buenos Aires' incomes, and began to show some impressive gains after 1831, yielding over 9 million pesos in 1833 (74 percent of total receipts). War and blockades, however, gutted the customhouse, plunging customs to scarcely 5 million pesos in 1840 and 6 million in 1846—these being the worst years of the blockades. In the brief respite of peaceful years, of course, revenues jumped significantly—reaching almost 58 million pesos by 1850 (over 93 percent of total receipts).[68]

Warfare crippled revenues at the very same time that the Treasury was most hungry for receipts. During the peaceful years, Rosas could almost balance the books, but the deficits of war years forced him to finance the shortfall. Essentially he relied on two instruments. First, the provincial government issued bonds, as it had in the 1820's, in the form of "public credit." Yielding 6 percent, the government placed 31 million worth of bonds on the market from 1831 to 1837, but they were entertained with such a discount that the government realized only 17 million pesos. In 1840, Rosas issued bonds worth 10 million to fight the Franco-Lavalle cause, which only brought in 6 million pesos. From the Treasury's point of view this was not a cheap means to finance shortfalls since interest and amortization payments were due on the nominal value of bonds, and not what they were earning in real terms. Without an effective bond market, for want of powers of credible commitment that the provincial government would honor its obligations, long-term financing through bond issues was becoming an expensive and unremunerative option. The absence of a constitutional order took its toll on methods of war financing, and eliminated the option of deferring the costs of war, and paying off debts when revenues recovered (tax smoothing by borrowing to cover wartime needs, and then servicing and amortizing the debts when peace restored commercial transaction and revenues). What Alexander Hamilton, with a constitution and a Bank of North America behind him, managed to do for the United States (create a proper funding system) and what Rivadavia tried to emulate in the 1820's, was inconceivable to Buenos Aires under Rosas.[69]

Instead, the mounting war debts were handled in ways more reminiscent of the French ancien régime and its revolutionary successor: currency (and not bond) finance.[70] Without credible commitments, monetary authorities simply printed the government through the wars. Just as French Jacobins let loose the *assignats*-making machine, so did Rosas with pesos. The administrations of the 1820's had bequeathed a stock of circulating paper pesos of 15 million—and even this had caused price turmoil by the end of the decade. To this, Rosas added the following emissions:[71]

March 1837	4,200,000 pesos
December 1838	16,575,000 pesos
September 1839	3,605,854 pesos
March 1840	12,000,000 pesos
January 1846	75,000,000 pesos
TOTAL	111,380,854 pesos

This massive injection of depreciating paper pesos rocked local commodity prices. Inflation soared during wars and blockades. With each bout of warfare, the delicate fiscal balance took a beating. Baring's envoy expressed a common sentiment: "It is impossible," he wrote back to London's merchant capitalists, "to give you an idea of the wretched state in which matters stand here. . . . The civil war absorbs all of the means of the country, and the finances, notwithstanding the confiscation of property to an immense extent, made available for the wants of the army, present a deficit of upwards of $13,000,000."[72] The reason things did not fare even worse was that the English and French navies were in no position to resolve a crisis that was in essence a regional constitutional problem (and they lifted their blockades when they saw how ineffectual they were), and that the other provinces wallowed in even worse funding circumstances. Whenever the anti-Rosas forces tried to print their own currencies to fund their war efforts (as General Paz repeatedly tried to do), these desperate measures immediately sent local merchants running for shelter behind more stable money, like Bolivian pesos. In these circumstances, Rosas's main fiscal and monetary weapon was his customhouse (which allowed him to recover *after* the wars) and the absolute penury of his rivals (who enjoyed no such luxury).[73]

Rosas's monetary prerogatives and military prowess may have solidified his public hold on power, but they frayed the ties with his clientele among Buenos Aires merchants. The depreciation of the peso, its constant oscillations, and wild commodity price variations created all kinds of trouble for business. One merchant moaned to *The British Packet*, that "the sudden and extreme fluctuations in our public currency [are] an evil that has long been preying on the very vitals of the state." Merchants need some control and predictability for their enterprises to survive, he argued. "But shackled with a fluctuating medium of exchange," our anonymous correspondent insisted, "all these virtues, deservedly the highest repute in every commercial community, may be overborne and rendered nugatory by the operation of causes over which the individual has no control. Hence, their operation becomes feeble and uncertain, and their gradual disappearance the inevitable result. In every transaction reference is necessarily made to the established medium of exchange, as likely to be affected by contingent events."[74] In 1840, on the heels of a large emission, a group of prominent merchants met to discuss how to cope with the difficulties. They agreed to form a delegation to meet with Rosas to "make him aware of the great inconveniences and the need to adopt our proposals [which they had outlined to the Minister of Finance six weeks earlier]." Later they urged monetary authorities at least to raise the interest rate on their bonds, and allow merchants to buy these instruments rather than accept worthless pesos. From their point of view, a move to bond finance and away from currency finance would recombine public and private interests.[75] By 1847, the situation had become so bad that peso notes were being printed on tattered paper (good paper was hard to find owing to the blockade) and dissolving in the hands of customers. Yet, for all their woes, merchants and consumers only grumbled; they did not dare protest.[76] In short, political change enabled the emergence of new forms of private wealth, but political conflict made this wealth vulnerable and war made it potentially ephemeral.

Conclusion

Rosas prevailed over his enemies because Buenos Aires enjoyed a strategic place as the mediator between emerging staple-producing areas and their Atlantic consumers. This also gave him an internal set of resources to protect local merchants' own hegemony over regional rivals. Along the way, he dispensed large tracts of land to his loyalists, which could be deployed to produce the staples shipped from Buenos Aires overseas. Warfare was thus functional to cronyism and helped build the rudiments of administrative organization from a provincial, but not national, base.

Littoral federalists wanted a national state precisely to deprive Buenos Aires of its monopoly so that other provinces could deal directly with the Atlantic world, but did not have the requisite fiscal-military powers. The only way to resolve the dilemma was to promote the idea of a federalist constitution—an idea completely anathema to Rosas, whose very quasi-legal rule enabled him to manipulate the strings of cronyism with dexterity. Rosas and his clientele, while more than happy to reintroduce the River Plate into an ever freer trading regime in the Atlantic, were unwilling to countenance the same open commercial pluralism within the region. The result was endemic conflict. But this pattern did not immediately devastate Buenos Aires in the way that earlier revolutionary conflicts did. In effect, cronyism and quasi-law helped solidify the province of Buenos Aires and reconstitute its propertied elite even as it animated the grief between the provinces.

This endemic conflict, the lack of credible commitment, and the toll it took on private contractual relationships, however, drained merchants' loyalty to the Rosas regime. They would have preferred stable money and the ability to forge long-term contracts, especially as emerging trans-Atlantic free trade presented so many opportunities for accumulation. Rosas offered them a constitutionless polity under whose carapace they enjoyed something of a regional monopoly. But the link between the private interests of merchant capital and public powers of the state was far from alloyed. So when a more credible alternative appeared on the horizon, Rosas's cronies defected from his alliance. They did so because they wanted sounder legal foundations for their private activities.

Herein lies the paradox of *caudillismo*. In the same breath, Rosas could proclaim himself the defender of laws while refusing to bend state powers to live by the same rules as private agents. Likewise, merchants of Buenos Aires could offer supine supplicants to Rosas and bankroll his assaults on competing ports, while at the same time privately fulminating about the instability of their "medium of exchange," the difficulties enforcing contracts, and the general malaise of business conditions. Rosas and his style of rule expressed the plight of post-revolutionary Latin American political economies. The Spanish empire had collapsed; but creoles shared no common vision of an alternative order. At the same time, the revolution redefined modes of collective representation while the state was extremely weak. This made it very difficult to forge a republican system from above—as the revolutionaries discovered in their failed efforts to integrate the old Viceroyalty under a unitary constitution. By the 1830's and 1840's, however, the bounty from the River Plate's reintegration into the Atlantic economy offered resources to manipulate the purse strings of cronyism. Rosas built an unstable successor to revolutionary regimes. The nub of the paradox, however, was the following: just as reintegration into the trans-Atlantic trading system enabled Rosas to create and dispense new property rights, it also implied (and in due course insisted) that legal-institutional systems be erected to defend the interests of capital as a whole. Rosas was the handmaiden of new property but refused to be its guardian.

6 ⌒ Chains of Obligation: The Duress of Merchant Law

> For he that performeth first, has no assurance the other will perform after; because the bonds of words are too weak to bridle men's ambition, avarice, anger, and other passions, without the fear of some coercive power; which in the condition of mere nature, where all men are equal, and judges of the justness of their own fears, cannot possibly be supposed.
>
> Thomas Hobbes, *Leviathan*

Institutions and Interests in Post-Revolutionary Merchant Law

Fernand Braudel once described the early modern economy as a world driven by many commercial wheels; commodities and people circulated along old and new trading routes with greater speed and distance.[1] As the gears churned, remote corners of these trading spheres, like the River Plate, aligned with the world market and fit into its rhythms. At the same time, long-distance trade also required money—as a medium of exchange and as small advances or credit on the promise of future compensation. Indeed, the two, money and goods, flowed synchronically across and through the commercial routes of the Atlantic world.

Yet, in Braudel's imagery, goods and money did not necessarily move at the same level, even if they followed parallel paths and conformed to a common pulse. As commerce intensified and regions concentrated on exports for distant markets of the Atlantic world, specialized agents, groups, and institutions emerged to handle merchandise and money. Eventually, the wheels of commerce spun with such velocity and complexity that merchant banks, exchanges, and markets for capital itself emerged to service trade circuits. Money handlers soon constituted the most cosmopolitan and puissant members of urban merchant classes of the Atlantic world. Their activities and interests created the chains driving the wheels of everyday commerce.

How did the interests of this upper-stratum of the Atlantic world adapt to deep political change? Not presuming that interests are precon-stituted and abstract, but arguing that they are shaped by context and even conflict, this chapter shifts to the process of interest-formation in the merchant class of Buenos Aires. It examines the role of private law to help understand the evolving interests of capital. If the upper stratum of mercantile activity provided the mechanisms for accelerating the rhythms of commerce, it was also linked by a set of legal norms and practices. Early modern commercial law enabled merchants and investors to de-liver and receive goods on the promise of future payment, and to invest in the hope of reaping later rewards. Law ensured traders' and finan-ciers' obligation to honor commitments; it provided a mechanism to se-cure cooperative behavior. This was especially important in light of the distance between bargainers and the complexity and the long-term na-ture of relations between them. To keep the chains of trade in motion, merchants subjected their notions of rights and entitlements to the some-times woolly criteria of reciprocity, fairness, and long-term obligation. They engaged in "relational contracts." Relational contracting was a way of coping with complexity and uncertainty before "will theories" of contract took over in the nineteenth century. Contracts, in short, rested on a public ordering system of norms and principles that provided the conditions for private transactions to occur. Accordingly, the chains of financial dealings were forged out of many small links of obligation binding merchants to one another through their promises, concern to keep good faith, and determination to nurture the right kind of person-ality to rank among the Atlantic world's patriciate.[2]

In this world, contracting involved a continuing relationship *within* communities, and not separable autonomous transactions. The mer-chants of the archipelago of Spanish American ports enjoyed their posi-tion thanks to their matriculation into guilds (*consulados*) that were themselves erected by royal charter. Membership and agreement to re-spect the collective ground rules of commerce entitled merchants to ply their wares and handle money protected by the artifice of the empire's mercantilist strictures and the guilds' zealous shelter of their members' prerogatives. In this respect, as Chapter 2 argues, merchant property rested upon agreements between the crown and the merchant class, and recognition among the merchants themselves that rights flowed from corporate membership. Far from absolute private property, merchants' domains were contingent and politically derived. The early modern wheels of commerce spun, but the chains of obligation depended on the ancien régime's ability to uphold the system of controlled membership and political enforcement against interlopers.

The Atlantic revolutions subjected the chains of obligation and relational contracting to extreme duress. Through the eighteenth century, talk of absolute private property became something of a mantra for reformers, especially physiocrats concerned that merchant rentiers were stifling economic progress. Others chimed the cant of Adam Smith in favor of more open competition and dismantling barriers to enterprise. Even as these aspirations mounted and flourished into sophisticated doctrines of political economy, they became more remote from reality.[3] In the end, across the British, French, and finally Spanish emporia, the coddled but effective mercantilist systems and colonial networks imploded into a generation of revolutionary war.

The latent schism of the eighteenth century blew open. For the descendants in the nineteenth century, the issue was how to create a system permitting private property and free-market competition without exposing merchants, especially those of the upper stratum, to the perils of uncertainty. For the citizenry of the new Spanish American republics, the challenge was even more vexing, since the very same body entrusted with the task of erecting institutions and encoding new legal machinery for the new order, the State, was itself a hobbled and splintered force. The revolution shattered the public law regime and did not create a stable order in its wake, save the very imperfect rulership of caudillos.

Bereft of a stable institutional system for the conduct of public affairs, how did merchant capitalists reconcile their private matters and disputes? The dilemma was obvious to Buenos Aires' merchant bankers. In a letter to the Minister of Finance in 1825, they explained that they were groping for a way to settle conflicting entitlements and obligations while "recalling the instability of public guarantees, no longer supported by the conviction and force of time, and detailing the risks to which this effort [the revolutionary program] exposes property, here annulled for the first time in a public form . . ."[4] The revolution shattered age-old commercial networks and intensified the rancor over property. Pedro Botet and Manuel Ortiz Basualdo had been longtime partners in the commodity trade between Cádiz, Valparaíso (Chile), and Lima (Peru), with Buenos Aires as the central clearinghouse. But with the eruption of war in 1810, their warehouses began to stink with the smell of rotting leather, bags of Paraguayan tea sat wasting on the quaysides, and revolutionary governments administered onerous forced loans on their fungible assets. Botet and Basualdo now squared off against each other in a bitter lawsuit, each accusing the other of violating prior commitments. Yet the very fragility of the judicial system condemned the proceedings to "acrimony directed against the judges, the hurried pronunciation of a dictionary of invective, reproach, and exaggerating to the clouds accusations of arbitrariness, injustice, and contravention against all laws."[5]

One solution to the intra-class conflict among merchants was to fall back on the pre-revolutionary jurisprudence of relational contracting—not so much because anyone thought that early modern conceptions of property were superior, but because modern notions of property, contract, and obligation appeared so difficult to introduce without an analogous transformation in public law.[6] In a sense, the revolution compelled merchants to rely on traditional private law less out of conviction than by default. In other revolutionary societies like the United States and France, public officials were the handmaidens of new private law because the constitutional powers of legislators and magistrates sufficed to effect changing notions of justice in matters of contract and property law. In these societies, "will theories" of contract supplanted relational contracting, subjecting exchange relations to private wills, and thus discrete ordering systems. The state stepped in and created modern contract law. Private actors obliged because the costs of violating the new order were so punitive. If litigants rejected the legitimacy of the emerging modern system, their legal adversaries stood to win their cases with ease. But where revolution gave way to civil war (as in Buenos Aires), the transformation of public law redoubled the reliance on pre-revolutionary private law: since the potential gains from embracing modern conceptions of property and contract law were so low, merchants clung to what they knew best, even if it delivered a less than optimal form of private justice. Paradoxically, then, the revolution in the River Plate (and elsewhere in the Spanish American world) gave archaic notions of relative and contingent property rights new leases on life well into the nineteenth century. The old chains of obligation not only survived political turmoil, but endured because of it.

Merchant Law

Eighteenth-century property jurisprudence rested on notions of relative dominions over things. Much as people aspired to absolute titles and invoked ideal-types of inviolable possession, relational-talk governed the legal language of exchange and production. This tension between absolute and relative dominions permeated the deliberations over how to usher in a new order without delivering fatal blows to the old—ones that might wreak more destructive havoc than yield to a virtuous recalibrated balance between private entitlements and public powers.

Governing property law was the purview of communities of merchants, and not direct state authority. In part, the location of legal sovereignty reflected the splintered and multilayered nature of the Spanish imperial polity. It is a mistake to treat Spain as an unwashed tight-fisted absolutist regime. Rather, efforts to centralize justice in the Peninsula collapsed in the seventeenth century, pushing the burden of dispute settlement back onto communities. Thereafter, Spain's tradition of parallel and independent court systems (*fueros*) of the church, military, and commerce abided by separable bodies of law dispensing justice according to a "law of persons."[7]

Colonialism splintered the jural spheres even more. By subjecting courts to a confusing and often contradictory mosaic of Castilian law and new imperial law (like the *Novísima Recopilación* or the *Siete Partidas*, both of which went through repeated updating until the late eighteenth century), in practice, courts on the ground reconciled disputes in less than coherent fashion and did not obey a single authoritative source of jurisprudence. Lawyers and jurists swung between appeals to a systematic body of law elaborated rationally by an external sovereign order and a legal style that decided right and wrong according to principles whose resolution varied depending on the concrete case at hand. This deep ambiguity was in many ways functional to the polity's need for flexibility in dealing with the unforeseeable and manifold difficulties dispensing justice in the remote corners of the realm—it gave authorities the ductile tools to administer law discretionally. In effect, the axioms of public law had little direct, linear imprint on private law.[8] The turmoil of post-revolutionary politics, and the sheer absence of durable public law, only sharpened the jurisprudential polarities of abstract principles and pragmatic dexterity. Community justice persisted in part because a public system was slow to emerge.

The decentralization, fragmentation, and then collapse of the Spanish imperial polity was not the only source of jural autonomy of private law and governance by communities. Just as important was the long-standing practice of merchant sensibilities eniphered in *jus mercatorum*. Merchants needed rules attuned to their needs and invariant across distance and cultural boundaries. Very loosely, this body of law emerged from centuries of customary practices among merchants of the medieval and early modern worlds. The notion of *consuetudo mercatoris*, or merchant custom, spread through the trading ports of Europe, principally from Venice and Genoa, through the fairs of France, especially in Champagne, and offered a cosmopolitan and secular legal referent for the behavior of and sanctions against merchants, thereby enabling them to trade across distances and frontiers without facing the risks of wildly different legal norms. Soon, ports and fairs hosted special tribunals to deal with merchant disputes—in England they were called the courts of piepowder; in the Spanish realm they were housed in the guilds. Guild courts operated autonomously from the public eye, and turned to their own codes, distilled from generations of commercial custom, for legal guidance.[9] This pattern persisted to the final days of the empire. Even after the revolution, custom continued to exercise a powerful influence on private law, especially in the absence of statute.[10]

In practice, throughout the Spanish empire, the tension between the aspiration to absolute domain and the reality of contingent entitlement was resolved through sets of norms and practices—a kind of legal culture—bequeathed from an age in which people enjoyed rights and entitlements depending on their station in life and the corporate group to which they belonged. For merchants (as for many others in urban circles), this meant belonging to commercial guilds, *consulados*. These guilds acted as the guardians of relational rules of contracting: norms governing proper behavior, respectability, and ultimately sanctions and penalties in instances of violations. All of this was designed to protect the interests of commerce as a whole. Community self-management of justice nestled in imperial guilds followed the design prescribed by the *Ordenanzas de Bilbao*.[11] The old guild of Bilbao drafted its own rules, and then refined them in the mid-sixteenth century. These then served as the template for commercial jurisprudence as Madrid chartered guilds across the realm. Revised again in the eighteenth century, the Bilbao Ordinances provided the architecture for community-controlled dispensation of justice.

This guild legal culture implied that rights flowed from membership and from the contracts forged among its constituents. Contracts were the links of the chains of obligation, binding merchants to each other as traders and financiers; they created relations of dependence on the will of peers. Especially when it came to debtor-creditor relations, deals were bound by a high degree of trust, respect, and shame should a partner fail to perform obligations. Relational rights implied a pattern of recognition among guild members, created and nurtured by the agents themselves. Unlike criminal law (invoking a coercive theory of social relations) or public law (about the legal powers to adjudicate and legislate), private powers of commercial law involved the practices and norms that were not created by explicit prescription from sovereigns, but emanated, as H. L. A. Hart noted, from legal habits of trust and obligation.[12] The law of property existed beyond the sovereign's coercive or legislative powers. Ensconced in guilds, commercial communities were entrusted with the job of allocating rights and dispensing justice.[13]

At the core of this doctrine—or really practices that aggregated into a quasi-formal set of norms—lay the notion of the personality of the merchant: a member in good standing of a guild, whose privileges (not quite a modern "right") depended on his (and they were, for the most part, men) recognized occupation. When merchants did invoke "rights," they did not imply rights that flowed from discrete acts of exchanging goods and services (or promises to perform these acts), but from their personhood.[14] As Dalmacio Vélez Sarsfield noted as late as the 1840's (the precise year is unknown), commercial law was a "legislation of exception," conferring privilege and levying penalties in a fashion inapplicable to any other legal realm precisely because it was so attuned to the corporate needs of members of the mercantile class, and because it required a recognized legal personality of a litigant, and less what he owned or did.[15]

Much of the job of preserving relational property by upholding community standards of personhood fell to the guild's court, the *Tribunal de Comercio*, a hall within the guild in which merchants gathered to settle disputes. Several features of this court system exemplified the merchants' faith in their own jural powers. First, judges had no formal legal training. By law, the magistrates came from the ranks of the guild's members, served short elected terms, and were not professionals—the idea being that merchants were most attuned to the needs of commerce and best apprised of the often arcane practices of transacting. Indeed,

the task of the magistrates was less to issue sentences of pure guilt or innocence (though they often did this in cases of clear malfeasance), than
to arbitrate between litigants, striking compromises that allowed traders
to continue their enterprise and avoid driving one or the other party out
of business.[16] In the words of one Tribunal official, "the base of all procedures of this court is the observation of good faith in commerce, without subjecting itself to the rigors of judicial formulae that, with good reason, are abhorrent in their peculiar institutions . . ."[17] Guild members
would accordingly avoid winner-take-all adversarial legal styles; the
community retained its collective fabric.

Second, litigants were forbidden from hiring lawyers to bolster their
cases. This practice echoed the suspicion of formally trained jurists in
favor of the practically tutored members of the guild as the custodians
of commercial law. Exclusion of legal professionals reflected the tradition of relying on commercial custom and local knowledge, the self-
evident principles enshrined in the notion of *verdad sabida y buena fe
guardada*, literally "known truth and good faith upheld" but perhaps
better translated as common sense and good faith. Intervention by outside agents threatened to introduce foreign principles and practices and
to obstruct the otherwise expeditious proceedings of the Tribunal—a
coveted aspiration of the guild. Indeed, the pressure to settle disputes
quickly was seen as the bedrock for preserving the harmony of the
community and serving the best interest of merchants, who loathed the
cumbersome, tiresome, inquisitorial style of other realms of private civil
law.[18]

Expeditious self-management was only one of the guiding axioms of
commercial law. Substantive justice was another. Since rights were not
treated as abstract entitlements flowing from the individuated exercise
of claims, but as relational powers derived from membership and from
the recognition of the upstanding qualities of other traders, reciprocity
was the name of the game. Merchants accepted that they should avoid
cut-throat dealing and naked abuse of other members of the community.
In principle at least, just price governed the value of commodities (so
gouging was frowned upon), and doctrines of usury forbade extortionate charges on loans. In the real world, merchants were shrewd enough
to bend the principles to make a good profit, but they could not break
them lest they face the sanctions of the community—which after all still
harbored the rights to expel a noncooperative member from the
charmed circle or (in the long run more troublesome) refuse to enforce

contracts struck with other merchants. Preserving the web of mutual dependencies required that justice follow substantive resolutions rather than formal a priori dictates. This was not, it should be stressed, an anti-legal *esprit*, but a belief in the notion that contractual obligations were inherently just and fair, and should be preserved as such. In the words of one plaintiff in 1806: "The order followed in this case violates all divine, canonic, and civil precepts. It has defected (with all due respect to the court) in substantive concerns, omitting what is the essence of all cases, no matter how privileged. Here we are not concerned with quantity, rather the substantive method that should be observed to determine the process."[19] In general, the letter of a contract itself did not distill fixed obligation. Rather, the personhood of the contracting merchants and their good faith determined that obligations would be fulfilled. The job of the court was to allow an insolvent merchant to find the means to preserve his identity, to be able to honor his commitment, and thus in turn be entitled to make future bargains.[20]

Substantive justice thereby reconciled a tension buried deep within the fabric of the guild: harmonizing the hierarchy of merchants (both within the guild and between the guild and the rest of the commercial world) and notions of equity that governed the early modern world of property-talk. Some merchants (especially wholesalers) were powerful controllers of trade circuits and big money lenders. But they could not be seen to be exploiting the community as a whole. Accordingly, they were willing to subject themselves to a jurisprudence that curbed their ability to use concentrated capital to earn impressive profits in dealings with lesser partners. In the long run, their profit flow required the survival of these lesser traders and producers and needed a legitimating framework for the unequal distribution of wealth. Substantive justice performed this function—not just in Buenos Aires, but across the Atlantic world, well into the nineteenth century.[21] However imperfect, commercial law, and the understanding of contracts as interlocking promises among members of a community of recognized traders with legal personality, enabled merchants to conduct their business immunized against moral charges of exploitation or pragmatic accusations of willful violation. Instead, justice flowed in contingent and arbitrated (not to be confused with arbitrary) fashion, thereby preserving the commercial fabric—even in the face of world market fluctuations and political turmoil.

The revolution convulsed commercial networks, dismantling some (especially involving trade to and from the Andes) and subjecting others to the caprice of Atlantic markets. But the legal pattern of *jus mercatorum* stuck, if only by default. While some legislators talked of reform, aspiring to emulate in particular Napoleon's exalted Commercial Code of 1808, nothing came of the deliberations. Revolutionary taxes and forced loans gutted the Consulado, which was abolished almost as an afterthought in 1820. But its Tribunal remained intact—indeed its role as the mise-en-scène of merchant litigation and dispenser of proprietary justice soared, not least because price shocks and shortages of money pummeled into non-existence the sheltered certainties of the old protected mercantilist world.

So important did the Tribunal become as a bulwark of private law (since other court systems, starting with the High Court, or *Audiencia* disappeared with no clear successor) that the unitarian regime of the 1820's issued a series of laws extending its jurisdiction. Flooded with cases involving litigants who hitherto did not belong to the guild, the government decreed in 1822 that the Tribunal cover all agents involved in commercial transactions beyond a specific threshold of value (though in practice, the Tribunal had to cope with even the most menial of disputes). Whereas the practice of *jus mercatorum* flowed from personality by virtue of membership in the merchant community, hereafter the community extended to anyone engaged in the act of market transaction. But rather than dispense with the notion of prerogatives flowing from status, the status was merely extended to a broader constituency— personality and prerogatives could be the entitlement of any citizen.[22] The principles of relational property and the practice of community-administered justice now extended to society as a whole. In effect, corporate law served a sustained function as long as a true *public* entrusted to stable political custodians remained more a liberal ideal than a social reality.

Negotiable Instruments

One of the clearest examples of the continuity, and contradictions, in commercial law was in litigation involving negotiable instruments— paper used to realize transactions. Promissory notes, bills of lading (for more long-distance deals), and bills of exchange were all devices used from medieval times to effect payment where liquidity was short, that is where purchasers could not admit immediate cash payment to vendors.

The most common instrument was the bill of exchange, and for simplic-ity's sake I will restrict my discussion to this type of paper. Effectively, bills implied two kinds of transaction: to exchange and to lend—because the note served as a kind of advance of funds in one place repayable af-ter some delay in another, sometimes even in a different currency. They involved four parties. Two contracted, the "taker" (A—sometimes called the purchaser of the bill) and the "deliverer" (B—or drawer), in the place in which the bill was issued, and then two others, the "payor" (C—or drawee) and "payee" (D—here people agree to the same term) contracted in the place of payment. In effect A was agreeing to pay D, but distance and time required that he pay B, who drew a bill on C. This bill ensured that C would make the money available to D by a certain date. Sometimes the roles merged into each other, when the deliverer was the same person as the payee. The loan aspect of the transaction (the interest charged on the advance of funds) was embedded in the rate of exchange to avoid usury charges.[23]

It was crucial that these notes or bills be "negotiable," that creditors transfer claims on a debtor to a third party, and that the third party en-joy powers to claim payment. Merchants could accept bills as payment or use them to compensate others by endorsing bills on the back, or even on the front of the scrip. This kind of commercial paper could, with time, carry a list of endorsements on the back as it made its way though the market. For this to work, two legal issues arose. First, these instruments had to be *enforceable* even when the deal involved parties who were not original signatories to the transaction. Creditors should be able to go to the courts and demand payment or compensation in case debtors lapsed. Second, these instruments had to be *assignable*: third parties ac-cepting the bills should have the same rights conferred to the original creditor. With both conditions met, and merchants confiding in the legal stability of the document, negotiable instruments could be endorsed re-peatedly and passed on from transaction to transaction, thereby allow-ing trade to flow.

Negotiable instruments could do the job of money when liquidity was in short supply, and provide the lubricant for the wheels of com-merce. For the River Plate, especially once the axis from the silver re-gions of the Andes to Spain was shattered, the circulation of bills was a solution to the chronic scarcity of liquidity. Merchants created their own money to allow trade to survive.[24] These instruments also served in ef-fect as short-term credit to allow accumulation to proceed. But keeping the machinery in motion required legal credibility. Only in this fashion could relations between debtors and creditors become more anonymous and stretch across longer distances without increasing transaction costs. Commodity money gave way to acceptable fiat money.[25]

Sustaining this private world of honor and credibility when the larger political context was a constant source of vexation was a daunting legal task. As a form of lending money, bills were subjected to innumerable abuses. This became the occasion for waves of litigation, especially in outbursts of high inflation. Guillermo Ford, a recently arrived importer in Buenos Aires rushed to the Tribunal in 1828 to demand that Pablo Lenormand honor a bill of exchange worth 5,000 pesos drawn by José Zapata. This was a bad period for commerce. Rivadavia had fled, the Brazilian navy sealed off the port, and Dorrego's government was hounded from all sides. Inflation careened. A standard Tribunal practice was to order the seizure of debtors' goods and gradual auction until the money could be raised, or the debtor knuckled under. This is what Ford clamored for. The problem was, just as bills of exchange became fiat money for a succession of transactions, forcing one transactor out of business threatened to detonate a wave of defaults. This is precisely what Ford's appeal elicited. Lenormand's defense was that Zapata still owed him money, and that the court could not force payment until the original debtor met the obligation. The court did not agree; rather, it sided with Ford, arguing that Lenormand's obligation involved a discrete transaction, and was thus liable irrespective of his contracts with others.[26]

This simple, crystalline resolution, however, was rare. More commonly, the Tribunal had to sort out thick webs of obligation. Outcomes were, to borrow Carol Rose's image, often muddy.[27] Despite the aspiration of expeditious justice, *jus mercatorum* had difficulty reconciling embroiled debts, as Ford himself discovered in a suit against Miguel Díaz de la Peña.[28] When transactions involved many overlapping obligations, the Tribunal relied upon equity arguments to settle disputes. The result, often, did not please individual creditors, but aimed to support the broader spectrum of creditors as a whole. Ruperto Albarellos's lawsuit presents a more typical dilemma and resolution to indebtedness involving bills.[29] Albarellos owed Juan Bautista Romero 4,572 pesos—no one disputed this fact; the former agreed to pay. The problem was, when? When the creditor began to lean on his debtor, the debtor appealed to the Tribunal for exemption, claiming that "the mix of unexpected circumstances that befell me, even though I had thought I might escape the ruin that has visited such damage on commerce. . . . But my efforts have been futile and plans frustrated by the fatality of the crisis . . ." Albarellos, firmly defending his "sacrifices," "good behavior," and upstanding membership, warned that liquidating his assets to pay Romero would deprive him of the means to pay off other creditors. Much damage would be inflicted on the market place as a whole. His wife, the aristocratic Isabel de Pueyrredon, chimed in, warning that she alone owed 10,147 silver pesos on four bills. In her words, "it will be incalculable, the ruin that his disgrace will bring to legitimate creditors." The Tribunal, always sensitive to threats that a single creditor's demands might shudder overindebted businesspeople into insolvency (and thus provoke a stampede to call in all loans), wavered. Romero protested. It took two years, however, for the court to sort out the mess, by which time the debtors recovered partially and the paper debt owed to Romero sank in value. This murky solution, while a blow to Romero, avoided full-scale default and therefore a blow to creditors at large.

This case exemplifies some of the difficulties sorting out the overlapping webs of credits and debts, and how the Tribunal handled disputes with an eye to preserving the health of the unstable market for tradeable financial instruments. Crystalline solutions to protect individuated property rights gave way to considerations of community relations to enable individuals to enjoy rights. Solutions, however, were not always so muddy, so attuned to relative justice. Often (when the litigants invoked such provisions), the Tribunal turned to the Bilbao Ordinances' provisions for "special rights." The Ordinances equipped courts to discriminate legally between obligations, conferring greater claim-powers to some creditors over others. If most cases, like Albarellos vs. Romero, reconciled themselves "equitably," by spreading the costs of temporary insolvency to avoid defaults, in some instances the Tribunal ranked obligations by priority. This offered some scope for intermediate position between crystalline individuated justice and muddy, relational justice.

Take the case of Philo Mills vs. Thomas Armstrong, two recent arrivals to the port, the former from the United States, the latter British.[30] Mills arranged to send a bill, drawn on the firm Zimmermann & Frazier (important brokers in the River Plate with dealings in England and France), to Armstrong, worth £2,000. Armstrong, who was by the early 1830's starting to have difficulties meeting payments, had arranged a similar deal with Bertram Chambers. When Mills went to collect his due, he found that Armstrong had paid Bertram but was unable to honor the obligation to Mills. The issue before the court was: whose obligation had more legal weight, which obligation trumped? The case is rich in muddiness. Pushing Armstrong to the wall to pay, especially given his impressive overcommitments, threatened to destabilize all confidence in the local market, as Armstrong, self-servingly, kept reminding the court. On the other hand, as Mills pronounced, with mounting umbrage (£2,000, a not unsubstantial sum, was converted by the court into paper pesos, which were plummeting in value), if basic contracts could not be honored, merchants would cease lending; the market would paralyze for lack of liquidity. Mills invoked a "special right" culled from bankruptcy provisions: his contract lapsed first, it was endorsed by a reputable house. The court dallied, and then denied the plaintiff's demand, arguing that Mills's appeal for privilege was "against all law, against good custom." Introducing Article 23, Chapter 17, of the Bilbao Ordinances, the Tribunal argued that all bankruptcy obligations had to be treated alike, "for the purpose of equalizing, meaning no credit is privileged." But it did argue that Mills was entitled to compensation along with other creditors of similar status, above common lenders. To expedite special rights for all creditors of Mills's ranking, the court ordered the creation of a fund to dispense among creditors, and whose value of compensation would be ordered by special rank. Then the court turned to Bertram, who, popeyed, watched as it ordered him to repay the debt (some 31,600 pesos) to a "common fund" (which would grow as Armstrong's assets were auctioned) that would then be redistributed to all the defendant's creditors in proportion to the size of their entitlements. In this case, equity arguments deprived Mills of absolute rights to collect his credits; but it did agree that Mills's rights eclipsed Bertram's. In this case, the court decided not to give Mills any special rights on his own, but did agree that his type of credit gave him rights over lesser categories.

It is important to note that where the stakes were much lower, the Tribunal did respect special rights claims—as in the case of de Cossio vs. Orma a few years later, in which it decided that an obligation from one bill of exchange trumped other obligations.[31] Here, equity arguments were less persuasive, and individuated special rights prevailed. So, not only was the Tribunal willing to rely on muddy equity arguments to forestall collective merchant crises, but it was prepared to administer justice in muddy, inconsistent fashion, at times letting crystalline solutions prevail in order to bolster the legal powers of credit instruments. The point is: both muddy and crystalline decisions coexisted to resolve the contradictory interests of merchants. On the one hand, merchants wanted obligations from single contracts to be honored, otherwise their property rights lost firmness. This endangered confidence in negotiable instruments. On the other hand, merchants respected the Tribunal's equity arguments to avoid large-scale defaults in such a shallow, uncertain capital market. A single failure could cause turmoil among merchants collectively. Both types of proprietary conflict and solution were necessary to keep the wheels of commerce in motion in such an unstable, uncertain environment.[32]

Liability

If disputes over negotiable instruments sometimes broke an obligatory link in order to protect the chains of obligation as a whole, how did commercial law treat problems of liability? Who was responsible, and who paid the price of insolvency? In effect, did the communal and relational sense of property rights limit liability (by not imposing costs on family members or partners in business)? Exploring this issue allows us to consider whether contract law was becoming generalizable. On the whole, across the Atlantic world, the nineteenth century witnessed a shift away from substantive justice, fairness, and equity, in which obligations flowed from what parties *did*, from their personhood prior to entering agreements. Increasingly, courts entertained the idea that the consequences of a contract were nestled in the will of its executors. Liability flowed from the fact of an agreement, an exchange of promises, and not from what they did or meant to do. People chose to enter contracts willfully; legally speaking this is what mattered; this is what determined liability; and this is what conditioned damage assessments.[33]

Buenos Aires was not exempt from this process, but the shift from customary to wholly executory contractual duties was fitful and halting. To begin with, the circumstances of a debtor's misfortune mattered. In 1824, Esteban Márquez agreed to sell cattle to Fermín Cuesta. Fermín's brother Manuel made payment. By year's end, with only a fraction of the cattle delivered, Manuel took the vendor to court. Márquez immediately acknowledged his obligation, but pleaded that the drought had wasted his herds. The court gave him time to muster the cattle into shape, or return the advance payment.[34] More troublesome than natural disasters were those wrought politically—for at the very least, people could recover from droughts or floods. In his drive to eliminate his opponents, Rosas began seizing assets of his foes. The dispute between Eugenia Aramburu and Felix Castro exemplifies the difficulties resolving unwillful breaches of contract. Aramburu, a wealthy widow, issued a bill of exchange in the name of Felix Castro to Ladislao Martínez in early 1840. When the bill came to term, Castro failed to pay. The source of the rub was Rosas's impoundment of Martínez's estate. "I do not deny the truth of this credit," exclaimed Martínez, "and I am not placing exceptions of any kind to the right." He would pay, save "for the disgrace [I] cannot. My rural establishment, which consists of the greater part of my fortune, is sequestered by order of Our Enlightened Restorer of the Laws." The Tribunal found this exculpation convincing. But Aramburu kept up her fight, citing Article 21, Chapter 13, of the Bilbao Ordinances holding debtors liable in principle. Still, the court refused to incarcerate Martínez or take the rest of his assets. Finally, in May 1847, Martínez paid the original 9,000 pesos, plus 2,160 in compensation for the delay.[35] In both instances, the Tribunal did not attribute liability according to the intent of the agreements, but waved contractual duties in an effort to consider the actions of the defendants and the reasons for their misfortune. In both cases, the plaintiffs were compensated, but with considerable delay and resources tied up in litigation.

Liability became even more thorny when the causes of default could not be ascribed to external, natural, or political circumstances. Inflation was a chronic source of breach of contract charges. Clearly no merchant was singularly responsible, but contracts normally discounted for future price instability. Did this make lapsed debtors liable for real losses? In some cases, yes. Using a promissory note for 20,899 pesos, Santiago Barrabine bought Geronimo Balleto's warehouse in 1828. But two years later, 10,000 pesos were still outstanding. The vendor insisted on the balance and interest; Barrabine acknowledged the former, but not the latter. The law was unhelpful. Traditionally, usury was a touchy issue, and for the most part excluded de jure from long-term agreements. On the other hand, the government had approved provisions in 1828 (since the paper peso was by then plummeting) committing contractual values to the silver peso rate of that year (so, with the devaluation, the paper peso price would adjust accordingly). Barrabine pleaded that the contract said nothing about conversion rates, and that inflationary erosion was not willful. The Tribunal, after much debate, sided with Balleto, thereby seeming to shift the burden of contractual liability to the execu-tor's intent.[36] But in another case, in the self-same year, the court agreed to place a moratorium on creditors' demands to seize and auction the assets of José Carvallo, a paint-store owner in the center of town. Wal-lowing in 27,000 pesos outstanding, and with an estimated 31,000 in as-sets, Carvallo pleaded that soaring inflation and the blockade of the port slashed sales, and thus prevented him from honoring obligations. The Tribunal sympathized with the retailer's plight and agreed to a morato-rium until sales revived. Here, the crucial difference was that the credi-tors themselves did not push their case, agreeing, by the end, to respect the suspension of payments given "the delicacy and fidelity of the debtor."[37] When it came to matters of market instability, Tribunal pro-ceedings do not evince any clear swing in favor of whole executory li-ability, but was willing, at least on an ad hoc basis, to administer justice according to the original will of the contractual parties. But in other cases, such a formal interpretation of obligation bent.

One pattern does emerge from the sample of over 200 contractual disputes until 1850: the Tribunal found it easier to administer crystalline solutions of formal property rights and full liability where the agree-ments were simple. Bilateral disputes between a debtor and creditor usually ended in the latter's favor; the chain of obligation held in favor of the protesting creditor. But when deals were multilateral, a relational logic figured in both the process and the outcome of litigation. The rea-son is fairly simple: given the ornate, interlocking obligations among merchants (among other things they tended to owe each other money in the form of ramified and multiple endorsed notes), forcing one mer-chant to honor debts to the point of insolvency meant that the same debtor would renege on other agreements. The result could be malaise for many merchants even if one was satisfied that the obligation was met.

Sometimes the multilateral nature of commercial concerns compelled merchants to be voices of relational property rights. Merchants were al-ways alert to unilateral contract failures. They often were the first to rush to the Tribunal invoking relational property-talk to defend the rights of helpless debtors against the demands of a single greedy lender. The case of the bankruptcy of the house of Aguirre & Ford, a major im-porter and distributor in the River Plate region, provides a good exam-ple.[38] To forestall any single lender's recalling immediate payment, a bloc of creditors, including some of the richest men of the city (like the

Anchorena brothers, Braulio Costa, Martin Iraola, and others) appealed to the Tribunal to place a moratorium on all payments from Aguirre and Ford, and to begin preparing an auction of assets lest a collective, amicable solution to the problem not be realized. A similar but much more contentious conflict between a single desperate creditor and a bloc of lenders willing to strike a compromise surfaced in the bankruptcy of Carlos Harvey.[39] In this case, however, one creditor, Tomás Whitfield (owed 25,000 pesos in five separate bills) balked at a collective solution. Fearing only a small cut, he angrily accused the Tribunal of violating fundamental contractual principles. The appeal went all the way to the commercial high justice of appeal (the *Juez de Alzadas*), to no avail. The communal cause of merchant capital prevailed over the capitalist debtor's singular demand.

Faced with an unstable political context, in which a large default in such a shallow capital market could send the market reeling, merchants themselves stood in the way of a transition to the kind of property-talk unfolding in other corners of the Atlantic world. Less out of conviction, they invoked traditional commercial practices to deal with coordination problems. In the words of one creditor threatened with the default of a debtor, "it is an axiom that the confession of a debtor in favor of one of his creditors . . . should not be allowed to harm all others who may have interests . . ."[40] In Buenos Aires, substantive, relational justice in matters of contract survived because merchants feared that an objective theory of obligation might benefit a single litigant, at the expense of the merchant class as a whole. They argued in favor of the defense of the chains, and not the rights of a single link, of obligation. Elsewhere, substantive concerns to defend the honorability of agents and arguments in favor of the good of the community of like-minded members gave way to more formal, abstract notions that obligation flowed from the willingness of executors to deal in the first place. What mattered, increasingly, was the legal power invested in the status of a single link in the chains of obligation. Chronic instability in the River Plate, however, compelled merchants to cling to substantive, relational justice.

The Powers of Personality

Subjective understandings of obligation survived. But what kinds of personalities of subjects did law valorize? Eighteenth-century writings about property intensified and made more explicit the links between property and personhood—a relationship ingrained in Locke and early humanist conceptions of society. By the middle of the eighteenth century, commercialization of social relations only highlighted the place of property in distinguishing ranks of society and as a determinant of behavior. But the meanings of the relationship between personhood and property were by no means unambiguous. Commercialization and a market rationale for human interaction only deepened a fundamental tension. On the one hand, social theorists and ground-floor traders in material possessions aspired to an ideal of personal independence buttressed by absolute private property. On the other hand, custom and relation rights, that is, other-regarding notions of justice pervaded rights-talk, even among those most fervently articulating the abstract ideal of absolute private property.[41] In Buenos Aires, this tension persisted. The revolution did not pave the way to a regime of absolute private property rights. It did the opposite; it gave new meaning to conventional notions of personhood.

Honor was possibly the most persuasive defense for a merchant's entitlement. Certainly it was the most ubiquitous. In the dispute between Juan Bautista Lima, a wood dealer in Paraguay, and Pascual Balbín, a Buenos Aires merchant, in the waning days of the colony, culpability turned on the honorable behavior of the defendant.[42] Lima, to clear his debt, offered to send Balbín some wood, lest recouping his loan cripple the Paraguayan, "given the poverty I have placed in your hands." Balbín refused; Lima went to the Tribunal, arguing that he had behaved honorably throughout, that he was offering a compromise, and that the creditor's intransigence would "bring ruin to my interests." Balbín, for his part, dwelt on his debtor's behavior: "His vulgar style and lack of attention, which you will appreciate in the character of this individual, and his complete deficiency of appreciation for the distinguished favor I have offered him in the form of my sacrifice of interests, and the notable damage to my credit by attending to his . . ." The Tribunal sided with the wood dealer, giving him a moratorium on his payments for one year to sort out his accounts. In another case, a debtor-defendant denied misdemeanor charges: "This claim is false, and there is no doubt how calumnious and completely offensive the charge is to my reputation and credit, the only base upon which I estimate and conserve the establishment of my fortune."[43] Indeed, the defendant confessed to being much more concerned about his honor and reputation than the funds involved in the dispute, and argued that the Tribunal should care more for protecting merchants against slander as for the defense of specific monetary claims. Ten years later, the same plaintiff reappeared in court, this time on the other side, as a debtor in arrears.[44] The revolution, responsible for "the continuous blows to credit . . . and to my purity and *hombría de bien* (honor as a man), has reduced me to a state of losses . . ." Like his erstwhile foe, he appealed for a moratorium on debt payments so that his honor and reputation not vanish completely. In both cases, the Tribunal sided with the defendants' efforts to uphold their personality.

It might be argued that honor was a self-serving (and effective) referent for defendants. It was, to be sure, more commonly found in the depositions of merchants on the verge of losing assets—but not exclusively. Honor claims worked for plaintiffs as well. One creditor argued that, while the laws defended the "specific rights of each individual . . . which is an indispensable good to maintain his credit, it is just as indispensable that they preserve [the credit] between men. The painful experience has shown that the faith of men alone was not enough security to sustain the commerce of society. . . . Without this mutually recognized assurance of our respective obligations, it would be the end of the community."[45]

This concern for honor and reputation was a common-sense concern for merchants—a man deprived of *hombría de bien* would not be a respected signer of commercial paper, but rather a suspected potential debtor, a poor bet. Honor and reputation, a public recognition of one's upstanding place in the community of merchants, served as a sort of informal credit-rating system where no public assessment of market liability existed. J. G. A. Pocock labels this "commercial humanism," a sensibility among men who made their livelihood for extensive participation *in* the market, but for whom the legal apparatus of a formal, anonymous, and law-imposing agent like the State was still a remote idyll.[46]

Honor and personality could also be deployed against the Tribunal itself. As the guardian of reputations and standings, the Tribunal was especially concerned not to be seen to violate its own purpose. Litigants, especially plaintiffs, used this to their advantage. One aggrieved creditor charged the Tribunal in the following terms: "With all due respect and with the most sincere cooperation, the course adopted by the Tribunal [of postponing a debtor's payment] in this promised business [sic]; I honestly cannot find the reason why the Tribunal is accepting these papers, asking for precedents, allowing obstacles, and entertaining exceptions in the dispositions of the arbitrators. . . . Does the Tribunal not see the damages and costs this is inflicting on me with all this dallying?"[47] In another case, the creditor's fury could not be contained: "I find it completely useless, this discussion of the appeal, and I doubt any of its value. . . . I cannot convince myself that the Tribunal would in any instance, without my presence or that of my representative, judge and decide that the debtor . . . does not owe me the value of the bill . . . This would be a complete abuse of such a magnitude and transcendence of such despicable proportion, that it is inconceivable to ascribe it to such an the enlightened Tribunal, so experienced in law and commercial practices."[48] Both damnations of the Tribunal were effective; the court ordered prompt payment. But instances such as these are rare—perhaps because accusing the Tribunal of besmirching one's character ran the risk of undermining the legitimacy of the very custodian of proper behavior, the court itself.[49]

If merchants did share a code of honor and mutual respect, and entrusted the Tribunal with protecting this informal code, the fabric of this legal culture was not impermeable. Indeed, by the 1830's and 1840's—in the deep Rosas years—the legitimacy of this order faced constant attacks. These attacks came, for the most part, from within the merchant community. At stake was the elastic notion of "common sense and good faith," the loose set of principles underlying the customary practices and honorable behavior.[50] This conviction that merchants were the custodians of their own sense of proper justice was essential to the functioning of the court, and the determination to keep legal professionals and state regulation more generally outside the confines of private commercial jurisprudence. Let us return to Basualdo vs. Botet. Botet, the debtor, appealed to the Juez de Alzada, accusing the plaintiff of "arbitrariness and caprice," noting that the welfare "of an entire family, on which immeasurable misfortunes have been borne . . . and for which the sentence . . . against all laws and all principles of justice . . . will bring indigence on a numerous family . . . ."[51] He continued, impugning the credentials of the court's legal advisers and the prolonged amount of time taken coming to a decision (during which his assets were impounded). Botet brought a storm of affidavits, testimonies, and witnesses to the Tribunal, stretching the appeal for years. Basualdo's patience, in the meantime, snapped. "Señor Botet makes pompous ostentation of codes, laws, and doctrines of classical authors to support his concepts, and very strangely he overlooks the same authors, laws, and codes, to form or ratify his ideas, which appear very confused and inexact on very prominent and cardinal points of the issue, which is to say, a regular downpayment." The case took nearly twenty years to resolve, and ended with the auction of all Botet's assets in Buenos Aires—by which time, he and his family had returned to Europe, leaving Basualdo with only meager compensation. Increasingly, very simple and routine aspects of commerce found themselves mangled in the confusing doctrinal machinery of Buenos Aires' private judiciary.

To bolster their cases, litigants began to violate age-old customs. Many—defendants and plaintiffs alike—turned to lawyers. *De facto* permissible under the rubric of "special" or "private" "advisers," formally trained jurists prepared briefs for clients, who in turn introduced them to the court.[52] Still, they could not appear before the Tribunal or sign documents (and for this reason it is not always easy to distill the voice of the lawyer from that of the aggrieved client in the archival material). Almost as frequently, the Tribunal had to hire accountants to ponder the ledgers introduced as evidence—also by both sides of the litigious coin. Their reports could sometimes take years to compile and soon became themselves contested as inadmissible evidence.[53] Faced with mounting confusion in the Tribunal, the magistrates themselves began to hire *asesores*, legal advisers, with training mainly from the University of Buenos Aires Law School, who, while not exactly experts in commercial jurisprudence, could at least brush up on general principles and make sense of the vitriol flying across the hall.[54] Even the advisers to the Tribunal found the proceedings unbelievable. One, Ramón Udaeta, concluded that "everything that has been shown here has been committed as a great abuse, and has damaged the creditors with no regard to their correspondent rights . . . and the defendant has accumulated a surfeit of judicial costs and illegal resources . . ."[55] Another adviser moaned to the Tribunal that the functioning of the court is a display of collective dishonor and ill faith, "and no matter how much sincerity is supposed, in very short order the Judicial Tribunals will be swamped with lawsuits [and cause] a problem for all real contracts, and for all the appearances of reality, the parties and suppositions will have neither peace, nor secure fortunes between contractors."[56] By the late 1840's, lawyers and accountants (figuratively speaking) hovered outside the Tribunal, and the unfortunate advisers to the Tribunal shouldered the burden of trying to steer their overwhelmed magistrates through the storm of litigation.

If the communal world of self-contained dispute-resolution of the early modern years survived well into the nineteenth century, it was being sorely tested by mid-century. The polite, honor-obsessed, and almost gentrified manner of substantive justice among merchants was giving way to deep uncertainty. The revolution did not shatter the chains of obligation. But the post-revolutionary fallout of rapid commercialization, increasingly bruising competition, and political-fiduciary turmoil was stretching the chains of obligation to the point that few stored much faith in the future of private substantive justice.

Conclusion

Relational notions of property survived. Indeed, they appeared to thrive. As the revolution threw the gates of the old guild open to all parties engaged in commercial transactions, the manner and lexicon of litigation and settlement of aggrieved contracts characteristic of the sovereign eighteenth-century mercantile world became the language of commercial justice for a broad constituency.

But this institutional answer to a rapidly changing universe of interests introduced a double-order of ambiguity to transactions. First, at a micro-level, the very mechanisms for valuing contracts, trading, and advancing short-term credit—that is, negotiable instruments—were becoming embroiled in a hitherto unknown degree of uncertainty. At least the gentrified world of the guild assured a certain informal protocol for handling these devices. Information was kept to a defined circle, and this circle had a vested interest in protecting its own affairs by respecting collective jurisprudential rules. As the nineteenth century unfolded, this confidence unraveled.

At a more macro-level, the entire region centered in Buenos Aires underwent rapid commercial transformation, increasing tremendously the number, value, and complexity of exchanges in question. The result was an over-burdening of the archaic structures of merchant law. Elsewhere, a public system emerged to replace private mercantile rights-allocation and dispensing. In the United States and Britain, common law courts assumed the mantle of private commercial justice; private property entered the flow of public institutional life. The same transpired in France, this time through the creation of universal courts for commerce as a whole, dominated by publicly trained judges and lawyers to mete out justice. New structures served as the basis for a modern vocabulary of rights-talk—and tied private interest–formation ever more tightly to the process of state-formation. Accordingly, with the construction of a truly public world, economic relations became more abstract and anonymous.[57]

If the personalized, corporate system of the guild retained some purchase on judicial procedures and the very language of proprietary understanding in Buenos Aires, it was only because moving to a more impersonal, anonymous system lurked too far in the future. Merchants needed something, and they clung to what they knew best, even if they disliked it. Old justice provided at least a semblance of stability and continuity in a turbulent political context. The emerging formalism and objective criteria for assessing entitlement and property rights in other corners of the Atlantic world echoed only in the imagination of a few jurists and merchants who followed foreign developments with a public eye.[58] Resolving this dilemma required a resolution to decades of constitutional discord to create modern civic channels for justice, a public judiciary empowered as a sentinel for the interests of private capitalist property rights. To reorder the private world of property-talk and stabilize property relations, state-builders had to reopen the vexing institutional problem of public law and face the challenge of forging an ideological consensus of modern statehood. To this theme, Chapter 7 turns.

7 ⌒ Reconsidering the Republic

> Cómo podrían las instituciones liberales crear las virtudes y las luces, cuando ellas mismas necesitan del apoyo de las luces y la virtudes?
>
> Marcos Sastre, in *Antecedentes de la Asociación de Mayo*

Romanticism and Republicanism

As the memory of 1810 receded into the past, Argentines began reconsidering their earlier faith in change managed by enlightened men. The past provided a gloomy but instructive script of what had to be avoided. Yet the aspiration remained the same: integrate the political community and consolidate it under principles of the rule of law, holding rulers accountable to the same laws as the ruled. A new constitutional spirit emerged from the caudillo regime of quasi-law and the simmering crisis of private property, a mood determined to transcend old divisive polarities.

The struggle to forge new ideological principles for statehood was not a uniquely Argentine phenomenon. In the Napoleonic wake, the restored regimes of the Atlantic world began wrestling with creating systems capable of accommodating gradual reform in order to avoid reenacting old paroxysms. Alexis de Tocqueville, in his second book of *Democracy in America* (1840), wondered "why great revolutions will become more rare." He observed that eighteenth-century "revolutionary" processes of political transformation were giving way to a moment of "construction" of state powers by the middle of the nineteenth century. This drift from undirected upheaval to sagacious investment in public authority was rooted in an underlying change in property relations, especially the increasing interdependency among people with property. The unintended effect of the democratic revolutions of the Atlantic world was to spread property more widely. Since no man's claim was secure without mutual recognition of the rights of others, dispersing property rights thickened society's stake in preserving collective rules: "Not only are the men of democracies not naturally desirous of revolutions, but they are afraid of them. All revolutions more or less threaten the tenure of property; but most of those who live in democratic countries are possessed of property; not only do they possess property, but they live in the condition where men set the greatest store upon their property."[1]

What de Tocqueville observed in post-revolutionary France and the United States also obtained in Spanish America—with the quite obvious caveat that stable constitutional rule still eluded Spanish American republics. Spanish American constitutionalists joined this "constructivist" rush to build state powers, with even greater urgency precisely to rescue property and sociability from the endless storm of revolution. More like their counterparts in the fragmented polities of Italy and Germany, creole thinkers sought to unify state systems, not to transform society, but to stabilize it and prepare it for integration into the trans-Atlantic fold of trade, investment, and migration. What they shared was an instrumental approach to balancing public powers and private rights to put both on sounder legal foundations.

The agents of this shift in Argentina were a new generation of legal thinkers. Rules of order and social conduct, the meanings of exchange and the status of property, found their custodians in the legal world. If any single profession contributed to the transition from military to civilian rule after the Wars of Independence, it was law. Previous chapters have treated what may be considered doctrinal failure: the inability to render proposed juridical order into legitimate rule. By the late 1840's, however, a new constitutional spirit emerged to try to restore Argentina to the path to liberal constitutionalism—a process unfolding, as de Tocqueville observed, in other corners of the Atlantic world.

This chapter explores how legal architects of the Argentine state struggled to reconcile various sources of jurisprudence, most notably the spread of European Romantic notions of law, with reflections on their own predecessors' mistakes. The failure of the unitarian experiment, spreading disillusionment with classical liberalism, and the apparent success of rule-by-caudillos gave rise to a sort of *Weltschmertz* among young Argentine thinkers. This disillusion was a fount for reflection, at once a pessimistic reading of the recent past in order to transcend the enmities that led to civil war and the reign of the caudillos. From these manifold sources arose new constitutional convictions resting on highly pragmatic and instrumental notions of law shorn of many of the transformative qualities of the revolutionary generation.[2]

Three principal Romantic constitutional theorists led the way in reconsidering the legal foundations of statehood: Esteban Echeverría, Juan Bautista Alberdi, and Domingo Faustino Sarmiento. They represented a cadre of intellectuals, often gathered under the rubric of the Generation of 1837, united in their determination to learn from the past, adapt international trends, and prescribe solutions appropriate to their context. They were, in a word, bound by a style of thinking and a common anxiety to decipher an authentic source of constitutionalism. The most important single message of European Romanticism to the young intellectuals of Buenos Aires was the rejection of universal precepts in favor of a historicized notion of the political subject.[3] Each society was the bearer of its own laws of motion, and thus any viable legal regime had to respect the particularity of locally constituted political subjects. The historicist turn enabled writers of the Generation of 1837 to reappraise the liberal faiths of their forefathers. In so doing, they devised new principles of statehood based on local legal norms and practices by dropping universalistic claims of liberalism.

Law and the Romantic Turn

The University of Buenos Aires and the less formal academic world of its environs were breeding grounds for new ideas. From the inception of the republic, the University of Buenos Aires enjoyed an unrivaled role in the intellectual reproduction, propagation, and refinement of liberalism. There, lawyers, even while they still lacked the armature of a constitution and the principles of a legal-civic order, sought to sustain the cause of legalism. And it was in part within the precincts of the University that the skein of constitutionalism survived—not so much as a result of what was *taught*, but by what students *learned*.[4]

Legal education during the 1820's was the heyday of classic liberal education, stressing utilitarian approaches to law and political economy—though this may overstate the coherence of curricular design. With the rise of Rosas, all liberal pretensions retreated or were suppressed, ushering in a dark era for the University as whole. The heavy hands of Rectors Santiago Figueredo and Paulino Gari reduced law to obscurantist rote.[5] Within the formal realm of learning, students of the

1830's and 1840's could not embrace classical liberalism as their own. At the same time, the evisceration of the University prevented it from being the arena for dissent or a place for intellectual debate.

Not surprisingly, much theoretical, and indeed heretical, jurisprudence took refuge in informal circles created by the students themselves. The discussion and debate in the salons and bookstores of Buenos Aires shaped emerging discourses aimed at distancing young thinkers from the utilitarian rigidity of the 1820's, and the formal obscurantism of the 1830's. Within this informal realm a new self-consciously youth culture, modeled in part on Mazzini's "Italian Youth" movement, flourished—albeit briefly.[6]

Fueling this retreat to informal sanctuaries was the fallout of the overthrow of Bourbon monarchy in Paris in 1830. The rising tide of French Romanticism and humanism associated with the July Monarchy opened a flood of books to the River Plate. Victor Cousin, Jules Michelet, and the plays and novels of Victor Hugo and Alexandre Dumas were all made available to inspiration-starved readership in Buenos Aires.[7] During these years the major books of the French Romantic movement became a dominant theoretical arsenal with which Argentine youth would attack the vestiges of Spanish scholasticism and Anglo-Saxon liberalism.[8]

The spread of European Romanticism, at least in its politico-legal form, was in fact, short-lived. Rosista persecution had always driven opponents abroad, but hitherto, refugees were mainly the unitarians of the 1820's. By 1838, French naval attacks on Buenos Aires aggravated the repressive mood. The exodus increased, affecting most men and women of the opposition, and by 1840, the man most inclined to bend with the *caudillo* and the lodestar of Platine Romanticism, Esteban Echeverría, fled to the Banda Oriental, where he was to die a decade later, impoverished and spiritually broken.[9]

From a jurisprudential viewpoint, three authors in particular exercised a decisive influence on the legal imagination of *porteño* youth and a generation of law students: Jean-Louis Eugene Lerminier, Theodore-Simon Jouffroy, and especially Giambattista Vico. Vico's *Scienza nuova* (first edition 1725) found its way to Buenos Aires through various channels. One was Pedro de Angelis, a Neapolitan intellectual associated with the Muratist era (the Neapolitan client regime in Southern Italy from 1805–15) who wound up serving as an important propagandist for the Rosas regime.[10] During his Buenos Aires years, de Angelis translated Vico from Italian into Spanish, and began circulating his renditions in 1833, the same year as the publication of his *Ensayos literarios y politicos*.[11] These scattered tracts probably had only scant influence on local readers—besides, de Angelis was becoming Rosas's chief ideologue after 1835, and thus suspect among the readers gathered in the salons of city.[12] Joining de Angelis in Vico-dissemination was Vicente López y Planes, sometime University professor and one of the few public officials maintaining cordial relations across the federal-liberal fault line. López y Planes translated excerpts from Herder, Lerminier, and Pierre Leroux, as well as random passages from Vico.[13] Like de Angelis's, these too probably enjoyed only limited circulation, and were probably most diffused through public readings around the city.

Vico's influence was most likely spread through Jules Michelet's translated selections, though these arrived several years after de Angelis's and López y Planes's versions.[14] Michelet reconstrued Vico to fit the general upheaval and reaction to the Enlightenment and the perceived excesses of the revolution. Vico's own doubts about Cartesian rationalism served, in Mark Lilla's words, to "widen into the high road of the Counter-Enlightenment."[15] Views of human nature as universal, objective, and timeless were suspect, and blamed for having led to the Terror and Napoleonic imperialism. Human knowledge and consciousness had to account for ethnic, religious, and communal—in a word particularist—features of the human experience. While Lilla has recently questioned this particular appropriation of Vico, suggesting that the Romantics may have mistakenly portrayed Vico as a pluralist, it was certainly the interpretation seized by intellectuals in the River Plate.[16] Consequently, rather than treat history as a uniform linear movement leading to the triumph of reason, Vico helped Romantics appreciate the incommensurability of the past and the variety of social experience. From Michelet's point of view, all this served his moderately liberal and nationalist agenda to create post-Napoleonic polities based not on traditional dynasties or the universality of reason, but on a reconciliation of warring parties derived from a common linguistic and cultural experience.[17] Liberty could still be a shared goal, but liberals could advocate many paths to its realization; not all countries were required to fit a uniform plan.

Romanticism had a deep influence on legal thought, animating the Historical School of jurisprudence. There is no question that Friedrich

Carl von Savigny loomed very large, shaping Continental legal scholarship and the revival of Romanist jurisprudence—though this was as
much a cultural ideal as a juric model.[18] In France, Jean-Louis Eugene
Lerminier, and Theodore-Simon Jouffroy were among Savigny's most
important disciples. Together they filtered German historicism into the
River Plate, and their writings on legal history and general philosophy
of history were important ingredients in the new mix of legal
thought.[19] Lerminier reacted to encyclopedic rationalism and natural
law theorists who had informed early French revolutionary theory on
the one hand, and to arguments for regal restoration on the other. He
disentangled *droit* from *loi*, in Spanish *derecho* and *ley*, in an effort to
challenge classical formulations which argued that legal systems were
divinely inspired: *droit* was the domain of supra-human will, *loi* reflected the domain of the social, the product of human interaction. Jurists should concern themselves with *loi*, attuning it to local needs and
desires. Doing so permitted a subjective and particularist appropriation of legal mechanisms governing everyday affairs. Jouffroy was
more spiritual than others in his cohort. In applying ethical criteria to
natural law, he called simply for moral reform of classical doctrine.
This notion of a moral revolution—especially through education and
delicate preaching to statesmen—gave Platine thinkers the notion that
change came not through unleashing individualist material interests,
as the revolutionary generation once believed, but with careful moral
reform and legislation.[20]

Above all, what Vico/Michelet, Lerminier, and Jouffroy inspired
was a reappraisal of the Spanish and brief republican eras as specific
and unique historical experiences—and not the unfolding of a cosmic
drama of Enlightenment forces, or the persistence of the scholastic *pac-
tum subjectionis*.[21] They were the vessels transporting the French and
German Historical Schools to the River Plate—which had been arguing in a European context, that not all societies had to squeeze into a
single mold, and that what infused national spirits was society-
specific. Since each society bore particular traits, intellectuals must
dispense with faith in the universality of reason in favor of cognitive
relativism: members of society developed features that had meaning
only in specific contexts, and they learned from experience accordingly.[22]

Freeing the destiny of post-colonial societies from the path laid out
before them by more "advanced" European societies permitted local

intellectuals to search for the roots of their own particular experience. When Marcos Sastre addressed the Salón Literario on June 23, 1837, he urged his friends to advocate legislation, education, and literature "appropriate and particular to the Argentine being." Later, he condemned excessive borrowing from other examples, alluding to Rivadavia's uncritical reliance on utilitarian liberalism: "Guided only by exaggerated theories, and hallucinated by the example of peoples of other civilizations, we have done nothing but imitate foreign forms and institutions, when everything should be found in the study of the nature of our own society, her virtues, her vices, and her grade of instruction and civilization, her climate, territory, population, and customs, and only on these bases [should we] establish a governmental system that fulfills us."[23] In the eyes of Platine youth, Jacobin convictions of the moral superiority of universal reason, and its alleged corollary, historical predestination, were thoroughly discredited.

Embracing historicism allowed intellectuals to reconsider the experiments of their forefathers, revolutionary liberals from Moreno to Rivadavia. According to López y Planes, this liberalism vested excessive sovereignty in the individual and created rights accordingly. The problems were best exemplified in the realm of property: "The theory of property consists entirely of the relationship between man and society. If all rights are encased within the exclusive entitlements, the problem is simplified. . . . But on the other hand we are also concerned with social utility and faced with periodic revolutions."[24] Individualists, in López y Planes's view, failed to recognize social needs and the premium on stability. In so doing, they overlooked certain hard facts about local customs: people were not sufficiently prepared to pursue their individual interests in a reasonable manner. Instead, greed savaged responsible uses of property. For Alberdi, local revolutionaries placed ideology before local historical experience, creating a grotesque parody of French liberty: "France began with thought to conclude in reality; we did the reverse, beginning with the end. Consequently, we find ourselves with results, but without principles, and from this we can appreciate a number of anomalies of our society: the bizarre amalgam of primitive elements with perfect forms; of the ignorance of the masses with representative government."[25] Having shattered Bourbon tyranny, revolutionaries replaced colonial law with unworkable, abstract, indeed destructive principles imported from abroad.

This critique of the first liberal generation did not imply revalorizing the colonial model. In France and Germany, historicism revived studies of age-old institutions and *Volksgeist* antedating the Enlightenment; in Chile, Andrés Bello rekindled the study of Roman Law; conservatives in Mexico did the same in efforts to return to the only model that seemed to offer stability. In the River Plate, the only premodern roots were Iberian and colonial. Spanish codes only reminded Platine youth of the obscurantism they were forced to ingest at the University. Miguel Cané, writing to Alberdi during the height of the Salón's activities, lamented colonial jurisprudence: "What heads! With the exception of three or four, they all seem more like bullfighters than jurists to me!"[26] Youthful thinkers may have rejected many of the principles of their revolutionary forefathers, but this did not lead them to reembrace absolutism. They turned to the more immediate past for hard lessons, and not in nostalgic searches for alternatives imbricated in custom or ancient texts.

If colonial jurisprudence came in for ridicule, it was because Platine youth sought to transcend what they believed was a false dichotomy of extreme camps between liberals and conservatives—each side championing an imported model. By trying to forge a middle ground, as Tulio Halperín Donghi has argued, the Generation of 1837 redirected intellectual debates that were fulminating elsewhere in Spanish America between Europeanized liberals and Hispanophile conservatives, indeed obviating this debate in Argentine political life. The Generation of 1837 construed European Romanticism to justify an aversion to imported recipes and solutions for their problems. Europe was not the source of clues for a new jurisprudence; local experience was.[27]

Esteban Echeverría

The phoenix of the new generation of thinkers was Esteban Echeverría. While he never wrote a legal tract, and had not systematically studied law, his dissemination of French Romantic classics, and his philosophical contribution to the debates of the 1830's shaped the imaginations of his younger colleagues. From a well-off landowning family, Echeverría entered the Colegio de Ciencias Morales in 1822, studying philosophy there until he dropped out, disgusted, a year later. At the end of 1825, he traveled to Europe, where he took up a four-year residence. Initially a follower of Rivadavia and his liberal professors, he was soon swept up in the French Romantic movement and influenced by young Italian nationalists in exile, and brushed by the utopian socialism of Saint-Simon and Fourrier. In mid-1830, he returned to Buenos Aires, where he remained for almost a decade, by which time Rosas's persecution drove him to Colonia, and, urged by Alberdi and Gutiérrez who had preceded him, thence to Montevideo.[28]

Echeverría published much more in exile than during his Buenos Aires years. In 1846, he planned the publication of his complete works, including a revision of his 1839 *Coda* of the Asociación de Mayo. This billowed into a long introduction, called "Ojeada retrospectiva: sobre el movimiento intelectual en el Plata desde el año 1837," and a full re-composition of the *Coda* as *Dogma Socialista*. His purpose was to rein-vigorate the spirit of youthful creative dissent of a decade earlier, though by now Romantic intellectuals had faded into far-flung torpor. The "Ojeada" and *Dogma Socialista*, nonetheless, reflect the classic ex-amples of Platine Romanticism.

Echeverría urged his friends and collaborators to reconceptualize the Republic's short but tempestuous history. In his view, the revolu-tionary generation had believed that releasing Argentines from the Bourbon system would unfetter the healthy interests of the region's inhabitants. Free to choose and bearing natural rights to liberty and property, citizens of the new republic would translate their independ-ence into good, stable, and benevolent government. Revolutionaries achieved independence, but could not consolidate their efforts. At the banquet to celebrate the founding of the Asociación de Mayo and in commemoration of the independence struggle initiated by their fore-fathers in 1810, Echeverría delivered the following words: "We wished to be independent in order to become free. And, after so much sacrifice, are we? No. The great thought of the revolutionaries, and the only way to sanction and legitimize them, is political and social regen-eration: without it, there will come the greatest calamity that provi-dence might inflict on a peoples. Now we have independence, the ba-sis of our complete regeneration; but we lack the finest roof and shel-ter for the rights that must be the complement to any political edi-fice—Liberty—because our regeneration has barely begun."[29] By dis-tinguishing between independence and liberty, Echeverría subdivided two separate phases of the revolutionary struggle. Independence may have been a necessary condition for statehood, but it was not suffi-cient. Liberty, the second cornerstone of statehood, still had not been

won. The May Revolutionaries accomplished the first phase; it behooved the youth of 1837 to consolidate the latter.

If the initial step had been taken, how then to pursue? This by no
means invited an automatic reply. For the two decades after independence, even if there had been a normal path from freedom to liberty, events changed its direction. The liberals lost, civil war ensued,
and the *federal* forces emerged triumphant on the battlefield. Many
Argentines were little closer to realizing their aspirations than they
had been in 1810. By 1837, Argentina was plagued by a civil strife
between two irreconcilable camps: victorious *federales* "who were supported by the popular masses and were the genuine expression of its
semi-barbarous instincts," and defeated unitarians "with good intentions, but with no local base for a socialist cause (socialist in the utopian sense of Saint-Simon), and a dose of antipathy due to their arro-
gant exclusivism and supremacy."[30]

For Echeverría, how had the promise of independence degenerated
into civil war? Much of the blame is placed on the unitarians themselves, who considered their feat necessary and sufficient for liberty.
The basic mistake was to assume that Argentines were "mature"
enough to take advantage of their "material revolution." The May
Revolution freed the region materially, but spiritually and intellectu-
ally, Argentines remained in a colonial cast. "Such a beautiful and
magnificent program," Echeverría said of the revolutionary effort,
"but yet, the revolution's legislators only did what they could. They
were aware, no doubt, that the People's intelligence was not up to
valuing its importance, that in their feelings and customs, and in their
way of seeing and sensing, some reactionary instincts were embedded
against all that was new and that which they did not understand." To
have taken advantage of independence and created a state edifice
would have required this "maturity," or intellectual preparation.[31]
Premature granting of suffrage was the principal malefactor. In the
Province of Buenos Aires, male inhabitants over twenty years old won
the right to vote in 1821. Supposedly, the inspiration for this concession came from the United States. "Yet, so incredible!, our law sur-
passes in liberalism such laws that exist in all other countries; and we
cannot understand the mind of the legislator who promulgates such a
law, when the representative system was so recently introduced to our
society, while at the same time trying to foster solid institutions."[32] In

Dogma Socialista, he extended the error to include more than just suffrage rights, but also unleashing individual material greed: "The predominance of individualism is wasting us. Egotistical passions have sown anarchy in the soil of liberty, and sterilized its fruit."[33]

Otherwise well-intentioned revolutionaries came to commit such folly by emulating the example of others and overlooking local experience. "Mesmerized by the social theories of the French Restoration, they believed that they could implant, in one blow, representative institutions, and that the authority of government would suffice for them to acquire consistency." The revolution, Echeverría argued, had set Argentines free and made them sovereign, yet did not provide an agreed model of authority to occupy the vacuum left by Spanish collapse, and, catastrophically, offered to the people the right to choose how to realize their freedom under authority. When exercised, popular choice favored caudillos over Enlightened statesmen. The *fons et origo* was the French notion of equality, which universalized that which varied by historical and geographical context. Rejecting another eighteenth-century nostrum, Echeverría argued that "equality exists in relation to the intelligence and welfare of citizens. Enlightening the masses of their real rights and obligations, educating with the aim of making them capable of exercising their citizenship and infusing it with the dignity of free men, protecting them and stimulating them so that they should work and be industrious, and offering the means to acquire welfare and independence—here is the way to elevate them to equality."[34] Equality was not, as Rousseau or his Spanish translator Moreno had imagined, the natural attribute of man in a state of nature, which civil society had obliterated. Rather, it was a historical product of engagement in civil society, the work of uplift, education, and good example. Equality was earned, not natural.

It is important to note that Echeverría did not reject the liberals' aspirations or the essence of their prescriptions, but indeed insisted on the direct appropriation of their "progressive traditions." In this, he believed that his generation was the true heir of the May Revolutionaries, but that it had to correct the errors of its predecessors who could not have imagined the consequences of their actions. A new generation had to heal the wounds opened in 1810 while preserving the revolutionary legacy: "The principle of unity for our social theory is the thought of May [1810]—Democracy." The definition of democracy here is an important issue, and I will return to it shortly. Democracy may have been a revolutionary ideal, but the revolutionaries had conferred rights to people who had not earned them.

Making up for lost time required delicate work. The most pressing need was cultural, intellectual, and spiritual uplift, and not concession of yet more rights and claims to the masses—much less democracy. Echeverría urged diffusion "by means of a slow but incessant propaganda, of our fraternizing beliefs." In *Dogma Socialista* he wrote that "to emancipate the ignorant masses and to open the path to sovereignty, it is necessary to educate them. The masses have but instincts: they are more sensitive than rational; they want good, but do not know where to find it; they wish to be free, but are unaware of the route to liberty."[35] This education was necessary because the colonial heritage still gripped the mind of post-colonial society. Nothing, according the Echeverría, better exemplified this sclerosis than the servile attitude to the state and the inertia it provoked. "Before the revolution everything was concentrated in the sphere of public power. The *pueblo* did not think or work without the permission or benediction of the state's henchmen—and from this the *pueblo*'s inertia. After the revolution the government based itself on the same footing as in the colonial era: the sovereign *pueblo* did not know how to make use of its liberty, and left everything to authorities, doing nothing of good for itself."[36] Education and culture would stir Argentines from their lethargy, causing them to apply their faculties and, in so doing, to begin the slow march out of tyranny, whether of monarchs or caudillos.

Youth was the savior then of the republic. This new generation would "unitarianize the *federales*, and federalize the unitarians." Youth would take the best of the liberal inheritance, the institutions, the faith in learning, and respect for property, and fit them to the local mold. They must struggle, "if it is possible, to fuse both parties."[37] Any edifice, however, had to be built respecting local circumstances, exigencies, and customs. "The point of departure, as we have been saying, to tackle these questions must be our own laws, our own customs, and our own social condition." He insisted: "No departure from the practical terrain, no confusion in abstraction, keeping the eye constantly fixed on the intelligence in the bowels of our society."[38] This reflected the historicist aversion to universal truths. It also responded to a new political reality: any solution had to be made legitimate—a new word introduced to the political lexicon of the River Plate. New institutions, faithful to the culture of the republic's citizens, had to break beyond the confines of a few cities "to be delivered to their legitimate own- ers—to the People."

Here we come to the heart of Echeverría's democratic imagination, for while on the one hand he was prepared to deplore the lapses and immaturity of fellow Argentines, he was concerned that they be freed from the tyranny of caudillos. In order to be effective, this freedom had to be self-realized, otherwise the machinery for ensuring the dig- nity of freedom—the "edifice" of the state—would lack legitimacy. "We want," he argued, "that the people not be as they have been hith- erto, a material instrument for the enrichment and empowerment for caudillos and their henchmen, a mere pretext, a vain name invoked by all sides to reinforce and enhance personal ambitions."[39]

There is a basic paradox however: how were people, still unpre- pared to exercise their rights owing to their intellectual and spiritual prematurity, expected to know what was good for them, and therefore to be able to distinguish between the competing legitimacies of caud- illos and youthful *hommes de lettres*? Echeverría's resolution is some- what arbitrary: he distinguished between a socially constituted *pueblo* embracing all inhabitants of the region, and a politically formed citi- zenry including those able to exercise public rights responsibly. Only citizens, in the end, were entitled to choose their preferred legitimacy. Another solution, reminiscent of Madison's own reservations ex- pressed in the *Federalist Papers*, was to create gradations of citizenship, by segmenting spheres of authority vertically (through the division of three powers) and horizontally (by introducing levels of jurisdiction from the municipal realm of broad suffrage rights over limited mat- ters, to narrow suffrage rights at the national level over which the larger issues were controlled). Even at the municipal level, the "proletariat," according to Echeverría, could enjoy electoral rights, but would be forbidden from candidacy to public office—that being the exclusive right and duty of property owners.[40] Those inhabitants un- fortunate enough to be left out of the charmed circle of citizens would simply accept what they could get, assured only that their better en- dowed neighbors knew what was in the true interests of the disen- franchised.[41]

According to Echeverría's formulation, then, not all inhabitants were citizens even if they were members of society. Indeed, citizen- ship, along with the political rights that flowed therefrom, itself had to

be earned *through* the building of state institutions, and did not ante-
date the state. The rights of man—at least those understood by Thomas Paine or Jean-Jacques Rousseau and eighteenth-century revolutionaries who believed these rights to be the property of all individuals—were purely political constructs, earned through the experience
of responsible exercise of power. Citizenship "comes from democratic
institutions" rather than vice versa. The logic was circular: youth's
project would only succeed if legitimated—that is, accepted by the
"people"—but the composition of this "people" was arbitrarily defined and suspiciously closed. In the context of a trans-Atlantic concern to stabilize post-revolutionary societies, whether in Europe or
across Latin America, Echeverría's "democratic" clarion call is consistent with a broader political trend to wind down the effects of revolution, scupper any transition from political to social claims-making, and
to rebuild polities that endorsed the rights of property and not of
broad social membership. To the extent that Echeverría's message to
his youthful followers had repercussions on the contemporary reflections and later legal deliberations during the Constitutional Convention of 1852–53, it was deeply conservative.

Juan Bautista Alberdi

The principal champion of Echeverría's legacy, and ultimately the
author of the constitutional blueprint in 1852–53, was Juan Bautista
Alberdi. One of Echeverría's closest friends and collaborators during
the febrile days of the 1830's, Alberdi translated his companion's more
philosophical and historical work into legal doctrine, though as we
shall see, this was to go through several incarnations as Alberdi lost
his youthful optimism in exile (something Echeverría, no matter how
lonely and impoverished, never relinquished) and became a devout
fatalist. His fatalism, and a deterministic logic that marked a departure from an earlier voluntarism, would stamp his jurisprudence with
an even more conservative seal while at the same time giving it an
analytical rigor absent from either Echeverría's or his own earlier
writings of the 1830's.

Alberdi's *cursus vitae* is better known than Echeverría's.[42] Born in
1810, in a large, traditional family of Tucumán, Alberdi moved to
Buenos Aires to study at the Colegio de Ciencias Morales in 1824. As a
law student in the 1830's, he wrote a series of cultural essays and a

memoir of his Tucumán years after making a return trip home in 1834. But his best known works were his address at the founding of the Salón Literario, and what would have been his dissertation for the Law School had he chosen to remain (as it was, he dropped out and only picked up his degree in Chile a decade later)—the *Fragmento preliminar al estudio del derecho*, which best embodies the juridical aspect of Romanticism in the River Plate.

His speech to the Salón reinvoked the popular call to reject the models presented by other revolutionary societies, France and the United States. Foreign doctrines rested on a view of history as progressive, linear, and constant, when in fact the events that led to their revolutions were contingent, or even accidental. Alberdi did not doubt that the United States and France enjoyed such progress. His problem was that while earlier examples inspired the Spanish American revolutions, their evolution took them elsewhere, not toward "progressive development." Laws governing social evolution vary: "Development, sirs, is the aim and law of all humanity. But this law is itself also subject to its own laws. All *pueblos* necessarily develop, but each develops according to its own mode, because development operates according to constant laws in intimate subordination to conditions of time and space. And just as these conditions do not reproduce themselves ever in an identical manner, it therefore follows that no two *pueblos* develop in the same way."[43] Historical laws of motion are not universal and transcendent, but exposed to the vagaries of human volition, its contradictions, and its culture.

Like Echeverría, Alberdi argued that it was the failure to appreciate the singularity of the Spanish American character and culture that led to the post-revolutionary disaster. By subjecting ourselves "to a general progressive law of development, we have not subordinated our movement to the appropriate conditions of our age and our soil. We have not achieved the special civilization that is a normal result of our national forms of being. And this is the flaw to which we must refer all the sterility of our constitutional experiments."[44]

To initiate this search for constitutional foundations, which would remain true to universal yearning for progress but amenable to local circumstance, Alberdi published *Fragmento preliminar al estudio del derecho* in mid-1837 (though the book was written in the course of 1836). Paradoxically, Alberdi did not provide any diagnosis or inventory of the Republic's principal traits and problems. In his preface he confessed that his original urge to write a treatise on Argentine law which would reflect the country's historical particularity, gave way to philosophical concerns. "I conceived of law," wrote Alberdi, "as a living phenomenon worthy of studying the organic economy of the state."[45] He pointed to Lerminier's distinction between *droit* (*derecho*) and *loi* (*ley*). *Derecho* was the moral and spiritual essence of a people that accounts for "the living harmony of a social organism," the basis of its sociability; while *leyes* were their material manifestation that guided day-to-day interaction. The spirit of *droit* (as Lerminier and Alberdi understood in turn from Montesquieu) is prior and antedates the laws themselves. A virtuous state is one in which its laws appropriately reflect their spirit. For Alberdi, Argentina's quandary could be reduced to a misalignment of the moral law from its laws and constitutions. A solution required an exploration into the moral world of Argentines in order to frame appropriate legislation. Having discovered the spiritual key, jurists and legislators would then readjust their laws accordingly.[46] Without this spiritual discovery, any society is condemned to live by its instincts, and therefore in barbarism, or by foreign models, and thus in anarchy.

This notion of spiritual or philosophical self-exploration turned on an appraisal of recent history. Like Echeverría, Alberdi believed that the May Revolutionaries erred by conflating material independence with spiritual liberty: they achieved the former but forgot the latter. "Two chains tied us to Europe," Alberdi explained, "a material one that broke, and an intellectual one that still lives. Our fathers broke the first with the sword; we will break the latter with ideas." Chronologically, "the reign of action has passed, and we have entered that of thought. We will have heroes, but they will emerge from the heart of philosophy."[47] The spiritual revolution was the job of intellectuals, and their mission was to educate in order for the people to realize the liberties to which they were entitled, but unable to appreciate.

Alberdi refused to abandon the dalliance with revolution, but he translated Romantic notions into a fundamentally pessimistic diagnosis of Argentine ailments: the quest for liberty was spoiled from the start because liberals misunderstood the culture of the republic's new citizens. Whereas liberals provided the intellectual justification for freedom from Spain, they had no plan for the conquest of domestic liberty. This etiology, and indeed the foundations for modern Argentine historiography, served the purposes of young Romantics. It gave them a political cause and reinforced their claim that only youth, second generation Argentines, could initiate a proper search for legal and legitimate foundations for statehood, broadly speaking realigning Lerminier's *droit* and *loi*, moral law with constitutions and legislation.

As the Generation of 1837 fixed their attention on this moral task, events around them, especially European blockades and endemic provincial warring, turned Buenos Aires into a hostile territory for anyone engaged in critical reflections that did not pour accolades on General Rosas. The ranks of anti-Rosistas swelled, though not always voluntarily. Alberdi, like many of his friends, fled the city in late 1838, finally settling down in Chile. Exile—as involuntary flight or incarceration is wont to do—compelled him to rethink much of his early Romantic and somewhat voluntarist political theory. During these years, Alberdi took stock of the failures of anti-Rosista forces, both youthful and more traditional unitarian.[48] These were years of transition for Alberdi, during which Romantic utopianism gave way to pragmatic materialism.[49] Alberdi, without abandoning his commitment to a time- and location-specific solution, ceased to see ideas and intellectual change as the driving force in history, favoring instead material, and increasingly technological, developments as the motor of change.

From a constitutional viewpoint, the most important text during his exile years was "La República Argentina 37 años despues de su Revolución de Mayo," published to mark the May Revolution in 1847.[50] Like Echeverría's "Ojeada retrospectiva," Alberdi's historiographic essay, a reinterpretation of the sequence of past events, was meant to provide a guide to a new constitutional framework. Yet, whereas Echeverría's essay hearkened back to an earlier romantic spirit, Alberdi's was a marked departure, and anticipates much that will appear later in his 1852 *Bases y puntos de partida para la organización política de la República Argentina*—which would serve as the blueprint for the 1853 Constitution.

By the time Alberdi wrote "La República Argentina," Rosas was stronger than ever, and appeared solidly ensconced. Alberdi's point of departure, therefore, was a reconciliation with the apparently indomitable caudillo. Accordingly, he began with a genuflection in Rosas's direction: "There is no man who can deny that the condition [of Argentina] is respectable, and that there is nothing shameful in this. And why not say this openly? The Argentine Republic has not been able to move foreign sensibilities with her civil war; she appears barbarous and cruel; but she has never been ridiculous to anyone; and the disgrace that does not become a taunt is far from becoming the last disgrace." Solidity and defiance of European powers reinforced the sovereignty of the state—now more firm than anywhere else in Spanish America. Buenos Aires' strength made it the model of America, the mirror of the continent's future. Rosas is "the man of America . . . because he is a political type uncommon to the rest of America . . ." The result is that "Rosas is not a simple tyrant in my view. If in his hand there is a bloody rod of steel, I see in his head the insignia of Belgrano."[51]

Rosas, no tyrant, was but a product of his people and his environment. His deep base of legitimacy (at least as Alberdi saw things) provided a point of departure for constitutional rule. Intellectuals would be better advised, in Alberdi's view, to begin cooperating with the caudillo than to oppose him, since he would always command the loyalty of the Argentine people. If Rosas rejected the unitarian constitutional formula, this did not mean that he spurned all frameworks. The task was to study Rosas's practices of government, to delve into the common-sense material of consensus. Such an experiment would reveal that wars and struggles had indeed centralized power, had created the foundations of statehood rather than undermined them. "One notable development," said Alberdi, "that forms part of the definitive organization of the Argentine Republic, has prospered through her wars, receiving important services, even from her adversaries. This is the centralization of national power." Rosas in fact built on the unitarian legacy rather than dismantling it: "Rivadavia proclaimed the idea of unity, Rosas has realized it. Between the *federales* and the unitarians, they have centralized the Republic, which means that the issue is of voices that express the mere spirit of young peoples."[52] Rosas provided a foundation for future development, and did not represent a force that had to be expunged. It would not be necessary to introduce or to write a new constitution after a hypothetical victory of intellectuals, but simply to formalize what the caudillo was doing in practice.

Alberdi's message to his former friends and colleagues was clear: Rosas was not necessarily the diabolical tyrant they had come to claim. Rather, he symbolized a continuity of spirit, not a rupture. During their Romantic phase, Alberdi and Echeverría had called for a state that was attuned to the common sense of Argentines. Now, recognizing Rosas as the embodiment of the Argentine common sense, it was time for the "men of talent" to return. "The day that these men return to their country to reunite in deliberative assemblies, such useful and comparative applications, and such practical knowledge and curious allusions, they will not have to take from the memory of their time spent abroad." Intellectuals will only have an influence within the Republic, and never outside it. Moreover, by having fled, intellectuals left the state in the hands of "plebeian masses." The experience of power itself instructed and uplifted these masses, and "has softened their ferocity in the cultural atmosphere that the others left them."[53] Indeed, the absence of intellectuals, who tended to fuel ideological discord, allowed a period of stability to settle in and reinforced the power and legitimacy of Rosas. Whereas liberals had let the former Viceroyalty crumble into disunited elements, Rosas built a new order.

Alberdi was not letting Rosas off the hook, exculpating him of the violence and bloodshed of earlier civil wars. Caudillos committed the same excesses as the unitarians. The latter flooded the country with too many liberties, and the former took advantage of them to perpetrate all sorts of barbarities. But once the wars were over, caudillos switched tack, from campaigns against unitarians and liberals, to consolidating their own hold on power, shifting from questions of liberty to concerns with order. "In the first chants of victory, [the May Revolutionaries] forgot a word less sonorous than that of *liberty*, but representing a counter-weight that keeps liberty afoot: *order*."[54] Liberty and order had become unhitched in the first decades of independence at the hands of zealous liberal unitarians. So while caudillos like Rosas had been guilty of earlier barbarities, years of power instructed them in the art of government—something neither intellectuals nor unitarian statesmen achieved.

By the late 1840's, Alberdi clearly saw caudillos as potential allies rather than foes. His only concern was that they convert their victorious *order* into legal government. Their triumphs rested on their skills on the battlefields, and their hold rested on acknowledgment of popular common sense, but they still recoiled from formalizing power into law. Alberdi saw this as the next step: "Though the *carta* or written constitution is neither law nor pact [this being an informal relationship between leader and led], however, they prove it, and keep it invariable. The word is a necessity of order and harmony. It guarantees the stability of all important contracts, writing it down; and what contract

is more important than the great constitutional contract?" By advocating the legalization of caudillo rule, Alberdi made constitutionalism
out of the implied contract between caudillos and people in the name
of order, and not some liberal notion of a document meant to incarnate the abstract interests and liberties of possessive individualists.
Alberdi's formula was a self-conscious rejection of unitarian constitutionalism: "It is a progress that tyranny should be exercised by law,
rather than being the will of a single man."[55] The constitution was the
last step, the culmination of an antecedent process of state-formation
consolidated by caudillos, but still missing its final component. Legal
and constitutional rule would transform order into peaceable government: "Peace can only come through the legal road. The constitution is the most powerful means to pacification and internal order.
Dictatorship is a constant provocation for war; it is sarcastic, an insult
to those who obey without reservation or limitation."[56] Without a constitution, there was no way to ensure that the leader in power kept the
faith bestowed to him by the people. In a word, the constitution was
meant to transcend rule by the will of a single man, to foster legitimate
authority.

This was a remarkable about-face, a clear turn against earlier faiths
in constitutions as formative documents, as instruments to *make* society into a political community. Alberdi, in effect, reversed the causal
order of late eighteenth-century constitutionalism, touting a *magna
carta* as a device to consolidate statehood, and not abstract aspirational
goals for refashioning revolutionary societies from above. If the phi-
losopher still had a role in a constitutional republic, it was as adviser
to the caudillo or legalized tyrant. Like Machiavelli to the Prince, Alberdi presented himself as an intellectual resource for the caudillo.[57]

Domingo Faustino Sarmiento

Alberdi's contemporary, a latecomer to the Romantic movement in the
River Plate, Domingo Faustino Sarmiento is often seen as his com-
petitor and rival. Differences between the two became explicit, and a
source of bitter dispute, during the 1850's, but they were also evident
by the 1840's. They speak to the ambiguities within Romanticism and
historicism, since they bound legal recipes tightly with historiographic
interpretation.[58]

Born in 1811 and raised in San Juan, Sarmiento became a teacher at the age of 15. He never left the province until he was forced into exile in 1831, after having sided with the unitarians, and later again he fled to Chile in 1840. Sarmiento only returned to Argentina again in 1852, when he fought on the side of Justo José de Urquiza, and after the victory at Caseros, he entered Buenos Aires for the first time. Meanwhile, he had traveled extensively in Europe and the United States—the latter leaving a particularly indelible mark on his subsequent thought.[59] Two major works came from his pen, *Facundo*, prior to his visit to the United States, and *Argirópolis*, written upon his return but published while he was still in exile. Together, these works represent an alternative constitutional vision for the Republic—one that shares much of Echeverría and Alberdi's concern to forge an appropriate legal structure but also takes some important departures from their historicism.

Sarmiento followed the Romantic turn to local pasts as a guide for future trajectories. Whereas Alberdi had come to see the Viceroyalty as an integral unity, temporarily shattered by the revolution and the failure of the unitarian experiments, only to be reassembled by caudillo power based in Buenos Aires, Sarmiento took quite a different view. For him, the colonial heritage was the source of much of Argentina's problems, which caudillos in turn aggravated. The Viceroyalty, far from being a coherent unity, was a shell filled only with anarchic politics and localist sentiments. The problem began with the dominant economy: pastoral production. Rather than colonize the River Plate with yeoman farmers, Spanish authorities had let mounted plainsmen, *gauchos*, roam the pampas creating a "reign of brute force."[60] This was to become a familiar nineteenth-century trope: environment conditioned national characters; a kind of pastoral angst, isolation, lack of community, mobility, and uncontrolled and undisciplined work habits bred disrespect for order and property. In the "struggle of isolated man with untamed nature, of the rational being with the brute," nature and brutality won.

The May Revolution threw this barbaric order into crisis. Two alternative political movements arose, each representing rival forms of social organization and touting mutually exclusive plans for the state. The "commotion and the sound of arms" pit representatives of European liberal civilization based in the city against American ("native" was Sarmiento's term) barbarism of the countryside. The wars themselves only increased the powers of "Bedouin hordes," and "the

revolutionary movement finally brought about provincial, warlike associations, called *montoneras*, legitimate offspring of the tavern and the
field, hostile to the city and to the army of revolutionary patriots."[61]
Prior to 1810, gauchos lived in happy, if primitive and backward tran-
quillity. The wars of independence armed these nomadic peoples. In
warfare, nomads helped Europeanized patriots of the cities triumph
over Royalist forces. But in their strength, the *montoneras* denied the
patriots the wherewithal to govern at will.

In the ensuing civil wars, barbaric rule gained the upper hand.
Sarmiento went into lugubrious detail, chronicling the human waste
and depredation at the hands of the caudillos, exemplified by La
Rioja's Facundo. In the course of the war, however, Sarmiento de-
tected a reversal of positions: as the unitarian forces went on the defensive, and the *montoneras* claimed victory after victory, the caudillo
armies lost their "primitive strength" and became increasingly orderly
and disciplined while unitarians retreated into the "*montonera* system." Rosas, the caudillo, and Lavalle, the unitarian, "exchanged
parts."[62] This reversal meant that organizing the Republic fell to Rosas,
Facundo, and other caudillos. Hitherto, however, their organization
was nothing but a facade for personalist rule.

Just as Sarmiento turned to environmental determinism to account
for the social personality of the gaucho, so too history was predetermined, making the unitarian project a pipe dream. The character of
the region's inhabitants foretold the failure of liberal constitutionalism.
Argentina was "destined to a consolidation," not through imported
European and liberal notions to make a country out of an artificial
unity based in Buenos Aires, "but by the force of the barbarian they
[the provinces] sent upon her [Buenos Aires] in Facundo and Rosas."[63]
Like Alberdi and Echeverría, Sarmiento argued that caudillos were
the heirs to the May Revolution.[64] Sarmiento, however, reduced the
rightful (though loathsome) claims to legitimacy of caudillo power to a
hard demographic fact: the region, populated by mounted plainsmen,
would never be fertile ground for liberal constitutional rule. The only
solution, which remained a consistent pillar of his work as writer and
politician until late in his life, was to be demographic annihilation,
through the settlement of European farmers, and later, in the 1860's a
war of unparalleled brutality against the gauchos of the interior. For
now, Sarmiento saw in Rosas the artifice of the new state. Alberdi had
come to see Rosas as the champion of the unitarian cause, creating a

centralized state rooted in Buenos Aires. For Sarmiento, on the other hand, Rosas was Rivadavia's alter ego, holding together a loose coalition of provinces whose localist sentiment far outweighed any national *esprit*.[65] Constitutionally speaking, for Alberdi, Rosas could serve as a point of departure; for Sarmiento, this was inconceivable.

After the publication of *Facundo*, Sarmiento went on a long trip to Europe and the United States, and his travels left a strong imprint on his subsequent work. The United States loomed increasingly large as a federalist model for solving the Argentine riddle of reconciling localism with constitutionalism. He found in the United States a decentralized body politic designed to keep strongmen at bay. Returning from the United States, he began composing a blueprint state, subsequently published as *Argirópolis* in 1850. It is important to note that, in the meantime, General Urquiza, Governor of Entre Ríos and former Rosas ally, was in the midst of galvanizing an alliance of disgruntled Littoral provinces with Brazil to rid Argentina of Rosas. *Argirópolis* was meant as an undisguised program for the anti-Rosas alliance. Urquiza, in Sarmiento's words, "is the highest glory of the confederation, chief of an army that always wins, governor of a province where the press has risen, where the state has organized primary education."[66] By aligning with the Entre Ríos governor, Sarmiento changed his tone from an environmental determinism, in which federalist constitutionalism—in *Facundo* an oxymoron since localism would always stymie the proper process of state-formation—was now a viable means to "constitute the country."

Still, constitutional solutions could not be deracinated imports. "Those most able to realize the pacific idea we propose are *federal* governments or those independent of the Littoral of the rivers that form the River Plate. For them, this is a question of life or death."[67] How would federalism become a basis for organization? If open land and the mounted plainsman conditioned the political apparatus that would flourish on the Pampas as represented in *Facundo*, Sarmiento now relocated the geographic vector from land to rivers, from cattle rustling to riverine trade. Since Rosas had consolidated his power in the 1830's, he strengthened the grip of Buenos Aires over the River Plate drainage basin, creating a centralized monopoly over trade in the name of decentralization. The source of political power, then, shifted from command over gaucho armies to control over trade. The problem was, Rosas exercised a trade monopoly in favor of Buenos

Aires, at the expense of other provinces. What Sarmiento urged was a truer form of federalism. "The measures we propose, more than legitimate and perfectly legal, conform to federal law, which serves as the base of all actual powers of the confederation."[68]

Sarmiento explored the federalist antecedents to the confederation, finding here the path for the country's future. The difficulty was that Rosas had used Buenos Aires' monopoly over the trading system to undermine the federalist spirit. How did Buenos Aires come to subvert the federal structure? *Argirópolis* takes the reader back to the Independence Wars. By sheer cruelty of history, Buenos Aires usurped the right to speak for the rest of the region. Nothing better exemplified Buenos Aires' guile than the manipulation of the Pact of 1831 between Buenos Aires, Santa Fe, and Entre Ríos, which was supposed to have consolidated a federation, a promise Rosas cynically betrayed. Indeed, for Sarmiento, the letter of the 1831 Pact was a potential founding stone for the nascent Argentine state. According to the Pact, the Littoral provinces had to invite the rest of the provinces to gather at a "general federalist congress, to arrange *the country's general administration under a federal system, its external and internal commerce, its navigation, the charging and distribution of general revenues*, consulting in the best possible way the security and grandeur of the Republic, its internal and external credit, and the liberty and sovereignty of each of the provinces."[69] Here was a deal that could serve in a post-Rosas era as a precedent for a federalist national state without implying any deep rupture with local traditions. Sarmiento relocated the problem from caudillos in a general sense, to the caudillo-governor of one province, *primus inter pares*, Buenos Aires.

In the long run, Sarmiento envisioned a reunited viceregal state, based on federalist principles, with a capital seated in the neutral territory of the Island of Martin Garcia (and hence beyond the reach of any single province). Its appeal was its pure pragmatism. Like *Facundo* before it, *Argirópolis* did not refer to transcendent or mystical notions of nationhood. Unlike European Romantics, who reached back into a reified medieval Holy Roman identity, Argentine Romantics had little choice but to speak of interests rather than allude to an intrinsic and embedded *Volksgeist*. Because the colonial system and its failed liberal successor lacked claims to legitimacy, any new state had to demonstrate to Argentines that they were united because common interests outweighed local ones. "The objective of a Confederation is to unite the collective force of the nation to the betterment and advantage of each of the associated States [meaning provinces], and it would be ridiculous to suppose that there exists a State that would unite freely to renounce all hope, progress, and improvement for itself, abandoning the power, wealth, and glory and all the other commercial and political advantages enjoyed by a single State or a single individual."[70]

Conclusion

Romanticism advanced two important aspects that served a new generation of legal thinkers' political purposes. First, it helped them spurn the siren calls of models of predetermined paths of historical causation driven by the overarching and teleological power of reason. Sharing the Romantic turn away from universal paths toward modernity, Platine intellectuals instead invoked historical particularity. Accepting the failure of imported straitjackets, they looked above all to indigenous possibilities for consolidating republican rule, though without abandoning the long-term project of folding Argentina into a trans-Atlantic liberal mold. Each country provided its own clues to its destiny and recipes to create conditions for legitimate order and the protection of property.

Second, natural legal doctrines, whether clad in the notion of rights inherent to the individual, or hierarchies of justice elaborated through divine inspiration, did not provide doctrinal foundations for statehood. Rather, historicism led, somewhat indirectly, to instrumental and pragmatic notions of legality. Increasingly, Platine political thinkers embraced ideas of the political community that did not trumpet statehood as the realization of transcendental ideals—whether divined or reasoned. Order, not justice, became the goal.

Realizing order meant that, one way or another, intellectuals had to reconcile themselves with caudillismo. Of course, by 1850, it was an open choice which caudillo, the Governor of Entre Ríos, Urquiza, or the Governor of Buenos Aires, Rosas, to choose as ally. The difference is best exemplified in the affinities of Alberdi, who initiated an overture with Rosas, and Sarmiento, who reached out to Urquiza. Their choices reflected quite different images of the federal structure of the state. Sarmiento opted for a decentralized confederation, reducing the powers of Buenos Aires in the name of a commercial common sense. Alberdi alluded to a more centralized model, in the name of continu-

ity with the unitarians, in which Buenos Aires' privileges were the
price to be paid for unity and peace.

Historical particularity and responses to shifting political fortunes
helped lead to—in Isaiah Berlin's words—"a melting away of the very
notion of objective truth." Generally speaking, without an appeal to
universal foundations, legal thinkers backed into a kind of cognitive
relativism. Relativism posed problems when it came to forging commonly shared constitutional parameters, for this incipient constitutional movement offered no claims to a higher authority of moral law
(as natural lawyers maintained), nor did it propound any factual non-
moral criteria for evaluating law's validity (as legal positivists would
soon tout). Law, rather, was placed squarely at the service of constructing a state, a state fashioned in the eye of its intellectual architects—and in particular cast as narrative structures of emerging national historiographies. Instead of promoting law and constitutionalism as embodiments of transcendent values, the legal scholarship in-
forming the debates of the 1850's espoused an instrumental concept of
its subject.

In this sense, Argentina's second generation of constitutionalists
took one large step away from its predecessor's fateful belief in the absolute efficacy of politics and the privileged role of the intellectual in
its conduct—manifest in the use of constitutions as autonomous tools
to forge revolutionary societies. Broadly speaking, this shift away
from aspirational constitutionalism fit the trans-Atlantic tilt to a "con-
structive" legal mood depicted by de Tocqueville. Hereafter, much as
they feuded over ensuing decades, the architects of the Argentine state
saw themselves less as abstract inventors of a new republic, and more
as instruments in its own fitful emergence.

☞ The Age of Order, 1850's–1860's

8 ⌒ Constitutional Persuasions

> There is nothing more difficult to carry through than initiating
> changes in a state's constitution. The innovator makes enemies of
> all those who prospered under the old order, and only lukewarm
> support is forthcoming from those who would prosper under the
> new. Their support is lukewarm partly from fear of their adversar-
> ies, who have the existing laws on their side, and partly because
> men are generally incredulous, never really trusting new things
> unless they have tested them by experience.
>
> Niccolò Machiavelli, *The Prince*

Constituting the Republic

The instrumental approach to public law that had gestated during the
dark years of Rosas's reign finally triumphed in the 1850's. Not, however, without discord; not without another round of conflict over what
kind of state would consolidate the political community. This step of
state-formation would require one last bout of civil war to generate the
heat with which to forge constitutional consensus, one that would
privilege republican order to stabilize property relations.

Difference of opinion over the post-caudillo order lurked within the
anti-Rosista coalition itself. In fact, Rosas's grip had squeezed the scattered forces of his rivals, adversaries, and enemies into an unholy alliance. Exiles, the neighboring states of Uruguay, Paraguay, and especially Brazil, and finally the chafing provinces of the Littoral conspired
to form a Grand Army of South America, led by the Entre Ríos Governor, Justo José de Urquiza. On February 3, 1852, 24,000 Allied troops
took on Buenos Aires' force of 23,000. Rosas the political strategist was
no match for Urquiza the seasoned warrior. The Battle of Caseros saw
the Buenos Aires army crumble, and with it, Rosas's entire military and
political edifice. The General fled, in disguise, to the protection of a British man-of-war, and permanent exile in Southampton. The Rosista re-

gime, never much more than a series of contingent deals made with an uneasy new-propertied clientele, crumbled in a matter if days.[1]

The problem was: Urquiza's alliance more clearly expressed what it did not want than what it did want. The result, with Rosas gone, was immediate feuding over the future. What is more, Buenos Aires' vocabulary and rituals of politics immediately raised banners of open elections, unobstructed press, and free association. So quickly did *porteños* embrace constitution-talk, that "rights" and "liberties" soon became cudgels with which to assail the liberator Urquiza himself. Urquiza entered the city and clamped down on pillaging and rampaging in certain quarters of the city where Rosista police had withdrawn leaving behind a vacuum. In a move that shocked many *porteños*, Urquiza meted out a form of justice that resembled more that of the toppled regime than its successor: he ordered the execution of 200 men, including civilians. The entire Aquino regiment was taken prisoner, and without trial found guilty. Executioners sliced the throats of the Buenos Aires soldiers' one-by-one. This form of brutal justice deprived Urquiza of potential friends in the occupied city. The city soon seethed at its "liberator."[2]

This political *malentendu* provided the backdrop to a decade of legal debate. Caudillos introduced a pattern of rule and conferred a delicate stability to the remains of the Spanish empire in the River Plate. They ruled regimes, but they did not consolidate states. Closure of the caudillo era opened a new chapter of debate, contention, and conflict over what kind of constitution befitted the region, how to ensure that citizens debate the laws of particular governments without questioning the laws of state.

The allied victory gave Platine thinkers, assimilating the new mutations of Atlantic liberalism, the opportunity they awaited. But constitution-framers grappled with an implied problem of Urquiza's alliance: it much more effectively articulated what it wanted to topple, the rule of quasi-law, than boasted credible principles of legal alternatives. Abandoning the revolutionary faith that a constitution could mold a colonial society into a modern liberal one, new legal thinkers of the 1840's and 1850's embraced instrumental ideas that a *magna carta* should reflect the needs of a society yearning for credible institutions. If anything, constitutions should foster social stability and order, not generate social transformation. Accordingly, thinkers of state faced the awesome problem of drafting a historically situated and appropriate founding charter that would solve the riddle of political order.

Two issues dogged the caudillo's successors. First, statesmen grappled with the issue of how to integrate provincial polities accustomed, after four decades of disunion, to considerable autonomy. The revolutionary experience in the River Plate, unlike the United States or even France, did not forge a common set of political registers upon which to construct a national people whose own unity would serve as the social foundations for a nation-state. The only way to convince provincial peoples to invest in the new nation was to assure them that, at the very least, all provinces would be equal. This immediately confronted the new national state with long-standing claims of Buenos Aires to special status—the self-nurtured image of itself as the modernizing pole of South America.[3]

The second issue was not unique to Spanish America, but bedeviled constitutionalists across the Atlantic world: how to reconcile the powers and rights of a sovereign people with the need to stabilize a state. Anglo-American traditions resolved the problem through multilayered polities and a series of checks and balances to prevent majorities from exercising irresponsible power. For Spanish Americans, the riddle was slightly different: not only were unruly mobs to be neutralized (and many constitutionalists had come to see the caudillo as the political emblem of mob-rule), but so too was civil society. Left to its own devices, society (elites as well as popular sectors) splintered into fissiparous localisms and degenerated to rent-seeking behavior. Similarly, many constitutionalists felt that the republican state should be autonomous from civil society as a whole—that there be a wide gulf between political representatives and their constituencies.[4]

In tackling the dual challenge of provincial sovereignties and the menace of an unruly civil society, Argentine constitutionalists articulated their misgivings about the world they wished to induct into the fold of trans-Atlantic legalism. Jurists across Europe and the Americas aimed to immunize society, and property in particular, from potentially destructive propensities of states. But in Spanish America, revolutionary unraveling and decades of civil war had only intensified doubts about the self-governability of the people. If Alexis de Tocqueville could observe that the local community was organized before the country and the country before the state in the United States, and that the reverse order held in France, Spanish Americans found organization nowhere.[5]

Such pessimism shaped constitutionalists' approach to balancing public powers and private rights. How, for instance, would they deal with a priori concerns and vested rights of private property, that is, the autonomy of economic agents? The French Droit des Hommes and the U.S. Bill of Rights provided external constraints against state incursions on civil society and codified abstract rights of free agents. Spanish Americans were much warier about investing so much autonomy in a civil society that displayed such a proclivity to squabbling over rules rather than respecting them. To Dalmacio Vélez Sarsfield, one of the central figures behind the new constitutional consensus, the aim should be liberty and prosperity, but this meant that "the common good" had to be protected from "egotists," "small-minded interests," and "men of parties who exploit" the general will. In the end, to get the balance right, the framers obeyed their instrumental approach to public law: in the new persuasion, abstract rights of citizens paled beside the project of building public powers.[6]

The constitution was no neutral or purely formal document. It shaped admissible and inadmissible politics in two ways: by defining the rules governing the conduct of forces as they bargained over political positions, and by structuring the alternatives to remaining within bargaining contexts. In drafting these rules, by confining and channeling the terms of future political debate and contestation, the framers aimed to transcend decades of civil strife and enmity over the shape of the republic.[7]

Crafting the Constitution

Urquiza and the Allied cause made the drafting of a constitution the banner of unity. As early as April 1851, the Entre Ríos Governor issued a circular to his colleagues calling for "the triumph of public justice." Commemorating the overthrow of the Viceroy on May 25, 1851, Urquiza declared that "the great clock of destiny has now struck the hour for the Organization and the triumph of the Republic."[8] The Allied victory and the promise of a constitution was cause for celebration in the city. *Porteños* lit bonfires in the streets and threw the obligatory red vests, armbands, posters, newspapers, and Rosista propaganda into the flames (only to have to retrieve the garb under humiliating orders from Urquiza). The caudillo's press, the *Gaceta Mercantil* and the *Diario de la Tarde* were dismantled or smashed. *The British Packet* performed an abrupt about-face, decrying the abuses of the regime it had eulogized for decades. A new breed of press, indeed, a new style of journalism, erupted onto the public stage—much more combative, much more autonomous, prepared to wade into public debate with unprecedented powers to mobilize the citizenry into ideological camps. Indeed, over the ensuing decade, the Buenos Aires press would perform a decisive role shaping public opinion over constitutional matters.[9] "Oppression has disappeared" proclaimed one paper as the news of Caseros spread through Buenos Aires. "The empire of law will from today forward be a reality. Individual security will be guaranteed, and property and the rights, life, and status of citizens will no longer suffer from the caprice of a dictator."[10]

As the dust settled, however, cooler heads began to prevail. Dalmacio Vélez Sarsfield, soon to play a central role as a moderate force in Buenos Aires' struggle with Urquiza, characteristically urged caution. "We should be prudent and moderate," he warned; "liberty is not license; nor is it caprice or egotistic interests of privileged classes to consolidate their advantaged social position. . . . Liberty is a right limited by duty: without these conditions, human associations will slide into chaos."[11] Mariano Fragueiro, a respected politician from Córdoba and scion of a merchant family, echoed the call for modesty. Urquiza's triumph only brought down the caudillo; the real work lay before statesmen who, not lacking in will, exaggerated their means to forge a new consensus. "I do not doubt," he wrote from exile in Chile, "the right, convenience, and will of the people: I doubt that these people have the means to exercise their rights and to verify their will."[12]

In the wake of the post-Caseros celebration, the dispersed statesmen turned, with nagging anxiety, to the problem of building a new order. Urquiza recruited provincial delegates to meet in the town of San Nicolás, where they invoked the 1831 Littoral Pact to call for a Constitutional Congress. The San Nicolás Accord set the meeting place for Santa Fe, stipulating that each province was entitled to send two delegates. Importantly, the Accord enabled delegates to approve any draft, and thus freed constitutional ratification from troublesome provincial assemblies. In the meantime, the Accord vested interim national authority over all military, commercial, and international affairs in the hands of Urquiza as the interim national government's temporary "Director."[13]

From the start, however, Urquiza ran up against opposition in Buenos Aires. *Porteños* disliked his style of summary justice. They disliked even more what appeared as a maneuver to arrogate to himself the powers of a nation-state that did not yet exist, and filed down their criticism into cutting accusations that he was resurrecting Rosas's proclivities. Several of Urquiza's advisers wanted to sever the city of Buenos Aires from the province and to federalize the capital to dilute the imbalance of Buenos Aires' political weight—a move that horrified provincialists when Rivadavia had advanced it, and that remained anathema. To make matters worse, in his effort to restore order in Buenos Aires, Director Urquiza named the hapless Vicente López y Planes as Governor, snubbing Valentín Alsina, who aspired to the job. In subsequent elections, the champions of Buenos Aires autonomy, led by Alsina, swept the Provincial Legislature—driving a rift between the provincial legislators and the national executive. Buenos Aires protested that the Accord was illegitimate without the full approval of the Provincial Legislature. A lame-duck López agreed, much to Urquiza's chagrin, and sent the San Nicolás pact to the Legislature in mid-June. When López y Planes appeared before the legislators, they showered him, and the Accord, with a torrent of abuse.[14]

The conflict over the San Nicolás Accord vented a debate over the authority of constitutional delegates, and thus the sovereign powers of the emerging national Convention. The delegates had argued that they acted as ersatz law-makers, the legislative embodiment of provincially sovereign people. The opposition, led by Alsina and the young crusader Bartolomé Mitre, denied that the delegates had any legislative authority: they were merely emissaries to negotiate a pact that required ratification by the only sovereign power until a legitimate national state could be forged—the provincial assemblies. Constitutional wrangling became the occasion for a new breed of political leader, exemplified by the soldier-journalist and later president-historian, Mitre. Born in 1821, and having fled Rosas's Buenos Aires in 1837, Mitre bitterly opposed whatever smacked of residual caudillismo. His stand was framed in decidedly constitutional terms. Over the long arc of Mitre's political career, whether as a state-builder in the 1850's and 1860's, or an opponent in the 1870's and 1880's, he upheld the principle that conflict had to flow through the channels of rules of state. For those who imperiled and abused constitutional rules, Mitre reserved his venom and justified armed resistance. Such was the hallmark of the emerging political language of state-formation in Buenos Aires—it was legalistic and pragmatic in the same breath. Mitre and others wanted a deeper involvement of legislators and feared handing over the constitutional reins to Rosas's former ally. Urquiza, in their eyes, promised only a recalibrated version of rule by strong-men and not the rule of strong laws. Urquiza's opposition coded their critique as the over-empowerment of the executive branch. For Mitre, "the conflict is simply because the Executive has stepped out of its field of powers, and not the Assembly, which has always remained within its field." The process, for Mitre, annulled the principle of divided powers, a crucial constraint on abuse, and hence a recipe for "despotism."[15] Some voices called for moderation. Warning his more aggressive partners that the looming confrontation could be catastrophic, Vélez Sarsfield cautioned: "Sirs, we should seize the moment to constitute ourselves as a Nation; and the person charged with normalizing the existence of the Nation should bear this in mind. The Argentine Republic does not exist: these are the circumstances we face when a man comes along to offer us everything we now possess."[16] But even this elder jurist upbraided the concentration of powers in the hands of the Governors, whose delegates unilaterally signed the Accord without the assent of provincial legislatures.

As the debate unfolded, Buenos Aires drifted from the course Urquiza struggled to steer. Urquiza lashed out: he shut down the *porteño* press, closed the Assembly, and ordered Vélez Sarsfield, Mitre, Alsina, and others to leave Buenos Aires—permanently winning him the ire of the province he needed to recruit most. The Palermo artillery trained their guns on the Retiro Plaza while the cavalry patrolled the streets. Buenos Aires was an occupied city. In early September 1852, Urquiza left Palermo (his camp on the edge of Buenos Aires) for Santa Fe to convene the Constitutional Convention. Without the Director in command of the occupying forces, Buenos Aires became a cauldron of intrigue, and eventually revolted on September 11. Buenos Aires seceded from the Argentine Confederation and declared itself an independent state (see Map 5).[17]

The separation of Buenos Aires was a blow, but it did not scupper the provinces' eagerness to constitute a national state. Many, indeed, feigned optimism, hoping that Buenos Aires would rejoin once the Convention contrived a foundational charter.[18] Urquiza inaugurated the gathering with a promise that these labors would allow the long-suffering provinces "to rest from the weight of commitment they [had] carried since 1831," and urged delegates "to reconstruct the fatherland, to reestablish the pact of a dispersed family." He did not mean to offend Buenos Aires: "I did not wish to make ostentation out of a triumph over brothers, but simply to be the guarantor of a capitulation among mem-

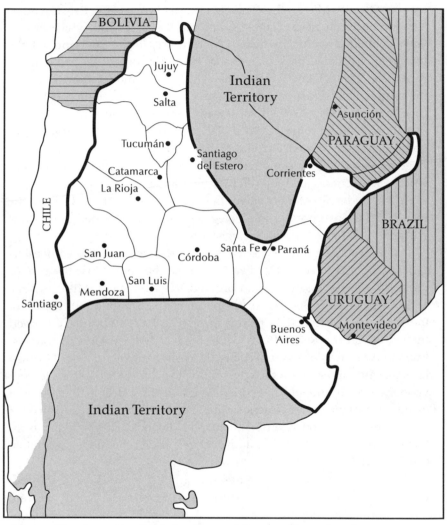

Map 5. The Argentine Confederation and Buenos Aires, 1852–62

bers of the same family."[19] With his promise to herald a federal charter, Urquiza withdrew to set up his makeshift capital in the Entre Ríos city of Paraná.

The Constitution bore all the hallmarks of the moment of its conception: a recipe for an emergency. As the country descended once again into civil war, the framers struggled to compile a charter whose process of inscription, and political substance, was designed to wind down endless disputes. As Vicente Fidel López (López y Planes's son and one of Urquiza's ministers) noted to the interim Director, the Convention had to run a difficult gauntlet. The delegates could not be seen to support tyrannical powers, and yet their decision-making had to avoid "discord among all the factions" in order to "create and settle a vigorous law." López held out little hope.[20]

Guided by this pessimism, the Convention submitted itself to Draconian rules. The Constitutional Convention opened in November 1852, and on December 24 struck a drafting committee whose dominant members were the young lawyer José Benjamin Gorostiaga and Juan María Gutiérrez, a central figure in the Generation of 1837 and now Urquiza's Minister of Government. Gutiérrez, like his friend Vicente Fidel López, held out little hope of success.[21] The Committee presented its report on April 18, 1853, and less than two weeks later, after eleven sessions, the Congress ratified the Articles of the new Constitution—miraculous speed considering the decades of wrangling preceding this founding moment. Urquiza feared that the Confederation would crumble and was desperate to be able to promulgate the Constitution on the commemorative date of May 25 (the day of the Viceroy's overthrow).[22]

Fear and pessimism informed more than the process of inscribing the Constitution: it also branded the outcome. By the 1850's, Argentine lawmakers had already begun to agree on some fundamental principles. They shared a legal culture rooted in a civil law tradition, one that shaped emerging republican dispositions in contrast to Anglo-American law. Trained in a jurisprudence that placed less weight on legal interpretation and emphasizing instead the immanent logic of statute, most of the men who gathered at the assemblies to work on the Argentine constitution did not embrace Anglo-American convictions that the meaning of the law depended on judicial scrutiny or oversight of potentially wayward legislators. Rather, they followed the path blazed by Napoleonic codification: rational statute governing public and private affairs could be made transparent and trans-historically applicable. Law

should not, in the eyes of the Argentine framers, be exposed to the subjective and arbitrary whims of magistrates. This orientation, it should be
stressed, owed less to some deep colonial tradition than to the superior
faith in the legislator over the judge as the source of rational law. From
as early as 1811, the question of judicial autonomy (James Madison's final check against majoritarian threats) was raised and debated, and for
the most part, lawmakers self-consciously opted to deplete judges of any
discretionary authority. This is an important consideration, because it informed the framers' views of checks and balances on state authority,
leading them to shift their concerns away from curbing public power
(unlike the North American framers) and toward building rational and
coherent state power free of arbitrary discretion.[23]

Second, all statesmen embraced federalism as the way to reconcile
local and national allegiances. Here, statists spurned the pieties of their
revolutionary forefathers and the example of the French Revolution. The
notion of a unitary polity—which, after all, was the primary form of political community imagined by state-builders across the Atlantic world
until the early nineteenth century—was bygone. The United States, a
great constitutional outlier, emerged as a much clearer alternative to
fragmented political identities. Still, North American federalism was
more useful in generalities than specifics. The United States, and to
some extent Canada soon thereafter, were still too decentralized as
models for states wishing to overcome decades of civil war. Yet the
question remained: how much and what kinds of power should be held
back from the supra-provincial political community?[24]

The answer was not too much and not too substantive. Reflecting the
framers' pessimistic and harried mood, they decidedly avoided the affirmative constitutionalism of their revolutionary predecessors. The
United States and French revolutions bequested aspirational talk for
public law; the wreckage of the River Plate's revolution did the opposite.
The drafting Committee's report insisted that federalism gird the state
structure—by default. Indeed, given the weakness of the federation, the
draft entrusted a national government with preserving harmony and
domestic peace within the political universe of the country as a whole,
even within jurisdictions previously assigned exclusively to provinces.
This was not a decentralized federation. Likewise, while the Constitution
made Argentina into a republic and a democracy governed by the rule of
law, steps had to be taken to avoid mayhem, by indirect presidential
elections and immunizing the polity from potential Congressional way-

wardness "after so many years of turbulence and administrative irregularity."[25] The framers, in a word, did not entirely trust the public. They
did not want a national state encumbered by obstacles to decisive action
should external or, more commonly, internal threats arise.

This fear of the public echoed through the most important inspiration for the framers, Juan Bautista Alberdi's *Bases y puntos de partida la
organización política de la República Argentina*, published originally in
Chile in May 1852, and shortly thereafter in an expanded edition in
Buenos Aires. This little book—which included a draft of a constitution—circulated more widely among the delegates at the Convention
than any other work.[26] Through the winter of 1851, Alberdi, hoping for
Urquiza's victory, had been publishing outlines in Chile and Montevideo. Indeed, he and his close friend Juan María Gutiérrez were traveling
together en route to Guayaquil when they learned of Rosas's fall. Gutiérrez rushed back to Buenos Aires, to become Urquiza's chief minister
and drafter, while Alberdi settled down in Valparaíso to design a blueprint constitution. In April he sent Gutiérrez and Urquiza the first version, and over the ensuing months, kept Gutiérrez, now the chief constitutional framer in Santa Fe, apprised of amendments.[27]

The chief brilliance of *Bases* lay in its crystallizing the legal sentiment
of day and shaping it into a workable formula for a state. Alberdi
tapped the historicist mood and eschewed the temptation to apply
models forged elsewhere, opting instead for a plan, not of the ideal republic, but, as he put it, of the "possible republic." He harbored no illu-
sions about what Argentina needed: unlike the United States, which
could create unity out of diversity through federalism, in Argentina diversity crumbled out of an original colonial unity. What was required
was a recomposition of central authority out of the natural powers
usurped by the provinces after 1820. If in the United States, unity was
artificial, decentralization was artificial in Argentina. This did not mean
that Alberdi did not want a federalist charter—far from it. What differed
was the model and purpose of federalism.[28]

The constitution, as far as Alberdi was concerned, should have a developmental purpose: to transform "the soil which we preserve as a de-
sert" into a civilization in its own right. A foundational law would invest virtue in politics and public institutions, thereby attracting European capital and settlers. This was the problem of earlier constitutions of
revolutionaries and unitarians. They were too concerned with inscribing
abstract rights and reproducing ideal types (both French and Anglo-

American). The 1826 Constitution in particular, obsessed with independence and liberty, overlooked the need for material progress. An appropriate charter, calibrated to circumstances, would provide the instrument for development—one that over the long run might spread the rights among a citizenry revolutionaries sought to allocate at the outset. Accordingly, Alberdi dispensed with talk of universal, unimpeachable rights and entitlements, stripped his code of expansive, florid language, and parsed it down to the unambiguous coinage of direct public powers of state and not private rights of civil society. The only concessions he made to a priori rights were to freedom of worship (to recruit European settlers) and private property (to enlist capital).[29]

Having dispensed abstract liberties to a second-order priority in order to uphold developmental goals, Alberdi turned to what the state should actually resemble. He wanted, based in part on what he saw as the success of Portalian Chile, a centralized federation and a powerful presidentialist polity to maintain order and peace and instill respect for the rule of law, to make of the state an instrument for capital accumulation. Constitutions, argued Alberdi, must be "types of merchant contracts of collective societies, formed especially to give our deserts to settlers." Indeed, for Alberdi, there was close homology between foundational charters of societies and commercial contracts between economic agents: "Though the written charter or constitution is not itself a law or pact, however, it proves, fixes. and maintains it invariable. The letter is a necessity for order and harmony. It guarantees stability for all important contracts by inscribing it—and what contract can be more important than the constitutional contract?"[30]

This notion of the constitution as a contract with reciprocal obligations between a people and a state was by no means original. But it harbored important implications for the future of Argentine democracy. Alberdi's quest for public stability compelled him to diminish a longstanding liberal image of a people endowed with rights to accept or reject the contract with governments. By the nineteenth century, elections had emerged as the ritual to ratify or reject the bonds between states and society. As far as Alberdi and many of his generation were concerned, this way of preserving the overarching contract (by giving people rights to support or reject their political representatives) threatened the no less important flip side, investing in the state the obligation to promote general welfare. Enfranchising people in a society deprived of norms weakened the state's ability to preserve an order necessary to foster market-driven activity and commercial prosperity. The contractarian balance had tilted too far in favor of society. Alberdi wanted to restore the state's ability to fulfill its commercial purpose. The only way to do this was by assuring political stability, thwarting popular demands and even curbing representation, which might upset collective goals, and protecting the rights of property. He confided to Gutiérrez that wide suffrage "has yielded the fruit it always will: so long as the masses [*populacho*] are called to vote, the masses [*populacho*] will elect boys who say nice phrases so that they may represent them. Electoral reform for the sense of order is the first thing to be considered."

The result: Alberdi ditched the North American checks-and-balances system and notion of states' rights. Internal constraints by creating autonomous branches of legislative, judicial, and executive powers were to be avoided. The same applied to external constraints of giving citizens unimpeachable rights to defend themselves against an intrusive state. He conceded that a measure of provincial sovereignty was an expedient to enlist short-term support, and admitted that some semblance of divided powers would be necessary to prevent the republic from sliding into dictatorship, but neither of these measures should obstruct a strong central state. Alberdi was fond of saying that he wanted to replace the despotism of one man with the despotism of law.[31] The 1787 Constitution in the United States, much as Alberdi admired it, was fit for a preconstituted society, not one that needed reconstituting like Argentina's. In the United States, society transformed state power; in Argentina, the state would transform society.

There were, to be sure, other, more remote influences on the framers. The United States Constitution ("the model of rapid aggrandizement of civil and political liberty," as the drafting Committee told delegates) provided specific clues as to how to divide powers between central and local authorities, and how to contour the presidency. Gorostiaga in particular seems to have looked to the U.S. charter as a baseline for equilibrating state and federal powers.[32] Other documents, the U.S. Declaration of Independence, Thomas Paine's *Common Sense*, constitutions of other Latin American republics, and even Chief Justice Joseph Story's *Commentaries on the Constitution of the United States* (translated into French in 1843) shared the stage. It is safe to say that no single external model shaped the framers' blueprint. At best, the Argentine Constitution of 1853 represented a bricolage of influences (exemplified in Alberdi's *Bases*) assimilated to give the republic a charter it immediately needed, not necessarily what it ideally wanted. In the words of one delegate, prior concerns with theory and abstraction should be avoided. "This exaggeration of exalted principles resulted in a furor of their proclamations. . . . These same Constitutions have been among us the focus and pretext and the greatest anarchy, positive lessons in upheaval and scandal, beginning with the destruction of the Congresses gathered to avoid them." He urged instead that these "principles be fit to the na-ture and peculiarity of the country where they should be applied."[33] Ar-gentina's constitutional spirit of the 1850's distilled the "systematic eclecticism" of the Generation of 1837, shaping ideas of statehood with an instrumental zeal to apply them to a convulsive reality.[34]

The debate itself was remarkably bereft of discord, and even deep reflection on the significance of the blueprint at stake—especially com-pared with the deliberations in Philadelphia and Paris. Most articles were not even discussed—the potpourri of U.S., Chilean, and Swiss charters, blended from Alberdi's *Bases*, for the most part stuck. Two camps emerged, one more liberal and concerned with constructing a state to mold a new national community, and another, more conserva-tive, concerned above all with preserving the toeholds of the Catholic church over education and civil law (these concerns, as several delegates repeatedly insisted, were not matters for the Constitution, but for subse-quent specific legislation, and were easily assuaged). Others sometimes expressed concerns about the prematurity of a constitution, arguing that without Buenos Aires, any charter would become the document solidi-fying disunion; others brushed off Rosas's earlier views that a meta-law could only come at the end of the process of social transformation through the exercise of public power. In general these objections were quickly squelched, and if a delegate persisted, Gutiérrez marshaled his peerless intellectual skills (especially in an Convention populated with an unremarkable majority) to put uneasy minds at rest. He argued forcefully that citizens would only learn respect for law if the state itself were beholden to a meta-law itself. Forty years of disorder had shown, he argued, just how a constitutionless polity left the rights of citizens and property rights in perpetual insecurity.[35] With very few exceptions, the drafted articles were approved without serious amendment.

The Committee's draft can be broken down into three segments. Prefaced with a brief prologue, it outlined state powers and the rights of citizens. First, the Constitution outlined the federal structure of the state, rejecting the pretensions of the unitarians in favor of the tradition of inter-provincial pacts, with the Federal Pact of 1831 and the San Nicolás Accords as the landmarks of federalism. Provinces were sovereign, independent, and to be governed by institutions outlined in their own constitutions. The federal government, based in a capitalized city of Buenos Aires, was vested with powers over foreign affairs and represented all the provinces in matters of general welfare—including trade and customs. By default (Article 101), all other responsibilities were matters for the provinces. One crucial clause (Article 6), however, curbed the autonomy of provinces. With the proverbial threat of regional insurrection or outright secession on their minds, the framers vested in the federal government the power to "intervene" in provincial affairs to defend "republican principles"—without much elaboration on what these principles might mean. This clause, with time, performed the task it was assigned: stabilize provincial affairs in the name of national unity and prevent civil strife that would imperil property.

Second, the federal government was to be comprised of three powers: an executive (Articles 71 to 90), a bicameral legislature (Articles 32 to 70), and a judiciary (Articles 91 to 100), each with a designated role—though not necessarily enjoying autonomy. Indeed, in the name of creating political powers to maintain the stability of the union—and reflecting the suspicion held for legislative assemblies (Buenos Aires' Assembly's behavior only fueled this impression) and averse to investing powers in the subjective wills of magistrates—the Constitution promulgated a powerful executive branch. The President enjoyed sweeping powers to govern by decree in the event of emergencies. Congress did not enjoy powers to vet Ministers or Justices. The Senate merely had to "agree" to the Executive's choice of judges (Article 83, Section 5). This last deliberate oversight ensured that the magistracy reflected executive will. Very seldom has the Supreme Court held the executive to be *ultra vires*, often finding—not without reason—provincial interventions and roughshod treatment of Congress to be permissible by the Constitution.

Finally, as a brake on state powers, the Constitution (especially Article 14) outlined a set of basic rights and guarantees for the citizenry: citizens were free to travel, work, trade, publish without censure, associate, worship, and enjoy their property. But what did these rights *mean*? Rights were vested in persons before the state, as would befit an enlightened charter. But these rights were more clearly upheld in matters of conflicts between citizens than between the citizen and the state. Indeed, if the state trod on basic rights of one or some individuals (so the Supreme Court tended to argue, often paraphrasing justifications issued from the Presidency), it was so that the abstract rights of the community of individuals as a whole would not be menaced. Moreover, in light of the weight given to the federal government to preserve stability, and the powers of the executive branch in particular, external checks on state powers of the sort trumpeted in the U.S. Bill of Rights were, in the breach, more often ignored than respected.[36]

The approval of the Constitution was as expeditious as its deliberation. There was nothing akin to the broad, public debates held in the United States when the Articles faced state ratification.[37] This was, of course intentional: the framers sought to reaggregate the political location of sovereignty into a new framework without dealing with the obstacles thrown up in the wake of the eclipse of the Empire. On May 1, 1853, the Convention approved the Articles; on May 5 Urquiza was apprised and in turn dispatched the news of the ratification to the provinces. According to the terms of the San Nicolás Accord (a point to which the Buenos Aires Assembly vociferously objected), the provinces alienated their right to examine and vote on the charter. The approval of the Convention and the acting Director of the Republic sufficed. This foundational practice set the stage for a centralized and executive-dominated system of public law. There is no evidence of any provincial opposition outside Buenos Aires—a fatigued people accepted the new terms of political association. The Convention heralded the démarche of a new federalist spirit, transcending the old federation's "dangerous, vague, and absurd significance . . ."[38]

Pragmatism and urgency shaped the form of ratification and eventual contents of Argentina's charter. Argentina ran the gamut from the florid, aspirational language of eighteenth-century constitutionalism, which appeared to bring the republic nothing but malaise, to the dour, constructivist statism of the nineteenth century.

It is important, however, to note that the apparent republican differences between the United States and Argentina were latent. The Argentine Constitution did divide powers and did inscribe prior rights of citizens (especially property rights), though such internal and external constraints were more muted than in the United States. As important as the text was in creating a polity to defend public order was a context that made that order all the more elusive. In the end, persistent conflict eroded constraints on state authority and intensified efforts to use that authority to generate social order.

Constitutional Discontents

By hitching hitherto sovereign provinces to a centralized and presidentialist polity, the Constitution of 1853 immediately confronted the basic component without which the Constitution was bereft of meaning: the independent state of Buenos Aires. It took time, but Buenos Aires would find in this new brand of Spartan constitutionalism the opportunity to hitch the polity to the lodestar of its capital. It took another eight years to integrate Buenos Aires into the federation, by which time it assumed the center of a hobbled and exhausted Confederation.

Buenos Aires greeted the news of a Constitution by heating up the rhetoric. Since the charter transferred some coveted powers from provinces to the federal government, Buenos Aires dug in its heels.

The obstacles to reunification were as political as they were doctrinal, reflecting a wariness about *how* power would be wielded, as well as for what purpose. On both sides of the border, the defense of property and the promotion of economic growth through strong public institutions were common goals. Part of the trouble was the continuing presence of Urquiza, elected as the Confederation's first President on February 22, 1854. *Porteños* aimed their viscera at the man who once freed them from Rosista tyranny but who now, in their eyes, proposed to reassert an even more diabolical regime. Vélez Sarsfield was unusually graphic (for him): "The word constitution is a lie on the lips of General Urquiza, vomited between his disrespectful cackles and drowning in the waves of despotism."[39] *La Tribuna* argued that Urquiza was none other than a reincarnation of Rosas. This secular infidel, illegitimately arrogating powers to himself as the President, threatened to cripple civil society, the "essence of liberalism," and despoil the rule of law.[40] The Buenos Aires press so saturated the public sphere with the blended metaphors of personalized hatred that it became very difficult for any politician to venture a more compromising tone as long as Urquiza ruled in Paraná—lest he was prepared to bury his political career.

There were also substantive reasons given for spurning the Confederation's invitation to join the state-building exercise. If the Confederation framers followed Alberdi's injunction to reaggregate political authority in the hands of the national executive, some *porteños* had misgivings about the costs this would imply for the charter's legitimacy. The people, according to Vélez Sarsfield, had to be present at the moment of the constitution's conception. And the people were not solely incarnate in the provisional Director, who was not elected, nor in the delegates to the Convention, who were not required to follow specific instructions from their Assemblies, nor to deliver their product for legislative approval. "It is not enough," Vélez Sarsfield wrote, "that a Constitution work for the happiness of a people. To realize it, it is necessary that the people take part . . . and from its origin they be consulted in all the acts that proceed until its promulgation, the seal of legality." Vélez Sarsfield, like others, objected less to the final document than to the way it was promulgated: "We accept the medicine, but we reject the doctor."[41]

More troublesome was the proposal to sever the city of Buenos Aires from the rest of the province—an idea floating about from Rivadavia's failed 1826 Constitution. Not only did this threaten to reduce the province of Buenos Aires to the same political latitude as the rest of the provinces, but it deprived the city of its own constitutive bodies—for without an elected governor of its own (but merely a mayor designated by the national executive), metropolitans in effect would enjoy fewer powers to exercise sovereign rights than citizens elsewhere in the Republic. What was designed as a means to neutralize the imbalance of the federation was a double incursion, as far as Buenos Aires was concerned, on its autonomy.[42]

It is important, however, to underscore *porteño* ambivalence. Essentially they agreed with the framers that splintered sovereignty led to decades of turmoil, and thus moved, more or less, in the same direction toward a centralist presidentialist system. But the process of skirting legislative ratification and depletion of judicial autonomy frightened not a few jurists—not least because, in the way Urquiza sought to rush the Constitution into existence, it threatened to deprive Buenos Aires of any control of the language or outcome of the process. If pessimism led framers to augment national executive state powers, it inspired inverse fears on the part of Buenos Aires that it would have to relinquish provincial powers involuntarily. They did not disagree in their suspicions and misgivings about the unruliness of Argentine civil society; they disagreed on how to create public rules to tame it. As Carlos Tejedor, a fervent Buenos Aires autonomist, wrote to Gutiérrez in Santa Fe, *porteños* wanted a constitution as badly as the Confederation to put an end to upheaval; they just resented their sacrifice to the method and language of constitution-framing implied by Urquiza's hurried agenda.[43]

Not to be outdone in the job of constituting the political community to rescue it from itself, Buenos Aires also rushed to promulgate a charter—even more quickly, with even less deliberation and concern for ratification or review than the framers in Santa Fe.[44] Not surprisingly, the Buenos Aires Constitution of 1854 is an uninspiring document: a catalogue of attributions to various branches, dividing up powers with the same asymmetry Alberdi contrived for the nation. Vélez Sarsfield, for one, wanted an executive-dominated polity for the province: "Liberty and order are constantly disputed, and very rarely does one of these principles sacrifice itself for the other. The friends of liberty have fallen into the painful trap of depriving the Executive of action and force." Indeed, the Constitution should bequeath the Governor so many faculties that he should not even have to turn to the Assembly for extraordinary emergency powers—as Rosas had done. For Vélez Sarsfield, "a strong constitutional power is to dictatorship what order is to slavery. The first is the most solid base of liberty, the other is the pedestal of despotism."[45] He echoed the sentiment among many of Buenos Aires' leading men: the constitution should restore and preserve order, and worry about liberating homilies later. Above all, the charter should not proclaim goals and inscribe aspirations for a people unprepared to realize them.[46]

The mood going into Buenos Aires' round of constitution-making resembled Santa Fe's. The recently elected Governor Pastor Obligado, named a Commission in September 1853, charging it with presenting a draft by the end of the year. In early March, the Assembly opened debate; on April 8, 1854, it approved the last article of the Constitution, and on May 23, a public ceremony in the Plaza de la Victoria promulgated the charter. Throughout, the only real source of discord came from a minority group, led by Mitre, against the fierce autonomist strain of the constitution. For Mitre, Vélez Sarsfield, and a few others, there was never any question that Buenos Aires would rejoin the Confederation—the question was when and on what terms. The autonomists, led by Valentín Alsina, held out no hope for the impoverished and teetering Confederation—for all intents and purposes Buenos Aires could retain its economic grip on the region with the port and the most coveted Pampa land as its backyard. Political union only brought trouble.[47]

Perhaps even more than Alberdi's formula, Buenos Aires sought material advancement as a basis for political unification. By the mid-1850's, Buenos Aires was in the throes of experiencing the full impact of trans-Atlantic free trade. New exports were booming. Foreigners poured into the city. In Europe, there was much talk of setting up agrarian colonies in the Pampas. In both Paraná and Buenos Aires, the feeling was that economic progress would be the salve of unity. The issue was which side would prove the more powerful engine of expansion and thus the force behind incorporation. Both sides agreed that the charter should be a trade-promoting instrument above all, for commerce was the true source for stability and unity. "The laws of politics are human," noted Sarmiento, but "laws of commerce and material interests are divine laws, and men must forcibly recognize this if they do not wish to violate natural laws."[48] The charter should promote good administration, especially in the Pampas, where most of the investment activity was unfolding. This meant protecting property rights. "The guarantees of property and persons will be an illusion in the countryside as long as there is not good administration. . . . Without achieving this, and other indispensable complements to the Constitution, the Constitution on its own is nothing more than a promise awaiting fulfillment."[49] Like the 1853 national Constitution, Buenos Aires aimed to depoliticize the public sphere and modulated the charter to promote the free flow and deployment of resources for trade and production.[50] Trade, colonization, and foreign investment dominated the news and, in the way *porteños* were formulating their political future, were becoming the baselines for assessing the efficacy of constitutionalism.

There is something of a paradox here. On the one hand, Argentines were more divided than ever, with Buenos Aires severed from the rest of the provinces. Yet, among statesmen on both sides, there was never more consensus about the lexicon and conduct of politics: that it should be stripped of aspirational intents for public virtue and deliver good administration for private purposes. In some respects, the paradox is less real than apparent. Moderates on both sides continued to nurture plans for reunification. The secession crisis bore little in common with the crisis engulfing the United States at the same time over much more fundamental constitutional principles. But the paradox was enough to sustain a clash between Argentina's two greatest nineteenth-century thinkers: Juan Bautista Alberdi and Domingo Faustino Sarmiento. What is remarkable about the debate, in spite of the venom they directed at each other, is the convergence in the way they imagined the Argentine public sphere and the role of the state.

Trouble had been brewing even before Urquiza defeated Rosas. Sarmiento felt spurned when the General did not accept his *Argirópolis* as the blueprint for reintegration in 1852 and gave him only a modest post within the Great Army.[51] Alberdi and Sarmiento had disagreed over things before, but the promulgation of the 1853 Constitution drove a permanent wedge between the two. Sarmiento issued the first strike in a series of essays published in several newspapers in Buenos Aires, attacking Urquiza, and then went straight for the 1853 Constitution.[52] For Sarmiento, the critical issue, following on his reflections in *Facundo*, was the legacy of colonialism. The viceregal experience had sowed propensities to anarchy and localism—forces barely contained by the mystified, personalized, and charismatic authority of the monarch. The only people with more than a provincial, localist consciousness were the port-dwellers of Buenos Aires—subjects, by location and vocation, whose cosmopolitanism served as a beacon of civilization. With the collapse of the empire, the irrepressible forces of provincialism clouded Buenos Aires' light. Thus, as Argentines approached their constitutional moment in the 1850's, in Sarmiento's view they were following a path opened by the U.S. framers in the 1780's: trying to build a union out of diversity. What made Argentina different was the incapacity of provincial sovereignties to guarantee liberty, which made the need for a true union all the more urgent. Only in this fashion would Argentina be able to turn its back completely on its Spanish heritage. There was simply no integrative legacy to be built upon; it would be better to follow the path of the United States.[53] This position offered intellectual arsenal to Buenos Aires autonomists' claims to enter and shape the constitution on its own terms, and thus enjoy rights to secession if the charter did not meet the Province's demands—hence acting as the herald for an enduring unity.[54]

Alberdi inverted the causal order. In four open letters to his erstwhile friend, followed by a long meditation on the 1854 Constitution of Buenos Aires, Alberdi's historicism led him to quite a different appreciation of the colonial heritage.[55] For the architect of the 1853 Constitution, what was natural was unity. The revolution and its aftermath simply fractured the body politic. The task of the framers was then to restore a natural propensity to centralization. The provinces of the River Plate bore, consequently, little resemblance to the North American states on the eve of ratification of the Articles of the 1787 Constitution. For the United States, unity was a concoction; for Argentina it was a return to a natural political universe temporarily shattered by the actions of an inept crown and zealous revolutionaries. "We are the product" of Spanish public law, argued Alberdi, "and while we should strive to change the ends, the *means* must be, for a long time, those in which we have been educated."[56] The notion of provincial sovereignty prior to the nation was an obstacle to unity, and without unity, the entire region was condemned to festering conflict. Instead, to realize lofty ends, statesmen and jurists were going to have to work within the framework of their institutional heritage based on a prior existence of a larger political community, pitiable as the nation might be. Alberdi, instead, advised that the only way to "perfect liberty" was through "imperfect liberty."[57]

If their federalist sensibilities differed, Alberdi and Sarmiento disagreed less when it came to locating the agency of society in the formation of public powers.[58] The former saw the charter as a force for stabilization through the restoration of a more natural order. The Constitution should be the passive protector of property rights and contractual obligations. In this fashion, it would sow the political preconditions for settlement and capital accumulation. With economic growth, citizens could realize their private potentials and acquire the virtues necessary to contribute to the good public life. Alberdi did not deny the possibility that people might learn to become more affirmative participants in collective decisions governing the public world, but he did not think it was the role of public institutions to tutor people. They could only learn by taking advantage of the minimal conditions set down by the charter for the terms of coexistence: the inviolability of contracts, both public and private. People would learn to become upstanding public agents through purposive private activity.[59]

Sarmiento was more sanguine when it came to the potential for public institutions to wean people from unfortunate habits. The constitution could be active. By proclaiming the state's role of transforming society into a more salubrious and harmonic entity, Sarmiento imagined a different constitutional purpose. This is one of the reasons he was to make such a fuss later in his career about education and public schools. But it also underscored what he saw in the 1787 Constitution of the United States: a charter with affirmative goals, designed to nurture society into a democracy. But Sarmiento agreed with Alberdi about the dangers of transposing a North American–style universal Bill of Rights to less fertile terrain. This did not mean that these rights had to be dispensed equally, nor that the state could not uplift or transform social classes unfit to exercise rights. "They tell us," Sarmiento argued, "that the people are not of a state to use such perfect institutions. Should we judge by the Argentine Republic, we would say that these people are prepared only for strangling, thieving, lounging about, devastating, and destroying. . . .

Now, a constitution is not the law of public conduct for everyone. The constitution for the popular masses is ordinary laws, the judges who apply them, and the police for security. The educated classes are those that need a constitution to assure freedom of action and thought, press, justice, property, etc., and it is not difficult for them to understand the game of institutions they adopt."[60] Differential allocation of rights ensured that the entitled citizenry would enjoy the privileges and immunities of their North American cousins. Moreover, those left out would aspire to the good life, learn proper public and private manners, and earn the rights that enlightened eighteenth-century men mistakenly considered natural. As a result, Sarmiento was prepared to champion the notion of external constraints on state powers (and he cited Madison agreeably on this point) by inscribing a Bill of Rights; he simply did not believe that these rights should be allocated equally, precisely because most of society was ill-prepared to use these rights in virtuous ways.

Thus, if Alberdi and Sarmiento disagreed on the function of public powers and the status of the constitution in framing the language of the state, they at least agreed that Argentine society (or at least a majority) was not prepared to be the willful agent of its own future. Whether through private activity or public nurture, the republic would only realize a robust notion of citizenship at the end of a very long process of social change—one the citizens were not necessarily invited to define or elect.[61]

Reunion

Upon this paradoxical consensus of a public unprepared for its own destiny, political leaders in Paraná and Buenos Aires in the end found a basis for convergence. To pursue their respective state-building missions, the Confederation and the Province waged crippling and, from the Confederation's point of view, ruinous economic war against each other. The conflict exhausted the battle over the bargaining terms of politics (the ability of contending forces to occupy political positions or ability to nurture alternative bargaining rules). It created a political convergence by default.

The unity finally achieved by 1861 was a *de facto* rapprochement forged out of fatigue from a half-century of civil war. In the words of *El Plata* editorialists, "liberty has degenerated to license, and as in so many other instances, the fruits are bitter and the consequences, with some perspective, are horrifying. The depth of our plight demands a swift and energetic remedy."[62] For Vicente Fidel López, lawlessness bred unbridled rent-seeking and political turmoil: "The individuals in a disordered society want an order to oppress competition while external passions tie the hands of others but not their own passions; and from this we get tyranny of factions, reactions, and disorder."[63] Even Sarmiento pleaded for imperfect accommodation in the name of peace. Buenos Aires should accept some loss of autonomy to avoid another cycle of warfare.[64]

It became clear that Urquiza could not win the fiscal war: bereft of a port and customs revenues, his union wallowed. Urquiza had to drag Buenos Aires back into the fold or else let the Confederation crumble. The long-awaited showdown finally took place on the outskirts of Buenos Aires, as Urquiza took on Mitre's Buenos Aires armies in the Battle of Cepeda on October 23, 1859. Urquiza's triumph was a pyrrhic victory.[65] Buenos Aires accepted the terms of the Pact of Union on November 11, 1859—but unhappily. This agreement inducted Buenos Aires back into the Confederation. It also made some concession to long-standing provincial demands: a Buenos Aires convention would examine the 1853 Constitution and could propose amendments; the city would not be federalized and severed from the province without the provincial Legislature's approval; and in fiscal terms, Buenos Aires resources would remain provincial, except for customs receipts that passed to national jurisdiction, but the national government had to back the province's expenditure needs for five years.

This was important: the peace terms shattered Buenos Aires' unity. Factions emerged that could then negotiate each successive stage of integration.[66] By paving the way to reunion, the Pact displaced the discord between Paraná and Buenos Aires to Buenos Aires itself, opening up a latent dispute between autonomists, who feared that Buenos Aires would be hamstrung by unstable and poorer provinces, and nation-builders who felt that Buenos Aires could help transform its fellow provinces. Through late 1859 and early 1860, the city was in the grip of a raging debate over whether and how much power should be transferred to national authorities. Finally, in April 1860, the amending committee presented its draft, edited by Mitre, and after three weeks of deliberation, the Legislature approved the proposal for Paraná.[67]

To consider Buenos Aires' amendments, the Confederation convoked a Convention in Santa Fe in September, and on the whole approved Buenos Aires' recommendations. The 1860 reforms to the Constitution did not alter the essential components of the 1853 version, but refined issues concerning federal-provincial balances of power: the provincial legislature had the right to vote on the federalization of the city; Article 6 was recalibrated to allow federal government "interventions" in provincial domains to repel invasions from abroad or other provinces and "to guarantee the Republican form of Government"—a sweeping concession to national power, and one that would be used repeatedly to dismantle governments with which federal authorities had conflicts; the national Congress did forfeit some authority to scrutinize reforms to provincial constitutions (Articles 5 and 64) or to suppress provincial impeachment procedures (Article 41). In judicial matters, the Supreme Court was mandated to decide on appeals concerning jurisdictional conflicts within provinces, and emerging national codes (commercial, civil, penal, and so on) were binding throughout the Republic. If anything, national powers were slightly enhanced.

The new framers did not enhance civil society's autonomy from the state by inscribing abstract rights. The slim concessions to legislative autonomy or judicial powers stuck. The only modification to social checks on state power was a new clause prohibiting Congressional (but not Presidential) curbs on freedom of the press and the abolition of execution with spears or daggers. The drafting Committee's report explained to the Buenos Aires Assembly that individual rights were primordial, but the only way to uphold them was through social respect for law in general. The result was, any specification of rights was redundant. A good constitution would limit public powers anyway, obviating the need to specify private, anterior rights. The framers grazed the issue when they considered Article 6—mandating federal authorities to intervene in provincial matters to preserve the republican form of government. Some Deputies rumbled about the menace of federal powers and potential abuses and attacks on individual liberties in the name of a capacious cause like republican defense. But the clause, with minor tinkering, survived.[68]

Reforms sharpened the purpose of the 1853 charter, and as the Buenos Aires drafting committee noted, the goal was essentially modest: "Whatever has been (the 1853 Constitution's) origins and the irregularity of its application, seven years of experimenting with free institutions have proven that there exists in this Constitution an essentially conservative principle; as accumulated experience over these years confirms the need and convenience of perfecting it, this is the occasion for the reunion of the ancient and glorious Argentine Republic under the auspices of a freely discussed common law accepted by all the Provinces and a common reformed agreement informed by the lessons of time and the needs of a new era and a new situation."[69] After a brief debate, focused primarily on the logistics of customs unification, the Convention in Santa Fe approved the reforms.

To get to this point, Mitre had to do some fancy political tacking to navigate through the shoals of local autonomist opposition. Urquiza, as it turned out, was a less successful helmsman. The post-Cepeda realignment shattered Confederate consensus. Some were desperate for unity; others grew increasingly angry at Buenos Aires. The Confederation quickly slipped into an advanced state of political decomposition. The election in March 1860 brought Santiago Derqui—a schemer aligned with many of the forces embittered by Buenos Aires' stranglehold on the union's fortunes—to presidential power. The loser was Mariano Fragueiro, the aged Cordoban merchant, and much the preferred candidate for moderate nation-building forces on both sides. To José Benjamin Gorostiaga, this was the last straw. The co-author of the 1853 Constitution and once Minister in Urquiza's Cabinet was so thoroughly disgusted by the factionalism and ineptitude surrounding Derqui, that he conceded to Sarmiento that the only hope for the republic lay in Buenos Aires.[70]

Unfortunately, the fragmentation of the blocs on either side of the struggle temporarily favored the more resistant factions. Thus, in spite of the progress marked by the Pact of Union and Buenos Aires' terms of incorporation, more recalcitrant parties on both sides dug in their heels and forced a final clash. Some members of the National Legislature, still smarting from Buenos Aires' arrogance and pretensions, subjected the deputies from Buenos Aires to humiliating abuse when they tried to join the Santa Fe Convention. Buenos Aires autonomists howled in indignation.[71] Worse, the penury of the Confederation wrought hardship across the region. Provinces throughout the republic began to tumble into civil war. As the Convention entertained the debate over the constitutional reforms, the provinces began lining up along pro–Buenos Aires or pro-Confederation lines (in effect meaning allegiance to Mitre or Derqui). In long-festering San Juan, a band of pro-Mitre supporters assassinated Governor Virasoro in November 1860 and put the "liberal" Antonio Aberastain in power. Derqui rushed to "intervene" and restore order, culminating in Aberastain's public execution and a revanchist campaign against "liberals." Buenos Aires pilloried Derqui as the author of the carnage. And as Corrientes likewise lapsed into political bloodletting, Confederate and Buenos Aires authorities retreated once again to their bellicose positions. Even President Derqui secretly confided to Mitre that the entire country was in arms and that he feared complete degeneration to a savage war of recrimination—to which Mitre replied with unminced words: "What have you done with the bloody triumph of your commissioner against the people of San Juan? What will you do with a defeated San Juan, enslaved and brutalized by *puntanos* and *mendocinos* [the provincial garrisons sent to crush the unrest]?"[72]

Across the region, people sank into despair. For Lina Beck-Bernard, the Alsatian wife of Charles Beck, a representative of a colonization agency, the crisis of 1861 was the worst in a series of unremitting misfortunes. Colonists patrolled their plots to protect their crops against bandits and starving soldiers. Horses were sealed up behind barricades to prevent rustling. For weeks on end, families hid in their homes; women sewed their jewelry and the family's gold into their clothes.[73]

Urquiza, meanwhile, dismayed by the spectacle of spreading butchery and the furious rhetoric flowing from pens in both camps, struggled to keep up negotiations. His efforts were futile. He agreed, once again, to a last-ditch effort to force Buenos Aires back into the union. In the year and a half since Cepeda, however, the Confederation had lost much of its ability to win a war, even if it could triumph on the battlefield (Urquiza was still the better warrior): many of the provinces had already begun to drift to the Buenos Aires orbit, Buenos Aires could now blockade the rivers effectively and choke all traffic, and the Confederation's finances were reduced to Urquiza's own personal bankrolling. In this context, on September 17, 1861, the two armies met again in a battlefield, near the shore of the Pavón River. The battle produced no clear victor.[74] General Urquiza withdrew before humbling Mitre once again. It seems likely that he recognized the pointlessness of the entire exercise, and in the heat of the struggle opted to disband the war and to negotiate a deal with Mitre and Buenos Aires.

The Battle of Pavón did not immediately decide things either way, but it quickly tilted the balance of forces against recalcitrants on both sides. With Urquiza now playing a neutral arbiter's role, Derqui enjoyed only spectral authority. In November, he fled to Montevideo; the Confederation resistors possessed no more political resources. Mitre now enjoyed the undisputed upper hand. He marched into Santa Fe and set about reconstructing a semblance of national authority. Lina Beck-Bernard was struck by the orderliness of Mitre's troops, and the entire region found the Buenos Aires soldiers' habit of paying for goods they appropriated along the way a pleasant shock.[75] Buenos Aires' armies under General Wenceslao Paunero marched across the provinces restoring "order" (by which they meant purging local governments of any Derqui-supporters and placing loyalists to Buenos Aires in control).[76] For the next decade, Buenos Aires and later National Armies crushed the remnant voices of provincial sovereignty and the fading federalism of the revolutionary era. These voices, led above all by Vicente "Chacho" Peñaloza in La Rioja, now called themselves "federalists" and waged a determined—if tragic—struggle to resist the centralizing designs of the Buenos Aires political leadership.[77]

Mitre also turned on his Buenos Aires autonomist rivals. He could not use the sanguinary tactics of the Interior and instead brokered an agreement to support some of the autonomists aspiring to high offices (Alsina went to the Senate, but his son Adolfo donned the mantle of recalcitrant autonomism) and postponed the Constitution's edict to separate Buenos Aires city from the province (this problem had to wait until 1880 to be resolved) while at the same time making Buenos Aires city the capital of the republic—thereby allowing Buenos Aires to have the cake of national integration and eat it too. By the end of September 1862, the struggle in Buenos Aires was over, all sides agreed to this costless compromise. Buenos Aires, in effect, rejoined the confederation on terms that clarified to all the location of the nation's political center of gravity. As if to confirm the reaggregation of concentrated public power, General Bartolomé Mitre was sworn in as the first constitutional president of the Argentine Republic on October 12, 1862. A week later, the new President appeared before Congress to share with the Legislature their mission: "We are convoked and reunited here by the will of the people, in the midst of chaos . . . without any conservative principle of political society but the sentiment of law. Your mission has been to put an end to the revolution by constitutional means, without upheaval, without pain."[78]

Conclusion

Argentina's road to constitutionalism, once the unifying force of the monarch vanished with no legitimate political heir to step into the breach, was both long and winding. The reintegration of what was left of the Viceroyalty under a Constitution in 1862 was a major turning point in the country's history. To be sure, some business remained unfinished. Some provinces still chafed under the centralist garb of the Constitution. The exact status of the city of Buenos Aires, as simultaneous capital of the province that bore its name and the republic over which it ruled, still had to be disentangled. But Mitre's address to the Congress signified an irrevocable change in the rules of the political power game.

First, the new alignment defined the rules by which political actors would conduct their struggles. Centralization and presidentialism shifted the orbit of public representation and dispute resolution to new spheres, away from governors, away from the militaries (that were often the institutional girders for caudillos), and now away from legislative assemblies (which enjoyed unparalleled, if fleeting, prominence for the ten years of disunion). To be sure, regional politics, military power, and legislatures remained important—indeed, decisive—arenas reconciling public matters. But now they had to contend with a base of political authority emanating more from the office of the president than any other source. This transformed the conduct of agents vying for political space as they bargained and jostled with each other, creating a commanding height from which to negotiate public disputes that, until that moment, had wrenched the fragmented sovereignties of the River Plate. A keystone of state power was put in place. As Miguel Cané noted, Argentines could finally discuss public laws without questioning the principles of public power.[79]

If the Constitution inscribed the rules governing the conduct of parties during the bargaining process, it also set boundaries structuring alternatives to staying within the bargaining process. Without stable national authority, and without accepted means to channel collective demands into decisions, the opportunity cost of "exiting" the rules of the game, and playing by separate rules was low.[80] Hitherto, there had been little power—save the brutal hand of the caudillo vindictiveness—to enforce the rules, and therefore scant penalty to violating them. Furthermore, there was little incentive to be loyal to the makeup if one party arrogated to itself the yields of the game. This was, not surprisingly, the nub of the issue when it came to customs revenues: it was simply not worth any province's sacrifice to bankroll national authorities so long as the Province of Buenos Aires cornered the taxes on trans-Atlantic trade.

And there was no incentive for Buenos Aires to forfeit this power as long as national authorities were too weak to enforce a project that Buenos Aires advocated, such as the integration of a national market and an end to unruly neighbors. In the end, this logjam extended much more than just to customs (though their absolute and relative prominence in fiscal matters of state made them such a touchy—and decisive—matter). It involved all matters where public goods (like the supply of money, protection of property, and administration of justice) depended on state authority. As provinces embraced the Constitution, the costs of "exiting" the framework became punitive. In a positive sense, they would lose access to priceless fiscal spoils; negatively, they had to contend with an ascendant military power of Buenos Aires. From the 1860's forward, dissenters increasingly accepted "voice" as the means to express their discontent. Thus the Constitution crystallized the bargaining rules and increased the cost of trying to reshape the rules unilaterally or exiting from them altogether. In these senses, the Constitution finally provided the carapace of political integration—the original revolutionary goal.

But this Constitution came into being in an entirely different juncture and mood than the type of charter imagined during the revolution. If the revolutionaries ultimately believed in the immanent potential of freed colonial peoples, mid-century framers harbored a much more dismal outlook on society. They did not believe that removing mercantilist controls or lifting onerous obligations would, on their own, unleash the behavior of virtuous citizens. Decades of freedom led only to "license" and "vice," habits that in turn undermined the social fabric and made the River Plate practically ungovernable—except of course under the helm of caudillos, who were seen as the organic political expression of unruliness. The Constitution and the mode of its implementation— text and context—curbed checks and balances, thereby limiting the *internal* restraints on state power. Argentine framers wanted to create a less constrained executive authority than, for instance, the United States. "The Constitutional Congress," noted one writer, "did well to rescue the country from a heritage of disorder and anarchy encased in laws of universal suffrage."[81] What Argentina needed was a strong state with a relatively unimpeachable authority.

Framers did not stop at internal powers. The "constructivist" thrust also depleted constitutional commitments to upholding sweeping and universal rights of citizens, thereby curbing *external* restraints on state power. U.S. constitutionalism, in theory and in practice, embraced vested rights as a cornerstone for ensuring the rights of private persons independent of the state. For political reasons, Argentine framers decided not to inscribe sweeping private rights into the Constitution. The modified 1853 Constitution was harnessed to a conservative vintage of liberalism because erstwhile faiths in autonomous possessive individuals had taken such a beating.[82]

Constitution-making began to resolve the age-old challenge of generating pre-commitment powers of state, the meta laws of government. Argentines increasingly upheld political bargains, not so much because public institutions served private interests, but because Argentines adhered to the rules of bargaining. Respect for bargaining rules inscribed in the constitutional persuasions of the 1850's enabled public bargaining and eclipsed public fighting. Public bargaining in turn stabilized public life.

This was only the beginning of the end of the process of state- and market-formation. Restoring the internal ligaments of state power and immunizing it from the claims of a legally autonomous citizenry was but one side of a complex story of the legal reconstruction of River Plate society. Public authority created the necessary institutional conditions for markets to function. But consolidated political power, on its own, was an insufficient guarantor of the private interests of capital so long as vested rights remained ill-defined. Statesmen had created a capital for a republic, but only partially solved the riddle of how to make the republic serve the interests of capital. So how were private properties to survive without the precommitments provided by constitutions? To resolve this problem, Argentine statesmen had to shift the legal job of reconstructing property relations to other public domains: the creation and regulation of a legal tender by consolidating monetary authority, and the formalization of contract law through a commercial code. The next two chapters turn to these themes.

9 ⌒ The New Property of Merchant Capital

> Civil government supposes a certain subordination. But as the
> necessity of civil government gradually grows up with the
> acquisition of valuable property, so the principal causes which
> naturally introduce subordination gradually grow up with the
> growth of that valuable property.
>
> Adam Smith, *An Inquiry into the Nature and
> Causes of the Wealth of Nations*, book V

On the Road to Legal Formalism

By the middle of the nineteenth century, Buenos Aires' merchants hovered between two phases of commercial capitalism, two "structures of the conjuncture" of the world economy. The first phase, the political economy of mercantilism destroyed in the course of revolution, no longer defended guild rent-seeking. Andean silver was a bygone preciosity. A new generation of staple exports fostered an emerging successor phase of open competition and reintegrated the River Plate into the Atlantic world, eclipsing the old pattern of political trade and property rights. "Free trade," by the 1840's, meant that the only barriers to market activity were economic, not political. It also, at least in theory, implied that market participants enjoyed equal entitlements to bargain over the rights to procure and dispose of commodities. The state was no longer the sentinel of any single private group, including the promotion of dynastic ambition.

The movement from the first to the second phase of capitalist development was anything but smooth. Although the external conditions and terms of competition evolved, the bargaining rules did not follow apace. Faced with this exogenous transformation without local legal accompaniment, merchants redoubled their reliance on old regime jurisprudence. They did so not out of conviction but because they needed some mechanism to allocate rights and adjudicate conflicts over them—even if, as they were aware, the system in place was deeply imperfect. Thus as Buenos Aires merchants folded into the trans-Atlantic commercial revolution, they clung to the frayed and torn fabric of a legal order de-signed to defend corporate, guild concerns. *Jus mercatorum* provided a basis for relative, situational rights—a community jurisprudence that would allow individuals to engage in economic activity. Buenos Aires merchants and jurists still faced the issue of how to create new rules to defend individual rights and reflecting new concepts and sensibilities about property. How would they invert the legal sequence and replace the old corporate universe in favor of an alternative in which prosperity depended on individuals' enjoyment of untrammeled rights to exploit property? How would shifting notions of private rights create a new image of community, bound not so much by status but by contracts ne-gotiated between autonomous parties?

This was, of course, a vexing issue—one that has been skirted by re-cent political economists of the new institutional school, for whom laws adjust according to shifting interests, since in a competitive world agents abandon redundant or retardative laws in favor of better ones. Winners come; losers go. In this view, the transition from one property rights re-gime to the next is itself fairly seamless since it does not disrupt any sense of the merchants' own identity, not to mention the idea of collec-tive virtue. In other words, there are neither personal nor community politics involved in the legal commercial revolution, simply an evolution of law toward clear and enforceable rights. In effect, the pioneering work of Douglass North and others conflates the role of institutions in economic development with an actual theory or explanation of what causes some institutions to emerge, decay, or persist.[1] This unpunctu-ated adaptation of property rules misses the rich complexity of the po-litical process—for what made the transition so vexing was that the very public institutions required to monopolize and enforce legal sanctions were themselves the subject of open discord over the shape of the politi-cal community and the meanings of public sovereignty.

Chapter 9, in exploring this transformation, shows how the process was deeply political. It disrupted merchants' sense of property rights, posed a new set of collective action problems, and, accordingly, recast the balance of private rights and public powers. In the end, this trans-formation redefined bourgeois concerns and state powers to realize class identities and to create a juridical framework to mediate the interests of capital. This process did not unfold outside politics, but was an intrinsic part of the process of state-formation.

Change at the top enabled this transformation to unfold. Toppling the caudillo rulership of quasi-law opened the way for a new pattern of lawfulness. A decade of debate about the purpose and meaning of law for the political community at large—a theme explored in the previous chapter—converged around a constitutional persuasion favoring a centralized federation short on checks and balances, with weak provisions for vested rights, but touting an executive-dominated polity to resolve conflicts within the political community with greater legal ease. This constitutional turn created public spaces for deliberating other facets of legalizing the social order. In this sense the constitutional turn enabled other realms of law to evolve. As Urquiza himself acknowledged, public law channeled conflicts over public order into sanctioned and legitimate institutions. In matters of private rights law, however, the constitution said comparatively little.[2] Since the foundational charter of state offered scant guarantees for private rights, society required an ancillary process of institutional encoding—one that ran parallel to inscribing public powers. In effect the constitutional convergence of the 1850's did little for private rights directly, but it did nurture public spaces for second-tier public institutions to address matters of private justice.

But this was more than just a top-down process; it was also political from the bottom up, responding to developments within civil society itself. What Urquiza did not imagine was that merchants themselves had already embarked on the road to redefining commercial law, if not *de jure* then *de facto*. Within the ambit of the Commercial Tribunal, plaintiffs, defendants, and the custodians (judges, advisers, accountants, and a panoply of court officers) had revised the terms of their legal interactions autonomous from the state. Indeed, this arms-length, private reform initiated by society could only come from below so long as caudillos with a determined aversion to the rule of law were governing from above. Private agents had struggled to fashion a public court with transparent and intelligible rules to transcend collective action problems that mired commercial affairs in costly litigation in the decades after the revolution. With the Rosas years behind them, merchants and jurists advanced this transition more openly, debouching into a full-fledged movement to codify private rights, first with the Commercial Code of 1859, followed by Rural, Civil, and Criminal codes.

If this offers us a window onto the social side of state-formation, it also reveals a third political facet of the business of encoding private property: through collective conflict within the merchant class, a new sense of community interests emerged. In the ancien régime, merchants pandered to dynasts and their own guild concerns in the name of a pre-modern universal but absolute sovereign. The new order asked that merchants justify their property rights in different universal—public and republican—terms. Doing so required a level of legal abstraction and formality unfamiliar to the merchants of the early modern Atlantic world. By the 1850's, the day-to-day language of commercial litigation dispensed with property-talk of personal righteousness and honor in favor of abstract contractual freedoms and rights to demand that public courts uphold commitments inscribed in contracts, irrespective of the plaintiff's or defendant's personality. What mattered was the formal stipulation of the contract, not who signed it. In effect, the rules governing property obeyed a logic independent of particular, situational concerns. Freedom replaced fairness; will eclipsed equity; relational property gave way to discrete exchange relations.[3] A new private ordering system of property was emerging. What it lacked was the external force to brace these new rules and sensibilities of bargaining in place.

Defenders of the new order advised that property-talk subsist beyond politics. Getting there, however, was deeply political.

The Legal Consciousness of Merchant Capital

Trans-Atlantic trading transformed the setting of post-revolutionary state-formation in the River Plate. If independent Latin America embraced free trade from the start, Europeans dropped their protection to native producers gradually. Thanks to a series of measures starting with the abrogation of English Navigation Acts and the Corn Law in the 1840's, and culminating with the French abolition of tariffs on wool imports in the 1860's, primary producers of the Pampas faced flourishing and unobstructed markets.

The nature of exchange itself began to change. What had started in the 1830's—the shift from primitive jerked beef and hide exports to a more diversified portfolio of commodities—accelerated. Leading the way was wool. Insignificant in the 1820's, by the 1850's wool accounted for over 10 percent of Buenos Aires exports; and by the 1860's it was the dominant staple. At the same time, sheep-herding did not elbow out other agrarian staples—indeed, jerked beef and hides sales continued to flourish so long as slavery remained an important mode of production in the Atlantic basin. And by the 1860's, the Pampas began to show signs of commercial arable agrarian exports.[4]

Accompanying the new commodity trades were a host of intermediaries. Rising exports allowed imports to increase apace. More and more consumer goods entered the port to supply the growing ranks of Buenos Aires' retail outlets. The city was home to emerging strata of stores. As much the scene for legendary knife fights, gambling, and cockfights, the catch-all *pulpería* serviced a wide array of consumer needs, all the way to libations of the neighborhood tavern. The *pulpería* shelves groaned under the weight of petty tinware, clothing, and drygoods—and increasingly farm and ranching implements. These modest general stores, frequently run by Basque, Catalan, or Northern Italian families, dotted the urban and rural landscape of the Pampas.[5] Then there was the middleman importer, such as the seasoned American partnership of Zimmerman & Frazier, or the creole magnates of Jaime Llavallol & Sons, also mainly immigrants, generally from Germany or Britain, who handled business between the port and retailers. Finally, there was the big merchant who frequently emerged from the ranks of wholesalers to become an integrated outfit, importing, exporting, and in constant contact with partners and dealers throughout the Atlantic basin.[6] This was, to be sure, not a highly demarcated hierarchy of family businesses. With such a vibrant market, the opportunities for rapid social ascent—as well as catastrophic misfortune—perpetually erased the social boundaries within the merchant class. From bottom to top, merchants operated through extended formal and informal networks and family ties, becoming an important Atlantic outpost of a trans-Atlantic cosmopolitan bourgeoisie.[7]

More than any other factor, credit kept this cosmopolitan world alive with opportunity. Financial flows both unified the merchandising world and demarcated the hierarchies within it. At the apex of the commercial system was not just the integrated importer-exporter as handler of goods, but the financier—indeed it was importer-exporter family's access to finance capital that gave it the ability to merchandise from the commanding heights. At the bottom of the merchant pyramid was the general store and its sales employees (traveling salesmen) often working on consignments. They were invariably a class of debtors. Accordingly, finance flowed from the hands of a few big merchant families in Buenos Aires with links to Antwerp, Paris, and especially London and Liverpool, out to wholesalers and petty retailers in centrifugal form, to lubricate flows of remittances and commodities in centripetal directions.[8] What remained constant from the eighteenth century was that flows of capital enabled flows of commodities. In this fashion, the capitalists of Buenos Aires reshaped the trading space of the River Plate and sustained the commercial transformation of the region into a free-trade hub.

Thriving new staples inflated the opportunity cost of legal uncertainty. These wealth-creators repopulated the ranks of a Buenos Aires merchant class that had been wracked by revolutionary and civil warfare. They also placed greater strains on the old fiduciary system, requiring more liquidity from the cumbersome circulation of merchant money (like bills of exchange) and longer horizons for stable fixed-capital-formation. Reintegration into the Atlantic economy and the emergence of new property heightened anxieties about the laws governing obligations of contracts.

The ability to contract depended on two factors beyond the control of single bargainers. First, it depended on trust: vendors had to trust that purchasers would honor obligations; creditors stored faith in debtors' ability and willingness to make future payments. In the merchandising world of the River Plate, where money was in chronic short supply, these two types of transactions often fused into one hybrid deal. Wholesalers advanced goods to retailers, and retailers to consumers, in the hope of future payments. This was especially common in a vibrant and rapidly growing export economy that was by definition highly seasonal in the flow of expenses and revenues in the production and handling of staples. Wholesalers, importers, and exporters conducted their business in similar fashion—selling goods on consignment, thereby injecting credit transactions into commodity exchange. Even purer credit relations, like the use of bills of exchange (for shorter-term bargains) and mortgages (for longer-term investments) relied on trust. The second aspect of creating a contractarian culture was credible commitment of authorities lest trustful relations between bargainers be violated. Contractors had to be able to rely on or fear the prospect of enforcement by outside officials. If public officials failed, private thuggery was always an option—though it was an alternative short on legitimacy. Trust and credible commitment were two public components of the emerging contractarian society that enabled private competition to function. The transactional nature of exchange rested on internal solidarity and external enforcement mechanisms.[9]

This was the aspiration for many merchants of Buenos Aires. Their

problem was that, with weak public authority, and the many temptations to shuck obligations, move on, in general to free-ride on creditors'
collective need to do their business, how were merchants to create a regime of trust and credible commitment?[10] Early modern jurisprudence
had an answer: rely on a moral and paternalistic model of enforcing be-
havioral norms. This was, as Chapter 6 has shown, a system in duress
by the 1840's. To prevent the costs of transacting from rising (letting the
implied cost of borrowing—interest rates, commissions, and constrained
redemption periods—for instance, to mount) and choking commercial
circulation, merchants began working out rules for themselves to befit
modern needs. Since, as it were, the sovereign was in no position to resolve merchants' collective action problems, traders and financiers began to do it on their own.[11] In effect, merchant capitalists undertook their
own self-refashioning as a class.

The Commercial Tribunal remained the clearinghouse for commercial justice. Accordingly, it was also the forum for merchants to explore
autonomously legal practices of modern contract law. The dominant
business of the Tribunal was enforcing petty obligations. Here, the move
to stricter compliance was most immediate and less contested—even by
guilty defendants. In the 1840's, after decades of monetary instability,
the court began responding to creditors' insistence that loans be paid
upon demand. In 1844, Carlos Benavides signed over a bill of exchange
(worth 2,897 pesos) payable to Francisco Anzó in four months. When
the maturity date arrived, Benavides reneged. Anzó went to court and
secured an order for Benavides to pay in three days or face debtors' jail.
The threat worked.[12] Such expeditious justice was not, however, restricted to small contracts. Tomás Giraldes owed Manuela Campana for
a six-month mortgage loan on a house on Suipacha Street.[13] Signing in
December 1844, the parties renewed the contract several times and
added to the principal—by late 1845, the debt reached 34,000 pesos.
When Giraldes failed to comply with his obligations, Campana went to
the Tribunal in December and secured an order that the debtor pay in
three days. Giraldes could not comply, and on January 21, bailiffs seized
and auctioned his possessions, raising 11,274 pesos. Broke and humiliated, Giraldes left the city; Campana had clearly lost a sizable fraction of
the loan. This resolution may not have pleased either party, but it was a
sign that the Tribunal acted with fewer obstructions of equity concerns.
When the shoemaker Cayetano Davico let his mortgage payments to Nicolas Dodero lapse in 1845, the court ordered payment within eight

days.[14] Davico appealed: "It is a constant rule that when a man is reduced to subsisting with only the wages from his trade, extraordinary
claims cannot continue." This did not persuade the court. Cases such as
these suggest that the Tribunal adapted to the mounting demands by
creditors that their rights be legally upheld without much consideration
for the personality of debtors.

Partnership disputes got the Tribunal into murkier legal waters. Especially when it came to dividing assets when the association lapsed,
contractors could not rely on clear guidelines for sorting out assets and
liabilities. Consider the case of Nicolas Arca vs. Ramón Durañona
(1843), erstwhile partners in a cattle ranch near the Areco Fort. Arca
leased Durañona's land for four years for 5,000 pesos per annum. The
deal stipulated that they would split the returns at 35 pesos a head of
cattle (also furnished by Durañona). When their *sociedad* lapsed, the defendant Durañona tried to sell off the cattle (estimated worth: 150,000
pesos), claiming it to be "his capital," and promised to pay Arca his
share. The problem was, Arca discovered that his partner was selling
"not just the cattle, but wool, horses, the buildings, corrals, and even the
brand" to Mariano Gache. Worse, Durañona stuck Arca with a bill of
25,000 pesos in back-wages for the peons (this latter grievance was soon
rectified). The contract clearly underspecified the terms of the partnership—it also left the Tribunal with the muddy business of sorting out
shares of compensation. An obvious solution might have been to meet
halfway. Yet each side took adversarial positions on the rights to the
capital-formation on the estate. Arca argued that the capital was a
"social part" of the estate—the result of the mutual agreement and
therefore partible. Durañona maintained that the tradition of rural enterprises implied that the vendor of the cattle claimed title to the capital—as this capital was an extension of cattle and land assets. The defendant argued to the court that splitting the proceeds violated his
property rights, "especially when comparing the capital I spent with
what I am getting back." The court tried to reach an amicable solution,
in the convention of trying to keep intra-mercantile harmony through
persuasion and notions of reciprocity. But the adversarial tone prevailed. Witnesses appeared for both sides. To make matters worse,
Gache refused to present the bill of sale, arguing that since he had made
no deal with Arca, he was in no way liable. The three magistrates set a
date for the hearing, but a full resolution took two and a half years.
Eventually, they agreed that Durañona owed Arca 26,666 pesos.

This case exemplifies the murky terrain of property rights and the ways in which merchants and their jural representatives groped away from relational notions of justice. What we would now call a leasing or franchise arrangement in which property holders furnish assets and a partner the labor and entrepreneurial skills, they called partnerships. The dispensation of rights over capital-formation within the arrangement was not, as the judges noted in their decisions, clear at all. Unlike most cases, where judges did not feel compelled to reason their decisions, in this case they did, leaving behind a remarkable juridical document, a testimony to this era of legal transition. The most suggestive and reflective—and meticulous—statement came from the pen of Ventura Arzac. Having carefully weighed the evidence and scrutinized the contract, Arzac found that the plaintiff's accounting records demonstrated that Arca spent money on improvements. More important still was the contract itself: in a partnership, *sociedad*, proceeds (as well as losses) were meant to be shared, whereas Durañona was selling the capital "for the object of his own convenience." Durañona's repeated invocation of "traditional" notions of estanciero rights could not support claims that he alone could alienate the capitalized value of their joint venture. To justify this move, as the judge argued, the contract should have been a simple share or labor-hiring contract, not a partnership. In effect, Arzac pointed to the centrality of the contract itself and the rights that flowed therefrom. Neither litigant's social position or proprietary status could condition the meaning of the contract. Contracts carried their own designations as to who was entitled to what.[15]

As a judge, Arzac was forward-looking, illustrating a growing propensity to settle disputes by reference to the formal stipulations of the contracts. But he could not help but lament that "a deal that, by its natural condition, should lead to an easy and brief resolution, has become very difficult, resulting from the moment in which the parties ceased to feel good faith and in which we had to follow the evident greed and clumsy partiality of the litigants." Gone was the old era in which good faith, reputation, and mutual respect bound the behavior of disputants. Amicable solutions (at least rhetorically) were giving way to adversarial relations. Honorable statements could no longer be accepted at face value. This made the job of the Tribunal, as all three judges observed impatiently, very difficult because they lacked modern criteria for assessing evidentiary validity and objective means to dissect partible property. Arzac's decision lamented a bygone era of guildlike sociability.

Cumbersome as partnership jurisprudence was, delivering sentences was relatively simple in bilateral deals, where losers did not whiplash other contracts. The court had an even tougher time resolving multilateral obligations. Given the complexity of the financial world of the River Plate, many disputes embroiled one or more parties who were not immediate signatories to disputed contracts. Here dispensing justice was an even more troublesome affair, and should qualify any rush to conclude that changing contract law aimed to help creditors at the expense of debtors. When a debtor lapsed on loan payments or, more commonly, failed to honor a bill of exchange, his or her insolvency often provoked a stampede by the other creditors to recall their loans. It befell the Tribunal to reconcile endemic collective action problems in a volatile market—an increasingly onerous task as the jural language of amity and corporate reciprocity gave way to individuated adversarial litigation.

Bankruptcies were the most common source of multilateral-obligation collective action problems. In these instances, legal procedure stuck to the convention of arbitrating solutions for the health of the merchants as a whole by invoking equity and substantive justice. When Pedro José Díaz failed to keep up mortgage payments to Simón Pereyra (who was himself becoming one of Buenos Aires' most powerful landowner-merchant-financiers) and Francisco Balbín on his sheep estate in 1843, he asked the court to call all his creditors to arrange a collective settlement.[16] Pereyra and Balbín balked, claiming that their contracts were "private" and therefore enjoyed privileges over other debts that were "public" (mainly maturing bills). The court defied the mortgagors in favor of the creditors as a whole. The same transpired later, in 1858, when the important German importing house of Leinau & Bros went belly-up, allegedly because of the commercial crisis in Europe following the Crimean War.[17] In pressing for payment, another merchant house, Bieber, forced Leinau under. When the Tribunal ordered a liquidation of Leinau's assets and proportionate distribution of the proceeds among creditors, Bieber protested vigorously, claiming that their credit was "privileged" by being the first to come due. But under pressure from other merchants, the Tribunal stuck to its decision.

Relational solutions persisted well into the 1850's because merchants still worried that privileging one creditor might sacrifice merchants in general and yield a wave of defaults.[18] However, the court was not without recourse to methods of distinguishing among classes of entitlements. In handling the failed jewelry store of DuMayne in 1857, the Tribunal dispensed "rights according to the nature and grade of each one of the credits . . ."[19] Arbitrating judges created two types of obligation: the first involved payment of rent and outstanding pledges from work done on the store; the second (and by far the greater amount) went to lenders. The first group should be paid in full; the second (in the somewhat opaque legal language of the day) "get the remainder . . . subject to the *pro rata* of their suffering to those who are mere personals and therefore belong to the last class of creditors to whom must be apportioned their respective credits from the sum left over after having paid the privileged creditors." By the late 1850's, traditional equity decisions were even overturned in appeal. In Deetjent & Co. vs. Enrique Sinclair (1857), the plaintiff contested the Tribunal's decision to resolve a default by distributing the burden among all creditors. The Superior Tribunal de Justicia (a newly created body to which I will return later) upheld the appellant's case and gave him the privilege to recoup his credit.[20] This pattern of credit-hierarchy, distinguishing between private and public agreements (the latter covering cash loans), signified the turn to formal readings of individuated contracts over the concern for the merchant community at large.

Legal reasoning struggled to refine crystalline rules, even without statutory guidelines. In the case of Jonathan Downes vs. Nicholson, Green (1851), both sides urged that the judges rely on clear principles to assess whether or not the defendant owed Downes money for a shipment of hides to Liverpool.[21] This case eventually drew in the young lawyer José Benjamin Gorostiaga (later a drafter of the Constitution) and Norberto de la Riestra (the prominent associate of Nicholson, Green, and the wizard of public finance in the 1850's and 1860's), both of whom echoed the call for straight rules. De la Riestra, in a losing plea, insisted that equitable, arbitrated solutions be avoided, even if this implied costs to the defendant. These kinds of procedures and outcomes, he felt, crippled commerce. By the late 1850's, this sort of petition for crystalline judgments was a trope. When Juan Labastie approached the court to ask for legal sanction of monthly payments of 2,000 pesos to a consortium of creditors so that he could restore his business and pay more fully later— a standard procedure well into the 1830's—the court faced a tough choice.[22] Many creditors still wanted an equitable solution because they wanted fuller redemption down the line. But a minority wanted prompt seizure and auction of all assets. The latter faction—supported by the Commercial Tribunal's aides Francisco Balbín and Mariano Fragueiro (both of whom were acquainted with the travails of creditors as notable merchants themselves)—prevailed handily. Within two months Labastie was in the debtors' jail and his property on the auction block.

Within the Tribunal, then, merchants and merchant-judges shifted away from relational or customary notions of property, to more formal rights inscribed in willfully contracted obligations subject—at least this was the recurring injunction—to crystalline rules and process. As Dalmacio Vélez Sarsfield noted as early as 1852, there was no inherent fairness in contracts, merely the presumption that people had entered them freely and were thus fully liable.[23] Of course, this did not diminish commercial litigation, far from it. Collective action problems still arose— especially when forcible defaults imperiled third-party rights. The emerging legal consciousness helped sort out who enjoyed prior entitlements and specified compensations with greater clarity. But an essential ambiguity survived: a competitive economy required impersonal contracts, yet market uncertainty without an external legal referent often threw the court back onto subjective notions of litigants' personhood. In the end, giving trust and credible commitment robust foundations required more than a shift in consciousness, an embrace of an early kind of legal formalism within the private community of merchants itself. Changing consciousness may have been necessary, but it was not sufficient to transform contract law. To give legal formalism some bite required an equally profound change in institutions and statute.

Contracts Go Public

Creating trust and credibility was more than an affair arranged within society itself. The very nature of the court and the absence of statutory referents to clarify ground rules soon prompted merchants to address the reconstruction of political powers to reconcile private interests. In doing so, merchants prepared to relinquish a centuries-old zealously guarded practice of being the exclusive custodians of private commercial law. By the 1850's, merchants were disposed to entrust to legal experts and public officialdom the powers to define and arbitrate private property rights. They wanted public courts, ruled by a sovereign, to hold autonomous individuals to their bargains. A new "jurisprudential ideology" championed formal rules of law to sweep away ambiguous legal reasoning.[24]

All this pointed to the problem of statute as a provider of uniform rules. To animate discussion and to foster consensus over the need for statutory rigor, Mariano Fragueiro, a prosperous merchant from Córdoba and seasoned veteran of failed state-building ventures, issued a series of articles reflecting on Chilean legal and economic reforms and advocated a similar cause in Argentina. His *Organización del crédito* (published in Santiago in 1850) and *Cuestiones argentinas* (published in Buenos Aires a few months after Alberdi's *Bases* in 1852) became touchstones advocating a new image of society, held together by reciprocal utility-seeking exchange relations and buttressed by modern law.[25] Bald individualism, Fragueiro argued, corroded social harmony, and the perils were more than apparent. Indeed, the prolonged caudillo era, he felt, could be attributed to people's, especially capitalists', unbridled egotism: men with capital (he used the term "credit" and "capital" to mean the same thing) accrued to themselves all the advantages of possessing property and manipulated public offices to reinforce their private powers. In this, the new order resembled the old rent-seeking mercantilist era without the magnanimity of the crown in checking abuses. "The study of our past shows us that all the social upheavals are the effects of the lack of harmony between the individual and society regarding the staples of life—material goods—the property in things and of persons." As Fragueiro was fond of noting, all political disputes "are questions of property."[26]

The issue was: how to ensure new, less rent-seeking property relations. Conveying individual interests into more harmonious social purpose was the job of jurists and enlightened merchants concerned to establish more open and durable channels for commerce. For Fragueiro, the solution was to create "public property" rights that could be enjoyed by the political community at large and could then deflate accusations against capitalists that they were cornering the market of property rights. "All legislation resides on material goods possessed exclusively. . . . Well, then, if property is the mainstay of man, and if man must live in society, then society must also have its own life and property, public property." Readers might find this notion of property meaninglessly capacious. When the author got around to defining it, he was content with "all the acts of life," hardly an unambiguous formulation. What he did imply was that actual physical property belonged to individuals; he did not advocate expropriation. But this did not exhaust the sum total of proprietary possibilities, for the state could behave in ways to create new physical properties for individuals. This state power is what he meant by public power. "Governments have property and in this a capital; this capital must be reproductive."[27]

Two public properties deserved urgent attention. The first, which dominated his work, concerned "public credit," the creation of a sound monetary regime so that all of society could rely on a stable currency. This in turn would motivate an emerging market for money and private credit, which, under the right guidance, could also spread private property, even to the hitherto dispossessed. Public property could allocate private property, thereby "moralizing" society. The trick hinged on a second concern, the creation of a legal framework for dispassionately apportioning and defending property rights—locating struggles over property beyond the public, and placing it in the hands of the custodians of a universal rule of law. This was the job for binding codes: "The codes are the dispositions of power to harmonize relations between man and other men, and between private and public property."[28] With laws, people could enjoy their rights without the threat of arbitrary abuse. Their quest for individual utilities could aggregate into social virtue.

Fragueiro's injunctions echoed through the emerging public world of merchant capital. *Porteño* readers were greeted with a flurry of like-minded tracts, urging legal reform to harmonize individual interests and social good, private property and public powers.[29] This chorus agreed that matters of private property were too important, and too delicate, to be exposed to the whim of private persuasions of individual capitalists, or to the caprice of an arbitrary ruler like a caudillo. To be really secure, the definition and reconciliation of private rights had to be nestled in public bodies beyond the reach of individual merchants' egos or governors' volatility, in a stable, independent judiciary. In turn, this judiciary should be bound by immutable principles inscribed in statute.

The message spread. Rapidly evolving commerce spawned a network of institutions that gave expression to the collective interests of the merchant class. In 1841, 148 merchants formed the Society of Resident Foreigners, which maintained a small library, supported a chess club, and operated as a stock exchange from noon to 1:00 P.M. With the fall of Rosas, *porteños* flooded to new public spaces reminiscent of the 1820's. Merchants joined the rush. In June 1852, British merchants created their own fraternity. But the most important new association was the Stock Exchange (the Bolsa), founded in 1854, and guided by the British potentates Daniel Gowland and Tomás Armstrong—both of whom integrated easily into the local creole elite. Both were also veterans of bankruptcy and the devastating oscillations of the Atlantic market. In due course, the Bolsa, which opened a branch in Rosario in 1858, doubled as an important gathering house for merchants and as a base for lobbying governments.[30] "Commerce without a stock exchange," noted one author, "is like religion without a temple."[31]

Credit institutions also began operating, albeit hobbled by the persistent monetary and political turmoil of the 1850's. Banks and financial firms came and went, mainly operating as family outfits and arms of integrated merchant houses. When the Bank of London and the River Plate opened its doors in 1862, and the Mitre government finally settled the unresolved rancor over the old Baring Brothers loan of 1824, British capital reentered the Buenos Aires market in tow. Incorporated lending institutions flourished thereafter to take advantage of the relaxation on credit supply.[32] All told, commercial and financial institutions and meeting places contributed to the emerging publicness of business affairs. This publicness helped nurture an emerging market for capital itself.

Trading and public gathering, though necessary, were insufficient conditions to create a proper capital market. As participants in this market were well aware, some formal rule-changing was also, and increasingly, necessary. Merchants used their thickening network of partnerships and gathering places to join a symphony of calls for public reform. Sometimes the lobbying aimed to promote investment or dispense concessions, such as Juan Baratta's appeals to the young politician Mitre to back public works (Baratta wanted to import steamships for riverine trade and begin dredging canals).[33] But most were part of a steady stream of demands that public institutions perform up to scratch. A constant source of grievance was the unruly peso (see Chapter 10). Daniel Gowland himself was caught holding a consignment of imports from Britain, which he had to pay for in sterling but had already committed for sale at rapidly depreciating peso prices. The squeeze nearly crushed this powerful merchant, and fueled his resolve to create merchant public venues to vent class interests.[34] These concerns prompted the main organ of Buenos Aires' cosmopolitan merchants to urge that "leaving the brilliant theories of Rousseau and the French School, we must now enthrone, enshrine, and deify, if possible, the abstract principle of legality."[35]

Aside from the proverbial complaints about monetary instability, merchants rumbled about the absence of statute for commercial affairs. It was not uncommon for litigants to find the operations of the court wanting. In José Clemente Cueto vs. Manuel Villafañe (1847), the defendant successfully appealed his case on the grounds that only two judges presided, when the old Bilbao Ordinances stipulated three.[36] Evidentiary disputes raged. Defendants held up cases when documents were not properly notarized—hardly a regular practice during the reign of *jus mercatorum*, but one that often helped debtors postpone visits by court bailiffs. One livid plaintiff, tired of running in appellant circles, argued to the Alzada (the chief Appeal Judge) that his debtor was abusing laws in order to violate his rights: "You are obliged," he told the Alzada, "to prevent people from usurping the property of others by resting themselves on the protection of superior decrees to introduce delays and resources that are absolutely rejected by laws."[37] At the same time, the increasing complexity of transactions and the somewhat amateurish position of untrained judges (recall that the judges came from the ranks of the merchant class itself) meant that judges needed the help of notaries and accountants to sort out the veracity of evidentiary claims. "The Commercial Tribunal is a constant chaos," noted one paper, "and we have never seen a decision resting on even the most minimal natural reason."[38] Echoing the trope of chaos, another paper noted that "when these scandalous events combine with the crisis [referring to the fissure between the Confederation and Buenos Aires], commerce is in chaos, no one has credit because all confidence has disappeared."[39] In the eyes of many, this sort of malaise only aggravated shortages of capital. "This disorder, this absolute absence of principles of justice and administration, influences not only the demoralization of society, but dries up and sterilizes the powerful elements of wealth of our fecund soils."[40] Even the Directors of the Banco de la Provincia de Buenos Aires chimed in on the same note.[41]

Such concerns prompted the merchants of Buenos Aires to press the government more directly for legal action. Both the Confederation and Buenos Aires governments of the 1850's created wings of their finance ministries for merchants to represent their concerns directly. The Stock Exchange created its own "Cámara Sindical" in 1856 to thwart any government efforts to curb freedom of commerce. Its chief proponent and Trustee was Amancio Alcorta, a powerful merchant well acquainted with the Commercial Tribunal—in one case he spent months trying to enforce redemption of a bill of exchange, and when he finally secured a court order to auction the debtor's property, the defendant had disposed all his goods and fled the city.[42] The Buenos Aires Finance Minister in

1855, Norberto de la Riestra, a fellow-merchant, enlisted Alcorta's support for a special Consultative Council comprised of "distinguished citizens" to oversee public administration reforms, promising that a delegate from the Stock Exchange and the President of the Provincial Bank were guaranteed representation.[43] By the late 1850's, Alcorta ranked among the most politically puissant merchants of the city, as a Director or member of all the main public institutions representing merchant capital or organs of the state designed to service merchants. He personified merchants' drive to push the state to take seriously the cause of private law reform—and authored a popular set of essays calling for juridical reform. "Law was created," Alcorta maintained, "to guarantee the fact established by the nature of property rights: law cannot violate what it is obliged to respect . . ."[44]

Merchants had allies within the legal establishment. In a sense, the convergence of mercantile and legal concerns had already begun within the bowels of the Commercial Tribunal itself. At stake was the whole notion of *verdad sabida*, merchants' common sense and moral rectitude as a framework for assessing guilt and liability. Convention maintained that merchants be the carriers of their own sense of law and mete out justice efficaciously and in a manner that fit the particular needs of the merchant world. Faced with the growing complexity of financial instruments and higher stakes in commercial contracts, merchants began to hire legal representatives to wage battles in the courthouse—a proscribed practice under early modern rules of corporate self-management by merchants. Merchant judges of the Tribunal found the legal experts' discursive style and command over legal arcana too intimidating to rebuff. And as hiring an attorney or councilor began to show dividends in the form of triumphal court decisions, more and more merchants—plaintiffs and defendants alike—hired legal allies in court.[45]

The fabric of *verdad sabida* was so frayed and the presence of lawyers so intrusive in the court that the judges themselves began leaning on legal experts, *asesores*, to bail them out of legal trouble. According to the old Bilbao Ordinances this was permissible only in appeals and was not supposed to become regular practice. Merchants were supposed to govern their own affairs. Magistrates flaunted these restrictions—and by the 1850's, lawyers like Roque Sáenz Peña (later President of the Republic), Dalmacio Vélez Sarsfield (the most prominent jurist of the day), and Francisco Balbín and Miguel Esteves Saguí (two influential lawyers and politicians in their own right) were regulars in the courthouse, filing depositions for clients and even helping out the judges by writing their sentences. Indeed, much of the litigation was so complex that the court hired a full-time team of accountants since so much in the evidentiary disputes rested on the maelstrom of commercial legedermain.[46] By the 1850's, *verdad sabida* was little more than a quaint archaism invoked by defendants grasping for legal straws.

Legal insiders berated the commercial judiciary for its flawed habits. Vicente López y Planes, a longtime Appellant Justice during the Rosas years and later Governor of the Province of Buenos Aires, moaned to his son, the aspiring liberal lawyer temporarily exiled in Montevideo, that the court system was a circus of legal confusion, in which medieval laws, Roman codes and digests, and French romantic dissertations jos-tled for center stage as legal referents.[47] One exasperated *asesor* gently upbraided the magistrate for mishandling a suit over the delivery of stale beer. What should have been a simple affair, noted the adviser, be-came a long, drawn out, and cumbersome process because the judge unwittingly admitted false testimonies and doctored books from both sides. Sorting out the mess was nearly impossible. (To be fair to the judge, the litigants hired a couple of long-winded obfuscating lawyers to bamboozle the court.) In his prelude to a long and thoughtful disentan-gling, the court adviser urged "that no prominent deed must be omitted, especially those generally used and consecrated in commerce and sanc-tioned as necessities to lend a certain character of legality to all transac-tions, which, like all human acts, should be based on the good faith and rectitude of procedures."[48]

As a source of legal experts' and merchants' ire, however, nothing rivaled the capricious and often despotic domain of Justices of the Peace—the outer-edge of the state's legal phalanx. JP's were the main ju-ridical figures in the countryside, chosen by the Executive, often at the behest of landowners themselves in an effort to introduce discipline to the relative freedom of a porous and untamed frontier. They were also legal henchmen (literally) in urban parishes, acting mainly as bailiffs at the behest of criminal and commercial courts, and even serving as judges in the most petty disputes. Short on training and hired for their ability to enforce rather than interpret, they were more commonly known for the inconsistency of their rule and, among the most plebeian sectors of the population, its naked brutality. What incensed merchants and legal experts most, however, was the arbitrariness and vulgarity of JP justice. For many it was a powerful relic of Rosas's quasi-legal rule deliberately designed to make of the rule of law a malleable instrument to promote social stability.[49] In one instance, a cart of wool and merchandise was impounded in the county of Morón in a dispute over a bill of sale. Having reached an agreement, the Tribunal's magistrate ordered the cart to be released so that the defendant might raise the cash to pay his obligation—only to find that the JP had pilfered the cargo of wool.[50] This was not untypical, and only animated the chorus of demands to establish a regular commercial court system both for petty disputes and in the countryside. Doing so, as legal reformers insisted with mounting urgency, required the overhaul of the judiciary and the creation of a more unified and integrated court system. Even the JP's complained of the vagueness of their mandates. The JP of Chascomús, Domingo Facio, claimed that contradictory demands on his office "give rise to continuous discord and acrimony given the informality with which these documents [his orders] are drafted, either for exploitation, out of trickery, or in bad faith tolerated owing to the ignorance of many." "It is clear," concluded Facio, "that a judge cannot issue decisions himself without instruments of a public or judicial character."[51]

The convergence of merchants and legal experts behind the cause of judicial overhaul did more than advance reform for the sake of reform. In publicly trumpeting legal deficiencies, partisans of change decried the whole idea that justice could be realized through common sense and merchants' *verdad sabida*. Reform was the wedge to separate legal professionals from the legal laity. In the ancien régime private law, the latter prevailed. But republican justice, noted *La Tribuna*, required a modern judiciary, guided by formal statute and informed by specialized, up-to-date jurisprudence. "The importance of this reform is incontestable; it helps us consecrate the principle of the independence of the judiciary."[52] The jurist-cum-politician José Barros Pasos argued that reform should begin with the replacement of merchant judges with legally trained magistrates.[53] To become truly impersonal theaters of justice, noted Dalmacio Vélez Sarsfield, the courts had to be ruled by judges chosen for their specialized rigor and therefore ability to refer to objective criteria, rather than make decisions predicated upon subjective perception.[54] In short, legal knowledge, to be truly impartial, could not be subjected to the domain of common sense, but had to subsist in an autonomous realm, accessible only through training and professional promotion. The freedom of the legal profession, as *El Industrial* argued, was a necessary analogue to freedom to trade in the making of a modern commercial society.[55]

The drive for juridical reform presents us with the following para-dox: the growing chorus for a shift in legal epistemology (from a subjec-tive community-oriented basis of legal consciousness, to an objective positivist understanding) implied that the courts should become in-struments of open and public adjudication, while at the same time ar-guing that legal knowledge should become increasingly segregated and privileged. From the point of view of a rising legal establishment and ascendant class of merchants, the balancing act between publicness of rules and fora for justice with greater formality and a hierarchy of legal knowledge was a necessary compromise. In trying to construct public powers to service private interests, jurists and merchants had to concede that property rights and claims had to be universally available to avoid any charge that the form of justice was illegitimate—an indictment that devastated merchant privilege during the revolution. To legitimate post-revolutionary rights-talk, a consensus was building in Buenos Aires to defend universal economic freedoms, and to place the custody of the rules governing these freedoms in the hands of legal cognoscenti.

Codification

By the mid-1850's, the shifting private consciousness of merchant capi-talists and the mounting public demands for juridical reform set the stage for a drive to modernize, update, and consolidate commercial ju-risprudence, and inscribe it in the immutable form of a code. There was, of course, an existing body of legislation. But it sprawled across the centuries, came from a mosaic of sources, and was altogether too un-wieldy to be of much use to merchants or jurists. The Ordinances of Bil-bao (revised in 1737) remained the primary touchstone—but they chief-ly addressed matters of juridical procedure, accounting, and how to form a corporation, and were unhelpful with contracts in general. The public laws of Spain were even more anachronistic. Book IX of the Leyes de Indias (*Nueva Recopilación*, 1567), for instance, tackled insurance and liability, but encumbered itself with very long discussions of boat con-struction, material types, permissible cargoes, and a vast mélange of cu-riosities, little of which spoke to the concerns of nineteenth-century commercial capitalism.[56]

Legislators did promulgate a few laws in Buenos Aires. After much talk of reform and codification in the 1820's, the implosion of the uni-tarian effort to put the republic on a constitutional track swept aside any incipient statutory moves. The Rosas government, in response to the increasing malaise in the Commercial Tribunal, especially by creditors who found the court too shackled to early modern equity concerns and defending relational rights over individuated ones, promoted a Bankruptcy Law in 1836, essentially to eliminate bad faith by suspending the tradition of *concursos* (open meetings of creditors to sort out relative compensations). On the statute books until Governor Alsina finally abrogated the law in 1858, it was not enforced (though occasionally invoked by debtors). Some provinces pushed through legislation—but here too there is no evidence of much juridical effect. The only real judicial reform came in October 1857, when the legislature of Buenos Aires, in response to the weltering appeals within the Commercial Tribunal and the outcry that merchant capital was agonizing in legal uncertainty, created a Superior Tribunal of Justice. To a limited extent, this court did defuse some of the conflict, and was the first public body to take commercial jurisprudence out of the hands of the legal laity. It became, in effect, the precursor to the modern courts, eclipsed once the state began constructing full judicial powers in 1862.[57]

The drive to codify gathered speed after the fall of Rosas and the approval of the constitutions. It is worth saying that even in the last years of Rosas's reign, several writers—including Dalmacio Vélez Sarsfield himself—offered to draft a code specifically for merchants.[58] But it was the collective representative bodies of merchant capital that spearheaded the initiatives. The Buenos Aires Commerce Commission drafted laws to regulate storage and maritime trade regulations to try to fill some of the gaps.[59] The Stock Exchange did not have any publications, but its members were actively encouraged to visit upon their friends in the government the need for statutory reform.[60] Amancio Alcorta, through the Commerce Commission, as a Director of the Provincial Bank and the Stock Exchange, as well as through his friendship with the Finance Minister Riestra, sustained the lobby for commercial legal reform.[61]

The press, much of which was owned and edited by merchants and prominent jurists, chimed in loudly. "The best way to preserve order," noted one paper, "is to work in the interests of liberty and justice. Industry and commerce cannot prosper without beneficent laws, and above all, without judges and tribunals that issue decisions promptly and equitably. In the end, the prosperity of the state is intimately linked to these modest concessions to commerce."[62] *El Nacional* lambasted the delays and confusions of the court: "In transfers and business, commerce is suffering on account of the lack of a Tribunal before which individuals may resolve issues and claim security or the payment of their credits. . . . Each person's property is time, even for just a minute . . . and property must be guaranteed as one of the primary rights, by divine and human law, of man in society."[63] Just as important, a specialized legal press emerged to reinforce the cause: *El Plata Científico y Literario* ran regular pieces on legal matters, and in its first issue it published a long treatise on replacing merchants with legally trained judges as magistrates in the Commercial Tribunal; the College of Lawyers began publishing *El Foro* in 1859; and by the 1860's, several legal periodicals circulated in the region.[64] *La Tribuna* excoriated the legislature for holding up the business of codifying by entertaining all kinds of idealist projects: "Everyone clamors for reforms instead of committing themselves to the enterprise of codifying according to the exigencies of our time and the specifics demanded by commerce in all its transactions; the legislature is holding up indefinitely this duty. The laxity characteristic of deliberative bodies should be borne in mind when advocating this constitutional mandate."[65] The public and behind-the-door barrage to overhaul commercial law was finally arguing that the issue was too important to be left to the caprice of legislators.

The push to codify came from the Confederation and Buenos Aires governments more or less simultaneously. Article 24 of the national Constitution of 1853 called on Congress to reform existing legislation, and Article 64 called specifically for civil, commercial, penal, and mining codes and forbade provinces from legislating on the matter. In 1855, Urquiza created a Codifying Commission, including Vélez Sarsfield, Vicente López, Francisco Pico, and José Benjamin Gorostiaga. The latter, entrusted with the commercial code, enlisted the help of his lawyer friends López and Pico, as well as two merchants, veterans of Commercial Tribunal battles, Francisco Balbín and José María Rojas. In the end, the persistent warfare between the Confederation and Buenos Aires, and the fiscal collapse in Paraná, eclipsed the urgency of private law reform.

The decisive move came from Buenos Aires. Dalmacio Vélez Sarsfield, then Minister of Government, joined with the noted Uruguayan jurist Eduardo Acevedo in 1856 to draft a code. After ten months' labor, in which Acevedo wrote and Vélez Sarsfield edited, a blueprint emerged in April 1857. The pair delivered the draft to the Executive on the 17th, and Governor Pastor Obligado signed it on the 30th. On May 1, the Senate got its copy, where it got gummed up in a jurisdictional squabble between committees. Sarmiento, recently elected Senator, wanted immediate promulgation "closed book" (i.e. with no discussion of the articles). His opponent, José Mármol, finally agreed, lamenting that "the houses are not prepared for this kind of work." The Senate and House of Deputies approved the Code hastily, closed book, on October 6, 1859, and it was slated to become effective law six months later. The only point of discussion was whether the Commercial Code was not premature because it presumed the existence of statutory civil law— which still awaited its code.[66] Most legislators agreed that in an ideal world the Civil Code would come first, but that the exigencies of merchants and the pressing needs of investors required a legal bedrock. Later, once the Civil Code passed the national legislature in 1869, the Commercial and Civil codes were homologized in 1889 to remove inconsistencies. When the discord between the Confederation and Buenos Aires abated, and Mitre assumed the presidency, the Buenos Aires Code became national on September 10, 1862. A month later, the Commercial Tribunal, the clearinghouse for merchant justice since 1794, closed its doors, making way for divisional courts (Tribunales de Primera Instancia) and special Commissary Judges chosen to handle bankruptcies. 1862 brought to a close a long era of commercial law without statute and self-governing merchant justice, paving the way for future legislation governing private law in the consolidated republic.[67]

What of the Code itself? Comprised of four books and 1,755 articles (these were later winnowed to 1,611 when a committee integrated the Civil and Commercial codes), the treatise was a monument to practical guidance. Book One defined merchants and who was subject to the Code; Book Two governed private contracts; Book Three stipulated rights and obligations in navigation; Book Four covered bankruptcy. Bereft of any general statement of principles or guiding framework (by the 1850's, after the debacle of the 1820's, jurists decidedly avoided ideal, aspirational legal language), the "General Rules" stated that the enclosed technicalities' intent and meaning were designed to be absolutely unambiguous. It stated, furthermore, that judges were forbidden from basing decisions and sentences on general principles, but should always refer conflicts to specific legal dispositions.[68]

In accordance with the pronounced aversion to the notion of judge-made law (magistrates, since the law was self-evident, enjoyed no interpretive role) and of legislators' right to approve subsequent ad hoc laws governing matters of commercial jurisprudence, the Code sought to place commercial and contract law on an unimpeachable pedestal—in effect enjoying the same legal status as the Constitution in matters of private commercial law between individuals or corporations. The drafters and promulgators acceded to the wishes of Buenos Aires' capitalists to keep their legal world of defining the day-to-day matters of locating and reconciling property rights beyond the reach of politics. Reflecting on the new Code, the young lawyer and eventual President, Nicolás Avellaneda, hoped it would usher in a new era: "Commerce is the marvelous agent called upon to populate and civilize these peoples . . ." New legal machinery, by vivifying commerce after half a century of turmoil, would help tame social passions so long as these same inflamed citizens could not tamper with the rules governing property.[69]

The early decisions of the new court vindicated the pressures to free commercial law from the juridical legacies of the ancien régime. In the squabbling partnership between two French barbers, the court flexed its expeditious muscle and insisted that protocol be upheld: the litigants were kept to a tight schedule for their depositions, the evidence had to prove guilt or innocence on the matter of dispute (and not testify to their personhood), witnesses were summoned and queried, and the judge issued his sentence referring to particular clauses of the Code.[70] José Leon vs. Venacio Caballero (1863) shows just how binding contracts had become—and the power this implied for creditors. Caballero leased a locale in the business district, but owed money to a third party, Elías O'Donnell.[71] When payments lapsed, O'Donnell won a court order to transfer the store as compensation. In the course of the investigation, it became clear that Caballero and O'Donnell in fact were partners in a separate venture. Not only did Judge Pinedo argue that Caballero was liable for keeping up the rent, but when the owner discovered in the trial that a *sociedad* existed, he successfully secured a court order making O'Donnell equally liable. Mariano Pinedo, the presiding magistrate in the reformed court in the early years, stuck to his codified guns, operating expeditiously to champion the principle of contractual freedom and full liability.

Furthermore, the Supreme Court reinforced this crystalline approach to contracts and the autonomy of the judge in applying (not interpreting) the Code. Indeed, the very first case facing the new Supreme Court involved the appeal of a creditor aggrieved because his debtor died and the case had gone to a general *concurso* for all the creditors and the divisional court allocated shares according to the principles of hierarchy of privilege. Otero objected on the grounds that the Code placed the proceedings in the hands of a trustee of the estate, and not the court. It did not matter. The Supreme Court dismissed the appeal, arguing that all divisional and provincial courts' decisions on matters dealing with codes (though so far only commerce was codified) were not appealable unless the complaint involved a jurisdictional violation of matters inscribed in the Code or the Constitution. Consequently, when it came to stipulations within the Code, the Supreme Court made the field of commercial jurisprudence autonomous and reinforced the power of objective statute.[72]

Conclusion

Codification did not do away with ambiguities within contract law. And it certainly did not end litigation. But it did change the jurisprudential structure of rights-making. It was the capstone of a long process of defining contractual freedom, the right to acquire and dispose of property, and to have public powers invoked to enforce these rights lest they be violated. And as the national judiciary began to be built over the 1860's, this kind of legal transformation created a national framework for credit and property transactions. The transactional approach to contract law empowered public courts to impose a formal ideal of contracts. What mattered was the freedom and will of transactors, not their intention or personhood. If equality entered the picture, it was the formal guarantee that all litigants enjoyed equal rights to represent themselves in court, but without guarantees of equitable outcomes. This did not herald any objectivist consensus about property, simply a growing faith that public institutions could act as domains to reconcile and to shelter unequal distributions of private interests.[73]

This did not happen out of the blue, but in response to several decades of gradual transformation within the community of merchants. On one level, the very legal consciousness of merchant capitalists shifted away from old regime relational rights and norms. If relational property-talk survived, it was because the framework for new rights-making seemed so elusive—especially as the early constitutional efforts gave way to civil war and caudillo rule. By the 1850's, the idea of public institutions to uphold private interests and the idea of contractual freedom (and not personhood) was no longer a pipe dream. Increasingly, hap-hazardly, and not without slippage and contradiction, merchants ar-ticulated more formal notions of their entitlements. Integration into the Atlantic trading system, rising stakes of contracts, and the greater pre-mium placed on commercial ventures raised the opportunity cost of older forms of transacting.

In the process, commercial consciousness laid the groundwork for an ad hoc alliance between merchants and legal experts. In ancien régime commercial jurisprudence, merchants loathed interloping lawyers be-cause they obstructed common-sense solutions and confused conflicts that might be resolved "equitably." But as consciousness began to shift, lawyers entered the daily activities of litigation to champion greater clarity and formality in legal reasoning.

Eventually, this convergence pushed changing jurisprudential ideol-ogy into the public sphere. Lawyers, merchants, and jurists actively and loudly championed the cause of judicial modernization and codification. Lampooning the "chaos" of the existing structure, the voices of reform called for a system that would place this private law beyond the sphere of politics—making commercial law a fully public ambit, but inscribing rights in an unimpeachable and universal code applicable to all con-tractual disputes. Private rights in property were, it was believed, best safeguarded by an autonomous court under a judge beholden to the contents of the Commercial Code and it alone. This was legal formalism at its most rigorous—and would become the tenor of juridical delibera-tion for at least the next half-century. What mattered hereafter was not an agent's intention or personhood before entering transactions, but the properties of the contract itself. If the idea that freedom to contract pre-sented a nimbus of equality, it rested purely on the formal notion that all agents enjoyed unobstructed rights to sign contracts. In no way did the new contractual consensus imply that intentions or capacities of trans-actors were at all equal before the fact of the contract itself. This is pre-cisely what large capitalists of Buenos Aires, and especially the core of creditors at the heart of the commercial system, yearned for as Buenos Aires folded back into the Atlantic economy.

The upshot of all this was the consecration of the private autonomy of the legal subject, a liberal aspiration since the unitarian days of the 1820's. Ancien régime personality and public dependence of the legal subject had finally passed. But this did not mean that individualism tri-umphed of its own accord, for, as Mariano Fragueiro had once argued, it took public powers to create and enforce private rights. Merchant capitalists of the River Plate agreed that individual rights made no sense without public authority. Faced with the sorts of collective action problems in moving to a different legal framework for rights-making, they deliberately rejected a sharp distinction between public and private realms. In this sense, class-formation unfolded in the process of struggling to realize individuated interests: with the collapse of the Spanish empire, revolutionary warfare, and the sundering of political property, a class of merchants in itself evolved into a class for itself through legal contestation over the meanings of their rights and entitlements.[74] To be sure, securing the private, legal autonomy for capital was an end that merchants learned to covet—but getting there required patching a much broader constitutional tapestry.[75]

Codification and judiciary-building were important, but not the exclusive preoccupations of the ascendant propertied classes in the River Plate. The other great nagging issue was the power to create, and control, money and credit. If lawfully binding contracts were the form in which exchange transpired, money became the means. To finalize the creation of a republic for capital and consolidate the power of the capital of the republic, officials and private interests turned to the problem of constructing monetary authority.

10 ☞ Making Money: The Battle for Monetary Authority

> The individual carries his social power, as well as his bond with society, in his pocket.
>
> Karl Marx, *Grundrisse*

Interests and Institutions in Money Making

The rise of free trade, flourishing new exports, and changing business practices brought prosperity to far-flung corners of the Atlantic world. Interlocking commerce and investment across borders also transmitted cycles—up and down alike—of commodity and capital flows within borders. The crisis years 1857, 1867, 1873, and 1890 demarked the increasingly trans-national nature of capitalism. At the same time, the competitive world of commercial capital ceded to the combined might of finance capital. By century's end, Baring, Rothschild, Morgan, and Rockefeller exercised unprecedented and unrivaled, but imperfect and incomplete, dominion over the economic fortunes of others. Faced with new uncertainties and the rising stakes of losses to capital in the event of unbridled crises, trans-border trade and investment compelled states to create new powers within their borders—powers to intervene in market forces to soften their occasional ravages. Especially in the north Atlantic societies, central monetary authority emerged as a means to immunize capitalists from potential political repercussions of downturns and to socialize, as much as possible, the losses inflicted upon capitalists' interests. In theory, public institutions enabled capitalists to navigate the stormy waters of financial crises and to restore prosperous environments once market relations stabilized. Only with the Depression of the 1930's did the idea of immunity and autonomy of finance capital finally come under assault.[1]

Latin America and Argentina folded into this international division of labor and capital as no other region. There was an important twist, however, to the Latin American story: these emerging export economies joined the Atlantic system while their foundational public institutions were still very much in formation. Thus, on the one hand, market integration fostered new interests: economic power shifted to owners of landed and financial assets while the state itself was still very weak. On the other hand, ideologues of state and politicians grappled with the job of institution-building without being able to rely on the backing of a solid elite bloc capable of giving private muscle to public power. Buenos Aires exemplified, with remarkable synchronicity, the coeval rise of private financial capital and consolidation of domains of political capitals across the Atlantic urban archipelago. This was a double legal transformation in the public and private domains.

This double and simultaneous legal transformation confuses the stock-in-trade accounts or causal lines of state and class-formation. States are supposed to defend and uphold property rights by lowering the costs of obtaining information and settling accounts—in a word, easing the transaction costs of contracting.[2] In the main, public-choice theorists approach capitalism's institutional life by stressing the functions of rules, but not their formation, what rules did, but not how rules themselves became encoded. Conflict over rule-making and its resolution are flattened into consequential explanations: because rules help individuals or groups, these same agents act as the handmaidens of these rules.[3] Yet Buenos Aires' public institutions were neither solid nor legitimate enough to exercise the functional roles to which private interests aspired. Moreover, the fact that a financial and large propertied class was in-formation meant that it could not assert its hegemony with anything rivaling the authority it enjoyed by the end of the century. Capitalists, at least on the surface, desperately wanted a stable medium of exchange to make the definitive shift away from the commodity money of the mercantilist era, to fiat money of modern fiduciary systems. But they did not possess the clout to translate private yearnings into publicly enforceable rules.[4] Functional accounts presume a coherence of class interests that did not yet exist, because this class was in-formation, and imply, with the same disregard for some uncomfortable facts, a credibility of institutional potential that was also more pipe dream than reality.[5] The indeterminacies posed by large-scale collective conflict over the ideas and institutions of public power mangle functional explanations of how law serves the interests of property. While the effects of institutional rules might have been functional to private interests, this chapter is more concerned with the process of rule-formation, a history or sequence that, at any given moment, might have followed a number of paths. And the choice of path is decisive, because it established the range of potential rules that in turn governed public and private affairs.

Nor was the state emerging as some sort of autonomous field, monopolizing the legitimate means of coercion (as Weber maintained) or embodying an ethical ideal (Hegel's post–French revolutionary claim).[6] States-in-formation, like Argentina's in the nineteenth century, hungered for fungible resources. Bereft of solid fiscal machinery, public officials depended on private backers and used various voluntary and involuntary means to enlist their support. Aspirants to the polity's commanding heights spent as much time grubbing about for the financial means to realize their ambitions as they did translating their secular dreams into the hortative language of nineteenth-century *pronunciamientos*. The state, as the current argot goes, was "embedded." The problem was: it was embedded in a highly unstable and rapidly changing milieu.

This chapter is concerned with the dual legal transformation that led to a convergence of public power and private interests. That meeting point was a monetary regime. Creating a monetary regime combined the public cause of state-formation with private interests in class-formation. At the heart of such a system was a market for financial assets— paper instruments that states could issue to marshal resources to support its objectives, and tender that traders could use to swap goods and services.[7] Negotiable instruments had to be expressed in monetary terms, while money relied on confidence instilled or deprived by the semblance of immutable objective laws.[8] This is why, in the nineteenth century, across the Atlantic world, jurisdiction over the issuance of money migrated from private capital–holders to states. In the process, societies, and especially certain classes (financial-asset holders above all), created public powers to reinforce private interests.[9] Monetary authority exemplified—as anyone who has lived through hyperinflation will attest—how public power conditions private property rights.

So long as creoles of the River Plate could not resolve their disputes over the ground rules for the political community, creating this monetary regime was as remote as it was coveted. This chapter explores the emerging monetary deal between finance capitalists and state-builders. The former agreed to finance the latter's project to integrate the polity; the latter agreed to stabilize the value of paper pesos. The revolution had shattered the old world of silver and bequeathed an anarchic and destabilized monetary regime; state-builders responded with centralized and concentrated powers to regulate money, culminating in a decision to peg paper currency to gold.[10] The monetary deal finally allowed the region to overcome the chronic shortage of liquidity that had encumbered commerce since the shattering of the Potosí–Buenos Aires–Cádiz silver axis of the early modern Atlantic economy.[11]

Because Buenos Aires was the context of a double legal transformation—building public institutions and consolidating private class interests—this was not a story of smooth mutual convergence of private elites and public authorities. Some financiers backed dissenters; some dissenters redoubled their resistance to the emerging power bloc in Buenos Aires. The opposition came in the form of the Confederation, the political experiment to forge a polity independent of Buenos Aires, the port, and its merchant elite. The underlying trouble was: while state-builders aimed to strike a monetary deal to weld an alliance with financiers, they also struggled to integrate the political community—a process whose means did not often mesh with monetary objectives; easy money could win quick allies but undermine the goal of autonomous financial control. What is more, many financiers may have aspired to an alternative monetary regime, but they did not find the preexisting one without its opportunities. Instability was a breeding ground for—very risky, to be sure—speculative profits and rent-seeking. Finding expounded evidence of this sort of interest in instability is, of course, notoriously difficult (who, after all, proclaims inflation and speculation to be a social good?). But it was (and is) a fact of all transitional economies.[12] In effect, the challenge was to create a republican regime for the political capital while concocting a monetary regime for private capital. The very double nature of this transformation complicates, violates, neat causal lines.

The crucible of this process, the dual legal transformation of public institutions and private interests, was warfare. In this sense what transpired in the River Plate was part of a trans-Atlantic process of what Lawrence Stone, John Brewer, and others have called the emergence of a "military-fiscal state."[13] The Argentine pattern of state-formation through warfare, however (and, for that matter, the Latin American pattern in general), differed from the European in one important respect: Europeans states waged wars against rival states. In Argentina the guns were directed at other Argentines; civil wars conducted over rival republican ideals, and not foreign wars over regional supremacy, provided the backdrop for fiscal and monetary developments. The out-come, since it was confined to sovereign boundaries, was one of winner-take-all. In Buenos Aires, by the 1860's, this is precisely what transpired, giving merchant capital unrivaled economic powers, and giving the re-publican capital unimagined political command over rival political proj-ects.[14] Out of the centrifugal crises of civil wars emerged unanticipated centripetal forces. The result was not foreordained, predictable at the outset, but the consequence of a struggle over the shape of the republic, a saga detonated by the collapse of mercantilist empires and the social upheaval of mass warfare.

The Monetary Deal and Political Disunion

State-builders had to contend with a deep legacy of post-revolutionary disunion. The caudillo era bequeathed an unstable inconvertible paper that was accepted as a medium of exchange throughout Buenos Aires, somewhat in the Littoral, and even as far as the Andes. But it was far from a happy medium. In the words of an agent dispatched by Buenos Aires' London financiers, "this wretched currency is in every respect injurious to the community, being based upon no tangible security and having only a fictitious and conventional value; the fluctuations are enormous and trade is thus to a considerable extent reduced to the level of a mere speculation."[15] Rosas's legacy was an inauspicious beginning for his successors.

One might have expected the fall of Rosas to change venal habits. Certainly this is what many capitalists hoped, rhetorically. But, Rosas's fall unleashed a decade of conflict within and between the provinces. To make matters worse, each side used money, or their own notes, as a weapon to wage war, as a cudgel to force rivals into submission. By ne-cessity, a financial war implied resorting to monetary emissions—sometimes reckless and flagrant printing. This in turn fueled inflation and aggravated uncertainty. Thus, as much as the Confederation and Buenos Aires sought to vanquish the other, they also brought their own economies to near ruin. By 1859, the specter of catastrophe forced them to reconsider the grounds of their feuds.

Urquiza's victory and efforts to form a broad alliance behind a fed-eralist union flew in the face of Buenos Aires' interests, for whom the prospect of equal footing with other provinces was humiliating. Re-opening the debate over Buenos Aires' autonomy highlighted the prob-

lem of who would control money-printing powers. This presented constitutional wranglers with the following Gordian knot: as long as Buenos
Aires enjoyed some measure of sovereignty over fiduciary issues, jurisdictional transfers from Buenos Aires to the incipient National Government implied forfeiting control over local currency. *Porteños* were all the
more reluctant since control over money was their last-ditch defense
against incursions by interloping centralizers. Buenos Aires, wanting no
part of such a loss of sovereignty, bolted from the Confederation, and
for the next decade managed an independent existence.[16] This decade of
conflict brought monetary affairs to new lows and a full-scale crisis by
the early 1860's.

Publicly, no one wanted monetary anarchy—it was an unintended
consequence of political discord. Urquiza and his followers initially
called for unity precisely to restore order to monetary affairs. At the
same time, stable monetary unity was a linchpin to integrate the fragmented units of the state: "without revenues, without money, without
regular commerce and means of communication," unification was chimera, and thus "it is imperative to create these and meanwhile use those
that exist in the provinces with more resources and a sense of national-
ity." The biggest obstacle was the lack of single monetary base: "Among
all the inconveniences, the greatest is the absence of uniform money."
This impeded trade within the national market that could help forge a
growing sense of national unity. It also menaced private property rights,
which Urquiza and his entire political generation treated as the foundation for a salubrious polity.[17] The interim Governor of Buenos Aires,
Vicente López y Planes, urged the province to respect the authority of
the new national regime in the following terms: "The commerce of our
province and that of her sisters, has immensely improved, having been
freed from the innumerable shackles that ruined exports of our fruits
and, without exaggerating, have been the principal cause of our poverty,
our backwardness, and of our political dissolution."[18] *Porteños* shared
this spirit. A customs and monetary union, argued the influential *El Nacional* on the eve of secession, would surely revive commerce, both domestic and international, and provide the basis for elusive prosperity.[19]

Unfortunately, a currency crisis undermined cooperation between
provincial and national leaders. Secessionist battles in the countryside
forced the provincial government to print 87 million pesos between July
1852 and June 1853—increasing the supply of pesos by 50 percent in less
than a year. To this were added another 8–10 million pesos in "gratui-

ties" to victorious officers.[20] The interim Provincial Finance Minister, José Benjamín Gorostiaga, named by Urquiza, strove to support the peso. To solve the currency crisis, the Minister consulted the city's most prominent merchants for their advice and help.[21] Gorostiaga especially solicited the support of the Casa de Moneda, the money-printing house erected during the Rosas era to replace defunct national and provincial banks. The Casa, a stronghold of merchant power, was understandably wary: Gorostiaga had to confess that the Province's unfunded debt surpassed 73 million (33 million left from Rosas's last battles, and another 40 million from this very brief administration). Merchants recoiled from extending even the most usurious loan, and instead aligned with Buenos Aires autonomists. Unable to enlist merchants' confidence, Gorostiaga resigned. Financiers' refusal to back the emerging regime came back to haunt them: shortly thereafter, *porteños* flocked behind the September 11, 1852, revolution. With the provinces now in full civil war, Casa emissions intensified and the peso plummeted. Merchants howled in protest against the use of paper money to fund wars and thus the debasement of their medium of exchange. In the words of one group of financiers, "the oscillation of metal [plummeting peso values] bring daily calamities to the country."[22]

Once secession was complete, each side quickly moved to establish respective monetary institutions. Political polarization intensified monetary fragmentation. Autonomous Buenos Aires most successfully created the foundations of a sovereign fiscal-military state. The initial step toward a monetary deal between finance capital and state-builders emerged in reaction to outside, Confederate ambitions. Buenos Aires statists, to enlist the support of financiers and to place provincial finances on more credible foundations, looked to the heart of the monetary nervous system. The first challenge was to redraft the powers of the Casa de Moneda to loosen its ties to "political" authorities, provide it with a greater measure of autonomy, and lend it latitude in open-market operations and rediscounting—or make it less an instrument of deficit financing and more a tool for maintaining monetary stability. In the words of one exponent of Bank autonomy, "I foresee with sorrow that as long as the fluctuations of our currency make every merchant's credit, and every proprietor's wealth uncertain, and at the same time victims of the most terrible, unaccountable, and sudden changes, it will be almost impossible to prevent the recurrence of the periodic crisis that afflicts our market."[23]

The Bank became a citadel of merchant power. After some debate over the new charter, the renamed Banco de la Provincia y Casa de Moneda opened its doors on January 1, 1855. Assuming responsibility for old Bank notes (between 204 and 212 million pesos in circulation), the new bank was supposed to receive deposits, make easier commercial loans, and most important, issue discounts at the judgment of the Directors. Bank Directors in turn came from the ranks of the city's most puissant merchants: the Llavallols, the Alcortas, the Gowlands, and the Armstrongs. By executive order, the Bank was also required to honor diligently all bills of exchange it had discounted, thereby reversing arbitrary payments on bills depending on the Bank's accounts.[24] In the first four years of its existence, the new Bank desisted from any emissions and appeared to be well on track to stabilizing the peso.[25] Constitutionally speaking, this reform reconsolidated monetary authority and placed it in the relatively independent hands of the city's merchant capitalists. Here was the first cornerstone of the monetary deal.

Creating autonomous monetary authority may have been necessary, but it was not sufficient for fiduciary stability. Several factors undermined Buenos Aires' unilateral efforts. First, the Bank succeeded only in raising 4,112 in metal pesos and 5.3 million in inconvertible paper. One observer wrote years later that this amount of capital "could never serve as base of an organization capable of restoring notes to their old value."[26] The capital shortage was evident to Directors. In turn, increasing interest rates and lowering charges on accounts to augment savings did not offset persistent lack of confidence.[27] There was also concern about speculation and liberal credit. The Finance Minister constantly pressured Bank Directors to keep interest rates over 10 percent to tame the "speculators" responsible for the peso's tremors. In mid-1855, he reminded Bank President Jaime Llavallol that rates must remain high, and that the Bank should call in all dubious rediscounted notes from agents involved in "demoralizing and prejudicial traffic, and to whom we must deny all the credit they have thusfar enjoyed, thus ending all types of transactions with them."[28] Merchants, as patrons and clients of the monetary regime, could not reconcile the contradictory pressures to raise Bank capital through the open market, maintain a tight reign on dubious notes, while at the same time offering credit to merchants in a bid to raise the institution's profile.

Explicit collaboration between merchants and officials waited for the government to address the disorder in its own fiscal house. In February

1855, Norberto de la Riestra took over the Provincial Finance Ministry. He brought extensive experience as a commercial agent for the firm of Nicholson & Green in London and Buenos Aires, and enjoyed a collegial rapport with the Buenos Aires financial and mercantile clique.[29] For the first time, this Ministry was in the hands of a businessman who played his political cards with unremitting determination to create a sound money regime. More than any other individual, Riestra, the Robert Walpole or Alexander Hamilton of Argentine financial history, laid the foundations of monetary and fiscal stability in Argentina; his efforts were an important step in the discontinuous path to convergence of merchant capital with *porteño* state power.

The hallmark of the Minister's efforts was to replace short-term deficit financing with longer-term public credit—reversing Rosas's own preference for issuing money over public credit. Bond finance was to replace currency finance. Doing so would help alleviate the pressure on the Bank to print pesos. In September 1856, the Provincial legislature approved a law creating a sinking fund of 10 million pesos bearing 6 percent interest, which would assign 100,000 pesos yearly to amortize existing debt, and into which the government could dip to cover current expenses. The same law requested that the Bank issue bonds on the open market for sale at not less than 75 percent of their face value.[30] According to one observer, "even private persons came forward offering to take it at a more favourable rate than that proposed to the Bank, shewing the facility with which the government can raise means whenever their own requirements oblige them [sic]."[31] Bit by bit, the government turned to this new fund to take the pressure off Bank emissions. Two years later, the government created another 12 million pesos in public funds for the same purposes. By all accounts this modest initial effort succeeded, and set the stage for a much more dramatic program of debt reconsolidation and amortization after political reunification.

The second prong of Riestra's strategy addressed the peso's volatile relationship to gold. The Minister, like a growing chorus of reformers across the Atlantic basin, figured that the long-term solution to monetary instability was to peg inconvertible paper money to the unimpeachable and "objectively" determined value of gold. Gold-backed pesos, fiduciary money, would chase away other monetary forms: commodity money, foreign coinage, and merchant bills—media of exchange that still possessed intrinsic value in creating a nimbus of reliability. Stabilizing the external rate of exchange for pesos would reinforce the internal use of government scrip. Such a transformation implied converting government liabilities (that is, after all, what notes and coins are) into an abstract means of payment and measure of worth with no innate value in and of itself. If anything, the value of public money depended on the credibility of administrations' promises to honor liabilities and merchants' faith in these pledges. The Directors of the Stock Exchange sustained a constant campaign to peg the peso to gold.[32] This would remove the shackles between monetary authority and political authority, in favor of new shackles to an international gold standard. The United States began to abandon bimetallism in favor of gold in 1853; similarly too Continental Europe and Brazil (Mexico opted to remain pegged to silver). Resolving the gold question, or rather, forging the political alliances to back the discipline of hard convertibility, was a sort of collective mantra. Many, Riestra above all, were impatient to impose some discipline on the unruly peso by making it convertible to specie. This would give paper, as the Minister was fond of saying, a "certain value."[33]

If gold was a goal, it was a long-term objective. Finance Minister Riestra had to confront two structural problems. First, chronic trade imbalances drained Buenos Aires of precious metals. Without stable reserves, civilians fled from paper whenever the peso's security was questioned. Getting reserves required positive trade balances or capital inflows. Either exports had to rise or foreign investors had to rekindle interest in the region.[34] As it turned out, exports were rising quickly, but their ability to brace the peso to gold still had to wait. In the case of foreign investors, here too there was a delay: external lenders still wanted to see financial discipline at work.

Second, the effort to stabilize and discipline the peso remained a constitutional problem. Buenos Aires' trade deficits with foreign trading partners could only be offset by surpluses with neighboring provinces. This triangular balance descended from colonial days, when Buenos Aires thrived off Andean silver, and persisted in modified form into the nineteenth century. Disunion impeded the triangular relationship between Buenos Aires, the provinces, and the Atlantic market. Only later, with the boom in agro-pastoral exports, and the massive shift in economic balance from the Interior to the Pampas, would Buenos Aires free itself from its dependence on the provinces. In the meantime, civil war shattered the triangular equipoise. The Paraná government saw the weak point in Buenos Aires' finances and sought to create its own autonomous base, and thus lashed out against *porteño* trade. With Buenos Aires' finances still wobbly, in July 1856 the Confederation imposed strict differential tariffs on trans-shipped cargo through Buenos Aires to redirect traffic to Confederation ports such as Rosario.[35] To this was added the international crisis of 1857 and a slump in exports.[36] Buenos Aires tried, but could not yet rely on trade surpluses to stabilize local money.

These obstacles notwithstanding, Riestra was determined to implement interim measures aimed mainly at putting a lid on paper note circulation. In a grim report to the Directors of the new Bank, he urged the Bank to limit emissions to metal coins so that "they may circulate and be received without depreciation outside the country." To give the region an even more solid trading currency, in July 1857 the Legislature endorsed several foreign currencies as legal tender. Moreover, the Bank should accumulate reserves in order to better defend its own notes. While his policies took time to bite, they signified an important change in priorities—previous rulers had paid only lip service to emission control and had paid even less attention to bank reserves, preferring to leave the peso exposed to civilian flight because money was such a powerful weapon for their political designs.

The trans-Atlantic crisis of the late 1850's forced Riestra to abandon calls for convertibility and issue emergency relief. He began urging the Bank to issue emergency credit and lower interest rates "that are paralyzing [commerce] and impeding the development of industry in the country."[37] With debtors unable to collect their own receipts, bills of exchange were going unhonored. To help out the most desperate merchants, Riestra appealed to the Bank to postpone the due date on its own 90-day bills (*letras de receptoría*). The Minister worried that malaise in Buenos Aires would inspire the Confederation to force Buenos Aires back into the union. But in pleading to monetary authorities to obey his political concerns, he had to face the consequences of his own monetary deal and the autonomy his government had given to the Bank. The Bank Directors cared less about Buenos Aires autonomism than the worth of their bills; they were truer champions of stable currency than even the Minister. Even Norberto de la Riestra, the paladin of peso-stability, could not control the urge to rely on emissions to print the government out of the political jam. Internal unpopularity in the wake of the 1857 downturn and external threats from the Confederation tore away at the Minister's currency convictions. The Bank President, on the other hand, did not find emergency measures necessary and, while acknowledging a general crisis, believed that policy should remain consistent, offering credit "to all mercantile houses that present real guarantees, as we are doing, and above all to ensure that on this base . . . the resources of the Establishment [meaning the Bank] remain sufficient to uphold future needs of the Señor Minister."[38] Riestra challenged, but in the end could not violate, the Bank's 1855 autonomous charter. This small showdown was a crucial step less for what it did than for what it did not do; political authority did not rescind the autonomy of private financial authority.

In the end, the provincial government survived the commercial crisis of 1857, but Buenos Aires was left in anything but a solid position. What was clear was that a durable solution to monetary instability required some alleviation of the tension with the Confederation. Without this constitutional resolution, the monetary deal still labored under the weight of the provincial state's noncredible commitment to uphold the rules of financial autonomy.

So how did republican architects resolve the riddle of political conflict? In retrospect, the solution was almost inevitable: let the Confederation implode. But at the time, Norberto de la Riestra and financial managers did not know that affairs in the Confederation were even more parlous than in Buenos Aires. In Paraná, policy-makers struggled to create parallel institutions to Buenos Aires' Bank and private market for funds. Their efforts failed for the same reasons that Buenos Aires' hung in a delicate equilibrium: Confederation exports simply could not match imports; the bulk of customs receipts were siphoned by Buenos Aires; and most important, warfare ravaged state finances.

Still, Paraná aimed to create an autonomous monetary regime. Things started badly, however. Then they got worse. Urquiza, without a Bank (and hence unable to print his way through the wars with Buenos Aires), and without an indigenous capital market (from which to borrow), turned to the Spanish merchant José de Buschenthal, who was fast becoming the Confederation's informal agent and was accumulating a significant—but risky—fortune off Paraná's insecurity. Buschenthal raised 225,000 silver pesos in Montevideo, charging 16 percent.[39] To escape this extortionate funding, the government issued a wave of reforms. The Confederation's first Finance Minister was Mariano Fragueiro, the champion of "public property," legal reform, sound finance, and a Chilean-style banking system. In late 1853, he helped author the financial blueprint for the regime, prompting the President of the Constitutional Committee in Congress to claim that the plan was the key to general constitutional survival.[40] Urquiza himself announced to the opening National Legislature that the scheme would be the "bases for the revenues of the State, having an origin equal to the right of property, so that nothing may be arbitrary, nor be the product of a forced service [*servicio prestado*] or loan [*capital anticipado*]. . . ."[41] The day of the statute's promulgation, Fragueiro sent a circular to the Provinces advising them of the new Confederate peso (worth 20 Buenos Aires pesos—the initial issue being worth some 6 million silver pesos). These moves aimed to staunch the drainage of money from the region to Buenos Aires, and to start re-importing silver.

By decree in February 1854, the National Bank of Rosario opened its doors, and in March, the new offices of the General Administration of Finance and Credit began operations. The Bank was supposed to act as the national Treasury, receive deposits, offer credit, and monopolize the handling of legal tender. But without stipulations on reserve levels or guidelines on the exact convertibility of notes, and most important, bereft of a nascent capital market populated with merchants willing to mop up government securities, it is hard to imagine how the statute might have worked. To make matters worse, bonds were to be denominated in national pesos, obligatory legal tender in all transactions. The first essay was a complete disaster: Chilean gold, Bolivian silver, old Spanish doubloons, and even *porteño* paper were preferable to Confederation scrip; the Rosario bank never got off the ground. 1.7 million pesos in notes were withdrawn from circulation, and Fragueiro himself resigned from the Cabinet in September 1855.[42] By the end of that year, the Confederation was demonetizing at an alarming rate.

Confederation statesmen redoubled their dependence on foreign financiers. Buschenthal lined up meetings with the French financial group Trouvé-Chauvel & Dubois in April 1855, to finance public works and lend the government money for current expenditures. After a brief *tripotage*, the French lost interest. In 1855, Juan Bautista Alberdi left for Europe to help raise funds directly, to little avail.[43] In May 1856, the Spaniard Esteban Rams y Rubert floated government bonds valued at 300,000 silver pesos (which raised 250,000 Bolivian pesos). At the end of 1857, Brazilian Baron Mauá set up a branch of his bank in Rosario, which closed two years later. Wanting to help cripple their rivals in Buenos Aires, even the Brazilian government lent 300,000 silver pesos to Paraná.[44] No amount of foreign "help" (this was a lucrative though very risky business) could overcome the Confederation's lack of a port, weak ties to domestic private finance capital, and persistent doubts about the solvency of the national regime. In short, the Confederation, deprived of customs and with only shredded ties to local private merchant capital, simply could not muster the revenues to finance daily operations, enjoyed no recourse to bonds, and finally could not even resort to emergency short-term currency finance.

Financial collapse loomed. Hit with the international downturn in 1857, the Confederation was in full economic crisis by 1858–59. Foreign merchants in Rosario who had been accepting government bills scrambled to redeem what little scrip they had accepted on payment from the Rosario customshouse.[45] Faced with penury, Urquiza realized the only way out was to force Buenos Aires back into the union. But even here, the Confederation invasion of the city had to be postponed to raise money. By the time the armies finally met at the Battle of Cepeda on October 23, 1859, though Urquiza soundly beat Mitre in the field, Buenos Aires had won the economic war. The armistice agreement of November 11 paved the way for national reintegration. It also set the stage for the next component of the monetary deal.

Convergence, 1859–1862

From the ruins of 1859, Buenos Aires and the Confederation converged—out of necessity more than out of conviction. Since neither side held the other in high regard, any talk of reconciliation was treated with a fair measure of suspicion and not a little duplicity. This was especially evident in talks over monetary controls, for here state-builders reopened the debate over political sovereignty. Who would control money, the national government, or Buenos Aires and the *porteño* merchant class? The dispute, in the end, led to war again, by which time the Confederation was a shadow of its former self. If disunion from 1852 to 1859 helped create the Bank of the Province of Buenos Aires, the next phase shaped how its legal tender would fare in the integrated national market.

In the months leading to Cepeda, both Buenos Aires and the Confederation resorted to measures that would burden the political apparatus emerging from the armistice. The Confederation leased the rights on Santa Fe customhouses for two years in return for a special monthly credit of 12,000 silver pesos; Buenos Aires opened another fund created out of a 10 percent surcharge on imports, and in mid-July 1859, returned to monetary emissions (by October, the Bank had printed 60 million pesos).[46] Across the country real money was becoming scarce as civilians fled from worthless paper and scrambled to hoard metal. Llavallol warned Riestra that "a million and a half [metal] pesos is very exiguous in proportion to the amount of paper in circulation, as the daily supply rises in our market."[47] Both sides were utterly bankrupt and the peso was worthless.

The Pact of November 11 provided the terms for economic convergence. First, the Constitutional Convention would tackle the problem of inducting Buenos Aires into the 1853 magna carta. Second, Buenos Aires ceded control of customs, but the province would receive transfers from the national Treasury at a rate of 1.5 million pesos per month. Third, Buenos Aires agreed to help build national economic public institutions. The new President Derqui gave Norberto de la Riestra command of the process of economic reconstruction. The President and his Minister, however, locked horns repeatedly. The former placed a higher premium on a political design to reintegrate the national government without ceding too much power to the political capital; Riestra was determined to transfer as much economic authority as possible away from politicians to private capital.

Riestra tried to apply to the Confederation the formula he used in Buenos Aires: convert short-term debt to long-term bonds. He began by trying to sort out the Confederation's obligations, settling accounts with Buschenthal and reclaiming authority over the nation's customhouses. Remonetizing the economy proved more difficult. Using an expedient tried in Buenos Aires years earlier, Riestra declared foreign currency legal tender to try to stymie fluctuations between metal and paper notes. He then negotiated an arrangement to declare the Buenos Aires paper peso legal tender, with the idea that the Provincial Bank would open branches across the Confederation.[48] This was important: it implied creating the first semblance of national monetary authority—which, if approved, would have enhanced the sovereign powers of the national government over *porteño* authorities.

Next, Riestra pushed for an overhaul of the national governments' revenue machinery. In November 1860, he presented a plan to nationalize customs, convinced that without a sound fiscal base the peso was not worth its weight in paper. Payments would be centralized at the port of entry, the money belonged to the national State, and no province (including Buenos Aires) could impose levies on merchants who had already paid their dues to the Confederation.[49] Buenos Aires accepted this arrangement (which should qualify lingering claims that Buenos Aires zealously guarded the customs monopoly).[50] On December 12, 1860, the provincial government ratified the accord, which included an amendment guaranteeing 65 million pesos per month payment from customs to the Treasury of the Provincial Bank. This money was earmarked to redeem debts and to stabilize the peso—and therefore strengthen its monetary authority. Gradually, authority over customs shifted to a national domain.[51] Buenos Aires financiers and governors were willing to forfeit fiscal jurisdictions to retain monetary sovereignty.

But persistent political turmoil soon aborted this convergence. In the first of a series of blows to Riestra's authority, the national Legislature refused to ratify a bill to reduce duty levels until Buschenthal was repaid (the legislators felt an obvious special affection to him for having financed the government thusfar). To break the logjam, Riestra proposed to buy off Buschenthal by raising a 4-million-peso loan to be negotiated at not less than 75 percent of its face value and bearing 6 percent interest, to be covered by a new sinking fund.[52] Given the ragged shape of the local money market, the success of this venture was unlikely. Then came the real setback: members of the national Constitutional Convention rejected the Buenos Aires delegates. Riestra began taking a bitter dislike to the unpredictable and somewhat impetuous President Derqui, and repeatedly complained to Mitre that he was dealing with a capricious helmsman who was less interested in financial affairs than political intriguing. When Derqui sent an army to put down open insurrection in San Juan, Riestra could take no more. The Finance Minister found the bloody intervention loathsome and the financial cost of the warfare a blow to his efforts to sort out the Confederation books. Every time the Paraná government needed money, Riestra had to appeal to his friends in the Bank of the Province to bail the government out. With each political downturn, the Finance Minister had to swallow his pride an ask for more transfers to the national Treasury. Finally, after so much humiliation, he quit in January 1861.[53] As Riestra packed his bags and prepared to return to Buenos Aires, a dismayed British envoy groaned to his Minister, "How much I regretted that he should have abandoned the government and the President at so critical a moment."[54]

Buenos Aires was also sinking into a maelstrom. In May 1861, Riestra reassumed the Provincial Ministry of Finance, inheriting a disaster there too. By March of that year, the Province had accumulated 45 million in obligations but raised only 28 million. Throwing in the costs of new public works, the government owed 18 million pesos. Riestra set about immediately to raise 5 million from "local capitalists," slashed spending and struggled to amortize recent debts with a special 24-million-peso reserve fund to restore the credibility of government bonds.[55]

The Minister also intensified efforts to collect direct taxes. This was never an especially easy task in Argentina, and Riestra tightened the screws on local tax collectors (especially Justices of the Peace) to reap license charges on petty merchants and "direct contributions" from landowners. Contributors moaned in protest, issuing a flood of petitions and appeals to the Minister for clemency and exemptions from fines and jail terms. One small landowner and retired public official pleaded with Riestra to release him from the direct levies on his lands. The new taxes of 1860 and 1861 visited penury upon his family, forcing him to mortgage the house. "You may judge," wrote Calisto Almeyra, "that in this year 1861 of war, misfortune, and paralysis . . . he who has nothing for subsistence but his meager pension from the state will have less to pay the Direct Contribution."[56] Even the collectors warned that rural producers were nurturing resentments against the government for the exactions they were being asked to sustain. Some worried about rural unrest.[57] The fiscal machinery ground to a halt.

Without revenues and unable to float more bonds on the local market, the provincial government turned to the printing press—this time forcing a reluctant Bank directorship to emit or face closure. Relations between political and monetary authorities reached an all-time low; paper money's relationship to gold followed suit, breaking the 400-peso ceiling in the winter of 1861. Rearmament, from 1859 to 1861, forced the Bank to issue 185 million pesos—almost as much as the 202 million issued from 1836 to 1859. By May 1862, the price of gold peaked at 426.[58] The Bank's metal stock vanished, and in April 1861, Directors voted to honor metal-denominated bills only in inconvertible paper, causing a storm within the Board. One Director claimed that gold reserves should be increased by increasing interest rates, for "it is cruel to give paper pesos to debtors so that they consume their own sacrifice buying gold at a time of rising premiums, with great damage to the credit of our currency . . ."[59]

In the end, warfare scuppered peaceable convergence on both sides. The clash finally came in late 1861. It left the Confederation completely bankrupt. Urquiza had to use his own personal fortune to finance this last campaign, and even then recoiled from spearheading the last fight. The national government collapsed; Derqui fled with his family to exile. Across the region, Confederation governors aligned with Paraná toppled—often in cruel and brutal recrimination (especially in Córdoba and Corrientes). By the end of 1861, most of Argentina was convulsed in insurrection. One by one, northern provinces fell to Mitre's forces led by General Paunero. The news from the hapless Vice-President was sobering: "We resorted to the emission of one hundred thousand pesos in treasury notes . . . and because of the poverty, lack of patriotism or bad faith of these capitalists, or for other reasons, despite the backing of that paper, it suffered a loss of value of some 70 percent before fifteen days had passed. . . . Our penury is absolute and complete. Our credit amounts to nothing."[60]

Buenos Aires emerged scarcely better. But the outcome was a decisive triumph for the republic's capital and a potential watershed for the private capital of the republic. First, the capital retained a greater measure of sovereign powers over economic policy-making thanks to its grip on revenues. Second, the basic monetary instruments remained the purview of Buenos Aires financiers, so that policy governing national legal tender was centralized in *porteño* hands. Buenos Aires, as the republic's capital, could dictate more easily the terms of political integration. Third, the opportunity to broaden the base of the national money market was lost: rather than create a regionally interlocked banking structure along the lines of the United States, the fallout of the crisis gutted regional financial bases. Rather than making the money market multipolar, warfare intensified concentration. Hereafter Buenos Aires financiers would be the near-exclusive source and conveyor of private money. The capital of the republic could more easily become a republic for capital.

Stabilization

Buenos Aires' triumph paved the way for the capital's financial hegemony over the rest of the republic. But it inherited a daunting economic legacy of civil war: massive debt-overhang. The government(s) and creditors had become reluctant partners; the debtors held creditors hostage. Debtor power over creditors was all the more troublesome since debtors were sovereign states and thus enjoyed alternative instruments: borrow more, raise taxes, or, as a last resort, just print more money.

However, sovereign debtor power was limited: debtors might depend on creditors for more money in the future. This quasi-voluntary alignment tied debtors and creditors into a common but conflictual plight.[61]

To right this malady, and resolve the conflict between sovereign debtors and private creditors, financial authorities initiated what we would now call a kind of stabilization package. First, a means to reconvert short-term debt to longer-term obligations had to be found to alleviate immediate and mounting charges. Second, the surfeit circulation of pesos had to be addressed to restore confidence. And third, fiscal discipline had to be imposed to rebalance revenues and expenditures so as to avoid future lending. The first option was a tricky business of convincing financiers to accept a long-term bargain with a hobbled state. The second and third implied dramatic austerity for society, especially holders of non-financial assets and wage earners. This was no easy task: at the same time that rulers introduced deep adjustment to shrink the debt and restore currency stability, they faced the enormous task of integrating a divided and literally bleeding political community. Stabilization was a trial by fire for republican capital.

As the smoke of battle began to lift, the extent of the financial devastation became clear. The economy was reeling from inflation and plummeting peso-values. By the end of the war, Buenos Aires had resorted to direct borrowing from merchants to keep their operations afloat: the peso was worth so little that emissions were pointless. A local capitalist, Antonio Fragueiro, lent the government 500,000 silver pesos to pay for intervention in Córdoba, and smaller merchants bought promissory notes to cover the defense of Rosario. By early 1862, the market was awash with 378 million pesos—more than triple the supply circulating when Rosas was overthrown a decade earlier. The news of Urquiza's withdrawal from the battlefield in early December 1861 brought brief respite for the spiraling peso.

The new government stumbled through its policy options. Debased pesos meant money shortages. Authorities had to balance rebuilding confidence with injecting liquidity into the market to revive economic activity. Provincial paralysis, warned one report, threatened to do more damage to unity than any loss on the battlefield.[62] Mitre himself, riding his triumphant wave in Rosario, wrote back to one of his Ministers in Buenos Aires that a much harder economic task awaited the Buenos Aires cause.[63] To save the Confederation, Buenos Aires leaders created an emergency 50-million-peso fund, backed by another round of bonds bearing 9 percent, specifically earmarked to cover national expenditures and alleviate fiduciary scarcity outside the capital. The Buenos Aires government lobbied hard to encourage the use of pesos in all official transactions. Riestra personally met with the owners of rural slaughterhouses (the region's largest economic enterprises), urging them to adopt paper in their own transactions. Then, in an effort to restore peso-confidence by mopping up the wash of notes, the Minister proposed gradually withdrawing pesos from the market by selling 6 percent bonds. He had to deal with an unruly and ungenerous provincial legislature, which balked at the scheme, arguing that peso-removal would accentuate "shortages" (not realizing that the sense of liquidity shortage had more to do with lack of confidence than lack of notes). Riestra responded. Exasperated, exhausted, and increasingly ill after handling provincial and national financial malaise single-handedly, he resigned from the Cabinet, claiming that immediate withdrawal of banknotes and stabilizing the currency were the "basis of all my financial plans."[64] He remained, however, the *eminence grise* of national finances and the unofficial mediator with Buenos Aires capitalists. But the conflict foretold acrimony between the executive bent on national unification and a legislature concerned with Buenos Aires' provincial prerogatives.

Dealing with the sagging peso led to currency and banking reform. The peso continued to sink from an annual average of 344 pesos per ounce of gold in 1860, reaching a nadir in February 1863 at 449. In December 1862, Riestra reminded the President of his proposal, now eight years old, of moving toward convertibility, "of fixing an exchange value relative to circulating paper money, with the objective of avoiding great oscillations, which cause such great unrest for commerce . . . not only to maintain morale and public faith, but also to prevent the demonetization of paper itself . . ."[65] A week later Mitre invited Riestra to meet in the Presidential Palace with Finance Minister (since October) Dalmacio Vélez Sarsfield to discuss immediate Bank policy governing note supply.

The Executive presented Congress with two important steps toward currency reform—what Norberto de la Riestra called "moralizing" money. First, in October 1863 the government made the paper peso national legal tender and established a preliminary schedule of exchange rates. A year later, in November 1864, Congress created a sort of dual exchange standard, declaring paper fixed at 25 per silver peso (400 per gold ounce), and banning all future unbacked emissions. The former measure really made *de jure* what was accepted *de facto*, that paper be the dominant means to settle accounts beyond the boundaries of Buenos Aires. As for the latter, although full convertibility had to wait for the 1880's and the restoration of foreign borrowing, the determination to curb emissions did tame wild peso oscillations.[66] Both declarations had to be backed by massive slashing of liquidity. The Bank began ritual burnings of piles of notes. From a stock of 378 million paper pesos in circulation in early 1862, the Directors managed to slash supply by 150 million by early 1865.[67]

If loudly proclaimed bonfires of pesos were meant to invest confidence in the peso, they elicited an even louder chorus of complaints from producers and merchants. *El Nacional* denounced a decision to torch 4 million pesos in June of 1863 as "barely rational."[68] *La Tribuna* accused the government of being dazzled by gold and willing to martyr its producers to satisfy investors.[69] Landowners of the county of Mercedes pleaded to the Bank for some respite from the credit shortage, wondering if some of the useless bills might not be loaned to them before the harvest to meet expenses.[70] Liquidity-starved non–financial-asset-holders saw peso withdrawal, correctly, as a boon to bondholders—represented as rich metropolitan fat cats. For their part, Buenos Aires financiers kept up their own campaign in favor of austerity. The President of the Bank warned Riestra that more pesos would visit "ruin and perturbation" on commerce, and invited the Minister to a meeting with other merchants and investors to discuss a sinking fund to mop up the supply of paper.[71] Amancio Alcorta, Senator and founder of the Stock Exchange, issued a series of essays defending short-term peso-burning for long-term fiduciary confidence.[72] A group of merchants warned that further instability would harm not just investors, but the whole country, adding that if the government did not honor its obligations in acceptable money, it would deprive itself of potential future investor generosity.[73]

There remained a pressing "constitutional" problem involving the sources of sovereignty governing monetary affairs. The principal means to issue and redeem remained in the hands of the province of Buenos Aires: the Provincial Bank. This split was a clear violation of the 1853 Constitution, which vested monetary authority in the hands of the federal government. Banking reform was a key to monetary stability—but it required an amendment of the provincial charter. Two principal schemes dominated the debate. The first was the brainchild of national Finance Minister Dalmacio Vélez Sarsfield: the Provincial Bank charter was to be amended to make it national, further emissions of paper illegalized, and existing paper made convertible. Norberto de la Riestra proposed a slightly different formula, based perhaps on the United States model of private sector "free banking." Also concerned to stabilize paper, but less concerned about the actual territorial jurisdiction of the Bank, Riestra urged that the Bank be reformed from top to bottom to remove all "political" holds over issuing authority—to place the regulation of money supply in the hands of the Bankers (and financial asset holders) themselves. Neither scheme flourished, for both threatened provincial autonomy and implied the transfer of this cherished jurisdiction to national state-builders—in the words of one defender of the status quo, "a people, when making deposits in its own sovereignty, decides the greatness or disgrace of its future."[74]

The failure to resolve the Bank issue threatened to shred the delicate alliance of national state-builders and capitalist financiers. The financial situation, despite earlier interim measures, appeared to worsen as 1863 unfolded. Bank Directors staunched the failing peso by accepting foreign currency deposits, raising interest rates, and accelerating the withdrawal of paper from the market. Hundreds of merchants gathered in the Colón Theater to express their concern, and struck a committee to pressure provincial and national governments into adopting some version of the Vélez Sarsfield-Riestra schemes. Meanwhile, budget cuts left the administration bereft of operating funds. The Minister of Interior canceled all transfers to provinces, restoring penury to the Interior and aggravating the civil strife. Unilaterally, the provincial government of Buenos Aires initiated talks with Baring Brothers to try to raise a loan.[75] Matters worsened with "El Chacho" Peñaloza's revolt in La Rioja, followed by General Flores's invasion of Uruguay; the peso resumed its tumble. With rumors that Urquiza would join Peñaloza in a pincer movement on Buenos Aires and a return to civil war, the flight to metal became a stampede, and merchants complained loudly of liquidity shortages. With the Buenos Aires legislature refusing to cede monetary sovereignty, Vélez Sarsfield abandoned Mitre's national cabinet.[76]

Historical contingencies came to the rescue. National armies eventually overwhelmed the rebels, subjecting much of the Interior to military occupation. Financially, a combination of desperate appeals by provincial governments, emergency loans by *porteño* merchants and the new London and River Plate Bank, and a trade boom based on wool exports to Europe and the United States (thanks to the U.S. Civil War), and hence customs receipts, brought relief.[77] In addition, earlier measures had now begun to bite. The fiscal deficit halved; the government tackled Buenos Aires directly by creating a 5-million-silver-peso fund, and authorizing the Provincial Bank to withdraw 2 million paper pesos a month on this fund. To afford this, Riestra devised a scheme to raise extraordinary funds, selling the Western Railway and auctioning frontier land to bidders.[78] Even the Bank's internal fortunes began to revive. Prudence and caution by the Directors helped nurture capital stocks. By 1864, reserves rose to 4.7 million silver pesos and 12 million paper pesos (up from 704,000 and 9.7 million respectively in 1860). Personal interest-bearing deposits rose from practically nothing to 2.3 million silver and 292 million paper pesos.[79] If we include bank deposits and capitalization as part of a generic monetary base (and not just notes in circulation), this suggests that the region was rapidly remonetizing.[80]

If the Province would not relinquish its monetary domain, the national government found other ways to convert the Bank into an instrument of monetary centralization and bestow autonomy from political forces. It was estimated that by December 1861, the Confederation's consolidated and floating debt reached 3.7 million silver pesos, with Buenos Aires' over 11 million silver pesos. The total public debt amounted to 16 million silver pesos (320 million in paper). The government made the Bank more than a crucial player in restoring currency credibility; the Bank became the instrument to reconvert short-term debt to long-term obligations through open-market operations.[81] Merchants had long since been arguing for such a solution.[82] Bank President Mariano Saavedra worked closely with Riestra in late 1861 to create a generation of Treasury bills backed by a special floating fund. Even the Provincial Legislature's Treasury Commission supported this sort of solution (it publicly preferred this to burning notes). By early 1862, the Finance Ministry operated through the Council of Public Credit in consultation with the Bank in the management of public, national bonds.[83]

Now the Bank could be put to the service of a national project of integrating the regional money market. Moreover, since the Bank was the citadel of *porteño* financiers, it transferred much of the work of handling sovereign debt to private capitalists. Not surprisingly, Amancio Alcorta of the Stock Exchange welcomed the use of tradeable financial instruments as a source of activity for the local capital market. In this fashion, he argued, money speculation, a venal "gambling operation," would give way to "free exchange . . . subject to laws." Open-market operations in public bonds would bring financiers and state-builders into a more harmonious relationship while subjecting public finance to market rules.[84] The move made the government's reluctant partner into an avid partisan. State power consolidated coeval with the emergence of a money market. Capitalist interests, national institutions, and liberal ideals began to converge.[85]

By 1865, political power rested in the hands of a new national state, but the authority to manage monetary affairs had clearly passed to the *porteño* financial elite, and in particular the city's merchants. The paradoxical outcome of a decade of civil war and nearly half a decade of post-war stabilization was to construct centralized political authority while divesting political representatives of the jurisdiction over a major allocator and invigilator of property rights: the power to confer or deny value to legal tender. Instead, a market for money monitored the rules and behavior of its participants—including governments themselves.

Stabilization and consolidation of a monetary regime—while it would undergo substantial modification over the next generation as Roberto Cortés Conde has recently shown—provided the foundation for Buenos Aires' integration into trans-Atlantic money markets. Boasting a more stable and credible monetary order, foreign banks moved into the region in droves. The Banco de la Provincia opened branches across the republic, becoming one of the New World's largest banks. Receiving deposits and issuing credit, it looked much like a wheel, with spokes radiating out of the capital city to the Argentine hinterlands. It was also the premier handler of government securities, capable of punishing wayward authorities by spurning their appeals for loans. Later, the Banco Nacional (1872) and the Banco de la Nación (1891)—likewise banks controlled by Buenos Aires' merchant-financial patriciate—aligned with the more seasoned Banco de la Provincia. Centripetal financial institutions served as the backdrop to the emergence of a national market for money. One could not imagine a more centralized contrast with United States–style free banking.

Money market centralization and stabilization quickly earned Buenos Aires a reputation as a lucrative haven for foreign investors. European financiers, especially British, turned to the republic as a destination for investment. Baring Brothers patched up their grievances with Buenos Aires in the mid-1860's. By 1870, European money was flowing in unparalleled quantities. Argentina lined up with the United States and Canada as a premier host for European investment. With capital moving in, and staple commodities flowing out, the peso at last lived up to Riestra's ambition. In the 1880's, monetary authorities in Buenos Aires folded local currency into the Atlantic world's rush to place regimes onto the inflexible, stable, and supposedly apolitical rules of the gold standard.[86]

Conclusion

By the 1860's, Argentina could boast unprecedented political authority based in the capital while upholding the private rights of capital. Delineating sovereign powers governing monetary policy had moved from being a dispute between federalists and Buenos Aires to conflict between Buenos Aires autonomists and national state-builders. In the end, antagonists compromised, letting the Bank remain a Provincial entity but allowing its actual control and management to pass to private financial interests who commanded a national vision of market integration. From this arrangement, a money market for public and private securities emerged. The guardians of this order were, in the main, finance capitalists themselves. Accordingly, state-builders and financiers reconciled the difficult balance between the public powers of sovereign debtors and the private interests of creditors. Political consolidation and fiduciary stabilization created a monetary regime able and willing to use public powers to encode private property rights.[87]

The creation of a stable medium for commercial transactions in a nationally unified market and the formation of an authority to govern monetary policies were clearly interdependent. This very interdependency also constituted the nub of fiduciary conflict. Without stable legal tender, political factions enjoyed greater incentives to assault adversaries since inflation and monetary oscillations undermined confidence in authority. Moreover, economic hardship accompanied instability, creating likely constituencies for armed opposition. This helps explain the cycles of civil war throughout the post-colonial era. Conversely, without constitutional consolidation, currencies were easy vehicles for short-term political gains. Rival parties relied on autonomous powers to create their own monetary base and used these prerogatives to print their way through endemic warfare.

The very interrelatedness of the dual legal transformation—creating a covering law for the political community and juridical foundations for private property—means that sorting out cause-and-effect sequences in the monetization of economic relations while integrating nation-states is, to say the least, complex. If nothing else, this chapter draws attention to the often contradictory and circular paths toward the constitution of property rights—that is, the contingencies presented by collective action when the rules of behavior were still in their formative stage. In this sense, encoding new notions of property, and the rights and duties they entailed, was above all a conflict-ridden, collective, and thus ultimately political process. There is no clear, parsimonious, and to say the least, universal causal relationship between the process of formation of public institutions of state and the private interests of capital.

However, it is safe to say that the alignment of the republic's capital with the private interests of capital in the republic produced two long-term *effects* that recast the rules of political struggle in the republic. First, this new monetary regime ensured a more universal basis for extracting fungible assets from society. Hitherto, the state had been too weak to rely on direct extraction through taxation or voluntary loans. This weakness had meant that short-term debt (like emissions) was often the only expedient. Emissions, inflation, and instability narrowed the scope of market activity. In this sense, currency-stabilization and concentration of monetary authority restored confidence to the circulating medium and bolstered open-market activity. This meant that the state—national and provincial—could more easily mold to society's productive structure, tapping into pools of capital where and when these resources accumulated. Extractive powers gave the state unrivaled ability to marshal resources to channel conflict (through war or coercion) or direct energies into productive enterprise (through investment).

Just as important, monetization reinforced state powers indirectly by making public notes, once and for all, the dominant medium of exchange. This deflated the risk of using legal tender, stimulated a nascent private credit system, and enabled the final eclipse of the colonial tradition of using merchant money. But as civil society increasingly accepted paper pesos, that is exploited money as a public good, the costs of withdrawing from open-market relations—or exercising the "exit" option in the words of Albert Hirschman—rose.[88] Once citizens agreed to play by market rules, they could not easily challenge authorities that controlled and invigilated these rules. In political terms, the opportunity costs of insurrection, rejecting the prevailing monetary regime, rose. This was not the language of General Urquiza, but it surely was the problem he faced. His Confederation could simply not survive so long as monetary authority lay outside his jurisdiction. The futility of winning armed battles but losing the economic war finally prompted him to withdraw from the battlefield at Pavón and to support General Mitre's efforts to galvanize a new national state, even if it was now on terms dictated by the Buenos Aires elite. The monetization and commercialization of civil society placed severe limits on the autonomy of dissenting political groups, forcing them to accept minimal rules of political conduct. Increasingly, the promise of issuing and regulating public goods such as money-generated societal respect for state power and forced political rivalries to be directed through constitutional channels. The coeval process of state-formation and money-market–formation transformed a centrifugal political and commercial region into a highly centralized political economy.

Out of warfare the interlocking pieces of an institutional jigsaw puzzle fell into place. Public power arose to uphold stable money, while a class of moneyed interests emerged able to be voluntary bankrollers of public power. The politics of financial transformation in the 1860's created the conditions for six decades of market-led, outward-oriented economic development. After a half-century of struggle, Buenos Aires rejoined the Atlantic world as a vibrant outpost of commercial capitalism in time for the golden age of free trade. Out of the rubble of mercantilism and the ancien régime emerged a capital capable of ruling over a republic, and a republic safe for capital.

11 ⤒ The Unfinished Revolution of the Republic of Capital

> It was only in the course of the eighteenth-century revolutions that
> men began to be aware that a new beginning could be a political
> phenomenon, that it could be the result of what men had done and
> what they could consciously set out to do. From then on, a "new
> continent" and a "new man" rising from it were no longer needed
> to instill hope for a new order of things. The *novus ordo saeclorum*
> was no longer a blessing given by the "grand scheme and design in
> Providence," and novelty was no longer the proud and, at the same
> time, frightening possession of the few. When newness had
> reached the market-place, it became the beginning of a new story,
> started—though unwittingly—by acting men, to be enacted further,
> to be augmented and spun out by their posterity.
>
> Hannah Arendt, *On Revolution*

Revolutionary Aftermaths

Ambiguity, paradox, contradiction, and contingency flow through this narrative as capital, commodities, and convictions flowed across the Atlantic in the nineteenth century. No single factor accounted for the causes, sequence, or outcome of Buenos Aires' revolution. Does this mean that there was no overall trajectory to the pattern of imperial crisis, upheaval, and emergence of republican statehood?

No. *Republic of Capital* has tried to offer a narrative comprised of a sequence of indeterminacies. The decade of the 1860's marked the final stage in Buenos Aires' long revolution. The process opening with Spanish imperial collapse culminated in the reaggregation of state power in the hands of creole civilians based largely in the Argentine capital and in close alignment with the interests of finance capital. By the 1860's, a half-century after the Viceroy stepped aboard a British man-of-war and reluctant rebels assumed the mantle of their own destiny, Argentines had some sense of what their future foretold. A new ruling coalition was in power, determined to fold the region back into the trans-Atlantic flow of commodities, people, capital, and ideas. The late nineteenth century recombined merchants' interests, public institutions, and ideas of political community—elements that had once combined within the shell of dynastic mercantilism, but now converged within the liberal blend of openness of markets and equality of legal subjects.

If this was the outcome, it was the unintended consequence of upheaval. The revolution had begun with the British occupation of the River Plate in 1806-7 and came to closure two decades later with the downfall of the unitarian administration.[1] In this phase, the political armature of formal rule trembled, then fell, giving way to efforts to use a liberal charter to reconstitute the old Viceroyalty on new legal foundations. Constitutions, the first generation of state-builders hoped, would create an emerging political community and fold it into the idealized republican form that appeared to be triumphing in other post-revolutionary societies of the Atlantic world. Paradoxically, constitution-making through public deliberation and debate was the catalyst of discord, not the creator of order. Creole conflict over the makeup of this new regime, coupled with mass mobilization for revolutionary warfare, only dimmed the prospects of a consensual transition to state legality. The United States' route to constitutionalism, as precarious as it was, was sealed off in the River Plate. What is more, fragmentation of the revolutionary elite and mass mobilization inhibited the fusion of ancien régime classes into a new restorationist alliance as in France, Brazil, or even Mexico before 1824.

Bereft of sovereign authority, the warring fragments of the River Plate coexisted within a membrane of caudillismo. The local chieftains eschewed the rule of law in order to squelch internal discord, but engaged in constant military jousting with neighboring political communities to preserve their local grips and to dispense patronage to their cronies. Inward ferment replaced a centralizing will.[2] In Buenos Aires, contingent agreements between the ruler, Juan Manuel de Rosas, and potentates enabled a new propertied class slowly to emerge from the anarchy. Yet, as in any instance when power rested on personalized arrangements and not legal enforceability, the emerging private elite could not count on state power to defend its immediate interests—let alone invest in public goods as states elsewhere in the Atlantic basin were beginning to do.

Civil war

Thus by the 1850's, revolution, civil war, and the loss of control over trade networks had shredded the old mercantile elite's fortunes. The revolution had forced the *porteño* patriciate to adapt to a new order of things, but it had not given this emerging class the legal wherewithal to *Legal* consolidate its private claims. In this sense, the rights of capital hovered between ancien régime jurisprudence and modern individuated notions of entitlement. The revolution expunged colonial vestiges of political property, where the legal enforcement of rights rested on non-neutral identities of rank and privilege, but it did not create the means to express and uphold a new notion of propertied interests.

The moment to shape a new legal order came in the 1850's. Guided now by the principles and reality of free trade, the River Plate folded back into the Atlantic system, commerce flourished, local and foreign merchant-financiers saw Buenos Aires as a magnet for enterprise, and trade and investment began enriching landholders. Herein, Atlantic transformations helped generate a social bloc able and willing to exercise its will over the far-flung constituencies of the region. In turn, jurists expounded a revised set of constitutional ideas, purging the idealist projects of using the charter to make society. Now constitution-talk tilted in favor of stabilizing the existing society, and not molding a new one. In turn, statesmen nurtured an approach to private law to separate the jural field of property from the discretion of lawmakers (whether legislators or judges), preferring to inscribe rights into a formal code that *contract* would doctrinally exhaust—and therefore make unassailable—contract *Property* and property law.

On two parallel dimensions, in private contract law and public law, the regime rationalized itself as a sequence of deals, monitored contracts among interest groups. This notion of legality as the expression of inter- *legality* est group pluralism, as Roberto Magabeira Unger has noted, was part of the nineteenth-century institution-building purpose of creating the appearance of neutral rules and standards for private and public behav- *neutral* ior.[3] The promulgation of constitutions and codes in the 1850's and 1860's heralded a new mood of legal formalism. Legal formalism—the commitment to deducing legal solutions from abstract and apparently neutral principles—freed the business of making choices over individual *Ideological* and collective rights from ideological concerns. In this fashion, markets for goods, labor, and especially capital could function according to their *economy* own laws of motion, beyond social classes. Now, to arbitrate disputes, legal agents appealed to doctrinal principles supposedly outside the

Legal formalism—

control of any class, sector, or region. This was an important material, political, and ideological triumph: no longer would social class determine which citizens engaged in market activity (as the colonial model implied); market activity would begin to contour emerging social classes.

If these were all necessary components of a reordered commercial world in southern South America, they were not, however, sufficient. Several final capstones still had to be placed on this republican edifice, as Alberdi, the architect of the republican order, observed.[4] First, the remnant unruly provinces—and there were fewer of these left as the decades passed—had to be subdued. The civil wars of the late 1850's and early 1860's finally broke the political impasse, by crippling the provinces and emboldening the capital's commercial and financial prowess. By the late 1860's and early 1870's, the caudillos of the Interior were on the run. In some western provinces (notably La Rioja) and Littoral provinces (especially Entre Ríos), federalists never relinquished their hope of a different proprietary and decentralized order, harboring dreams of a bygone era. Centralizing forces ultimately prevailed by forcible pacification. The most serious clash came when the last large-scale federalist uprising overlapped with the last regional challenge to Buenos Aires' hegemony, in the War of the Triple Alliance (1865–70). In this conflict, Argentina, Uruguay, and Brazil levied Latin America's most gruesome war against Paraguay and against their own hinterlands. Whatever one might think of this carnage, it capped the political and economic consolidation of *porteño* authority over the River Plate region. By the 1880's, local provincial patriciates emerged to eclipse their personalist forerunners, and alloyed themselves to the commercial and financial power of the capital. Argentine leaders finally reconciled the problem of how to reorganize the political community under the carapace of a constitution. Now, however, this constitution eschewed aspirational-talk, part of it once inscribed in the vocabulary of federalism; public law was not the maker of a new order, but a defender of the order that was.

Having subdued the provinces of the Interior, the capital had to reconcile its emergence with the most powerful province of all: Buenos Aires. Hardline autonomists, the offspring of the 1820's civil wars, did not want to sever the links between the province and the capital. The new emerging bloc, progeny of the capitalist transformations of the 1850's, was less concerned about the inter-provincial weight of the province, and aimed to consolidate the puissance of the capital within the Republic as a whole. With the Interior provinces kneeling, and the power of capital ascendant, autonomists lost their excuse for defending the province of Buenos Aires' unequal status. Friction between Buenos Aires provincial autonomists and national-centralizers finally came to a head in 1880, only to be followed by the foregone solution of federalizing the city.

The final capstone was the consolidation of the capital's financial power. The construction of a central state rested on a group of urban financiers willing and able to bankroll the operations of the public regime. These same agents soon became the magnates in an emerging "national" capital market dominated by banks with quasi-public functions. The Banco de la Provincia—nominally public—was dominated by private merchants of the capital, and ruled over a network of branches across the country by the 1880's. The Banco Nacional, created in 1872, was privately owned, and also enjoyed its reach into the provinces, though it was much smaller than the Banco de la Provincia. Both operated as agents of the emerging regime, as crucial handlers of public debt, and thus spared governments' need to rely on short-term loans or currency finance. This gave the national state unrivaled financial resources. To boot, both banks extended the reach of urban financial power into the commercial hinterlands of Argentina. The idea of free banking and decentralized credit structures was a bygone pipe dream

Internal pacification, external warring, the neutralizing of provincial Buenos Aires' itchy chauvinism, and the consolidation of the city's financial clout all built on the institutional, intellectual, and interested transformations of the previous half-century. What emerged was not just a politically centralized polity based in the capital, but the consolidation of an economic regime whose ruling heights were controlled by capital. The equipoise of public authority and private rights shattered in the revolution coexisted tensely through the years of civil war, and finally reconverged symbiotically half a century later. The private rights of capital and the public power of the capital locked arms to usher Argentina into the pluralist, multilateral liberal Atlantic order of the late nineteenth century.[5]

Two Revolutions in One

How should we characterize Argentina's revolution? One strategy presents the events following May 1810 as an extension of the trans-Atlantic

Trans Atlantic revolutionary process

revolutionary process ignited by the American and French revolutions. The Spanish American revolutions represented the final episode of an Enlightenment struggle against imperial anciens régimes. Uprisings in British North America, Saint Domingue, and Hispanic America sundered the formal political grip of Europe in the New World, unraveled protected, exclusive and monopolized commercial networks, and toppled monarchs in favor of republican notions of equality and autonomy of the legal subject. The revolutionary arc opened in the British polity in 1776, and closed in the second decade of the nineteenth century in Spanish America. Spanish American revolutions marked the final saga in the long decline of the early modern Atlantic system.[6]

That Buenos Aires and the rest of mainland Spanish America was one large corner of the Atlantic world's revolutionary conjuncture became the dominant interpretation of the republic's founding historians. In the view of mid-nineteenth-century liberal writers such as Juan Bautista Alberdi, Vicente Fidel López and Bartolomé Mitre (each with their own hue), Enlightenment creoles aimed to destroy ancient arrangements with a great rupture. In this sense, the revolution was the last great struggle for liberty and equality. If, late in their lives, Alberdi and López bemoaned the unfortunate downturn of their forefathers' goals, they nonetheless agreed that there was a democratic kernel embedded in a project that seemed only to lead to chaos. It was not surprising that the Enlightenment's last heroic—and most convulsed—battle against aristocracy, monarchy, and scholasticism should unfold in the corners of Europe's oldest, greatest, but most decrepit empire: Spain.

Ouch! Spanish revolution

The revolutionary heritage, however, did not—could not—generate the sort of triumphal narratives that soon flowed from the pens of other post-revolutionary writers in the United States and France. Indeed, it was the very inability of the revolutionaries fully to dismantle old ways that inhibited an easy North American–style transition. This led to civil war. So, to solve the riddle of republican governability, they embraced, as a necessary evil, a political structure bolstering order over liberty. Mitre, less pessimistic, formulated the revolution in similar ways, but saw himself, his generation, and the city from which he governed as the

creole

inheritor of the creole mission. He was determined to place the republic back on its virtuous path after the unfortunate lapse into provincialist anarchy. Either way, creole thinkers could draw a line, twisting perhaps, between the revolutionary heralds of 1810 and their state-building heirs of the 1860's.

Revolution

This understanding of the revolution enjoys a long and distinguished vintage. For good reasons. If the romantic narrative exaggerated the like-mindedness of creole elites championing a new order, and saw its forefathers as willful rather than reluctant revolutionaries, this narrative *Saga* appreciated two cornerstone aspects of the saga. First: the revolution was a revolution. Subsequent revisionist scholarship has tended to see *1810* the fallout of 1810 as nothing but colonial elite reconsolidation of power in republican drag. This book has argued that the revolutionary sequence and outcome did not restore old notions of public rule; rather, they bequeathed a liberal sensibility about politics to be governed by *liberal* appeals to reason. Argentines spoke differently about public affairs: citi- *Reason* zens were putatively equal—the rule of law applied to everyone, ruled and rulers alike. This was the meaning of republicanism, and it offered a vocabulary for legitimating claims to power and denouncing power holders. Revolutionary Buenos Aires was an Enlightenment birthright.

Second: rights-talk also inflected the language of personal claims. No *2* longer did people speak of privilege or prerogative according to membership in special circles, derived from one's station in life. People made material claims by referring to their autonomous rights to enjoy prop- *Rights* erty to the exclusion of others, and to strike bargains that were enforceable precisely because contracting parties entered the private bargaining world as willful, free, and independent agents. This was the meaning of new property-talk, and this was the language that percolated through *Property* the courtrooms of the republic to arbitrate private conflicts over property rights. The legal transformation of the River Plate Viceroyalty uncoupled the ancien régime fusion of qualification to participate in public life and entitlement to enjoy personal possessions. The revolution separated property from sovereignty, splitting rights to own and alienate possessions from the public constitution of a citizenry.   *Citizen*

But separation is not the same as opposition, for neither property nor politics subsisted in entirely autonomous domains.[7] This is important to *Property* appreciate, for although the revolution put Argentina on a liberal capi- *Rights* talist path, it did not mean that private property relations would cease to shape politics, or that public decisions never entered the autonomous field of personal claims-making with its contract law sentinel.

The process of transformation created only partial, not absolute, immutable, "end-of-history" kinds of resolutions. The transformation from colony to statehood and from monarchy to republic was so profound, so far-reaching, that unforeseen contingencies could not help but intrude upon and deflect the transformation. This is why this book has spent so much time on the narrative ("mere description" in the unfortunate words of one political scientist) course of change.[8] In the long run, the revolution created the legal foundations for liberal capitalism, even though the kind of public and private equality that emerged did not fit what the revolutionaries in fact had envisioned. It was, indeed, far easier for revolutionaries to define themselves in oppositional terms against the ancien régime than it was to express a coherent set of alternative principles, much less feel secure that these principles enjoyed any consensus. While they tried to negotiate the difficult post-colonial and republican transitions, as for instance, North American patriots barely succeeded in doing, creole political wills alone could not prevail. Subsequent upheaval meant that any arrangement for rule would face difficulties legitimating itself. Even the United States' smoother transition still faced considerable contestation and persistent opposition, and only eventually formulated a liberal constitution as a blind, transcendental ideal for the political community.[9] Argentina (and for that matter the rest of Spanish America) was less fortunate. By the 1860's, the *porteño* patriciate got order, but they had some distance to cover before making it seem universally benevolent.

The reasons why the revolution debouched into civil war and not the consolidation of a new order are both circumstantial and structural. Deeper social tension, the loss of the primary commercial silver axis, and more entrenched counter-revolutionaries presented structural obstacles to what already promised to be a difficult transition. But the combination of friction with neighbors (especially Brazil), internal discord among the revolutionary leaders, and the inability to get a public funding system to bolster political authority aggravated the improbability of smooth reordering. The United States' triumphal narratives ironed out the tricky business of forging political communities and stabilizing property relations in the wake of revolution—providing stories of state-building that were as misleading and misguided as they were triumphalist. If anything, Spanish America and Buenos Aires exemplify more authentically the paradoxes and contingencies revolutions pose: how to build new orders—as Hannah Arendt elegantly notes in the passage cited as the epigraph to this chapter—when the public and private means to do so were hobbled remnants of the old system or mere foundlings of a future promise.

How, then, do we account for transformations which do not pre-

sume that new political communities were automatic postcursors of
revolution? One way is to treat revolution and its aftermath as a tragic
saga. Indeed, at first blush, the trans-Atlantic Enlightenment purpose in
the River Plate comes to us as a failed venture. This is certainly the impression conveyed by later historians. Revisitonists have tended to see
nineteenth-century transformations as a counter-revolution in republican drag, as a betrayal of the liberal promise, as a reconsolidation of a
deeply entrenched colonial order. If the revolution had a liberal mission
at the outset, illiberal sectors (in the form of personalist caudillos) and
classes (landed baronies) hijacked it. The spirit of the revolution was
betrayed. Indeed, the fate of the figure of Mariano Moreno, the firebrand of 1810 who died mysteriously at sea, is often treated as the embodiment of the tragic narrative.

To be sure, history did not work out as intended. The reasons a
tragic narrative has proven so compelling are easy to understand: the
upheaval of 1810 did not lead to a new order with deep legitimacy or
lasting momentum of affirmative rights for a developing citizenry. Such
pessimism, and revisionist historiographic handiwork exaggerate the
denouement. While the eventual outcome paled beside its original aspirations, need we describe it as a non-liberal order? It certainly was not a
restoration of the ancien régime. Nothing of the counter-revolutionary
resilience of Congress of Vienna Europe emerged in the River Plate. The
post-revolutionary reordering of the River Plate republics may not have
fit the idealized templates of the United States' triumphal narratives, but
this need not deprive Argentina's outcome from qualifying for a liberal
pedigree.

Just what kind of revolution was this if it did not measure up to its
founding aspirational goals? To characterize it, other narrative structures free from idealized comparisons may help. We have agreed on
some of the long-run effects of revolution—it sundered the legal foundations of mercantilist colonialism and bequeathed a new kind of rights-
talk that emphasized contractual will and individual entitlements free
from status. But the revolutionary saga can also be the source of a *different* interpretation, one that did not square easily with original Enlightenment goal of separating sovereignty from property. Indeed, this other
interpretation and process emerged precisely as a response to the unanticipated, and unfortunate, consequences of the 1810 rupture.

The Atlantic world hosted a subsequent, overlapping state-formation
story that characterizes some aspects of what transpired in the River

Plate. The half-century of upheaval, turmoil, and feeble public or private authority pushed the sequence of Argentine state-making into a second Atlantic constitutional conjuncture. If the first moment was a late eighteenth-century phenomenon associated with imperial and monarchical crisis in the pursuit of liberty, the second, gestating in the post-Napoleonic decades, placed greater emphasis on the political construction of state-forms from above in order to avoid the threat of insurrection from below. Paying less attention to abstract notions of autonomy and freedom of political subjects, a new constitutional paradigm gripped the Atlantic world. This paradigm is best captured in de Tocqueville's reflections on a new "constructionist" mood among public authorities of the 1830's and 1840's, and characterizes regimes across the Atlantic world, from responsible governors in Canada, to Brazilian constitutional monarchs, to Italian *Risorgimento* architects. A new brand of public leadership began unifying political communities to create stable foundations for commercial capitalism in the age of the nation-state.[10] Order overshadowed equality; political unity eclipsed sovereign autonomy. Juan Bautista Alberdi, writing in 1853 as his blueprint for the constitution was sailing through the National Assembly, captured the spirit with characteristic economy: rather than aspire to an "ideal republic" and "perfect liberty," Argentines should aim for the "possible republic" and "imperfect liberty."[11]

Buenos Aires' revolution straddled the two constitutional conjunctures of the Atlantic world's transformation, the constitutional moment associated with the democratic revolutions of the late eighteenth century, and the mid-nineteenth-century movement of integrated state-formation. It exemplified both a republican aspiration to dismantle the girding of the ancien régime in America, and a later top-down effort to consolidate the power of a political capital while creating a new legal framework for private capital. As such, it was internally ambivalent: the revolutionary situation and its unfolding *combined* both types of collective action, purposive struggles for equality and popular sovereignty, with efforts to unify the political community from above while upholding the rights of property. While the former has often been seen as more "revolutionary" and the latter almost as "counter-revolutionary," this book has tried to present these constitutional sagas as two sides of a liberal coinage.

In this sense, revolutionaries, from the very start agonized over how to reconcile liberty with modern authority. If, in the early stages of their political peregrinations, they tended to see liberty as something they could introduce to a society capable of playing by new ground rules, civil war soon chastened such voluntarism. As the decades passed, constructing authority came to be seen as the necessary condition for liberty, and not vice versa. This did not make Argentina's experience of state-formation any less liberal, any less capitalistic. Argentina did not deviate from the liberal mold. It just exemplified an internal contradiction between private property and political representation—a tension shared across the Atlantic world that gave rise to a variety of arrangements for rule. The revolutionary heritage was, then, internally ambiguous, torn between disparate visions of what liberal modern political economies should resemble. In effect, the separation of property and sovereignty was a revolutionary accomplishment, but it did not absolve the future of potential tension between the two domains.

The Republic of Capital in Crisis

In Argentina, liberalism tilted in the direction of a pragmatic effort to stabilize rulership and set the economy on a path of market-driven growth. Notions of popular sovereignty took a beating from the 1820's onward in order to consolidate a particular proprietary regime and to defuse political rancor. The constitutional convergence of the 1850's and 1860's narrowed the scope for countervailing powers within the fabric of constitutionalism. Internal checks on the political regime, whether it be the decentralized authority of federalism or the balancing of powers between executive, judicial, and legislative branches, were deliberately curbed. Effective at bonding the core of political power from the capital outward, expunging the possibility of legal, constitutional contestation against rulers from *within* the state pushed oppositional movements outside the formal political arena. So good at creating order, the political system was less effective at incorporating or channeling political pluralism. What is more, deliberate weakening of external checks on public authority—for instance, diluting vested rights of citizens before state power—deprived actors of the means to make claims on the state from within the vocabulary of Argentine liberal constitutionalism. Once again, this pushed more expansive notions of citizenship outside the formal arena of public power. And as the twentieth century began to wean new sensibilities about collective entitlements, especially with the rise of social-claimsmaking, it proved increasingly difficult to accom-

modate new rights and patterns of representation to the parsed ideas
and institutions of nineteenth-century Argentine statehood. Constitutionalism consolidated a state to squelch fissiparous dissenters, but it did
not create the legal machinery for this state to handle future opposition
movements. In effect, the republic of capital was such a triumph that it
made it difficult to imagine—never mind assimilate—alternative, countervailing and evolving republican sensibilities.

The ambiguities of Argentine constitutionalism meant that the multiple legal transformations, from monarchy to republic, from rent-
seeking to competition, from relative to absolute property, did not necessarily imply closure. Consolidation of a republic of capital did not settle public and private discord for good—it simply set up the terms for
future clashes. Indeed, once the legal terms of rulership settled in the
voluntary and not so voluntary alignments of the 1860's, contested elections and political representation became increasingly heated matters.
Competition at the ballot box soon became the occasion for dissent
against the tightfisted rulers of the capital. Indeed, one of the revivers of
the language of popular sovereignty channeled into the electoral arena
was none other than Bartolomé Mitre himself, who, by the 1880's, lam-
pooned the sort of "oligarchic" deals made among the capital's rulers
and their provincial allies.[12] This kind of oppositional talk finally animated the formation of Argentina's first modern political party, the
Unión Cívica Radical, whose leaders self-consciously styled themselves
as the inheritors of a Jacobin, "radical" esprit born in 1810. Furthermore,
the mantra of popular sovereignty was to carry this party to victory in
the republic's first open and universal male elections in 1916, a century
after the revolution erupted. It appeared that, finally, Argentina by the
1920's, had legitimized its public law domain in the guise of suffrage
without destabilizing the private legal domain of capital.

History, however, soon dashed the hopes of combining wide political representation with the legal immunities for the rights of capital.
Elections and the practice of universal suffrage did not reconcile property and sovereignty. If competitive elections stripped the ruling bloc of
its ability to act as sentinels of the regime but did not upset the power of
private capital, the democratizing polity still failed to integrate peoples,
classes, and sectors who were not present at the debate and negotiations
over the terms of rulership in the 1860's. The Radical Party did champion the cause of competitive and robust elections; but it did not solve
the riddle of how to induct popular sectors into the mainstream of po-

litical society. Social Democrats and Conservatives fared even worse.[13] Thus, on the eve of industrialization, substantial sectors of Argentine society did not identify with political authority as the legitimate incarnation of a popular will ratified through the rituals of electoral brokerage. Indeed, to many, the republic still appeared to be a haven for capital, even if suffrage were universal.

What was absent from the political settlement of the 1850's and 1860's was the institutionalization of any countervailing forces built into fabric of constitutionalism itself. Not only was the legal fabric of the republic so alloyed to the interests of capital, but its legal image as a neutral and pragmatic compact among interest groups meant that any class or sector that expressed deep dissent over the balance of public authority or allocation of private rights was immediately tarred as a threat to the republic. Discordant rights-talk found little room for legal expression from within the heritage of nineteenth-century Argentine constitutionalism.

As the twentieth century unfolded, earlier notions of popular sovereignty and emerging ideas of social entitlements and group rights found ready constituencies among the burgeoning popular sectors of Buenos Aires. Indeed, the failure of political parties to act as the conduits for political integration left many workers and migrants to the New World's largest capital outside the realm of formal representation. Moreover, and perhaps more important, urban workers and middle sectors also embraced more than just amplified formal political rights, but extended the idea of collective representation into entirely new fields, like rights to bargain collectively for wage-labor contracts, rights to protection against the worst abuses of capital. And as popular ideas, emerging institutions (like unions), and surging interests trumpeted this new rights-talk, it flew in the face of the dominant legal fabric of the republic of capital. Since the constitutional apparatus of the nineteenth century had purged the foundational rules of politics of aspirational content and very self-consciously designed the architecture of state to preserve order rather than accommodate countervailing forces, Buenos Aires' popular folk did not channel their ideas, interests, or institutional energies within formal legal domains.

When popular rights-talk led to mass mobilization, strikes, and calls for social and economic justice, rulers responded by invoking the constitutional language of stability and republican order. The cause of shop-floor and ballot-box popular representation became unfulfilled goals in the inter-war years, and soon deprived "liberal" arrangements of their legitimacy. To make matters worse, segments of the elite even violated the agreement to let electoral competition legitimate state power. In 1930, the military toppled the hapless Radical government. Then republican rulers secured the vindication of Argentina's first coup d'état from the Supreme Court—realizing what the framers had originally intended: for the judiciary to act as ballast for the executive branch. By the 1930's, the regime was wallowing in a deep crisis of legitimacy, supported by fraud and modern cronyism. It was able neither to respect its own internal formal controls nor to embrace the emerging popular demands for new rights. The republic of capital was smothering itself, spoiling the old system and refusing to come to terms with a new one.

The crisis of the republic of capital finally came to a head during the Second World War, with the next military coup in 1943, followed by the triumph of Colonel Juan Domingo Perón at the polls in 1946. What Perón offered was a new vision for the republic. To resolve the unsettled problem of balancing political representation and the autonomy of property, he was willing to intrude on the rights of capital. Perón, in effect, reintegrated the republic by opening the public sphere to popular sectors and creating new legal avenues of social and economic claims-making—in a word, enabling the countervailing forces to champion their own law-clad ideas, institutions, and interests that had once been forced out of the constitutional framework of nineteenth-century state-builders. Perón's effort to induct this new legal spirit into a populist constitutional arrangement, however, was an affront to its precursor. It destabilized an almost century-old agreement to leave untrammeled the private world of contract. The rights of property took a beating.

While this arrangement lasted, it was remarkably successful. It transformed the republic, integrating sectors and classes that hovered on the margins of the old republic of capital. But, in mobilizing society while polarizing it, Perón's realignment of power also created the conditions for its own implosion. The Peronist alliance simply reconstrued the tension between private property and political representation, and did not transcend it. He did not—and in this, he followed in the footsteps of his constitutional predecessors—create a constitutional carapace to accommodate the tensions between property with sovereignty within the same legal framework. Perón opted, just as Alberdi had done a century earlier, for a regime that tilted one way at the expense of the other. If for Alberdi, law-making had to serve the goal of republican stability and the needs of capital to transform the political economy from above, for Perón, law-making was put at the service of republican transformation and the claims of popular sectors from below.

In the end, this was a dramatic, but short-lived experiment in populist constitutionalism. Its brevity contrasted with the depth of its scars. Argentina was divided between warring camps. It was a republic tearing itself apart over irreconcilable images of republicanism. What survived still was the hope—at least among many—that reasoned discourse could lead the republic out of its maelstrom. But even this faith faded. With Perón's downfall in 1955, Argentina entered a long tunnel whose light slowly dimmed, and then went out in March of 1976. In the name of republican stability and order, the Argentine military, at the behest of certain sectors in society, visited unspeakable acts of illiberty on a society clinging to a vision of a political community united by the faiths of its foundational, if deeply and agonizingly ambivalent, revolution: a republic to be governed by the compass of reason and not the power of force.

Yet the republic lives. Its unresolved revolutionary heritage emerged maimed and badly bruised, but it is still with us. The difficulties accommodating the tensions between property and sovereignty, and between personal claims and collective aspirations, however, should not be seen as evidence of failed precursors that are better forgotten. If at times the republic was a figurative—and literal—battleground, such conflict and warring proves the importance of enabling countervailing forces to participate in the constitutional life of the republic, for its own long-term health, and for the strength of its democratic fabric. Dissent and disagreement, especially from the weak and marginalized, can rescue the political community from its own self-satisfaction and propensity to reinforce those who already possess public authority and personal power. This is the lesson of Buenos Aires' republic of capital—a republic too triumphant and too successful for its own good that it could not make room for others.

REFERENCE MATTER

⌒ Notes

The following abbreviations are used in the Notes:

AA   Archivo Alberdi, Colección Furt, Argentina
ABPBA Archivo del Banco de la Provincia de Buenos Aires
AGM   *Archivo del General Mitre.* 28 vols. Buenos Aires: Museo Mitre,
        1911–13.
AGN   Archivo General de la Nación, Argentina
AHPBA Archivo Histórico de la Provincia de Buenos Aires
BBA   Baring Brothers Archive, Guildhall Library, Great Britain
BN   Biblioteca Nacional (in AGN)
FO   Foreign Office Archive, Public Record Office, Great Britain
PH   Papeles de Hacienda (in AHPBA)
TC   Tribunal Comercial (in AGN)

Chapter 1: Toward a Political History of Economic Life

1. "Santiago Esperon solicita moratorias por cinco años" (1815), AGN, TC, E-66 (1801–18).
2. Thelan and Steinmo, 3–8; Maier, 2–7.
3. Sahlins, xiv.
4. Eggertsson.
5. Chatterjee, 4–13.
6. On the comparative method, see Collier; Ragin; Elster, *Logic*, ch. 6; Roxborough.
7. Macpherson.
8. Polanyi, 68–76.
9. Marshall.
10. Hayek; for a discussion, see Flanagan, 335–57.
11. Marx, 279–81.
12. Cardoso and Faletto.
13. Véliz. Admittedly, these formulations usually have trouble dealing with the Argentine record from 1870 to 1930—a mere sixty years of transformation.
14. The theoretical literature is now massive, certainly more voluminous than

actual historical applications. For a recent survey, see Getzler. For suggestive histories of the approaches, see Stigler; Coase.

15. North, *Institutions*.

16. For a recent exception, see some of the essays in Stephen Haber, *How Latin America*.

17. Bates, "Contra Contractarianism."

Chapter 2: Imperial Reconstitution and the Limits of Political Property

1. Attman; TePaske, "New World Silver"; Vilar. A fine account of the later silver matrix of Potosí is Tandeter, *Coercion*.

2. Palmer, 1: 4.

3. Halperín Donghi, *Reforma*. For a different view, which argues that Spanish policies taxed, and snapped, creole loyalty, see E. O. Acevedo, and more generally on the parting of creole and imperial loyalties, see the majestic work of Brading, *First America*.

4. Guerra, "Spanish American Tradition" and *Modernidad*, chs. 2–3.

5. Jean Bodin was the supposed intellectual architect of French absolutism. See his *Six Books of the Commonwealth*, esp. book I. For critiques of Spanish absolutism, see Stein and Stein, *Colonial Heritage*; Anderson, 60–82. On Bodin's ideal-type, see Parker, "Sovereignty."

6. See Tilly, *From Mobilization*, 189–219, which disentangles conditions from causes, situations from outcomes.

7. Cited in Stein, "'Un raudal,'" 220.

8. Braudel, "Du Potosi"; Moutoukias, *Contrabando*; Villalobos; Zaefferer de Goyeneche; Parry, ch. 14; Walker. On the origins of Britain's use of the *asiento* as a wedge for broader commercial goals, see Nettels.

9. Elliott; Kuethe and Blaidsell; Castillo.

10. Burkholder and Chandler; Brading, "Bourbon Spain." It is worth noting that so poorly did the first mercantilist system operate that some authors argue that Carlos III's policies can be treated as Spain's belated acceptance of European mercantilism. See, for instance, Stein, "'Un raudal,'" 225.

11. Moutoukias, *Contrabando*, 26–31. The effects on the Limeño side are well traced by Jacobsen.

12. Ravignani, "El Virreinato"; Lynch, *Spanish Colonial Administration*; Socolow, *Bureaucrats*; Zorraquín Becú.

13. Klein; and for detailed commentaries, Amaral, "Public Expenditure Financing."

14. Halperín Donghi, *Guerra*, 51–60.

15. Ibid., 51.

16. Overland levies (*alcabalas terrestres*) grew as highland commerce with Buenos Aires flourished: from a meager 2,266 pesos in 1776, payments rose to 20,428 in 1780 and 32,978 pesos by 1795. Revenues from the Buenos Aires customhouse soared commensurate with ascending trade: between 1773 and 1777, average receipts yielded 23,474 pesos fuertes annually, but by 1791–95, average annual re-

turns jumped to 390,000 pesos. On the fiscal bureaucracy, see Socolow, *Bureaucrats*, 28–33. On highland remittances, see TePaske, "Fiscal Structure"; Klein, 451; Amaral, "El descubrimiento," 383. On overland levies, see Levene, *Investigaciones*, 2: 53. On customs, see Assadourian, Beato, and Chiaramonte, 315.

17. Viner, 76; Magnusson; Heckscher.

18. To be sure, the crown experimented with the creation of giant joint-stock companies (like England's East India Company), but these barely scratched the power and privilege of private mercantile establishments housed in the Cádiz *consulado* with satellites fanned out across the dominions. Haring; Ekelund and Tollison.

19. Root, ch. 1; Bien.

20. TePaske, "Spanish America," 515; Barbier; Christelow, "Great Britain" and "Contraband Trade." The fact was, Cádiz did enjoy a burst of trade in the wake of the reforms—but the real growth came not from Spanish merchandise movement, but from a soaring business in reexporting, especially to and from France.

21. Cited in Fisher, *Commercial Relations*, 9. Emphasis mine.

22. For a different account of the meaning of *comercio libre*, see Liss, ch. 6. On the effects of *comercio libre* elsewhere, see Fisher, "Effects" and *Commercial Relations*.

23. Cited in Brading, "La monarquía," 36.

24. Moutoukias, "El crecimiento"; Fisher, *Commercial Relations*, 46, 61, 77, 120; Garavaglia, "El Río de la Plata," 75–76.

25. Garavaglia, "El Río de la Plata," 77; Mayo, *Estancia y sociedad*, 31; Tjarks, *El Consulado*, 1: 40–41.

26. Assadourian, *El sistema*, intro. On silver output, see Tandeter, *Coercion*, 1–3; Garner; Cross.

27. Assadourian, *El sistema*, ch. 2; Garzón Maceda; Moutoukias, *Contrabando*, 50–55; Tandeter, Milletich, and Schmit; Ibarra de Roncoroni; Sánchez Albornoz, "Extracción" and "La saca"; Amaral, "*Comercio libre*"; Garavaglia, "De la carne."

28. Punta; Amaral, "*Comercio libre*," 26–27. A useful survey can be found in Tjarks, "Panorama."

29. Montoya, *Historia*, 9–25; Mandrini; K. L. Jones.

30. The most common pattern of privatization was the *censo*—conferral of rights to land in return for obligations to the crown (usually defense or security of territory, sometimes even settlement of families). Three types of *censos* prevailed: *reservativos*, *consignativos*, and *enfiteusis*. The latter seems to have been the most prevalent, creating a system of long-term inheritable leases for annual payments. Sometimes the crown gave land as a form of payment, a *merced*, for services already rendered—especially to soldiers. Mariluz Urquijo, *El régimen*; Ots Capdequí; Garavaglia, "Precios." Land prices in the countryside around Buenos Aires remained roughly the same from 1750 to 1820.

31. Garavaglia and Gelman, 81.

32. Azara, 15; Gelman, "Sobre esclavos."

33. For a pioneering revisionist case study, see Halperín Donghi, "Una estancia."

34. Mayo, "Landed," 709, and *Estancia y sociedad*, 38–45; Mayo and Latrubesse, 113–25.

35. García Belsunce; Gelman, "Los caminos" and "Producción"; and for a more skeptical note, see Amaral and Ghio.
36. Azara, 4–9; Mayo, "Estancia y peonaje"; Gelman, "New Perspectives" and "Sobre esclavos," 64–83; Salvatore, "Breakdown"; Amaral, "Rural Production."
37. Fradkin, "'Según la costumbre del país'" and "Producción"; Gresores; Salvatore, "Breakdown," 74–75.
38. Maeder, 167–80.
39. Montoya, *Historia*, 18–28.
40. "Dos noticias"; Sala de Touron, de la Torre, and Rodríguez, *Estructura*; Azcuy Ameginho, 39–60.
41. For a useful thumbnail sketch, see Mayo, "Estructura."
42. Gelman, "Mundo," "Los caminos," 113–16, "Venta," and "El gran comerciante"; Saguier.
43. José Martínez de Hoz to José Miguel de Tagle, July 26, 1798, in Romero Cabrera, 94. For a general description, see Tandeter, Milletich, and Schmit, 104–6; Halperín Donghi, *Politics*, 30–36.
44. Moutoukias, "Réseaux personnels"; Socolow, "Marriage"; *Merchants*, 27–52. I have also benefited from conversations with Zacarías Moutoukias on these matters.
45. Fradkin, "El gremio"; Mayo, "Landed," 775–76, and *Estancias y sociedad*, 64–68.
46. Fisher, *Trade*, 79; Cuenca Esteban, "Statistics."
47. Johnson, "Military," 32–35; Sala de Touron, de la Torre, and Rodríguez, *Artigas*, 28–29; Halperín Donghi, "Revolutionary Militarization," 85–86.
48. Amaral, "El descubrimiento," 383–92.
49. Tandeter, *Coercion*, 2, and "Crisis."
50. For a useful recent survey late colonial unrest, see McFarlane; Stern. For the Potosí region, see Serulnikov.
51. Larson, 225–28; Spalding, 111–13; Tandeter, "Forced and Free Labour."
52. José Miguel Tagle to Miguel Gregorio de Zamalloa, July 26, 1805, in Romero Cabrera, 126; Tandeter, "Crisis" and "Forced and Free Labour," 126–30.
53. For a classic depiction, see Rene-Moreno. Also Levene, "Intentos," 454–55; O'Phelan Godoy and Cahill, 127–32.
54. Ravignani, "El Virreinato," 144–50; Tjarks, *El Consulado*, 1: 48–57; C. A. Acevedo, 13–17.
55. AGN, Sala IX, Consulado, Actas, 29/1/1, 22 dic., 1795, f. 99.
56. Ravignani, "El Virreinato," 162–63; Galmarini; Molinari, 80–81; Levene, "Funciones económicas," 297.
57. AGN, Sala IX, Consulado, Actas, 29/1/1, 9 enero, 1796, f. 108.
58. "Memorial presentado al Ministro D. Diego Gardoqui por los hacendados de Buenos Aires y Montevideo en el año 1794," *La Revista de Buenos Aires*, 37 (May 1860), 302–9; also the report of hardship, AGN, Sala IX, Consulado, Actas, 29/1/1, 21 junio, 1795, n.f.
59. "Representación al Rey de los labradores de Buenos Aires (1793)," *La Revista de Buenos Aires*, 66 (Oct. 1868), 161–92.

60. See AGN, Sala IX, Consulado, Actas, 29/1/1/, 7 mar., 1796, ff. 134, 138–42 & 16 feb., 1796, f. 238.

61. Goebel.

62. AGN, Sala IX, Consulado, Actas, 29/1/1, 13 mar., 1797, ff. 245–60.

63. For effects on colonies closer to the United States, see Cuenca Esteban, "United States Balance of Payments."

Chapter 3: The Quest for Equipoise
in the Shadow of Revolution

1. Ingenieros, 1: 74. In more recent renditions of the intellectual origins of the independence revolutions, the Enlightenment plays an even more direct role in imperial disintegration—models of freedom and individual liberty inspired creoles to the chuck the Spanish yoke. In the words of José Luis Romero, a "creole spirit" lined up against an "authoritarian spirit." Romero, 55; Liss, 172–89; Pagden, *Spanish Imperialism*, 133–51, and "Identity Formation"; Levene, "Significación histórica," 490–93.

2. Rama.

3. Caillet-Bois, "El Río de la Plata" and *Ensayo*, 33–73.

4. Stein and Stein, "Concepts"; Reeder.

5. Sewell, *Rhetoric*, 114–20; Pocock, "The Mobility of Property and the Rise of Eighteenth-Century Sociology," in Pocock, *Virtue*, 103–23.

6. Pocock, *Machiavellian Moment*, 465–88; Pagden, *Lords*, 115–16, 180–84.

7. Hirschman, *Passions*.

8. Venturi, , 265–69; Galano, 401–29.

9. Chiaramonte, *La crítica*, 109–17, and *La ilustración*, 83–91.

10. Rípodas Ardanaz, *Biblioteca*, "La biblioteca de Mariano Izquierdo," and *La biblioteca porteña*.

11. Levene, "Significación histórica," 492; Fernández López.

12. Moreno, "Querella por cuatrerismo contra un militar," in Durnhofer, 235.

13. Góngora, 181–204; Griffin; Chiaramonte, "Ilustración" and *La ilustración*, 12–18.

14. Weinberg, 37.

15. Belgrano, *Autobiografía*.

16. Cited in Mitre, 1: 88.

17. Belgrano, "Memoria" (1796), in Belgrano, *Escritos*, 64. This message was the first of a series of reports read aloud before the members of the guild, and was intended to act as a sketch of general principles for the activities of the association. See also "Representación al Rey de los Labradores de Buenos Aires" (1793), *La Revista de Buenos Aires*, 66 (Oct. 1866), 174.

18. Belgrano, "Memoria" (1796), 65.

19. Vieytes, 137, 146.

20. Lavardén, 115. This tract was initially serialized in 1801 in the *Telégrafo Mercantil*.

21. 3 marzo, 1810, *Correo de Comercio de Buenos Aires*, in Belgrano, *Escritos*, 113.

22. Moreno, "Representación a nombre del apoderado de los hacendados de

las campañas del Río de la Plata dirigida al excmo. Señor Virrey Don Baltasar Hidalgo Cisneros" (Sept. 30, 1809), in *Escritos políticos*, 156.

23. For a sense of the disparateness of views on Moreno, see Levene, *El pensamiento*, 17–20; Bagú, *Mariano Moreno*.

24. Levene, *Vida y escritos*, 19–21.

25. Villaba, lxxx.

26. Rene-Moreno, 63–65.

27. Francovich; Mendoza.

28. Moreno, *Escritos*, 1: 5–35.

29. Lavardén, 119.

30. Ibid., 160–72; on parallel antecedents to the French Revolution, see Sewell, *Rhetoric*.

31. 3 marzo, 1810, *Correo de Comercio de Buenos Aires*, in Belgrano, *Escritos*, 115.

32. Lavardén, 178; Waldron, ch. 6; Ryan, 5–6; Rogers M. Smith, 15–22.

33. Chiaramonte, *La crítica*, 60–62; Sewell, *Work*, 120–25.

34. Moreno, "Representación a nombre del apoderado de los hacendados de las campañas del Río de la Plata dirigida al excmo. Señor Virrey Don Baltasar Hidalgo Cisneros" (Sept. 30, 1809), in *Escritos políticos*, 113.

35. 10 marzo, 1810, *El Correo de Comercio de Buenos Aires*, in Belgrano, *Escritos*, 117.

36. Belgrano, "Memoria" (1796), in Belgrano, *Escritos*, 70, 74.

37. Ibid. (1797), 97; ibid. (1798), 99.

38. Lavardén, 173; Vieytes, 158–61.

39. From the *Telégrafo*, cited in Lavardén, 62. *Nuevo aspecto* was serialized in 1801 in the *Telégrafo Mercantil*; Chiaramonte, *La crítica*, 39–42.

40. Lavardén, 175.

41. Jefferson, query eight; Lerner; Appleby, *Liberalism*, chs. 2 and 10.

42. In Belgrano, *Escritos*, 76.

43. Ibid., 86.

44. Ibid., 104.

45. Vieytes, 139.

46. Belgrano, "Memoria" (1798), in Belgrano, *Escritos*, 107; "Representación al Rey de los labradores de Buenos Aires (1793)," *La Revista de Buenos Aires*, 66 (Oct. 1868), 175.

47. "Dos noticias," 361.

48. "Representación al Rey de los labradores de Buenos Aires (1793)," *La Revista de Buenos Aires*, 66 (Oct. 1868), 184.

49. Vieytes, 143.

50. "Dos noticias," 345.

51. 10 marzo, 1810, *El Correo de Comercio de Buenos Aires*, in Belgrano, *Escritos*, 121.

52. Lavardén, 181; Belgrano also promoted colonization (see "Memoria I," 62), as did Vieytes, 214; Chiaramonte, *La crítica*, 66–74.

53. 23 junio, 1810, *El Correo de Comercio de Buenos Aires*, in Belgrano, *Escritos*, 158.

54. The term is from Chiaramonte, *La crítica*, 52.

55. Pocock, *Machiavellian Moment*, 467.

56. For more general reflections on this moment in political economy's history, see Hont and Ignatieff.

57. Chartier, 197; see also Keith Michael Baker, 20–25.

58. Moreno, "Constitución federativa asentada por la Convención de 17 de Septiembre de 1787," in Durnhofer, 85; Chiaramonte, "Modificaciones."

59. Keith Michael Baker, 238–41, has called this sort of position "social representation" in France.

Chapter 4: From Revolution to Civil War

1. Posadas, 1410.

2. Annino, 10.

3. Graham, 52–53; Anna, *Spain*, 8–19.

4. Moreno, "Memorias sobre la invasión de Buenos Aires por las armas inglesas, el día 27 de junio del año 1806," in Moreno, *Escritos políticos*, 78.

5. Gillespie, 50. For a general study, see Street, *Gran Bretaña*, 27–65.

6. K. Gallo; Street, *Gran Bretaña*, 69–89; Ferns, 27–45.

7. Rodríguez, 1516; Belgrano, *Autobiografía*, 16; "Discurso a favor de las familias pobres de la capital de Buenos Ayres que quedaron huerfanas de resultas de los sangrientos combates con los ingleses, pronunciado por el Dr D. Luis María de Moxo y López" (julio, 1807) and "Sucinta memoria sobre la segunda invasión de Buenos Aires el mes de julio de 1807" (1808)—both of these pamphlets can be found in the collection at Widener Library, Harvard University.

8. Moreno, "Escrito del Cabildo de Buenos Aires sobre la peligrosa situación de las Provincias del Río de la Plata por falta de armas. Julio de 1808," in *Escritos políticos*, 229–30; Williams; Street, "Lord Strangford."

9. Tjarks and Tjarks, 42; Tjarks, *El Consulado*, 1: 326–45; Socolow, *Merchants*, 129–31; Street, *Gran Bretaña*, 99–106.

10. Rodríguez, 1514–15; Mitre, 1: 202–38; Halperín Donghi, *Politics*, 126–27. On the debates within the Spanish Juntas and Cortes, see Halperín Donghi, *Reforma*, 115–17; Anna, "Spain"; Costeloe; Hamnett; Domínguez.

11. Mitre, 1: 241–310.

12. For a discussion of the Anglo-American sovereignty debate, see Morgan.

13. If Bartolomé Mitre's classic account of the revolution invoked the image of an "embryonic democracy," what deserves emphasis is the embryo. Mitre, 1: 210; Levene, "Asonada."

14. Belgrano, "Las causas de la destrucción o de la conservación y engrandecimiento de la Naciones" (19 mayo, 1810), in Belgrano, *Escritos*, 146.

15. Monteagudo, "Observación" (24 enero, 1812), in Monteagudo, 57.

16. Levene, "Los sucesos"; Halperín Donghi, *Politics*, 153–57.

17. For an outline of events of May 1810, see Carranza; Caillet-Bois, "La Revolución," 73–75; and more generally E. O. Acevedo.

18. *El Censor*, 21 & 28 enero, 1812, in *Biblioteca de Mayo*, 7: 5766–67, 5775–76; González Bernaldo, "La Revolución"; Fernández López.

19. Murrin; Greene, 94–95.

20. Monteagudo, "Pasiones" (12 enero, 1812), in Monteagudo, 46; for more on Monteagudo, see Araña et al.

21. Moreno, "*Prólogo* a la traducción del Contrato Social," in *Escritos políticos,* 265–67; Shumway, 27–42.

22. Halperín Donghi, *Politics,* 158; González Bernaldo, "La Revolución," 21, 25; Caillet-Bois, "La Revolución," 73; A. D. González, 36.

23. Moreno, "Sobre la misión del Congreso convocado en virtud de la resolución plebescitaria del 25 de Mayo," in *Escritos políticos,* 279.

24. Monteagudo, "Oración inaugural pronunciada en la apertura de la Sociedad Patriótica la tarde del 13 de enero de 1812," in Monteagudo, 144–60; *Martir o Libre,* 6 abril, 1812, in *Biblioteca de Mayo,* 7: 5864–65.

25. *Martir o Libre,* 20 abril, 1812, in *Biblioteca de Mayo,* 7: 5876.

26. Nedelsky; M. W. McCann.

27. Moreno, "Sobre la misión del Congreso convocado en virtud de la resolución plebescitaria del 25 de Mayo," in *Escritos políticos,* 279.

28. Appleby, *Capitalism,* 4.

29. Bushnell, "El sufragio," 11–13; Chiaramonte, "Vieja y nueva representación."

30. Moreno, "Plan de operaciones que el gobierno provisional de las provincias unidas del Río de la Plata debe poner en practica para consolidar la grande obra de nuestra libertad e independencia," in *Escritos políticos,* 301–68. There is some doubt whether Moreno was the author of this report, though few find it inconsistent with (though it is slightly more gory than) the rest of his revolutionary writings. See Ricardo Levene, "La obra," who finds the report at odds with Moreno's "democratic" impulses—an unconvincing argument in my view.

31. Moreno, "Sobre la misión del congreso convocado en virtud de la resolución plebescitaria del 25 de Mayo," in *Escritos políticos,* 290–93.

32. Caillet-Bois, "La Revolución," 154.

33. Goldman, "Los 'Jacobinos,'" 118–55.

34. Barsi.

35. Belgrano, *Autobiografía,* 58–59; Segreti, 18–22; for a description of the guerrilla warfare to restore a *utopía andina,* see O'Phelan Godoy and Cahill.

36. Belgrano, *Autobiografía,* 31–57; Whigham, *Politics,* 20–23; Ornstein; Pastore, 552–55.

37. Chiaramonte, "Acerca."

38. To date, the best single study of Artigas is Street, *Artigas;* see also P. B. Acevedo; Sala de Touron, de la Torre, and Rodríguez, *Artigas.*

39. Street, *Artigas,* 155–57.

40. Pasqualí; Beraza, 85–107.

41. Levene, "El Congreso," "Las Juntas," and "El 5 y 6 de 1811."

42. Even in Buenos Aires a provincial spirit began to eclipse the original centrality of the city. By 1816, weary of the urban bias of politics and inflected by *artiguismo,* some *porteños* invoked a "federal" solution for the city and its rural surroundings. Its leader, Manuel Dorrego, however, still hovered in the shadow

of *porteño* centralists. For an important recent study of Buenos Aires federalists, see Herrero; also Chiaramonte, "Acerca," 1–7, and "Legalidad."

43. Moreno's followers, purged from their offices, would contend that Cornelio de Saavedra conspired to murder his rival. Goldman, "Los 'Jacobinos,'" 15–17, and *El discurso*, 182–83.

44. Halperín Donghi, *Politics*, 191–94; Halperín Donghi, "Revolutionary Militarization."

45. Canter, "El Año XII" and "La Revolución"; Palcos, *Rivadavia*, 1: 252–320.

46. Caillet-Bois, "El Directorio," 556; Mario Belgrano, *Rivadavia*, 115–25, and *La Francia*, 21–25; *La Crónica Argentina*, 22 sept., 1816 & 9 nov., 1816, in *Biblioteca de Mayo*, 7: 6305–8, 6359–63.

47. Ravignani, *Asambleas*, 1: 941; Levaggi, "Espíritu"; for an important study of early federalist constitutionalism, see A. D. González.

48. Levene, *La anarquía*.

49. Coatsworth; Amaral, "Del mercantilismo."

50. Segreti, 20; AGN, Sala IX, Consulado, Copiador de Correspondencia con las Pcias, 4/6/16, 4 agosto, 1812; Prebisch, "Anotaciones"; Halperín Donghi, "La Revolución," 81–85.

51. AGN, Sala IX, Consulado, Correspondencia Potosí, 4/6/12, f. 549, 27 abril, 1806.

52. AGN, Sala IX, Consulado, Actas, 29/1/5, f. 180, 25 agosto, 1809; Gillespie, 58; Halperín Donghi, "La Revolución," 101–4.

53. Miguel Antonio de Saracívar to Tagle, 6 marzo, 1810, in Romero Cabrera, 159.

54. AGN, Sala IX, Consulado, Correspondencia, 4/6/2, doc. 543a, 16 feb., 1809; Belgrano in *Correo de Comercio*, 3 marzo, 1810, in Belgrano, *Escritos*, 113–17.

55. AGN, Sala IX, Consulado, Correspondencia, 4/6/2, doc. 570a, 28 sept., 1809 & doc. 588, 23 dic., 1809; Copiador de Correspondencia con las Pcias, 4/6/16, 4 enero, 1810.

56. AGN, Sala IX, Consulado, 4/6/16, 17 feb., 1810. For background on the 1809 decree, see Molinari, 174–83; Tjarks and Tjarks, 36–41; Tjarks, *El Consulado*, 1: 343–54; Socolow, *Merchants*, 129–33.

57. AGN, Sala IX, Consulado, Actas, 29/1/3, f. 88, 17 nov., 1800 & f. 147, 8 oct., 1801.

58. AGN, Sala IX, Consulado, Correspondencia, 4/6/2, doc. 459, 19 junio, 1806 & Cuentas y otros, 4/8/3, "Año 1806. Emprestito y donatibo hecho a S.M."

59. Ravignani, "Las finanzas."

60. AGN, Sala IX, Consulado, Copiador de Correspondencia con las Pcias, 4/6/16, 2 julio, 1810.

61. AGN, Sala IX, Consulado, Actas, 29/1/6, f. 19, 21 nov., 1811, and Copiador de Correspondencia con las Pcias, 4/6/16, 22 nov., 1811.

62. Ibid., f. 9, 30 enero, 1811; Halperín Donghi, *Guerra*, 119–21.

63. Halperín Donghi, *Guerra*, 119–21.

64. AGN, Sala IX, Consulado, "Copidaor de Correspondencia con las Pcias," 4/6/16, 23 mayo, 1812, 6 agosto, 1814, 22 agosto, 1816, 4 oct., 1816, 6 oct., 1816,

11 enero, 1817 & 21 junio, 1817; *La Crónica Argentina*, 26 nov., 1816, in *Biblioteca de Mayo*, 7: 6383.

65. AGN, Sala X, Gobierno Nacional, Guerra, 9/4/3, Hacienda, emprestito 1816, Juan Turnet, 21 marzo, 1816.

66. AGN, Sala IX, Consulado, Copiador de Correspondencia con las Pcias, 4/6/16, 16 oct., 1817; and Sala X, Gobierno Nacional, Guerra, 9/4/4, Hacienda, emprestito; Posadas, 1432–33; Amaral, "Del mercantilismo," 211; Amaral, "El descubrimiento," 398–402; Amaral, "Las formas."

67. AGN, Sala IX, Consulado, Actas, 29/1/1, 30 sept., 1814.

68. Ibid., f. 46, 1 sept., 1815; Halperín Donghi, "La Revolución," 114–16; Street, *Gran Bretaña*, 164–66. By 1816, even the foreign mercantile community was being asked to support the fiscal cause of the revolution. Pretty soon, British merchant voices joined the chorus of creoles complaining about state insolvency and the accumulation of arrears. AGN, Sala IX, Consulado, Copiador de Correspondencia con las Pcias, 4/6/16, 16 mayo, 1816 & 18 junio, 1816.

69. According to Emilio Ravignani, import tax revenues rose from 871,000 pesos in 1810 to 6 million in 1829, while export taxes yielded 197,713 in 1810 and 433,211 in 1829. Ravignani, "Las finanzas," 22; Halperín Donghi, *Guerra*, 119–21.

70. Nicolau, *La reforma*, 104.

71. Parish to Canning, June 25, 1824, in Humphreys, 8; Forbes, 77; AGN, Sala IX, Consulado, "Cuentas y otros," 4/8/3, 22 oct., 1819.

72. Álvarez, *Las guerras*, 44–48; Chiaramonte, "El federalismo."

73. This plan enlisted high marks from travelers, who started roaming the region in the 1820's. Caldcleugh, 191.

74. Ingenieros, 1: 203.

75. Williford, 39–40; Parish to Canning, June 25, 1824, in Humphreys, 9; Julián Segundo de Agüero, "De los fueros privilegiados," *La Abeja*, 15 agosto, 1822, in *Biblioteca de Mayo*, 6: 5363–68.

76. Cansanello; Ternavasio, 65–74; Chiaramonte, "Acerca," 12–17; Bushnell, "El sufragio," 13–15, 22–24.

77. In fact, federalists had been debating drafting a constitution of their own. One such plan, developed in Córdoba, was effectively squelched by Buenos Aires. See Ravignani, "El Congreso Nacional."

78. Ravignani, *Asambleas*, 1: 889–1133; Mayer, *Agüero*.

79. Moreno, "Vista política-económica de la Provincia de Buenos Aires," *La Abeja Argentina*, 15 abril, 1822, in *Biblioteca de Mayo*, 6: 5252.

80. Prebisch, "Anotaciones," 195–99. For a general appraisal of the 1820's, see Barba, "Notas"; Álvarez, "La evolución."

81. Moreno, "Vista político . . . ," *La Abeja Argentina*, 15 mayo, 1822, in *Biblioteca de Mayo*, 6: 5283; AGN, Sala IX, Consulado, "Cuentas y otros," 4/8/3, "Informe ex-prior Joaquin Belgrano," 18 enero, 1820; *Mensajes de los Gobernadores*, 1: 29–31.

82. AGN, Sala IX, Consulado, "Cuentas y otros," 4/8/3, 6 junio, 1821; Nicolau, *La reforma*, 113–18; Palcos, *Rivadavia*, 1: 612–15; Amaral, "La reforma." It did not take long for the reforms to begin to bite, as the U.S. envoy to Buenos Aires gleefully noted to his Secretary of State after the Customs Inspector Fernando

Calderón was arrested on corruption charges. Forbes to John Quincy Adams, Sept. 11, 1821, in Forbes, 137.

83. Along the way, Buenos Aires tried several colonization ventures. Starting on the wrong foot and fueled by exaggerated expectations on all sides, they ended in rude epistolary exchanges and pamphlets. Beaumont; Piccirilli, 2: 102–49; Infesta, "La enfiteusis."

84. "The properties of a state habilitate the administration that overseas them, not only to guarantee the public debt, but to support resources in times of extraordinary need, or to motivate further the progress of the country's prosperity." Piccirilli, 2: 136; Lamas, *La legislación*, 36–39; Moreno, "Vista económica . . . ," *La Abeja Argentina*, 15 junio, 1822, in *Biblioteca de Mayo*, 6: 5309–11; Coni, 45–48.

85. Piccirilli, 2: 88; AGN, Sala IX, Consulado, Copiador de Correspondencia con las Pcias, 4/6/16, 26 sept., 1818; Andrews; Head.

86. Cited in Dawson, 11.

87. The real losers in the end were the final holders of an asset whose value soon plummeted and which Buenos Aires would take almost half a century to repay. Amaral, "El emprestito"; Marichal, 13–53.

88. Manuel José García, 5 mayo, 1823, in *Mensajes de los Gobernadores*, 1: 30.

89. Parish to Canning, June 25, 1824, in Humphreys, 23–24; Parish, 370–72; Nicolau, *La reforma*, 105–12.

90. Nicolau, *La reforma*, 156.

91. ABPBA, Libros de Actas, 1: 1–2; Bagú, *El plan*, 37–39.

92. Amaral, "Comercio y"; Nicolau, *La reforma*, 161–65.

93. AHPBA, Libros de Actas, 1: 36–38, 91–92; Nicolau, *La reforma*, 159–65.

94. Lord Ponsonby to Canning, Oct. 20, 1826, Webster, 156; Rottjer; Caillet-Bois, "La Guerra"; Seckinger, 67–148.

95. Ravignani, *Asambleas*, 2: 424–73; Prebisch, "Desde el primer Banco Nacional"; Bagú, *El plan*, 72–89.

96. ABPBA, Libros de Actas, 2: 47–59, 117; Parish, 373–74; Amaral, "El descubrimiento," 413–15.

97. General Dorrego, the ballast of the anarchic year 1820, warned his president that "the masses want to unite, but in their own way." He added that "in a republican system the mass is the possessor of authority; I can only pray that you know what it wants." Palcos, *Rivadavia*, 2: 52–68.

Chapter 5: Rosas Agonistes, or the
Political Economy of Cronyism

1. For many observers and analysts, the caudillo emblematizes natural features of the region's politics: personalism (loyalty not to public office but to its occupant), lawlessness (arbitrary exercise of authority), and patriarchal ties with subject peoples (clients submit to the patron through personal, fictionalized family ties). Wolf and Hansen; Zorrilla. The classic studies of Rosas are Lynch's *Argentine Dictator* and *Caudillos*.

2. Caudillos are often seen as the incarnation of a timeless, persistent, and

enduring feudal system. The caudillo simply restored the medieval world punctuated by Enlightenment revolutionaries. Dealy, "Prolegomena" and *Public Man*; and for a more ambitious, but even more troublesome, effort to peg a "Spanish American" political culture, see Véliz.

3. Halperín Donghi, "Anarquía"; Chiaramonte, "Legalidad"; Chiaramonte and Buchbinder.

4. As the nineteenth century unfolded, state-formation passed (in de Tocqueville's formulation) from a revolutionary to a constructivist moment. "Why Great Revolutions Will Become More Rare," in Tocqueville, 2: 265–78.

5. Root, xii; Levi; Ekelund and Tollison; North and Weingast.

6. Elster, "Impact," and the skeptical reply by Przeworski.

7. "Mensaje del Gobernador Manuel Dorrego, 14 de setiembre, 1827," *Mensajes de los Gobernadores*, 1: 42; Ravignani, "El Congreso Nacional."

8. Manuel José Haedo to Blas Achaval, 20 mayo, 1828, AGN TC, H, leg. 125 (1834–39), doc. Manuel José Haedo c. Blas Achaval (1837).

9. Dorrego himself denounced "the aristocracy of money," and in an effort to restore stability to the peso, he ordered Bank authorities to begin to withdraw their depreciating notes from circulation and to close down merchants' credit lines with their financial arm. Roxas to Directors, Mar. 4, 1828, ABPBA, Ministerio de Hacienda, Correspondencia, 023-1-1, f. 1259; Nicolau, *Dorrego Gobernador*, 43, 72.

10. González Bernaldo, "Social Imagery"; Monsma, 201–4.

11. Parish, 374–75; ABPBA, Libros de Actas, 2: 4 marzo, 1828, p. 192; J. M. Forbes to Henry Clay, June 4, 1829, in Forbes, 548; Levene, *El proceso*; Saldías, *Historia*, 1: 246–54.

12. Ingenieros, 2: 17–20; Saldías, *Historia*, 1: 267–68.

13. Halperín Donghi, "Clase," 24–25; Halperín Donghi, *Historia argentina*, 301–3.

14. Ternavasio, 80–84. For a suggestive study of other popular rituals, see Salvatore, "Fiestas."

15. *Diario de la Tarde*, Mar. 13, 1840; Lynch, *Argentine Dictator*, 48–50; Barba, *Quiroga*, 57–92; Halperín Donghi, *Historia argentina*, 325–27; Saldías, *Historia*, 2: 11. Tomás Manuel de Anchorena, one of Rosas's staunchest backers and a business partner, captured the circularity of this drift to quasi-law in a pronouncement in the Legislature: "The path to the end is not the end itself; and the wish to see the reestablishment of the laws through the established laws themselves ... would be the same as taking the path to the end where we are now. It is impossible to constitute a government on this principle that the laws require, and it is for this reason that we invoke extraordinary measures. In this, there is no contradiction whatsoever." Cited in Ingenieros, 2: 9. For a general discussion of political discourse of the era, see Myers, *Orden*.

16. Rosas to Quiroga, 20 dic., 1834, in *Archivo Americano*, June 25, 1845; see also Rosas to Estanislao López, 12 mayo, 1832, ibid., Oct. 10, 1844; Sampay, *Las ideas*, 34–47; Chiaramonte, "Acerca"; Myers, *Orden*, 25–28, 62–74.

17. *Archivo Americano*, Oct. 10, 1844; Feb. 28, 1845.

18. *Agente Comercial del Plata*, July 18, 1851; *Gaceta Mercantil*, July 4, 1840; *Ar-*

chivo Americano, June 21, 1845; Apr. 8, 1851; Díaz Molano; Weiss, "Pedro de Angelis"; Myers, *Orden*, 37–38.

19. Juan Manuel de Rosas, Estanislao López and Pedro Ferré to José María Paz, Apr. 12, 1830, in *Documentos para la Historia Argentina*, 16: 107–10; Eusebio Agüero and Mariano Fragueiro to Rosas, Mar. 13, 1830, AGN, Sala X, 5/4/1.

20. Rosas to J. P. López, Apr. 15, 1831, AGN, Sala VII, Colección Farini, Archivo Adolfo Saldías, 3/3/8; "Mensaje de los Ministros," May 20, 1831, *Mensajes de los Gobernadores*, 1: 61–62; Goldman, "Legalidad"; Chiaramonte, "Legalidad," 193–94.

21. Barba, *Unitarismo*, for the distinctions between riparian federalism (my term) and Buenos Aires' own ideas of federalism. For the constitutional implications of the Pact, see Tau Anzóategui, *Formación*, 53–87.

22. Southern to Palmerston, May 17, 1850, FO 6/150, frame 173; Blondel, 23–25; Mariluz Urquijo, *Estado*, 113–19; Nicolau, 27–34.

23. "Comercio," *El Regulador*, July 16, 1831. On the absence of commercial policy debates, see Halperín Donghi, "Argentina," 105–7, and "Liberalismo," 145–54.

24. Nicolau, "Movimiento"; *The British Packet*, Aug. 5, 1845; Zaefferer de Goyeneche, 119–33; Reber, 74–75.

25. *The British Packet*, Feb. 12, 1842; Southern to Lord Palmerston, 6 Mar., 1849, FO 6/143, frame 229.

26. Garavaglia, "Precios"; Gorostegui de Torres, "Los precios"; Merediz.

27. The value of British exports to Buenos Aires rose from £369,123 in 1812 to £1,104,499 in 1824, only to decline after the speculative bubble burst, to £632,172 in 1830. In Latin America, only Brazil imported more British produce. Under Rosas, British imports rose even more dramatically (though the oscillations could be even more dramatic): in 1835, total British exports to the River Plate reached £658,525, and by 1849 they more than doubled to £1,399,575. "Appendix I," in Humphreys, 344–49; Great Britain, House of Commons, *Parliamentary Papers*, 39 (1842), 119–79, and 52 (1854–55), 176–256.

28. Adelman and Amaral; Parish; Nicholson to Lord Aberdeen, 22 June, 1846, FO 6/129, frame 278; Brown, *Socioeconomic History*, 81–82.

29. Halperín Donghi, "Bloqueos."

30. Ayres and Gertner; Bordo; and generally Barzel; see also Chapter 6.

31. Álvarez, *Las guerras*, 44–50.

32. "The right of a state over its interior rivers is inseparable from that of sovereignty and dominion, and is confounded with that of property and jurisdiction. If the rivers are interior ones and situated in the territory of the state, no one can reasonably dispute the right of disposing their navigation . . ." *Archivo Americano*, June 31, 1846, and July 30, 1846; *The British Packet*, Aug. 14, 1847; Saldías, *Por qué se produjo*.

33. Lucas to Lord Aberdeen, Dec. 1, 1845, FO 6/113, frame 5; *The British Packet*, Jan. 8, 1842, and Jan. 7, 1843.

34. Howden to Lord Palmerston, July 17, 1847, FO 6/134, frame 180, and Ruil to Howden, Mar. 15, 1847, frame 225.

35. Southern to Lord Palmerston, Nov. 21, 1848, FO 6/139, frame 213; *The British Packet*, Feb. 24, 1844.

36. "An Appeal on Behalf of the British Subjects Residing in and Connected with the River Plate . . . ," *The British Packet*, June 6, 1846, and Oct. 10, 1846.

37. From *The Morning Chronicle*, cited in *The British Packet*, Mar. 20, 1847. North Americans held the same opinion of the Foreign Office's faux pas. See Bent to Ouseley, Sept. 23, 1845, and Harris to Lord Howden, July 1, 1847, in Manning, 1: 293, 424.

38. Southern to Lord Palmerston, Oct. 8, 1849, FO 6/145, frame 52; Harris to Lord Howden, June 17, 1848, in Manning, 1: 456; Williams, 56–62.

39. Merchants to Southern, Oct. 27, 1849, AGN, Sala VII, Colección Farini, Archivo Adolfo Saldías, 3/3/11, f. 82.

40. Anderson, 24–42; Bonney; O'Brien, "Political Economy"; Kautsky.

41. Romano; Segreti, 87–92, 209–36; De la Fuente, 67–87.

42. *El Comercio del Plata*, Aug. 26, 1847.

43. Chiaramonte, *Mercaderes*, 147–63, and "Legalidad," 183–95.

44. Southern to Lord Palmerston, Sept. 10, 1850, FO 6/151.

45. Ratto; K. L. Jones, 111–16.

46. Avellaneda, 80–117; Rosas's Mensaje, Jan. 1, 1837, in *Mensajes de los gobernadores*, 1: 117–18. Of course, this did not dispense with the very real problem of how to define property—especially in the absence of surveying techniques. If the previous system tended to allocate land according to frontage along waterways, in the 1820's, especially as the frontier moved outward, officials (notably Justices of the Peace who waged front-line struggles to consolidate rural property) defined plots "physically," by which they meant square leagues. Not until the advent of barbed wire and the railroad did the demarcation lines enjoy much fixity. See AGN, Sala VII, BN, Informes, 387/6600, f. 26a–28; Montoya, *La ganadería*, 25–26. Now the definitive study of land legislation in this era is Infesta, "Usufructo," and Infesta and Valencia.

47. By 1840, some 2.5 million square leagues passed to private hands. Lands north of the Salado River (in effect the Indian frontier) became leaseholds and then freeholds, whereas south of the river lands were granted in sales or *premios*. Between 1836 and 1852, Rosas sold 1,500 square leagues and donated 714 square leagues. Coronel Antonio Ramírez walked away from the battle against Indians at La Cortada with a cool 2 square leagues, while his officers in the 2nd Cavalry Regiment each earned from one-half to a full square league. The average size of sales was 4.64 square leagues (the largest single purchase was made by Pedro José Vela, who bought 49.8 square leagues). The vast majority of buyers were former leaseholders. Infesta, 145–47, 160–63, 175–83.

48. Monsma, 67–77.

49. Sebreli; Carretero; Brown, "Cattle Empire."

50. W. McCann, 1: 81–86; Mayo, "Landed"; Johnson; Amaral, *Rise of Capitalism*; Sabato, *Agrarian Capitalism*, 159–61; Adelman, *Frontier Development*, ch. 3. This was also a feature of the Brazilian pampas. See Chasteen.

51. See Oddone; Rock, 107–8. For a critique, see M. Peña, who treats Rosas as the alchemist of a rural capitalist class producing for world markets.

52. Amaral, *Rise of Capitalism*, ch. 11; Sabato, *Agrarian Capitalism*, 107–10;

Adelman, *Frontier Development*, 159–84; Garavaglia and Gelman, 79–92; Garavaglia, "Tres estancias."

53. Halperín Donghi, "La expansión," 81–85; Monsma, 93–99; Chiaramonte, *Mercaderes*, 81–83; Whigham, "Cattle Raising," 324–25; Brown, *Socioeconomic History*, 146–59.

54. Szuchman, *Order*, 92–95, 213–27. On diversified business strategies within households or estates, see Sábato; Sabato, *Agrarian Capitalism*, 160–64.

55. Griffiths to John Bidwell, Sept. 15, 1844, FO 6/97, frame 47.

56. Chiaramonte, *Mercaderes*, 87–89.

57. J. M. Rosas to J. P. López, Apr. 12, 1839, AGN, Sala VII, Colección Farini, Archivo Adolfo Saldías, 3/3/8, f. 12; Santos Muñoz, for the most thorough description of this war; also Whigham, "Trade," 165–70.

58. *The British Packet*, Nov. 6, 1841.

59. Ibid., Feb. 9, 1840, Aug. 29, 1840, Nov. 13, 1841; Halperín Donghi, *Historia argentina*, 350–75; Lynch, *Argentine Dictator*, 170–74, 202–8. On the Interior, see José María Paz to Gregorio Araoz de la Madrid, Aug. 5, 1841, AGN, Sala VII, BN, Archivo Félix Frías, 677/9247; J. M. Paz to Mariano Villar, Mar. 27, 1842, AGN, Sala VII, Archivo Andrés Lamas, leg. 38, f. 81; Ravignani and Mandelli.

60. Ouseley to Aberdeen, Oct. 27, 1845, FO 6/105, frame 145; Saldías, *Porqué se produjo*.

61. Ouseley to Aberdeen, Dec. 20, 1845, FO 6/107, frame 14, for an extended discussion of the Paraná mission. On the blockade more broadly, see MacKinnon; Bustamante, *Los cinco errores*.

62. José Luis Bustamante to General Rivera, Aug. 29, 1845, AGN, Sala VII, Colección Farini, 3/2/1, f. 39; Falconnet to Barings, July 12, 1842, BBA, HC 4.1/14; *The British Packet*, Aug. 20, 1842, July 6, 1844, Sept. 6, 1845; Admiral Inglefield to Ouseley, Sept. 2, 1845, FO 6/105, frame 55; Ouseley to Aberdeen, Jan. 31, 1846, FO 6/115, frame 188; Ouseley to Aberdeen, June 6, 1846, FO 6/119, frame 53.

63. Adolfo Alsina to Félix Frías, May 22, 1849, AGN, Sala VII, 677/9447; Harris to Lord Howden, July 1, 1847, in Manning, 1: 424; Saldías, *Cómo surgió Urquiza*, for the best account of the military story.

64. Tilly, "War Making."

65. De Angelis, 4, 13; Nicolau, *Rosas*.

66. Budgets from 1837 to 1850, *Mensajes de los Gobernadores*, 1: 148–52, 172–75, 187–90, 200–203, 215–18, 226–29, 239–55, 269–71, 295–98, 2: 40–43, 91–94, 281–84; Burgin, 167, 197–98; Fitte; Halperín Donghi, *Guerra*, 255–57, 267–70.

67. Falconnet to Barings, Mar. 7, 1842, BBA, MS 18.321, HC 4.1, f. 14; AGN, Sala VII, Archivo Andrés Lamas, leg. 77/347, report of Dec. 7, 1841.

68. Burgin, 167, 195–96; Halperín Donghi, *Guerra*, 251–53, 258–60, 264–66. Rosas did try to supplement customs receipts with a tax on land—ineffectually. See Estévez.

69. Province of Buenos Aires, Memoria, 14–15; Swanson and Trout; E. Ferguson; Riesman.

70. E. Ferguson, 389. This system was also the pattern prevalent in the pre-

revolutionary English colonies. For a broader comparison, see Bordo and White.

71. "Emisiones sucesivas desde la creación del papel moneda," ABPBA, 017-1-16/4. In 1836, Rosas finally shut down the National Bank, creating in its stead the Casa de Moneda, endowed with banking functions, but operating as a manufacturer of paper pesos (it did not, for instance, even handle deposits or discounting operations). The financiers, of course, were unhappy with this move, but from the start the Bank had failed to win the confidence of the capitalist "public." For the government's assault on the Bank, see Comisión del Directorio del Banco al Ministro de Hacienda, Dec. 18, 1833, ABPBA, 017-1-6/10, and the bankers' response in "Informe y dictámen de los Directores del Banco Nacional a los Accionistas. 1834," ABPBA, 002-2-2, carpeta 5.

72. Falconnet to Barings, Mar. 7, 1842, BBA, HC 4.1, f. 14.

73. Halperín Donghi, "Bloqueos," 315, 323; Burgin, 260, for Buenos Aires price estimates from 1830 to 1850.

74. "Remarks on the Public Currency," *The British Packet*, Jan. 17, 1846.

75. Ibid., report of Dec. 7, 1841, leg. 77/348.

76. AGN, Sala VII, Archivo Andrés Lamas, leg. 77/354, report of Feb. 12, 1847. The concerns of merchants prompted the Cordoban merchant Mariano Fragueiro to publish *Organización del crédito* in 1850, based on his reflections on Chile's financial reforms of the 1840's. Not everyone was a loser in this system. Inflation is a great redistributor. Faced with a devaluing currency and lags in the adjustment of local wages and prices (they did not rise as fast as the peso was falling), exporters benefited. They sold their produce on the Atlantic market at world prices for hard currency and could convert their earnings into pesos. This was a windfall for landowners. The prospect of making such earnings only intensified the flight of merchants into rural property. Inflation was a way of taxing wage earners and merchants to pay for war, and along the way redistributed earnings to landowners. The problem was, the export system relied on merchant capitalists to provide credit and handle merchandise. Inflation may have temporarily enhanced the fortunes of some of Rosas's cronies, but not all of them.

Chapter 6: Chains of Obligation

1. Braudel, *Civilization*, 2: 134–37.

2. Goetz and Scott; Macneil.

3. Gordon, "Paradoxical Property"; Vandervelde.

4. Directors to Manuel José García, Jan. 8, 1825, ABPBA, Libros de Actas, 1: 92.

5. Manuel Ortiz Basualdo c. Pedro Botet (1835), AGN, TC, B-12 (1806–35).

6. Levene, "El derecho." Levene argues that private law evolved more gradually than the great rupture inflicted on public law by the revolution. While I would agree that they followed separate time lines, it is hard to see "evolution" in private law, at least until the 1850's.

7. Thompson, 222–23; Kagan, xxi.

8. Méndez Calzada, 31–48; Tau Anzoátegui, *Casuismo*, 31–32; Merryman, 73–100; Golbert and Nun, 2–19; Van Kleffens, 138–230.

9. Pirenne, 51–55; J. H. Baker; Rogers.

10. Trueba; Robert Sidney Smith; Tau Anzoátegui, "La costumbre."

11. Coronas González, 37–78, for the best description of this system. For a description of the law in practice, see Robert Sidney Smith.

12. Hart, 77–91.

13. Berman, 11–12.

14. See C. A. Acevedo, 19–22.

15. Vélez Sarsfield, "Pleito de Don Francisco Letamendi con el Dr D. Vicente Anastasio Echevarría," in Vélez Sarsfield, *Escritos*, 227.

16. "Juan de la Elguera pidiendo a Junta para tratar la avería padecida en la barca [sic] Nuestra Señora del Carmen" (1805), AGN, TC, E-66 (1801–18).

17. Juan Bautista Elorriaga c. Felix Alzaga (1820), AGN, TC, E-67 (1820–25).

18. For an extended meditation of these notions, see the testimony of Antonio Josef Escalada, and replies by the court's advisors in Antonio Josef Escalada c. Manuel del Arco (1822), AGN, TC, E-67 (1820–25), and "Informe sobre el recurso que ha interpuesto Felipe Botet quejandose de infracción de ley, marzo 23/1836," AGN, Sala VII, BN, 387/600, Informes, f. 145; C. A. Acevedo, 60–62.

19. José Hernández c. Ventura Miguel Marco (1806), AGN, TC, H-1800–1819.

20. José de Faria c. Guillermo Dalton (1817), AGN, TC, F-81 (1815–19); Berman, 340–46; Horwitz, 150–61.

21. Mensch.

22. Blondel, 48–49; AGN, Sala VII, BN, 387/6600, Informes, f. 66; Méndez Calzada, 134–35; C. A. Acevedo, 22–27. There were also minor changes to the internal makeup of the court. The members were chosen by the government (though in practice they still responded to the advice of big merchants), and only the senior magistrates could decide in cases involving bills of exchange, public funds, and commercial paper. Lawyers remained excluded, and judges still came from merchant ranks. The Bilbao Ordinances remained the jurisprudential touchstone.

23. The clearest description of these operations is Braudel's *Civilization*, 2: 142–48. See also the classic account of Roover, 210–19. On the effects of inflation on prices and means of production, see Amaral, "Alta inflación."

24. Even Buenos Aires provincial monetary authorities got into the business of endorsing and discounting bills to cover for cash shortfall. See the Libros de Actas insert for June 16, 1848, AGN, Sala VII, Archivo Andrés Lamas, leg. 77, f. 395. Amaral, "Medios" and "Las formas."

25. Carruthers, 127–28; Bordo and Capie, 2–3.

26. Guillermo Ford c. Pablo Lenormand (1828), AGN, TC, F-83 (1824–28). On the effects of inflation on relative prices, see Amaral, "Alta inflación."

27. Rose, ch. 7.

28. Ford c. Miguel Díaz de la Peña (1824), AGN, TC, F-83 (1824–28).

29. Ruperto Albarellos c. Juan Bayta Romero (1829), AGN, TC, A-1 (1806–31); Anderon, Weller & Cia c. Juan Mitchell (1843), AGN, TC, A-3 (1841–44).

30. Philo Mills c. T. Armstrong (1831), AGN, TC, A-1 (1806–31).

31. Juan García de Cossio c. Francisco Mariano Orma (1835), AGN, TC, G-98 (1835).

32. See, for instance, the discussion among the provincial bankers in January

1851, in AGN, Sala VII, Archivo Andrés Lamas, Libros de Actas, leg. 77, f. 417, and Dalmacio Vélez Sarsfield's defense of equity arguments in "Causa de los embargados por opiniones políticas" (1847), in Vélez Sarsfield, *Escritos jurídicos*, 15–17, relying on Roman law. Admittedly, he was speaking of involuntary debts in this case. But defendants almost always cited involuntary reasons for their inability to pay debts.

33. See the classic account in Atiyah, 400–408; Horwitz, 201–24.

34. Manuel Joaquín de la Cuesta c. Esteban Marquez (1825), AGN, TC, C-22 (1825–27).

35. Eugenia Aramburu c. Felix Castro (1840), AGN, TC, A-3 (1840–44).

36. Geronimo Balleto c. Santiago Barrabine (1835), AGN, TC, B-12 (1806–35).

37. "José Carvallo solicitando aprobación de las moratorias que conseden sus acrehedores" (1828), AGN, TC, C-23 (1828–32).

38. "Moratorias declaradas por los acreedores de Juan Pedro Aguirre y Guillermo Ford" (1828), AGN, TC, F-83 (1824–28), and the continuation in "Guillermo Ford Concursado" (1830), F-84 (1828–32).

39. "Concurso de Carlos Harvey" (1828), AGN, TC, H-122 (1821–28). For an especially bitter battle, see "Concurso de don José Espinola" (1810), E-66 (1801–18).

40. Juan Bautista Elorriaga c. Felix Alzaga (1820), AGN, TC, E-67 (1820–25). Sometimes even plaintiffs recoiled from driving their debtors out of business. See Laureano Almada c. Ventura Galicia (1840), AGN, TC, A-3 (1840–44).

41. Pocock, *Virtue*, 54–71; Waldron, ch. 11; Somers.

42. Pascual Balbín c. Juan Bautista Lima (1801), AGN, TC, B-12 (1802–35).

43. Santiago Esperon c. Caetano Rico (1807), AGN, TC, E-66 (1801–18).

44. "Santiago Esperon solicita moratorias por cinco años" (1815), AGN, TC, E-66 (1801–18). See also "Jorge Frank su concurso" (1828), F-84 (1828–32), for a remarkably similar appeal.

45. Josef de Elia c. Juan Josef Lahitte (1815), AGN, TC, E-66 (1801–18).

46. Pocock, *Virtue*, 50.

47. José Manuel Coronel c. Damaso del Campos (1828), AGN, TC, C-23 (1828–32).

48. Francisco Daniel Holterhoff c. Antonio Fontier (1836), AGN, TC, H-125 (1834–39).

49. I have found only one instance in which a merchant reached beyond the Commercial Tribunal, to appeal to the Governor. See Manuel José Haedo c. Blas Achaval (1837), AGN, TC, H-125 (1834–39).

50. C. A. Acevedo, 60–61.

51. Manuel Ortiz Basualdo c. Pedro Botet (1835), AGN, TC, B-12 (1806–35).

52. Geronimo Balleto c. Santiago Barrabine (1835), AGN, TC, B-12 (1806–35); Manuel de Achutegui c. Andres Elias (1832), A-2 (1831–35).

53. Ventura Arzac & Francisco Anzo c. Marchi, Viales & Cia. (1832), AGN, TC, A-2 (1831–35).

54. Bernardo Jonas c. Tomas Armstrong (1834), AGN, TC, A-2 (1831–34). For an early sampling of this thinking in the Law School, see Santiago Viola, "Pensamiento sobre el sistema de codificación" (Mar., 1838), in the manuscript collection of Law School theses in the Biblioteca Nacional.

55. Adeleyda Sequeza c. Concurso de Victor Furno (1828), AGN, TC, F-84 (1828–32).

56. Manuel José Haedo c. José Joaquin Esnaola (1827), AGN, TC, H-121 (1800–1819); Narciso Aguero & Santiago Sarria c. Sres. Frontan Hnos (1846), A-3 (1840–46). See also the thoughts of two seasoned British merchants, Robertson and Robertson, 3: 154.

57. Neal, 8–14, 180–226; Carruthers, 129–31.

58. Fragueiro, *Organización; El Comercio*, Aug. 14, 1852.

Chapter 7: Reconsidering the Republic

1. Tocqueville, 2: 265–67.

2. Watson.

3. Gossman; Cranston.

4. Gutiérrez, *Origen*, 337; Garro, 355–71; Pestalardo; Halperín Donghi, *Historia de la Universidad*. For a comparative view of the United States, see Samuel Haber, ch. 3; and for France, Fitzsimmons, 4–10.

5. López, 342; Candioti; Pestalardo, 52–61; Cutolo.

6. Alberdi, "Introducción," 20.

7. López, 336.

8. For a sample of their broadsheets, see *La Moda: Gaceta Semanal de Música, de Poesía, de Literatura, de Costumbres,* from Nov. 1837 to Apr. 1838. Myers, "Una geneología; Sarlo Sabajanes; Myers, "Revoluciones"; Sommer, chs. 2–3; Botana, *La tradición.*

9. Halperín Donghi, *El pensamiento*; L. C. González.

10. Díaz Molano; Weiss, "Pedro de Angelis" and *Los antecedentes*; Sabor.

11. "Recherches sur Homere par J. B. Vico traducido por Sr. Pedro de Angelis 1833," AGN, Sala VII, Archivo Pedro de Angelis, 1/6/7. Miscellaneous notes on *Scienza nuova* can also be found in Sala VII 1/7/2.

12. Juan María Gutiérrez to Alberdi, n.d., n.p., item 625, AA; Alberdi, *Fragmento*, 3. For translations of other examples of French Romantics circulated locally, see AGN, Sala VII, Archivo Andrés Lamas, leg. 51/153, "Consideraciones sobre los principios de la filosofía" by Victor Cousin; leg. 51/245–51, "Sobre la filosofía de Nuestra historia y sobre los deberes que ella impone a la Juventud" by Vicente Fidel López, based on the writings of Cousin and Lerminier; AGN, Sala VII, Colección López, 21/2/4, f. 5451, "Apuntes" of Herder, Hipolyte, and Fortoul.

13. Portions of these renditions can be found in AGN, Sala VII, Colección López, 21/1/11, Libro de Apuntes (1836); Castellano.

14. Michelet.

15. Lilla, 4.

16. Lilla, 6–13; Berlin, "Giambattista Vico" and *Vico,* xvi–xxi.

17. Michelet, 1: iii, xiv–xv; Gossman, 169–70.

18. Kelley; Whitman.

19. Félix Frías to Lerminier, Apr. 22, 1855, AGN, Sala VII, BN, Archivo Félix Frías, leg. 679/9924; Treves.

20. Quiroga de la Rosa, 21–41; Orgáz, 3–26.

21. For an alternative view, see R. Peña, who argues for the persistence of scholastic *derecho indiano* into the republican era.

22. AGN, Sala VII, Colección López, 21/1/11, Libro de Apuntes, 3.

23. Sastre; García, "Introducción al estudio de las ciencias sociales argentinas" (1899), in García, *Obras completas*, 1: 84–181.

24. AGN, Sala VII, Colección López, "Libro de Apuntes," 22.

25. Alberdi, "Doble harmonía," 42.

26. AA, Miguel Cané to Alberdi, n.d., Buenos Aires, letter 284.

27. Luís Domínguez to Félix Frías, Apr. 15, 1844, AGN, Sala VII, BN, Archivo Félix Frías, 677; Halperín Donghi, "Argentina," 99; Halperín Donghi, "Una nación." For an alternative view, see Shumway, 164–67.

28. Palcos, "Prólogo." Of interest also is Gutiérrez's "Noticias biográficas sobre Don Esteban Echeverría," originally written for the publication of Echeverría's *Obras completas* (vol. 5), and reproduced in the La Plata annotated publication of *Dogma Socialista*.

29. From Gutiérrez, "Noticias," 43. In *Dogma Socialista* he wrote the following: "The great thought of the Revolution has not been realized. We are independent but not free. The arms of Spain no longer oppress us; but its traditions are suffocating us" (193).

30. Echeverría, "Ojeada retrospectiva," 76; Daniel Torres (Montevideo) to Esteban Echeverría, Jan. 9, 1842, AGN, Sala VII, Colección Farini, 3/2/1.

31. Echeverría, "Dogma Socialista," 184, and "Ojeada retrospectiva," 78–79.

32. Echeverría, "Ojeada retrospectiva," 93.

33. Echeverría,"Dogma Socialista," 157. On the vexing problem of people's moral and material maturity, see Hirschman, *Passions*.

34. Echeverría, "Dogma Socialista," 164.

35. Ibid., 202.

36. Echeverría, "Ojeada retrospectiva," 87. Ontologically speaking, societies have domain over individuals—who are only constituted as social beings, and not as bearers of natural inherent rights—and hence the community is the custodian and guardian of a regime of rights. "Dogma Socialista," 155, 183.

37. Echeverría, "Ojeada retrospectiva," 77–78.

38. Ibid., 84.

39. Ibid., 87.

40. Ibid., 97, and "Dogma Socialista," 205–15; Madison, "Federalist Paper no. 37," in Madison, *Federalist Papers*, 227–31. On Madison, see Nedelsky; McCoy, ch. 2.

41. Daniel Torres to Echeverría, Jan. 9, 1842, AGN, Sala VII, Colección Farini, 3/2/1.

42. The most comprehensive biography is Mayer, *Alberdi*, 2 vols. See also Alberdi, *Autobiografía*.

43. Alberdi, "Doble harmonía," 41; Treves, 336; Orgáz; Ghirardi.

44. Alberdi, "Doble harmonía," 42. Echeverría celebrated Alberdi's analytical precision and struggle to search for concrete solutions, but lamented his polemical style, which tended to create more enemies than friends. See Echeverría, "Ojeada retrospectiva," 118–22.

45. Alberdi, *Fragmento*, 2.
46. Ibid., 11. Alberdi to Vicente López y Planes, Dec. 10, 1834, AGN, Sala VII, Archivo Andrés Lamas, leg. 59, f. 18.
47. Alberdi, *Fragmento*, 14; Dotti, 20–22.
48. Canal Feijóo, 2: 39–58.
49. Dotti, 22; Canal Feijóo, 2: 67–108; Feinmann, 82–90.
50. Alberdi, "La República Argentina 37 años despues de su Revolución de Mayo" (1847), in Alberdi, *Obras completas*, 3: 219–42.
51. Ibid., 222; Juan F. Mur (Santiago) to Alberdi, Nov. 24, 1848, AA.
52. Alberdi, "La República Argentina," 233; F. Gómez (Valparaíso) to Alberdi, Dec. 17, 1845, AA.
53. Alberdi, "La República Argentina," 234; Juan María Gutiérrez to Alberdi, n.d., AGN, Sala VII, Archivo Andrés Lamas, leg. 59, f. 52.
54. Alberdi, "La República Argentina," 237.
55. Ibid.
56. Ibid., 240.
57. Rosas liked Alberdi's pamphlet, and invited him to return to Buenos Aires. Liberals, of course, were furious. Juan Thompson to Frías, Nov. 4, 1848, AGN, Sala VII, BN, Archivo Félix Frías, 686/11175; Bartolomé Mitre to Alberdi, May 14, 1851, AA.
58. Halperín Donghi, "Una nación," xxxv–xlii, and "Sarmiento's Place." For other, quite different treatments in English, see Shumway, ch. 7; Brading, *First America*, ch. 28.
59. The best survey of Sarmiento's life is Bunkley.
60. Sarmiento, *Life*, 9, and "Vindicación de la República Argentina" (junio, 1841), in *Obras*, 6: 1–4. It is worth noting that Sarmiento was not above changing his views. In an earlier article he portrayed Buenos Aires as a vibrant entrepreneurial commercial hub. See "El 25 de mayo," in Sarmiento, *Obras*, 6: 33. Hereafter, I will cite the English translation and edition of Sarmiento's classic *Facundo*, though I am aware many of the deep inconsistencies between the English and Spanish vintages. The finest edition of *Facundo* is the edition of the Universidad Nacional de la Plata, edited by Alberto Palcos in 1938.
61. Sarmiento, *Life*, 55. Consequently, the struggle shifted from "civil war" to a battle against "tyranny." "La cuestión del Plata" (Oct., 1842), in Sarmiento, *Obras*, 6: 78–83.
62. Sarmiento, *Life*, 195.
63. Ibid., 131. Sarmiento's grim conclusions did not always earn him accolades. Echeverría, for one, noted "an emptiness in the work of Mr Sarmiento on Quiroga; we find him barely dogmatic [Echeverría used this term in Romantic, prescriptive sense]—there is much to learn in his work about reflexive spirits; but we would have desired that the author formulate a political thought for the future, and render to all the living lessons encased in the animated search presented by our own history." See Echeverría, "Ojeada retrospectiva," 115.
64. Sarmiento, "La cuestión del Plata," in Sarmiento, *Obras*, 6: 62–63.
65. Ibid., 62. For reflections on *Facundo*, see Sazbón; Piglia.
66. Sarmiento, *Argirópolis*, 11, and in (Sarmiento, *Obras*, 6: 247–50) "Los in-

tereses comerciales" (Dec., 1849). On the role of U.S. influence, see, for instance, Stoetzer, 311–18.

67. Sarmiento, *Argirópolis*, 10.
68. Ibid., 7, and "La cuestión del Plata," in Sarmiento, *Obras*, 66–67.
69. Sarmiento, *Argiropólis*, 17.
70. Ibid., 87.

Chapter 8: Constitutional Persuasions

1. *La Organización Nacional* (Corrientes), Dec. 5, 1851; Valentín Alsina to Félix Frías, Apr. 29, 1851, AGN, Sala VII, BN, Archivo Félix Frías, 677/9414; Sarmiento, "Congreso, constitución y libre navegación de los ríos" (Apr. 17, 1851), in Sarmiento, *Obras*, 6: 401–2; Vásquez, 42–46; Bosch, 151–74. On the final days of Rosas's reign, see Halperín Donghi, *Historia argentina*, 395–403; Lynch, *Argentine Dictator*, 311–33.
2. Cárcano, 149–52.
3. Chiaramonte, "La cuestión," 194.
4. Gargarella; Macpherson.
5. Tocqueville, 1: 61–62.
6. *El Nacional*, May 3, 1852.
7. Unger, *Critical Legal Studies Movement*; Gordon, "Critical Legal Histories"; Wolin, 3–5; Dearlove; Kennedy, 84–86. For a consideration of the long-term political implications of the Argentine constitution, see Nino; Botana, "Las transformaciones."
8. Tau Anzoátegui and Martire, 588; Bosch, 228–38.
9. Auza, 7–26.
10. *Agente Comercial del Plata*, Feb. 5, 1852; Valentín Alsina to Félix Frías, Feb. 4, 1852, AGN, Sala VII, BN, Archivo Félix Frías, 677/9436.
11. *El Nacional*, May 3, 1852.
12. Fragueiro, *Cuestiones*, 2; these essays were originally published in Copiapó, Chile, in August 1852.
13. "Acuerdo de San Nicolás de los Arroyos. . . ," in Sampay, *Las constituciones*, 333–39.
14. Luís Domínguez to Félix Frías, July 1, 1852, AGN, Sala VII, BN, 680/10286; *El Nacional*, June 16, 1852; *El Constitucional*, Sept. 9, 1852; Urquiza to V. F. López, June 17, 1852, AGN, Sala VII, Colección López, 21/1/17, f. 4462; Scobie, *La lucha*, 24–31; López Rosas, 503–22.
15. Discourse of Mitre, in Ravignani, *Asambleas*, 4: 296, 315; see also the ballistic Sarmiento, *El Pacto*.
16. *El Nacional*, June 22, 1852; for a more cautious appraisal, see *El Federal*, June 16, 1852.
17. *El Nacional*, June 14, 1852; Gore to Earl of Malmesbury, June 24, 1852, FO 6/168; *El Constitucional*, Sept. 20, 1852. The best description of the secession is Cárcano; and the less than impartial Bustamante, *Memorias*.
18. *El Nacional Argentino*, Feb. 23, Mar. 17, 1853.
19. Mabragaña, 3: 1–7.

20. V. F. López to Urquiza, Nov., 1852, AGN, Sala VII, Colección López, 21/1/16, f. 4290.

21. Juan María Gutiérrez to V. F. López, Sept. 14, 1852, AGN, Sala VII, 21/1/17, f. 4465.

22. Tau Anzoátegui and Martire, 591–96.

23. Levaggi, "La interpretación," is the most thorough survey of the debate over judge-made law.

24. See Ruíz Moreno, for the tracks of federalism up to the Constitution; see also López Rosas, 121–23; Stoetzer.

25. "Borrador del informe que la Comisión de Constitución eleva sobre el Proyecto de Constitución," Biblioteca del Congreso, Archivo Juan María Gutiérrez, Caja 11/Carpeta 44/leg., 6; "Informe de la Comisión de negocios Constitucionales del Congreso General Constituyente de la Confederación Argentina," in Sampay, Las constituciones, 354–58.

26. Alberdi, Bases. Even in Buenos Aires, this book was regarded as the cornerstone of the new constitutional movement. See El Nacional, July 22, 1852. For a more detailed discussion of this tract, see Adelman, "Between Order."

27. Juan Bautista Alberdi to Juan María Gutiérrez, July 8, 1852, in Gutiérrez, Archivo Juan María Gutiérrez, 2: 150.

28. Chiaramonte and Buchbinder, 4–5; Botana, La tradición, 338–84.

29. Alberdi, Bases, 29–35.

30. Cited in Ravignani, Historia constitucional, 1: 35.

31. Ibid., 182.

32. AGN, Sala VII, BN, Archivo José B. Gorostiaga, 706/14054, notes. The Federalist Papers were read for their ruminations on sovereignty, and the Constitution for state powers. Sarría. For a systematic comparison the Argentine and U.S. constitutions, see Padilla, La Constitución, 111–12, who aligns article by article, finding some rough homologies. In this vein, the Federalist Papers (translated into French in 1792) also provided touchstones, confirming, especially in Madison's writings, the concern about majoritarian menaces of civil society to private property and public virtue. What the Federalist said, however, is one thing (advocating internal and external constraints on the powers of state to immunize property from such threats); how it was understood is quite another. The Argentine framers and Convention delegates interpreted the text loosely as advocating a sober appraisal of society to justify investing state powers with sweeping authority.

33. Discourse of Zuviría, in Ravignani, Asambleas, 4: 470–71. Padilla, Lecciones; Stoetzer, 314–31.

34. Halperín Donghi, "Una nación," xvii.

35. Discourse of Gutiérrez, in Ravignani, Asambleas, 4: 479–80. In private, Gutiérrez found consolation with his friend Vicente Fidel López that the Convention's delegates were perhaps less than luminaries. But since they were "tolerant, modest, and discreet," the Committee might be able to sway the assembly without much resistance. Gutiérrez to López, Oct. 20, 1852, in AGN, Sala VII, Colección López, 21/1/17, f. 4468.

36. "Constitución de la Confederación Argentina 10 de mayo, 1853," in Sampay, Las constituciones, 358–72.

37. Wood.

38. Rivarola, 4.

39. *El Nacional*, Sept. 18, 1852. It is worth noting that many of Urquiza's allies warned him of the consequences of proceeding without Buenos Aires. See V. F. López to Urquiza, May 7, 1853, AGN, Sala VII, 21/1/16, f. 4294.

40. *La Tribuna*, Feb. 12, 1856.

41. *El Nacional*, May 30, 1853.

42. Ibid., June 11, 1853.

43. Carlos Tejedor to Juan María Gutiérrez, Oct. 22, 1852, in Gutiérrez, *Archivo Juan María Gutiérrez*, 2: 184.

44. *El Constitucional*, Sept. 9, Sept 22, 1852; *El Nacional*, Sept. 17, 1852.

45. *El Nacional*, Oct. 8, 1852.

46. Ibid., Oct. 19, 1852, Apr. 11, 1854.

47. Ibid., Sept. 5, 1853; *La Tribuna*, Aug. 12, 1853.

48. *El Nacional*, Sept. 19, 1853. For a fuller development of this formulation, see Rose, 3–5; Adelman, "Property Rules."

49. *El Nacional*, Apr. 18, 1854.

50. Bustamante, *Bosquejo*, 278–97, for an example of the weariness with which *porteños* entertained constitutional matters.

51. Domingo F. Sarmiento to Wenceslao Paunero, May 15, 1852, Museo Mitre, Archivo Paunero, 7/4/10/824; "Carta de Yungay," Oct. 13, 1852, in Sarmiento, *Las ciento y una*, 11–58; and Sarmiento, *Campaña*—these were the first salvos against Urquiza. Alberdi described *Campaña* as a "tawdry and puerile" book in *El Nacional*, July 23, 1853. This work was originally published in Rio de Janeiro in late 1852, dedicated, ironically, to Alberdi. See also Bunkley, 315–56.

52. Sarmiento, *Comentarios*.

53. Ibid., 58–61; *El Nacional*, Nov. 21, Nov. 23, 1853; Botana, *La tradición*, 341–43.

54. *La Tribuna*, Nov. 26, 1856; *El Comercio del Plata*, Mar. 8, 1860, for especially vitriolic blasts against Alberdi on these grounds.

55. See the compendium of Quillotana letters in Aberdi, *Obras completas*, vol. 4, and reactions to the Buenos Aires charter in *Obras escogidas*, vol. 3; *El Nacional Argentino*, Oct., 1854.

56. Alberdi, "Estudios sobre la Constitución Argentina de 1853," in Aberdi, *Obras escogidas*, 3: 37.

57. First "Quillotana" letter, January 1853, *Obras completas*, 4:17; *El Nacional Argentino*, May 14, 1854.

58. Vicente López y Planes to Vicente Fidel López, Oct. 12, 1854, in AGN, Sala VII, Colección López, 21/1/2, f. 2441. Outside observers saw this problem as something of a false dichotomy. *El Nacional*, Dec. 17, 1859, and Vélez Sarsfield's position in *El Comercio del Plata*, Apr. 28, 1860. Ravignani, *Historia constitucional*, 1: 36–46; Chiaramonte and Buchbinder, 3–5; Shumway, 176–86; Levaggi, "Espíritu," 239–301; Bushnell, "Los usos."

59. Alberdi, "Estudios sobre la Constitución," in Aberdi, *Obras escogidas*, 3: 53–63. This was also the thrust of Alberdi's subsequent work, *Sistema económico y rentístico de la Confederación Argentina según su Constitución de 1853*, first pub-

lished in Chile in 1854 and serialized in *El Nacional Argentino* through March and April 1855.

60. Sarmiento, *Comentarios*, iv.

61. This view was broadly shared. See *El Comercio del Plata*, Feb. 19, 1860.

62. *El Plata*, Feb. 25, 1855; *El Industrial*, Feb. 29 to Mar. 4, 1856.

63. V. F. López to Félix Frías, July 9, 1855, AGN, Colección López, 21/1/16, f. 4302; *El Comercio del Plata*, Dec. 29, 1859; *La Tribuna*, Jan. 8, 1860.

64. *El Nacional*, Nov. 23, 1859.

65. *La Tribuna*, Oct. 30, 1859.

66. *El Comercio*, Dec. 6, 1859; *El Nacional*, Nov. 22, 1859.

67. *El Nacional*, Jan. 21–31, 1860; Heras, xxv–xxxviii. This debate was the high-water mark of adulation and aspiring imitation of the U.S. constitution, especially from Sarmiento and Vélez Sarsfield.

68. Ravignani, *Asambleas*, 4: 802–16.

69. "Informe de la Comisión Examinadora de la Constitución federal presentado a la Convención del Estado de Buenos Aires," in Sampay, *Las constituciones*, 386, and, for a full text of the reformed charter, "Constitución de la Nación Argentina," 412–26; Tau Anzoátegui and Martire, 600–604; López Rosas, 607–25.

70. J. B. Gorostiaga to Sarmiento, n.d., AGN, Sala VII, BN, 706/14004 & Gorostiaga to Félix Frías, Mar. 13, 1861, AGN, Sala VII, Archivo Félix Frías, 677/9367.

71. Bartolomé Mitre to Santiago Derqui, Sept. 7, 1860, in *AGM*, 7: 20–22; *La Tribuna*, June 1, 1860; Scobie, *La lucha*, 197–261.

72. S. Derqui to B. Mitre, Jan. 8, 1861, and Mitre to Derqui, Jan. 22, 1861, in *AGM*, 8: 44–45, 66–67; *El Nacional*, Nov. 30, Dec. 29, 1860.

73. Beck-Bernard, 209–19.

74. *La Tribuna*, Oct. 3, 1861.

75. Beck-Bernard, 219–21.

76. *El Nacional*, Nov. 23, 1861; B. Mitre to Manuel Ocampo, Oct. 22, 1861, in *AGM*, 10: 20–27.

77. Gorostegui de Torres, *Historia*, 65–76; de la Fuente.

78. "Discurso del Presidente de la República Gen. Bartolomé Mitre en el acto de la clausura del Congreso, Oct. 20, 1862," Museo Mitre, Archivo Íntimo, 8/10/32/11916; Scobie, *La lucha*, 383–90.

79. Cané, "La Constitución de Mayo y su examen," *El Comercio del Plata*, Dec. 29, 1859; see also Juan María Gutiérrez to Vicente Fidel López, Jan. 21, 1861, AGN, Sala VII, Colección López, 21/1/19, f. 4718.

80. Hirschman, *Exit*; Kennedy, 84–86.

81. *El Imparcial*, Aug. 30, 1855.

82. Halperín Donghi, "Argentina," 102; Lettieri; Botana, *La tradición*, 367–85; Adelman, "Between Order."

Chapter 9: The New Property of Merchant Capital

1. North, *Institutions* and "Theory." For a critique of evolutionary contractarianism, see Bates, "Contra Contractarianism."

2. "Alocución del Director Provisorio de la Confederación Argentina . . . 20 de noviembre de 1852 en la ciudad de Santa Fe," in Mabragaña, 3: 2–3; also his inauguration of Congress in October 1854, "Mensaje del Presidente de la Confederación Argentina . . . ," ibid., 3: 10–12.

3. Drassinower; Williamson; Baird; and for a general reflection on economic history, see Libecap, *Contracting*, 3–10.

4. Sabato, *Agrarian Capitalism*, 24–29; Gibson; and for the later agrarian change, see E. Gallo; and Adelman, *Frontier Development*. For trade figures, see Adelman and Amaral.

5. Sabato and Romero, 225–41.

6. For a compendium on the merchant houses of Buenos Aires and their national origins, see "List of Mercantile Houses in Buenos Aires 1850s," BBA, HC 4.1/25; Sabato, *Agrarian Capitalism*, ch. 6; Mariluz Urquijo, "Las sociedades," 39–48.

7. Jones, *International Business*, 2–4.

8. White to Baring Brothers, July 1, 1852, BBA, HC 4.1/24:21.

9. Gordon, "Macaulay"; North and Weingast. See Rose, for an important defense of the publicness of the rules governing private transactions.

10. Baird; Bates, "Contra Contractarianism."

11. Kronman.

12. Francisco Anzó c. Carlos Benavides (1844), AGN, TC, A-4 (1844). See also Gervasio Castro c. Juan Piñero (1843), C-26 (1843–46), for a similar case.

13. Pedro Romero (in the name of Manuela Campana) c. Tomás Giraldes (1846), AGN, TC, C-28 (1846). See also Prudencio Dolzé c. Eduardo Gerding (1856), D-33, for a similar case.

14. Nicolas Dodero c. Cayetano Davico (1845), AGN, TC, D-60 (1845–49).

15. For a similar formulation, see Jonathan Downes c. Nicholson Green (1851), AGN, TC, D-62 (1850–51).

16. Concurso de Pedro José Díaz (1843), AGN, TC, D-59 (1841–45).

17. Concurso de Leinau Hnos. (1858), AGN, TC, 2nd deposit, L-1 (1858–63). For analogous cases, see Concurso de Casa Luchter & Dittborn (1858); and Concurso de Juan Lavazaille (1858), in the same legajo; Concurso de acreedores del prófugo Adolfo Delfou (1844), AGN, TC, D-59 (1841–45).

18. See Jorge Landgreve c. Carlos Federico Dominico (1850), AGN, TC, D-62 (1850–51); Francisco Delgado c. Dominga Barbosa (1857), AGN, TC, D-65 (1857).

19. Concurso de Leon DuMayne (1857), AGN, TC, D-65 (1857).

20. Deetjent & Co. c. Enrique Sinclair (1857), AGN, TC, D-65 (1857). For a commentary on and definition of credit hierarchies, see Vélez Sarsfield's "Jurisprudencia II," *Agente Comercial del Plata*, Mar. 23, 1852.

21. Jonathan Downes c. Nicholson Green (1851), AGN, TC, D-62 (1850–51).

22. Concurso del fallido Juan Labastie (1858), AGN, TC, 2nd deposit, L-1 (1858–63).

23. Vélez Sarsfield, "Jurisprudencia II," *Agente Comercial del Plata*, Mar. 23, 1852. Friedman, 235–46; Horwitz, 160–99.

24. R. B. Ferguson, 22; Van Caenegem, 115–22; Kronman, 5–6.

25. Fragueiro, *Organización* and *Cuestiones*; *La Prensa Nacional*, May 22, 1852.

26. Fragueiro, *Organización*, 114–15.

27. Ibid., 117–18.

28. Ibid., 128; *Cuestiones argentinas*, 33.

29. For a sample, see Huergo; Alcorta; Sarratea, which was more a response to Alberdi but advocated much the same view as Fragueiro's.

30. Actas de Fundación, July 10, 1854, AGN, Bolsa de Comercio, Sala VII, 1/4/3; Actas est. Bolsa de Comercio (Rosario, 1858), AGN, Sala VII, Archivo Andrés Lamas, legajo 38/307; *El Comercio*, Aug. 6, 1854; *La Tribuna*, Nov. 26, 1853, for early discussions.

31. *El Nacional*, July 29, 1854.

32. Reber, 45–50, 113–14; C. A. Jones, "British Financial Institutions," 3–22.

33. Juan Baratta to Bartolomé Mitre, June 1, 1852, Museo Mitre, Archivo del General Mitre, Archivo Íntimo, 8/19/54/13.461.

34. White to Barings, July 1, 1852, BBA, HC 4.1, 24:21.

35. *The British Packet*, Feb. 12, 1853; *El Comercio*, July 15, 1852.

36. José Clemente Cueto c. Manuel Villafañe (1847), AGN, TC, C-29 (1847). See also *El Nacional*, Aug. 25, 1853.

37. Adrián Cires c. Matteo Pintroli (1847), AGN, TC, C-29 (1847); for similar cases, see Bartolomé Carofino c. Estevan Lissandri (1847), AGN, TC, C-29 (1847); Nicolas Dodero c. Cayetano Davico (1845), AGN, TC, D-60 (1845–49).

38. *El Industrial*, Jan. 22, 1856; *El Nacional*, Dec. 2, 1854.

39. *La Constitución*, Jan. 27, 1857.

40. *El Imparcial*, Dec. 7, 1855.

41. ABPBA, Libros de Actas, 9: 1114, Jan. 30, 1855.

42. Amancio Alcorta c. Martin Posse (1844), AGN, TC, A-4 (1844).

43. Norberto de la Riestra to Alcorta, July 26, 1855, AGN, Sala VII, Archivo Amancio Alcorta, leg. 27/001876.

44. Alcorta, 81.

45. Cocqueteaux & Lavigne c. Luis Belaustegui (1843), AGN, TC, C-26 (1843–46); Narciso Aguero & Santiago Sarria c. Sres. Frontan Hnos. (1846), AGN, TC, A-3 (1840–43); José Agote c. Manuel Biedma (1844), AGN, TC, A-4 (1844).

46. For a suggestive case in which a bookkeeper's report determined the legal outcome, see Jorge Landgreve c. Carlos Federico Dominico (1850), AGN, TC, D-62 (1850–51). On the penetration of experts into the hermetic legal world of merchants more generally, see C. A. Acevedo, 61–62.

47. Vicente López y Planes to Vicente López, July 9, 1847, AGN, Sala VII, Colección López, 21/1/2, f. 2331.

48. Perez's statement in Sebastian Carreras c. Ramón Arriola & Hno. (1847), AGN, TC, C-29 (1847); for general ruminations along the same lines, see "Borrador de petición de los miembros del foro de la Pcia de Bs As elevan al gobierno en la que proponen un cambio en la organización de la Admin de Justicia" (n.d.), in Biblioteca del Congreso, Archivo Juan María Gutiérrez, Caja 26, Carpeta 54, leg. 4; *Registro Oficial de Buenos Aires* (1853), 137–43.

49. Bustamante, *Bosquejo*, 338–39; *La Tribuna*, July 29, 1854; *El Nacional*, Aug. 12, 1853. For a good history of the JP, see Díaz, *Juzgados de paz*.

50. Tiburcio Ayerdi pidiendo desembargo de una carreta cargada de lana . . . (1861), AGN, TC, A-9.

51. Domingo Facio to Eduardo Costa, Apr. 22, 1862, *Registro Oficial de Buenos Aires* (2ndo sem., 1862), 9.

52. *La Tribuna*, Nov. 22, 1853, Aug. 5, 1854.

53. José Barros Pasos, "Conveniencia de reemplazar el Consulado de Comercio por Jueces Letrados," *El Plata Científico y Literario*, June 12, 1854; M. Navarro Viola, "Jurisprudencia de sentencia" (1855), reprinted in *La Revista de Buenos Aires*, 19 (1869), 435–38.

54. Vélez Sarsfield, *Dictámenes*, 183–84. Vélez Sarsfield was the chief councilor to the Buenos Aires government, issuing in August 1857 a "dictamen" to the Commercial Tribunal that they should uphold the old *jus mercatorum* until a new code came along.

55. *El Industrial*, Feb. 27, 1856.

56. Díaz Couselo, 21–23.

57. *Registro Oficial* (1857), 156–57; C. A. Acevedo, 32–51; Guillamondegui, "Notas" and "Primer proyecto"; Mariluz Urquijo, "Las sociedades."

58. Vélez Sarsfield to Rosas, Apr. 6, 1850, in AGN, Sala VII, Colección Farini, Archivo Adolfo Saldías, 3/3/11, f. 158.

59. *Registro Oficial de Buenos Aires* (1852), 330–37.

60. *Le Commerce*, Aug. 28, 1853; *La Tribuna*, July 28, 1854.

61. Luis Domínguez to Amancio Alcorta, July 23, 1852, AGN, Sala VII, leg. 5, f. 000325; Francisco Balbín to Alcorta, Nov. 27, 1852, leg. 3, f. 000185.

62. *La Tribuna*, June 29, 1854; *El Constitucional*, Sept. 1, 1852; *El Plata*, Jan. 25, Jan. 26, 1855.

63. *El Nacional*, Aug. 1, 1862. For a general survey of the press of the era, see Auza.

64. *El Plata Científico y Literario*, June 12, 1854. On the legal press, see Tau Anzoátegui, "Los orígenes."

65. *La Tribuna*, July 29, 1854; *El Plata*, Mar. 8, 1855; *El Industrial*, Jan. 21, 1856.

66. *El Nacional*, June 8, July 13, Sept. 18, 1857, June 17, June 19, 1858.

67. *Registro Oficial de Buenos Aires* (2ndo sem., 1862), 123; *El Nacional*, Apr. 21, 1857, Dec. 4, 1862; *La Tribuna*, June 7, 1860; Díaz Couselo, 34–38; Martiré.

68. Perhaps the most useful annotated edition is Malagarriga.

69. Nicolás Avellaneda, "El Código de Comercio," in *El Comercio del Plata*, Oct. 6, 1859; Tau Anzoátegui, *Las ideas* and *La codificación*, 330–34.

70. Julio Bloy c. Jean Labarthe (1869), AGN, TC, 2nd deposit, B-11 (1869–70).

71. José Leon c. Venancio Caballero (1863), AGN, TC, 2nd deposit, L-1 (1858–61).

72. "Causa Primera: mercantil" (Miguel Otero c. José Nadal), *Fallos de la Suprema Corte de Justicia Nacional*, 1: 17–25. See also "Causa IV" (Adhel Fonteynes de Mezieres c. Ramon Martínez), 29–32.

73. For a suggestive comparison, see John; Wortman; H. S. Jones.

74. On the political dimension of class-formation, see Przeworski, *Capitalism*, 66–81; Block.

75. On the connection between private property and constitutionalism in the United States, see Nedelsky.

Chapter 10: Making Money

1. Gourevitch; Sklar; Livingston.

2. Buchanan; Roger Smith; March and Olsen. For useful reviews of basic principles, see North, *Structure* and *Institutions*; Libecap, "Property Rights"; Machina.

3. Basu, Jones, and Schlicht.

4. Bordo and Capie, 3.

5. On this inherited problem of entangled class and state goals, see especially Chapters 4 and 5; Burgin; Halperín Donghi, *Guerra*. For the later period, see Cortés Conde.

6. Alford and Friedland, esp. chs. 7–9; Giddens, ch. 3.

7. Zelizer, *Social Meaning*; Wayne Baker, 110–11.

8. Nussbaum, 1–7; Kemp. For recent pioneering studies of the social construction of money, see Zelizer, *Social Meaning*; Reddy.

9. Kindleberger, 9.

10. Scobie provided an early description. See his "Monetary Development." Although this remains the single most important essay on economic policy during this period, it exaggerates the coherence of interests and positions within the Confederation and Buenos Aires camps—overlooking the conflicts within each side.

11. The problem was raised by Raúl Prebisch in one of his earliest essays. See Prebisch, "Anotaciones."

12. Przeworski, *Democracy*.

13. For a useful overview of this literature, see Stone.

14. The pattern was not unlike the powerful centralizing effect of the Civil War in the United States, or the chronic domestic strife in Mexico. Benzel; Sushka and Barrett. This of course did not eclipse federal-state conflict over financial affairs. See, for instance, White. In this sense, centralization was much more marked as a result of civil wars in Latin America. The result, as Stephen Haber has shown for Brazil and Mexico, was a high degree of financial repression. See Haber, "Regulatory Regimes."

15. George White to Baring Brothers (1852), quoted in Reber, 31; *La Cronica*, Aug. 6, 1852; *The British Packet*, May 22, 1852.

16. Chapter 8; Gorostegui de Torres, *Historia*, 15–19; Scobie, *La lucha*, 7–34.

17. "Mensaje del Presidente de la Confederación Argentina, Just José de Urquiza . . . 22 de octubre, 1854," in Mabragaña, 3: 55–56.

18. Ravignani, *Asambleas*, 4: 304.

19. *El Nacional*, July 31, 1852.

20. "Buenos Ayres Paper Money," n.d., BBA, HC 4.1/24.4; *Registro Oficial de Buenos Aires* (1853), 30.

21. *Registro Oficial de Buenos Aires* (1852), 156.

22. Cited in an open letter in *El Plata*, Feb. 27, 1855; Gore to Malcolmson, Dec. 25, 1852, FO 6/170–71; 176/ Gore to Russell, Apr. 1, 1853; *El Nacional*, July 23, 1854; *El Plata*, Mar. 1, 1855.

23. *The British Packet*, Feb. 17, 1855.

24. *Registro Oficial de Buenos Aires* (1854), 104–5; *El Nacional*, Mar. 14–15, 1855.

25. Quintero Ramos, 40–41. For a strong dissenting remark on the reforms, see *El Nacional*, Aug. 12, 1853.

26. Pedro Agote (1881) cited in Prebisch, "Desde el primer Banco Nacional," 291; Lamas, *Estudio*, 47.

27. *Registro Oficial de Buenos Aires* (1856), 3; ABPBA, Libros de Actas, 9: 1144.

28. ABPBA, Libros de Actas, 9: n.p.; Riestra to Llavallol, June 26, 1855, ABPBA, Ministerio de Hacienda, Correspondencia, 023-1-3: 1207.

29. *El Nacional*, Feb. 9, 1855; *The British Packet*, May 9, 1857.

30. *Registro Oficial de Buenos Aires* (1856), 106; (1857), 30, 186, 321; ABPBA, Ministerio de Hacienda, Correspondencia, 023-1-4: 1276.

31. Parish to Clarendon, Oct. 20, 1856, FO 6/196.

32. *El Nacional*, July 23, 1857; AHPBA, PH, 50B/A1/L11 (1856–57), Bolsa petition to Riestra, Aug. 4, 1857, doc. 374.

33. *El Nacional*, Sept. 2, 1854, June 12, 1855; *The British Packet*, July 15, 1854; Gallarotti.

34. Riestra to Directors, Mar. 31, 1854, ABPBA, Libros de Actas, 8: 435. An amended version can be found in Norberto de la Riestra to Junta de Administración de la Casa de Moneda, July 5, 1854, in *AGM*, 15: 37–41.

35. *El Nacional Argentino*, May 10, 1856; *El Imparcial*, Apr. 16, 1856; *El Nacional*, Jan. 8, 1857; on the final abolition, see *La Tribuna*, June 14, 1859; Scobie, *La lucha*, 159–64.

36. Bolsa petition to Riestra, Aug. 4, 1857, AHPBA, PH, 50B/A1/L11 (1856–57), doc. 374; Province of Buenos Aires, *Informe*, 5–11; *The British Packet*, May 23, 1857; Adelman and Amaral.

37. ABPBA, Ministerio de Hacienda, Correspondencia, 023-1-4, p. 1331; Riestra to Saavedra, Feb. 25, 1858, AHPBA, PH, 50B.A2/L21 (1858), Documento 383.

38. ABPBA, Libros de Actas, 10: 9; Directors to Riestra, May 18, 1857, Ministerio de Hacienda, Correspondencia, 023-1-4, no number.

39. Scobie, "Monetary Developments," 61.

40. For the debate on the Statute, see Ravignani, *Asambleas*, 4: 616–55; *La Tribuna*, Aug. 12, 1854; *El Nacional Argentino*, Feb. 23, 1854.

41. Cited in Díaz, *Mariano Fragueiro*, 119. According to the British delegate to the region, the statute would eliminate "an evil which was the cause of great dissatisfaction," paper notes. Parish to Clarendon, Nov. 29, 1854, FO 6/186/184.

42. Quintero Ramos, 38–39.

43. With Alberdi's support, Buschenthal even returned to the House of Baring for money. See Buschenthal to Barings, Aug. 19, 1858, BBA, HC 4.1/38.

44. *El Nacional*, Nov. 22, 1856, Feb 5, 1857; Scobie, "Monetary Developments," 61; Gorostegui de Torres, *Historia*, 54–55.

45. Fagan to Malcolmson, Apr. 20, 1859, FO 6/218/126; Fagan to Malcolmson, Aug. 24, 1859, 219/100.

46. "Emisiones sucesivas desde la creación del papel moneda" (n.d), ABPBA, Documentación, 017-1-14, No.4; Vicente Cazon to Luis L. Domínguez, May 9, 1864, AHPBA, PH, A5B.L59.

47. Llavallol to Riestra, June 25, 1859, AHPBA, PH, 50b/A3/L30 (1859) Documento sin número.

48. Derqui to Mitre, June 23, 1860, *AGM*, 8: 13–14; *El Nacional*, June 28, 1860.

49. *Registro Oficial de Buenos Aires* (1860), 156–57; Thornton to Russell, June 19, 1860, FO 6/226/109; Mitre to Riestra, Oct. 22, 1860, Museo Mitre, Archivo del General Mitre, Archivo Íntimo 8/13/42/12.332.

50. See for instance, Scobie, *La lucha*, 271–79.

51. *Registro Oficial de Buenos Aires* (1860), 269. This was followed by Riestra and Mitre's agreement to national storage and handling charges. *El Nacional*, Nov. 5, 1861, Dec. 13, 1861, June 4, June 12, 1862.

52. Thornton to Russell, Oct. 12, 1860, FO 6/227/60.

53. Transfers began in August 1859 and were deposited in a national Colecturía General. ABPBA, Libros de Actas, 10: 77. For an instance in which Riestra's patience wore thin, see Riestra to Finance Ministry in Buenos Aires, Jan. 14, 1861, AHPBA, PH, 50B.A4.L4 (1860–61). For a statement of these concerns echoed by Mitre, see the "Mensaje del Gobierno de la Provincia de Buenos Aires a la Honorable Asamblea General Legislativa" (Apr. 30, 1861), *Registro Oficial de Buenos Aires* (1861), 69–78; Scobie, *La lucha*, 294–96.

54. Thornton to Russell, Feb. 6, 1861, FO 6/232/40.

55. *Registro Oficial de Buenos Aires* (1861), 116–17, 148.

56. AHPBA, PH, A5a.L57 (1863–65), doc. 771.

57. AHPBA, PH, A5a.L57 (1863–65), doc. 2722, for a report on Matanzas; doc. 2840 for Baradero; doc. 269 for Mar Chiquita.

58. Quintero Ramos, 41.

59. ABPBA, Libros de Actas, 9: 69.

60. Pedernera to Urquiza, Nov. 25, 1861, cited in Scobie, "Monetary Developments," 68–69.

61. Veitch; Carruthers, 3–6; Levi, 181–84.

62. *El Nacional*, Oct. 19, 1861.

63. Mitre to Rufino de Elizalde, Oct. 29, 1861, in *Correspondencia Mitre-Elizalde*, 76–77.

64. Riestra to Mitre, July 24, 1862, *AGM*, 8: 198; Doria to Russell, July 28, 1862, FO 6/240/101. It did not help that Elizalde, another Mitre Minister, saw Riestra as a rival and schemed with his opponents to bring Riestra down. *El Nacional*, May 13, 1861; Elizalde to Mitre, May 11, 1861, in *Correspondencia Mitre-Elizalde*, 70.

65. Mitre to Riestra, Dec. 9, 1862, AGM-AI, 8/13/42/12.352.

66. Agote, 1: 105–7; Thornton to Russell, Nov. 22, 1864, FO 6/251/249; Cortés Conde, 22. On the convertibility debate in 1863–64, see Rosa, 15–24.

67. Burning began in earnest in December 1862, ABPBA, Libros de Actas, 12: 24.

68. *El Nacional*, June 2, 1863.

69. *La Tribuna*, Dec. 5, 1861, Mar. 22, 1862.

70. AHPBA, PH, A5b.L62 (1864–65), doc. 295.

71. *El Nacional*, Nov. 28, 1861.

72. Ibid., Nov. 27, 1861; Alcorta, for a compendium. Actually, Alcorta wanted

the peso supply to be cut, but he also wanted the Provincial Bank to open a web
of new branches across the country to offer credit to producers. He did believe,
in the end, that peso stability was ultimately a confidence game.

73. *El Nacional*, Aug. 25, 1862.

74. Cited in *El Nacional*, Mar. 10, 1863; for appraisals, see *El Nacional*, Dec. 17,
23, 1862; Scobie, "Monetary Developments," 75–76. On the debate over the U.S.
model, see Ravignani, *Asambleas*, 5: 209, 244, 252–60.

75. Luís Domínguez to Barings, Jan. 27, 1863, BBA, HC 4.1/43.

76. Vélez Sarsfield to Mitre, Sept. 19, 1863, *AGM*, 23: 47–49; Doria to Russell,
June 26, 1863, FO 6/245/273. Mitre then turned to former Finance Minister Juan
Bautista Peña, who, after the example of Riestra and Vélez Sarsfield, turned
down the offer.

77. Adelman and Amaral.

78. See Riestra, "Informe sobre los proyectos de redención del papel moneda
y bancos particulares de emision," AGM-AI/8/9/29/11,789.

79. Agote, 1: 121. It is worth noting that there is some discrepancy in the
numbers: for the sake of caution, I am using the lower estimates. For the internal
discussion on how the Bank might augment operations, see *Registro Oficial de
Buenos Aires* (1862–63), v–xxi.

80. Cortés Conde, 58.

81. Agote, 1: 33–38. On Mitre's own doubts about this plan, see Mitre to Riestra, Aug., 1863 AGM-AI, 8/13/42/12.358.

82. ABPBA, Ministerio de Hacienda, Correspondencia, 023-1-6; Province of
Buenos Aires, *Memoria*, 49–51. Plans for reconsolidation began months before
the Battle of Pavón. See Riestra to Mitre, Nov. 29, 1861, *AGM*, 8: 190–91.

83. AHPBA, PH, A5a.L57 (1863–65), doc. 2653; *El Nacional*, Nov. 28, 1861, Oct.
12, 1863; Cortés Conde, 24–25. One of the first acts of the provisional national
government was to create, in January 1862, a public fund of 50 million pesos to
be raised with 9 percent bonds and amortized at 3 percent, to be administered
by an ad hoc Junta de Administración, and covered by a special tariff of 2.5 percent on exports and imports (which remained in place until the extinction of the
bonds in 1878). To consolidate the Confederation's floating debt generated from
April 1861 and the collapse in December of 1861, in November 1863 the national
government created an additional public fund of 7 million pesos bearing 6 percent and amortized at 1 percent. A final amortization plan for Buenos Aires
came in October 1866, by which time the nation was already making payments
on an ad hoc basis.

84. *El Nacional*, Mar. 11, 1862.

85. Carruthers, 6–9; Dickson, 11–14.

86. For a useful recent summary, see Regalsky.

87. Bordo.

88. Hirschman, *Exit*, 1–15.

Chapter 11: The Unfinished Revolution
of the Republic of Capital

1. The revolutionary situation, in Tilly's sense, could probably be extended to the 1850's. See Tilly, *From Mobilization*, 89–193, and *European Revolutions*, 10–16.

2. The best analogy is perhaps early modern Italian principalities. See Burkhardt, 4–13.

3. Unger, *What Should Legal Analysis Become?*, 46–53.

4. Alberdi, "De la anarquia y sus dos causas principales" (1862), in Aberdi, *Obras escogidas*, 3.

5. O'Brien, "International Trade"; Stedman-Jones.

6. For suggestive recent comparisons, see Langley; Maxwell.

7. Katznelson, 85–92; Hobsbawm, 22–23.

8. Bates, "Introduction."

9. Rogers M. Smith.

10. Tocqueville, 2: 265–70. De Tocqueville did add the caveat that if America faced any lingering "revolutionary" threat from the eighteenth century, it came from "the black race." There is also a loose homology with Antonio Gramsci's distinction between active and passive revolutions. I have chosen not to invoke this idea, because Gramsci meant it to apply to cases where feudal, pre-modern formations align with modern capitalist ones in the process of reconstituting a polity from above—in a word, where the age of revolution did not shake up ancien régime property. While this may apply to Mexico and Brazil, and possibly even the Southern United States, it did not apply to revolutionary Buenos Aires. See Gramsci, 106–13; Ginsborg.

11. Alberdi, "Carta Quillotana, enero 1853," in Aberdi, *Obras completas*, 4: 17.

12. Sabato, "Citizenship"; Sabato and Palti.

13. Rock, *Politics in Argentina*; Adelman, "Socialism"; Ansaldi; Botana, *El orden*.

❧ Bibliography

Archives and Manuscript Collections

ARGENTINA

Archivo de Juan Bautista Alberdi, Colección Furt
Archivo General de la Nación
  Sala VII
    Archivo Amancio Alcorta
    Archivo Andrés Lamas
    Archivo Pedro de Angelis
    Biblioteca Nacional, misc.
      Archivo Félix Frías
      Archivo José B. Gorostiaga
      Informes del Tribunal de Justicia al Gobierno
    Bolsa de Comercio
    Colección Farini
      Archivo Adolfo Saldías
    Colección López
  Sala IX
    Consulado
  Tribunal Comercial

Archivo Histórico de la Provincia de Buenos Aires
  Papeles de Hacienda

Banco de la Provincia de Buenos Aires
  Actas, Comisiones Especiales
  Asambleas, Memorias y Balances
  Directorio
  Documentación
  Libros de Actas
  Ministerio de Hacienda
    Correspondencia

Biblioteca del Congreso
  Archivo Juan María Gutiérrez

Biblioteca Nacional
  Law Theses of the University of Buenos Aires
Museo Mitre
  Archivo del General Bartolomé Mitre
  Archivo del General Wenceslao Paunero
  Archivo Íntimo

GREAT BRITAIN

Guildhall Library
  Baring Brothers Archive, MS 18.321, HC 4.1
Public Record Office
  Foreign Office 6
University of London, University College Archives
  Buenos Ayres and River Plate Bank Ltd.

Periodicals (from Buenos Aires unless otherwise noted):

Agente Comercial del Plata
Archivo Americano
The British Packet
El Comercio
El Comercio del Plata
Le Commerce: Organe des étrangers
  residant dans La Plata
La Confederación, Rosario
La Constitución
El Constitucional
El Correo Judicial
La Crónica
Los Debates
El Diario, Córdoba
Diario de la Tarde
El Federal
Gaceta Mercantil

El Imparcial, Córdoba
El Industrial
El Mercantil, Montevideo
El Mercurio
La Moda
El Nacional
El Nacional Argentino
La Organización Nacional, Corrientes
El Plata
El Plata Científico y Literario
La Prensa Nacional
Registro Oficial de Buenos Aires
El Regulador
La Revista de Buenos Aires
Revista del Plata
La Tribuna

Published Primary and Secondary Material

Acevedo, Carlos Alberto. *Ensayo histórico sobre la legislación comercial argentina.* Buenos Aires: Imprenta Alsina, 1914.

Acevedo, Edberto Oscar. *La Independencia de Argentina.* Madrid: Editorial Mapfre, 1992.

Acevedo, Pablo Blanco. *El federalismo de Artigas y la independencia nacional.* Montevideo: Casa Barreiro y Ramos, 1933.

Adelman, Jeremy. "Between Order and Liberty: Juan Bautista Alberdi and the Dilemmas of Argentine Liberalism." Forthcoming.

————. *Frontier Development: Land, Labour and Capital on the Wheatlands of Argentina and Canada, 1890–1914.* Oxford: Oxford University Press, 1994.

————. "Property Rules or the Rule of Property?" *Law and Social Inquiry,* Dec. 1996, 101–20.

————, ed. *Colonial Legacies: The Problem of Persistence in Latin American History.* New York: Routledge, forthcoming.

Adelman, Jeremy, and Samuel Amaral. "Buenos Aires Exports 1815–1865: Quantity, Composition and Destination." Mimeo.

Agote, Pedro. *Informes del Presidente del Crédito Público sobre la deuda pública, bancos, y emisiones de papel moneda y acuñación de monedas de la República Argentina.* 5 vols. Buenos Aires: n.p., 1881.

Alberdi, Juan Bautista. *Autobiografía.* Buenos Aires: El Ateneo, 1927.

————. *Bases y puntos de partida para la organización de la República Argentina.* Buenos Aires: Plus Ultra, 1981 [1852].

————. "Doble harmonía entre el objeto de esta institución." In *Antecedentes de la Asociación de Mayo, 1837–1937: Homenaje del honorable Consejo Deliberante de la Ciudad de Buenos Aires en su fundación.* Buenos Aires: Consejo Deliberante, 1939.

————. *Fragmento preliminar al estudio del derecho.* Buenos Aires: n.p., 1837.

————. "Introducción." In Gutiérrez, *Origen,* pp. 11–32.

————. *Obras completas.* 8 vols. Buenos Aires: Imprenta de La Tribuna Nacional, 1886.

————. *Obras escogidas,* vol 3. Buenos Aires: Editorial Luz del Día, 1953.

————. *Sistema económico y rentístico de la Confederación Argentina según su Constitución de 1853.* Chile: n.p., 1854.

Alcorta, Amancio. *Escritos económicos.* Buenos Aires: n.p., 1862.

Alford, Robert R., and Roger Friedland. *Powers of Theory: Capitalism, the State and Democracy.* New York: Cambridge University Press, 1985.

Álvarez, Juan. "La evolución económica (1810–1829)." In Levene, comp., *Historia,* vol. 7, pp. 439–68.

————. *Las guerras civiles argentinas.* Buenos Aires: Eudeba, 1985 [1918].

Amaral, Samuel. *The Rise of Capitalism on the Pampas.* Cambridge: Cambridge University Press, forthcoming.

————. "Alta inflación y precios relativos: el pago de las obligaciones en Buenos Aires, 1826–1834." *El Trimestre Económico* 56:221 (Jan. 1989): 163–91.

————. "Comercio y crédito en Buenos Aires, 1822–1826." *Siglo XIX* 5:9 (1990): 105–21.

————. "*Comercio Libre* y economías regionales: San Juan y Mendoza, 1780–1820." *Jahrbuch fur Geschichte von Staat, Wirtschaft und Gesellschaft Latinamerikas* 27 (1990): 1–67.

————. "El descubrimiento de la financiación inflacionaria: Buenos Aires, 1790–1830." *Investigaciones y Ensayos* 37 (1988): 379–418.

————. "Del mercantilismo a la libertad: Las consecuencias económicas de la independencia argentina." In Leandro Prados de la Escosura and Samuel Amaral, comps., *La independencia americana: Consecuencias económicas,* pp. 201–16. Madrid: Alianza Editorial, 1993.

————. "El emprestito de Londres de 1824." *Desarrollo Económico* 92:23 (Jan.–Mar., 1984): 559–87.

————. "Las formas sustitutivas de la moneda metálica en Buenos Aires (1813–1822)." *Cuadernos de Numismática y Ciencias Históricas* 8:27 (Jan. 1981): 37–61.

————. "Medios de pago no metálicos en Buenos Aires a comienzos del siglo XIX." *Cuadernos de Numismática y Ciencias Históricas* 9:30 (Apr. 1982): 45–55.

————. "Public Expenditure Financing in the Colonial Treasury: An Analysis of the Real Caja de Buenos Aires Accounts, 1789–91." *Hispanic American Historical Review* 64:2 (May 1984): 287–95.

————. "La reforma financiera de 1821 y el establecimiento del crédito público en Buenos Aires." *Cuadernos de Numismática y Ciencias Históricas* 9:33 (Oct. 1982): 29–48.

————. "Rural Production and Labour in Late Colonial Buenos Aires." *Journal of Latin American Studies* 19:2 (May 1987): 235–78.

Amaral, Samuel, and José María Ghio. "Diezmos y producción agraria. Buenos Aires, 1750–1800." *Revista de Historia Económica* 8:3 (Autumn 1990): 619–47.

Anderson, Perry. *Lineages of the Absolutist State.* London: NLB, 1974.

Andrews, Commander Joseph. *Journey from Buenos Ayres, Through the Provinces of Cordova, Tucuman, and Salta to Potosi.* London: n.p., 1827.

Anna, Timothy E. "Spain and the Breakdown of the Imperial Ethos: The Problem of Equality." *Hispanic American Historical Review* 62:2 (May 1982): 254–72.

————. *Spain and the Loss of America.* Lincoln: University of Nebraska Press, 1983.

Annino, Antonio. "Introducción." In Antonio Annino, ed., *Historia de las elecciones en Iberamérica, siglo XIX: De la formación del espacio político nacional,* pp. 7–18. Buenos Aires: Fondo de Cultura Económica, 1995.

Appleby, Joyce. *Capitalism and a New Social Order: The Republican Vision of the 1790s.* New York: New York University Press, 1984.

————. *Liberalism and Republicanism in the Historical Imagination.* Cambridge, Mass.: Harvard University Press, 1992.

Araña, María Margarita, Luis Marcos Bonano, Claudia Elina Herrera, Patricia Penna de Villalonga, and Gabriela Tío Vallejo, eds. "Monteagudo: Un itinerario del iluminismo en la revolución americana." In Noemí Goldman, ed., *Imagen y recepción de la Revolución Francesa en la Argentina,* pp. 101–28. Buenos Aires: Gel, 1990.

Archivo del General Mitre. 28 vols. Buenos Aires: Museo Mitre, 1911–13.

Arendt, Hannah. *On Revolution.* New York: Viking Press, 1965.

Assadourian, Carlos Sempat. *El sistema de la economía colonial: El mercado interior, regiones y espacio económico.* Mexico City: Ediciones Nueva Imagen, 1983.

Assadourian, Carlos Sempat, Guillermo Beato, and José Carlos Chiaramonte. *Argentina: De la conquista a la independencia.* Buenos Aires: Paidós, 1972.

Atiyah, P. S. *The Rise and Fall of Freedom of Contract.* Oxford: Oxford University Press, 1979.

Attman, Artur. *American Bullion in the European World Trade, 1600–1800.* Goteborg: Kungl. Vetenskaps-och Vitterhets-Samhallet, 1986.

Auza, Nestor Tomás. *El periodismo de la confederación, 1852–1862.* Buenos Aires: Eudeba, 1978.

Avellaneda, Nicolás. *Estudio sobre las leyes de tierras públicas.* Buenos Aires: Biblioteca Argentina, 1915 [1865].

Ayres, Ian, and Robert Gertner. "Strategic Contractual Inefficiencies and the Optimal Choice of Legal Rules." *Yale Law Review* 101:4 (Jan. 1994): 729–66.

Azara, Félix de. *Memoria sobre el estado rural del Río de la Plata en 1801 y otros informes.* Buenos Aires: Editorial Raigal, 1943.

Azcuy Ameginho, Eduardo. *El latifundio y la gran propiedad colonial rioplatense.* Buenos Aires: Fernando García Cambeiro, 1995.

Bagú, Sergio. *Mariano Moreno.* Montevideo: Biblioteca de Marcha, 1971.

———. *El plan económico del grupo rivadaviano (1811–1827).* Rosario: Universidad Nacional del Litoral, 1966.

Baird, Douglas, G. "Self-Interest and Cooperation in Long-term Contracts." *Journal of Legal Studies* 19:2 (June 1990): 583–96.

Baker, J. H. "The Law Merchant and the Common Law Before 1700." *Cambridge Law Journal* 38:2 (Nov. 1979): 295–322.

Baker, Keith Michael. *Inventing the French Revolution: Essays on French Political Culture in the Eighteenth Century.* Cambridge: Cambridge University Press, 1990.

Baker, Wayne. "What Is Money? A Social Structural Interpretation." In Mark S. Mizruchi and Michael Schwartz, eds., *Intercorporate Relations: The Structural Analysis of Business,* pp. 109–44. Cambridge: Cambridge University Press, 1987.

Barba, Enrique. "Notas sobre la situación económica de Buenos Aires en la década de 1820." *Trabajos y Comunicaciones* 17 (1967): 65–71.

———. *Quiroga y Rosas.* Buenos Aires: Pleamar, 1974.

———. *Unitarismo, federalismo, rosismo.* Buenos Aires: CEAL, 1994.

Barbier, Jacques. "Silver, North American Penetration and the Spanish Imperial Economy, 1760–1800." In Jacques Barbier and Allan J. Kuethe, eds., *The North American Role in the Spanish Imperial Economy, 1760–1819,* pp. 6–12. Manchester: Manchester University Press, 1984.

Barsi, Juan Carlos. "La expedición Libertadora al Alto Peru." In Levene, comp., *Historia,* vol. 5:2, pp. 167–88.

Barzel, Yoram. *Economic Analysis of Property Rights.* New York: Cambridge University Press, 1989.

Basu, Kaushik, Eric Jones, and Ekkehart Schlicht. "The Growth and Decay of Custom: The Role of the New Institutional Economics in Economic History." *Explorations in Economic History* 24:4 (Oct. 1987): 1–21.

Bates, Robert H. "Contra Contractarianism: Some Reflections on the New Institutionalism." *Politics and Society* 16:3 (1988): 387–401.

———. "Introduction." In Bates, *Analytical Narratives.* Forthcoming.

Beaumont, J. A. B. *Travels in Buenos Ayres and the Ajacent Provinces of the Río de la Plata with Observations Intended for the Use of Persons Who Contemplate Emi-*

grating to That Country, or Embarking Capital in Its Affairs. London: James Ridgeway, 1828.

Beck-Bernard, Lina. *Cinco Años en la Confederación Argentina (1857–1862)*. Buenos Aires: El Ateneo, 1935.

Belgrano, Manuel. *Autobiografía*. Buenos Aires: Emecé, 1942.

———. *Escritos económicos*. Buenos Aires: Raigal, 1954.

Belgrano, Mario. *La Francia y la monarquía en el Plata*. Buenos Aires: Librería García Santos, 1933.

———. *Rivadavia: Sus gestiones diplomáticas con España (1815–1820)*. Buenos Aires: Editorial Huarpes, 1945.

Benzel, Richard F. *Yankee Leviathan: The Origins of Central State Authority in America, 1859–1877*. Cambridge: Cambridge University Press, 1990.

Beraza, Agustín. *La economía en la Banda Oriental, 1811–1820*. Montevideo: Ediciones de la Banda Oriental, 1964.

Berlin, Isaiah. "Giambattista Vico and Cultural History." In Berlin, *The Crooked Timber of Humanity: Chapters in the History of Ideas*, pp. 49–69. London: John Murray, 1990.

———. *Vico and Herder: Two Studies in the History of Ideas*. London: Hogarth Press, 1976.

Berman, Harold T. *Law and Revolution: The Formation of the Western Legal Tradition*. Cambridge, Mass.: Harvard University Press, 1983.

Biblioteca de Mayo: Colección de obras y documentos para la historia argentina. 17 vols. Buenos Aires: Senado de la Nación, 1960.

Bien, David D. "Offices, Corps, and a System of State Credit: The Uses of Privilege Under the Ancien Régime." In Keith M. Baker, ed., *The French Revolution and the Creation of Modern Political Culture*, pp. 89–114. New York: Pergamon, 1987.

Block, Fred. "Political Choice and the Multiple 'Logics' of Capital." *Theory and Society* 15 (1986): 175–87.

Blondel, J. J. M. *Almanaque político y de comercio de la ciudad de Buenos Ayres para el año 1826*. Buenos Aires: Ediciones de la Flor, 1968.

Bodin, Jean. *Six Books of the Commonwealth*. (1576). New York: Barnes and Noble, 1967.

Bonney, Richard. "Absolutism: What's in a Name?" *French History* 1:1 (1987): 93–117.

Bordo, Michael D. "The Effects of Monetary Change on Relative Commodity Prices and the Role of Long-term Contracts." *Journal of Political Economy* 88:6 (Dec. 1980): 1088–1109.

Bordo, Michael, and Forrest Capie. "Introduction." In Michael Bordo and Forrest Capie, eds., *Monetary Regimes in Transition*, pp. 1–12. Cambridge: Cambridge University Press, 1994.

Bordo, Michael, and Eugene White. "British and French Finance During the Napoleonic Wars." In Michael Bordo and Forrest Capie, eds., *Monetary Regimes in Transition*, pp. 241–73. Cambridge: Cambridge University Press, 1994.

Borges, Jorge Luis. *Obra Poética, 1923–1977*. Buenos Aires: Emecé, 1977.

Bosch, Beatríz. *Urquiza y su tiempo*. Buenos Aires: Eudeba, 1980.

Botana, Natalio. *El orden conservador: La política argentina entre 1880 y 1916.* Buenos Aires: Editorial Sudamericana, 1985.

————. *La tradición republicana: Alberdi, Sarmiento y las ideas políticas de su tiempo.* Buenos Aires: Editorial Sudamericana, 1984.

————. "Las transformaciones del credo constitucional." *Estudios Sociales* 6:11 (2nd sem. 1996): 23–48.

Brading, David. "Bourbon Spain and Its American Empire." In Leslie Bethell, ed., *The Cambridge History of Latin America,* vol. 1, pp. 389–439. Cambridge: Cambridge University Press, 1984.

————. *The First America.* Cambridge: Cambridge University Press, 1991.

————. "La monarquía católica." In Antonio Annino, Luis Castro Leiva, and François-Xavier Guerra, eds., *De los imperios a las naciones: Iberoamerica,* pp. 19–43. Zaragoza: Ibercaja, 1994.

Braudel, Fernand. *Civilization and Capitalism, 15th–18th Century,* vol. 2: *The Wheels of Commerce.* New York: Harper & Row, 1982.

————. "Du Potosi a Buenos Aires: Une route clandestine de l'argent, fin du XVIe, début de XVIIe siecle." *Annales, Economies, Sociétés, Civilisations* 4 (Oct.–Dec. 1948): 546–50.

Brown, Jonathan. "A Nineteenth-Century Argentine Cattle Empire." *Agricultural History* 52:1 (Jan. 1978): 160–77.

————. *A Socioeconomic History of Argentina, 1776–1860.* Cambridge: Cambridge University Press, 1979.

Buchanan, James M. "Asymmetrical Reciprocity in Market Exchange: Implications for Economies in Transition." *Social Philosophy & Policy* 10:2 (Summer 1993): 51–64.

Bunkley, Allison Williams. *The Life of Sarmiento.* Princeton: Princeton University Press, 1952.

Burgin, Miron. *Economic Aspects of Argentine Federalism, 1820–1852.* Cambridge, Mass.: Harvard University Press, 1946.

Burke, Edmund. *Reflections on the Revolution in France.* New York: Penguin, 1969.

Burkhardt, Jacob. *The Civilization of the Renaissance in Italy.* New York: Random House, 1954.

Burkholder, Mark A., and D. S. Chandler. *From Impotence to Authority: The Spanish Crown and the American Audiencias, 1687–1808.* Columbia: University of Missouri Press, 1977.

Bushnell, David. "El sufragio en la Argentina y Columbia hasta 1853." *Revista del Instituto de Historia del Derecho Ricardo Levene* 19 (1968): 11–29.

————. "Los usos del model: La generación de la independencia y la imagen de norteamérica." *Revista de Historia de América* 82 (July–Dec. 1976): 7–27.

Bustamante, José Luis. *Bosquejo de la historia civil y política de Buenos Aires desde la Batalla de Monte Caseros.* Buenos Aires: n.p., 1856.

————. *Los cinco errores capitales de la intervención anglo-francesa en el Plata.* Montevideo: n.p., 1849.

————. *Memorias sobre la Revolución del 11 de septiembre de 1852.* Buenos Aires: n.p., 1853.

Caillet-Bois, Ricardo. *Ensayo sobre el Río de la Plata y la Revolución Francesa.* Buenos Aires: Facultad de Filosofía y Letras, 1929.

―――. "El Directorio, las provincias de la unión y el Congreso de Tucumán." In Levene, comp., *Historia*, vol. 6, pp. 527–82.

―――. "La Revolución en el Virreinato." In Levene, comp., *Historia*, vol. 5:2, pp. 73–75.

―――. "El Río de la Plata y la Revolución Francesa, 1789–1800." In Levene, comp., *Historia*, vol. 5:1, pp. 37–54.

Caldcleugh, Alexander. *Travels in South America During the Years 1819–20–21; Containing an Account of the Present State of Brazil, Buenos Ayres, and Chile.* London: John Murray, 1825.

Canal Feijóo, Bernardo. *Constitución y Revolución: Juan Bautista Alberdi.* 2 vols. Buenos Aires: Hyspamerica, 1986.

Candioti, Marcial R. "Bibliografía doctoral de la Universidad de Buenos Aires: Catálogo cronológico de las tesis en su primer centenario, 1821–1920." *Revista de la Universidad de Buenos Aires* 44 (1920): 19–80.

Cansanello, Oreste Carlos. "De súbditos a ciudadanos: Los pobladores rurales bonaerenses entre el antiguo régimen y la modernidad." *Boletín del Instituto de Historia Argentina y Americana 'Dr. Emilio Ravignani.'* 11 (1st sem. 1995): 113–39.

Canter, Juan. "El Año XII, las Asambleas Generales y la Revolución del 8 de Octubre." In Levene, comp., *Historia*, vol. 5:2, pp. 403–511.

―――. "La Revolución de abril de 1815 y la organización del nuevo directorio." In Levene, comp., *Historia*, vol. 5:2, pp. 203–44.

Cárcano, Ramón J. *De Caseros al 11 de septiembre (1851–1852).* Buenos Aires: n.p., 1918.

Cardoso, Fernando Henrique, and Enzo Faletto. *Dependency and Development in Latin America.* Berkeley: University of California Press, 1971.

Carmagnani, Marcello, comp. *Federalismos latinoamericanos: México/Brazil/Argentina.* Mexico City: Fondo de Cultura Económica, 1993.

Carranza, Adolfo. *Dias de Mayo: Actas del Cabildo de Buenos Aires, 1810.* La Plata: n.p., 1910.

Carretero, Andrés. *Los Anchorena: Política y negocios en el siglo XIX.* Buenos Aires: Editorial Astrea, 1970.

Carruthers, Bruce G. *City of Capital: Politics and Markets in the English Financial Revolution.* Princeton: Princeton University Press, 1996.

Castellano, Angel. "Cuando una afirmación se convierte en interrogante: Vico en Alberdi? Un ensayo de metodología del pensamiento." In Devoto and Rosoli, eds., *L'Italia*, pp. 17–34.

Castillo, Andrés. *Spanish Mercantilism: Gerónimo de Ustáriz—Economist.* Philadelphia: Porcupine Press, 1980.

Chartier, Roger. *The Cultural Origins of the French Revolution.* Durham: Duke University Press, 1991.

Chasteen, John. "Background to Civil War: The Process of Land Tenure in Brazil's Southern Borderland, 1801–1893." *Hispanic American Historical Review* 71:4 (Nov. 1991): 737–60.

Chatterjee, Partha. *The Nation and Its Fragments: Colonial and Postcolonial Histories.* Princeton: Princeton University Press, 1993.

Chiaramonte, José Carlos. "Acerca del orígen del estado en el Río de la Plata." *Anuario del IEHS* 10 (1995): 1–10.

———. *La crítica ilustrada de la realidad: Economía y sociedad en el pensamiento argentino e iberoamericano del siglo XVIII.* Buenos Aires: CEAL, 1982.

———. "La cuestión regional en el proceso de gestación del estado nacional argentino." In Waldo Ansaldi and José Luis Moreno, comps., *Estado y sociedad en el pensamiento nacional,* pp. 159–203. Buenos Aires: Cántaro, 1989.

———. *La ilustración en el Río de la Plata: Cultura eclesiástica y cultura laica durante el Virreinato.* Buenos Aires: Puntosur, 1989.

———. "Ilustración y modernidad en el siglo XVIII hispanoamericano." In Gazmuri R. Krebs, ed., *La Revolución Francesa y Chile,* pp. 83–109. Santiago: Editorial Universitaria Chile, 1990.

———. "Legalidad constitucional o caudillismo: El problema del orden social en el surgimiento de los estados autónomos del litoral argentino en la primera mitad del siglo XIX." *Desarrollo Económico* 102:26 (July–Sept. 1986): 175–96.

———. *Mercaderes del Litoral: Economía y sociedad en la provincia de Corrientes, primera mitad del siglo XIX.* Buenos Aires: Fondo de Cultura Económica, 1991.

———. "Modificaciones del pacto imperial." In Antonio Annino, Luis Castro Leiva, and François-Xavier Guerra, comps., *De los imperios a las naciones: Iberoamerica,* pp. 107–12. Zaragoza: Ibercaja, 1994.

———. "Vieja y nueva representación: Los procesos electorales en Buenos Aires, 1810–1820." In Antonio Annino, ed., *Historia de las elecciones en Iberamérica, siglo XIX: De la formacíon del espacio político nacional,* pp. 24–51. Buenos Aires: Fondo de Cultura Económica, 1995.

Chiaramonte, José Carlos, and Pablo Buchbinder. "Provincias, caudillos, nación y la historiografía constitucionalista argentina." Documento de discusión No. 1. Instituto de Historia Argentina y Americana 'Dr. Emilio Ravignani,' 1991.

Christelow, Allan. "Great Britain and the Trades from Cádiz and Lisbon to Spanish America and Brazil, 1759–1783." *Hispanic American Historical Review* 28:1 (Feb. 1947): 2–29.

———. "Contraband Trade Between Jamaica and the Spanish Main and the Free Port Act of 1766." *Hispanic American Historical Review* 27:2 (May 1942): 309–43.

Coase, R. H. "Law and Economics at Chicago." *Journal of Law and Economics* 36:1 (Apr. 1993): 239–54.

Coatsworth, John. "La independencia latinoamericana: Hipóteses sobre los costos y beneficios." In Leandro Prados de la Escosura and Samuel Amaral, comps., *La independencia americana: Consecuencias económicas,* pp. 17–27. Madrid: Alianza Editorial, 1993.

Collier, David. "The Comparative Method: Two Decades of Change." In Dankwart A. Rustow and Kenneth Paul Erickson, eds., *Comparative Political*

Dynamics: Global Research Perspectives, pp. 7–31. New York: Harper Collins, 1991.

Coni, Emilio A. *La verdad sobre la enfiteusis de Rivadavia*. Buenos Aires: Facultad de Agronomía y Veterinaria, 1927.

Coronas González, Santos M. *Derecho mercantil castellano*. León: Colegio Universitario de León, 1979.

Correspondencia Mitre-Elizalde. Buenos Aires: Universidad de Buenos Aires, 1960.

Cortés Conde, Roberto. *Dinero, deuda y crisis: Evolución fiscal y monetaria en la Argentina*. Buenos Aires: Sudamericana, 1989.

Costeloe, Michael P. "Spain and the Latin American Wars of Independence: The Free Trade Controversy, 1810–1820." *Hispanic American Historical Review* 61:1 (May 1981): 209–34.

Cranston, Maurice. *The Romantic Movement*. Oxford: Blackwell, 1994.

Cross, Harry E. "South American Bullion Production and Export, 1550–1750." In J. F. Richards, ed., *Precious Metals in the Later Medieval and Early Modern Worlds*, pp. 397–424. Durham: Carolina Academic Press, 1983.

Cuenca Esteban, Javier. "Statistics of Spain's Colonial Trade, 1792–1820: Consular Duties, Cargo Inventories, and Balance of Trade." *Hispanic American Historical Review* 61:3 (Aug. 1981): 381–428.

———. "The United States Balance of Payments with Spanish America and the Philippines Islands, 1790–1819." In Jacques A. Barbier and Allan J. Kuethe, eds., *The North American Role in the Spanish Imperial Economy, 1760–1819*, pp. 28–70. Manchester: Manchester University Press, 1984.

Cutolo, Vicente Osvaldo. *La enseñanza del derecho civil del Profesor Casagemas durante un cuarto de siglo (1832–1857)*. Buenos Aires: Instituto de Historia del Derecho, 1957.

Dawson, Frank Griffith. *The First Latin American Debt Crisis: The City of London and the 1822–25 Loan Bubble*. New Haven: Yale University Press, 1990.

De Angelis, Pedro. *Memoria Sobre el estado de la Hacienda Pública; escrita por el orden del Gobierno*. Buenos Aires: n.p., 1834.

De la Fuente, Ariel. "Caudillo and Gaucho Politics in the Argentine State-Formation Process, 1853–1870." Ph.D. diss., SUNY Stony Brook, 1995.

Dealy, Glen. "Prolegomena on the Spanish American Political Tradition." *Hispanic American Historical Review* 48:1 (Feb. 1968): 37–58.

———. *The Public Man: An Interpretation of Latin Americans and Other Catholic Countries*. Amherst: University of Massachusetts Press, 1977.

Dearlove, John. "Bringing the Constitution Back In." *Political Studies* 38:4 (Dec. 1989): 521–39.

Devoto, Fernando, and Gianfranco Rosoli, eds. *L'Italia nella società argentina*. Rome: Centro Studi Emigrazione, 1988.

Díaz Couselo, José María. *Código de Comercio argentino*. Buenos Aires: Editorial. Astrea, 1988.

Díaz Molano, Elías. *Vida y obra de Pedro de Angelis*. Santa Fe: Editorial Colmegna, 1968.

Díaz, Benito. *Juzgados de paz de la campaña de la Provincia de Buenos Aires, 1821–1854*. La Plata: Universidad Nacional de La Plata, 1952.

————. *Mariano Fragueiro y la Constitución de 1853*. Buenos Aires: Editorial Coloquio, 1973.

Dickson, P. G. M. *The Financial Revolution in England: A Study in the Development of Public Credit, 1688–1756*. London: Macmillan, 1967.

Documentos para la historia argentina, vol. 16: *Relaciones interprovinciales. La Liga Litoral (1829–1833)*. Buenos Aires: Facultad de Filosofía y Letras, 1922.

Domínguez, Jorge I. *Insurrection or Loyalty: The Breakdown of the Spanish American Empire*. Cambridge, Mass.: Harvard University Press, 1980.

"Dos noticias sobre el estado de los campos de la Banda Oriental." In *Revista Historica* 52–54 (Feb., 1953): 301–527.

Dotti, Jorge E. *Las vetas del texto: Una lectura filosófica de Alberdi, los positivistas, Juan B. Justo*. Buenos Aires: Puntosur, 1990.

Drassinower, Abraham. "Beyond *Contract as Promise* and *The Death of Contract*." Unpublished ms, University of Toronto Law School, 1997.

Durnhofer, Eduardo, comp. *Mariano Moreno inédito: Sus manuscritos*. Buenos Aires: Plus Ultra, 1972.

Echeverría, Esteban. "Dogma Socialista." In Echeverría, *Dogma Socialista*. Edición de Alberto Palcos, pp. 145–228. La Plata: Universidad Nacional de la Plata, 1940.

————. "Ojeada retrospectiva sobre el movimiento intelectual en la Plata desde el año 37." In Echeverría, *Dogma Socialista*. Edición de Alberto Palcos, pp. 75–144. La Plata: Universidad Nacional de la Plata, 1940.

Eggertsson, Thráinn. "A Note on the Economics of Institutions." In Lee Alston, Thráinn Eggertsson, and Douglass C. North, eds., *Empirical Studies in Institutional Change*, pp. 6–13. New York: Cambridge University Press, 1996.

Ekelund, Robert E., and Robert D. Tollison. *Mercantilism as a Rent-Seeking Society: Economic Regulation in Historical Perspective*. College Station: Texas A&M Press, 1981.

Elliott, J. H. "Self-Perception and Decline in Early Seventeenth-Century Spain." *Past and Present* 74 (1977): 41–61.

Elster, Jon. "The Impact of Constitutions on Economic Performance." *Proceedings of the World Bank Annual Conference on Development Economics, 1994*. Washington, D.C.: World Bank, 1995. Reply by Adam Przeworski.

————. *Logic and Society: Contradictions and Possible Worlds*. Cambridge: Cambridge University Press, 1978.

Estévez, Alfredo. "La Contribución Directa, 1821–1852." *Revista de Ciencias Económicas* 48:10 (Apr.–June 1960): 123–234.

Fallos de la Suprema Corte de Justicia Nacional con la relación de sus respectivas causas, vols. 1–5 (1864–1870). Buenos Aires: n.p., 1864.

Feinmann, José Pablo. *Filosofia y nación: Estudios sobre el pensamiento argentino*. Buenos Aires: Ariel, 1996.

Ferguson, E. James. "Political Economy, Public Liberty and the Formation of the Constitution." *William and Mary Quarterly* 40:3 (July 1983): 389–412.

Ferguson, Robert B. "Legal Ideology an¹ Commercial Interests: The Social Origins of the Commercial Law Codes." *British Journal of Law and Society* 4 (1977): 18–38.

Fernández López, Manuel. "La Revolución Francesa en el pensamiento de Manuel Belgrano." In Noemí Goldman, ed., *Imagen y recepción de la Revolución Francesa en la Argentina*, pp. 53–68. Buenos Aires: Gel, 1990.

Ferns, H. S. *Britain and Argentina in the Nineteenth-Century*. Oxford: Oxford University Press, 1960.

Fisher, John R. *Commercial Relations Between Spain and Spanish America in the Era of Free Trade, 1778–1796*. Liverpool: University of Liverpool Centre for Latin American Studies, 1985.

———. "The Effects of *Comercio Libre* on the Economies of New Granada and Peru: A Comparison." In J. Fisher, Allan J. Kuethe, and Anthony MacFarlane, eds., *Reform and Insurrection in Bourbon New Granada and Peru*, pp. 147–63. Baton Rouge: Louisiana State University Press, 1990.

———. *Trade, War and Revolution: Exports from Spain to Spanish America, 1797–1820*. Liverpool: University of Liverpool Institute of Latin American Studies, 1992.

Fitte, Ernesto J. "Los presupuestos de Rosas." *Investigaciones y Ensayos* 25 (July–Dec. 1978): 15–30.

Fitzsimmons, Michael. *The Parisian Order of Barristers and the French Revolution*. Cambridge, Mass.: Harvard University Press, 1987.

Flanagan, T. E. "F. A. Hayek on Property and Justice." In Anthony Parel and Thomas Flanagan, eds., *Theories of Property: Aristotle to the Present*, pp. 335–60. Waterloo, Ont.: Wilfred Laurier University Press, 1979.

Forbes, John Murray. *Once años en Buenos Aires (1820–1831)*. Buenos Aires: Emecé, 1956.

Fradkin, Raúl O. "El gremio de hacendados en Buenos Aires durante la segunda mitad del siglo XVIII." *Cuadernos de Historia Regional* 3:8 (Apr. 1987): 72–96.

———. "Producción y arrendamiento en Buenos Aires del siglo XVIII: La Hacienda de la Chacarita (1779–1784)." *Cuadernos de Historia Regional* 15 (1992): 67–96.

———. "Segun la costumbre del país: Costumbre y arriendo en Buenos Aires durante el siglo XVIII." *Boletín del Instituto de Historia Argentina y Americana 'Dr. Emilio Ravignani'* 11 (1st sem. 1995): 39–64.

Fragueiro, Mariano. *Cuestiones argentinas*. Buenos Aires: W. M. Jackson Ed., 1930.

———. *Organización del crédito*. Buenos Aires: Editorial Raigal, 1954.

Francovich, Guillermo. *El pensamiento universitario de Charcas*. Sucre: Universidad San Francisco Xavier, 1948.

Friedman, Lawrence M. *A History of American Law*. New York: Touchstone, 1973.

Galano, Giuseppe. *La filosofia in soccorso dé governi: La cultura napoletana del settecento*. Guida: n.p., 1989.

Gallarotti, Giulio M. "The Scramble for Gold: Monetary Regime Transformations in the 1870s." In Michael Bordo, and Forrest Capie, eds., *Monetary Regimes in Transition*, pp. 5–67. Cambridge: Cambridge University Press, 1994.

Gallo, Ezequiel. *La Pampa Gringa: La colonización agrícola en Santa Fe (1870–1895)*. Buenos Aires: Sudamericana, 1983.

Gallo, Klaus. *De la invasión al reconocimiento: Gran Bretaña y el Río de la Plata, 1806–1826*. Buenos Aires: A-Z Editora, 1994.

Galmarini, Hugo. "Comercio y burocracia colonial: A propósito de Tomás Antonio Romero." *Investigaciones y Ensayos* 28 (Jan.–June 1980): 407–39 and 29 (July–Dec. 1980): 387–429.

Garavaglia, Juan Carlos. "De la carne al cuero: Los mercados para los productos pecuarios (Buenos Aires y su campaña, 1700–1825)." *Anuario del IEHS* 9 (1994): 61–96.

————. "Precios de los productos rurales y precios de la tierra en la campaña de Buenos Aires." *Boletín del Instituto de Historia Argentina y Americana 'Dr. Emilio Ravignani'* 11 (1st. sem. 1995): pp. 65–112.

————. "El Río de la Plata en sus relaciones atlánticas: una balanza comercial (1779–1784)." In Garavaglia, *Economía, sociedad y regiones*, pp. 65–117. Buenos Aires: Ediciones de la Flor, 1987.

————. "Tres estancias del sur bonaerense en un período de transición (1790–1834)." In María Mónica Berg and Andrea Reguera, comps., *Problemas de historia agraria: Nuevos debates y perspectivas de investigación*, pp. 87–121. Tandil: Instituto de Estudios Histórico Sociales, 1993.

Garavaglia, Juan Carlos, and Jorge Gelman. "Rural History of the Río de la Plata, 1600–1850." *Latin American Research Review* 30:3 (1995): 75–105.

García Belsunce, César A. "Diezmos y producción agrícola en Buenos Aires Virreinal." *Investigaciones y Ensayos* 38 (1988): 317–55.

García, Juan Agustín. *Obras completas*, vol. 1. Buenos Aires: Claridad, 1955.

Gargarella, Roberto. *Nos los representantes: Crítica a los fundamentos del sistema representativo*. Buenos Aires: Miño y Dávila Editores, 1995.

Garner, Richard L. "Long-term Silver Mining Trends in Spanish America: A Comparative Analysis of Peru and Mexico." *American Historical Review* 93:4 (Oct. 1988): 898–935.

Garro, Juan M. *Bosquejo histórico de la Universidad de Córdoba*. Buenos Aires: n.p., 1882.

Garzón Maceda, Ceferino. *Economía del Tucumán: Economía natural y economía monetaria, siglos XVI–XVIII*. Córdoba: Universidad Nacional de Córdoba, 1968.

Gelman, Jorge. "Los caminos del mercado: Campesinos, estancieros y pulperos en una región del Río de la Plata colonial." *Latin American Research Review* 28:2 (1993): 89–118.

————. "Mundo rural y mercados: una estancia y las formas de circulación mercantil en la campaña rioplatense tardíocolonial." *Revista de Indias* 52:195/196 (1992): 478–83.

————. "New Perspectives on an Old Problem and the Same Source: The Gaucho and the Rural History of the Colonial Río de la Plata." *Hispanic American Historical Review* 69:4 (Nov. 1989): 715–31.

————. "Producción campesina y estancias en el Río de la Plata colonial: La región de Colonia a fines del siglo XVIII." *Boletín del Instituto de Historia Argentina 'Dr. Emilio Ravignani'* 6 (2nd sem. 1992): 41–65.

————. "Sobre esclavos, peones, gauchos y campesinos: El trabajo y los trabajadores en una estancia colonial rioplatense." In Juan Carlos Garavaglia and Jorge Gelman, eds., *El mundo rural rioplatense a fines de la época colonial*, pp. 45–83. Buenos Aires: Biblos / Fundación Simón Rodríguez, 1989.

―――. "Venta al contado, venta a crédito y crédito monetario en América colonial: Acerca de un gran comerciante del Virreinato del Río de la Plata colonial tardío." *Revista de Historia Económica* 5:3 (Autumn 1987): 485–507.

Getzler, Joshua. "Theories of Property and Economic Development." *Journal of Interdisciplinary History* 26:4 (Spring 1996): 639–69.

Ghirardi, Olsen A. "La filosofía y la historia en Alberdi." *Cuadernos de Historia* 2 (1992): 33–77.

Gibson, Herbert. *The History and Present State of the Sheep-Breeding Industry in the Argentine Republic*. Buenos Aires: n.p., 1893.

Giddens, Anthony. *The Nation-State and Violence*. Cambridge: Polity Press, 1985.

Gillespie, Alexander. *Gleanings and Remarks Collected During Many Months Residence at Buenos Ayres, and Within the Upper Country*. Leeds: B. Dewhirst, 1818.

Ginsborg, Paul. "Gramsci and the Era of Bourgeois Revolution in Italy." In John A. Davis, ed., *Gramsci and Italy's Passive Revolution*, pp. 31–66. London: Croom Helm, 1979.

Goebel, Dorothy Burne. "British Trade to the Spanish Colonies, 1796–1823." *Hispanic American Historical Review* 43:2 (Jan. 1938): 228–320.

Goetz, Charles J., and Robert E. Scott. "Principles of Relational Contracts." *Virginia Law Review* 67:6 (Sept. 1981): 1089–1150.

Golbert, Albert S., and Yenny Nun. *Latin American Laws and Institutions*. New York: Praeger, 1982.

Goldman, Noemí. *El discurso como objeto de la historia*. Buenos Aires: Hachette, 1989.

―――. "Los 'Jacobinos' en el Río de la Plata: Modelo, discursos y prácticas (1810–1815)." In Noemí Goldman, ed., *Imagen y recepción de la Revolución Francesa en la Argentina*, pp. 7–26. Buenos Aires: Gel, 1990.

―――. "Legalidad y legitimidad en el caudillo: Juan Facundo Quiroga y La Rioja en el Interior Rioplatense (1810–1835)." *Boletín del Instituto de Historia Argentina 'Dr. Emilio Ravignani'* 7 (1st sem. 1993): 31–57.

Góngora, Mario. *Studies in the Colonial History of Spanish America*. Cambridge: Cambridge University Press, 1975.

González, Ariosto D. *Las primeras fórmulas constitucionales en los paises del Plata*. Montevideo: Casa Barreiro y Ramos, 1962.

González, Liliana C. *Repensando el "Dogma Socialista" de Esteban Echeverría*. Buenos Aires: Instituto Torcuato di Tella, 1994.

González Bernardo, Pilar. "La Revolución Francesa y la emergencia de nuevas prácticas de la política: La irrupción de la sociabilidad política en el Río de la Plata revolucionario, 1810–1815." *Boletín del Instituto de Historia Argentina y Americana 'Dr. Emilio Ravignani'* 3:1 (1991): 7–27.

―――. "Social Imagery and Its Political Implications in a Rural Conflict: The Uprising of 1828–29." In Mark D. Szuchman and Jonathan C. Brown, eds., *Revolution and Restoration: The Rearrangement of Power in Argentina, 1776–1860*, pp. 177–207. Lincoln: University of Nebraska Press, 1994.

Gordon, Robert W. "Critical Legal Histories." *Stanford Law Review* 36:57 (Jan. 1984): 57–125.

―――. "Macauley, Macneil, and the Discovery of Solidarity and Power in Contract Law." *Wisconsin Law Review* 3 (1985): 565–79.

―――. "Paradoxical Property." In John Brewer and Susan Staves, eds., *Early Modern Conceptions of Property*, pp. 95–109. London: Routledge, 1996.

Gorostegui de Torres, H. *Historia argentina: La organización nacional*. Buenos Aires: Paidós, 1972.

―――. "Los precios de trigo en Buenos Aires durante el gobierno de Rosas." *Anuario del Instituto de Investigaciones Históricas* 6 (1962–63): 141–61.

Gossman, Lionel. *Between History and Literature*. Cambridge, Mass.: Harvard University Press, 1990.

Gourevitch, Peter. "Protectionism and Free Trade: The Crises of 1873–1896." In Gourevitch, *The Politics of Hard Times: Comparative Responses to International Economic Crises*, pp. 71–123. Ithaca: Cornell University Press, 1986.

Graham, Richard. *Independence in Latin America*. New York: Alfred A. Knopf, 1972.

Gramsci, Antonio. *Selections from the Prison Notebooks of Antonio Gramsci*. New York: International Publishers, 1971.

Great Britain, House of Commons, *Parliamentary Papers*.

Greene, Jack P. *Understanding the American Revolution*. Charlottesville: University Press of Virginia, 1995.

Gresores, Gabriela. "Productores directos o criminales: Miradas contradictorias sobre la población campesina. San Vicente, 1799." In Gabriela Gresores and Carlos M. Birocco, *Arrendamientos, desalojos y subordinación campesina*, pp. 9–43. Buenos Aires: Fernando García Cambeiro, 1992.

Griffin, Charles C. "The Enlightenment and Latin American Independence." In Arthur P. Whitaker, ed., *Latin America and the Enlightenment*, 2nd ed., pp. 119–43. Ithaca: Cornell University Press, 1961.

Guerra, François-Xavier. *Modernidad e independencias: Ensayos sobre las revoluciones hispánicas*. México: Fondo de Cultura Económica, 1993.

―――. "The Spanish American Tradition of Representation and Its European Roots." *Journal of Latin American Studies* 26:1 (Feb. 1994): 1–36.

Guillamondegui, Julio César. "Primer proyecto de Código de Comercio rioplatense." *Revista del Instituto de Historia del Derecho Ricardo Levene* 16 (1965): 204–18.

―――. "Notas para el estudio de la justicia mercantil patria en las provincias argentinas." *Revista del Instituto de Historia del Derecho Ricardo Levene* 20 (1969): 117–34.

Gutiérrez, Juan María. *Archivo del Juan María Gutiérrez*. 7 vols. Buenos Aires: Biblioteca del Congreso, 1979–1990.

―――. *Origen y desarrollo de la enseñanza pública superior en Buenos Aires*. Buenos Aires: La Cultura Argentina, 1915 [1868].

―――. "Noticias biográficas sobre Don Esteban Echeverría." In Esteban Echeverría, *Dogma Socialista*. Edición de Alberto Palcos, pp. 3–68. La Plata: Universidad Nacional de La Plata, 1940.

Haber, Samuel. *The Quest for Authority and Honor in the American Professions, 1750–1900*. Chicago: University of Chicago Press, 1991.

Haber, Stephen. "Regulatory Regimes, Capital Markets and Industrial Development: A Comparative Study of Brazil, Mexico and the United States, 1840–1930." In John Harriss, John Hunter, and Colin Lewis, eds., *The New Institutional Economics and Third World Development*, pp. 265–82. London: Routledge, 1995.

————, ed. *How Latin America Fell Behind: Essays on the Economic Histories of Brazil and Mexico, 1800–1914*. Stanford: Stanford University Press, 1997.

Halperín Donghi, Tulio. "Anarquía y caudillismo." In Enrique Barba, ed., *Iberoamerica, Una Comunidad*. Madrid: Ediciones de Cultura Hispanica, 1989.

————. "Argentina: Liberalism in a Country Born Liberal." In Joseph L. Love and Nils Jacobsen, eds., *Guiding the Invisible Hand: Economic Liberalism and the State in Latin American History*, 99–116. New York: Praeger, 1988.

————. "Bloqueos, emisiones monetarias y precios en el Buenos Aires rosista." In Francisco Miró Quesada, comp., *Historia, problema y promesa*, pp. 307–41. Lima: Pontífica Universidad Católica del Universidad de Peru, 1978.

————. "Clase terrateniente y poder político en Buenos Aires (1820–1930)." *Cuadernos de Historia Regional*, forthcoming.

————. "Una estancia en la campaña de Buenos Aires, Fontezuela, 1753–1809." In Enrique Florescano, ed., *Haciendas, latifundios y plantaciones en América Latina*, pp. 447–63. Mexico City: Siglo XXI, 1975.

————. "La expansión de la frontera de Buenos Aires (1810–1852)." In Alvaro Jara, comp., *Tierras nuevas: Expansión territorial y ocupación del suelo en América (siglos XVI–XIX)*, pp. 77–91. Mexico City: Colegio de México, 1973.

————. *Guerra y finanzas en los origenes del estado argentino (1791–1850)*. Buenos Aires: Editorial de Belgrano, 1982.

————. *Historia argentina: De la revolución de independencia a la confederación rosista*. Buenos Aires: Paidós, 1989.

————. *Historia de la Universidad de Buenos Aires*. Buenos Aires: Eudeba, 1962.

————. "Liberalismo argentino y liberalismo mexicano: Dos destinos divergentes." In Halperín Donghi, *Espejo de la historia: Problemas argentinos y perspectivas latinoamericanas*. Buenos Aires: Sudamericana, 1987.

————. "Una nación para el desierto argentino." In Halperín Donghi, *Proyecto y construcción de una nación (Argentina 1846–1880)*, pp. xi–ci. Caracas: Biblioteca Ayacucho, 1980.

————. *El pensamiento de Echeverría*. Buenos Aires: Sudamericana, 1951.

————. *Politics, Economics and Society in Argentina in the Revolutionary Period*. Cambridge: Cambridge University Press, 1975.

————. *Reforma y disolución de los imperios ibéricos, 1750–1850*. Madrid: Alianza Editorial, 1985.

————. "La Revolución y la crisis de la estructura mercantil colonial en el Río de la Plata." *Estudios de Historia Social* 2:2 (Apr. 1966): 78–125.

————. "Revolutionary Militarization in Buenos Aires, 1806–1815." *Past and Present* 40 (July 1968): 93–107.

————. "Sarmiento's Place in Post-Revolutionary Argentina." In Tulio Halperín Donghi, Iván Jaksic, Gwen Kirkpatrick, and Francine Masiello, eds., *Sarmiento: Author of a Nation*, pp. 19–30. Berkeley: University of California Press, 1994.

Hamnett, Brian. "Constitutional Theory and Political Reality: Liberalism, Traditionalism and the Spanish Cortes, 1810–1814." *Journal of Modern History* 49:1 (Mar. 1977): 1071–1109.

Haring, Clarence H. *Trade and Navigation Between Spain and the Indies in the Time of the Hapsburgs*. Cambridge, Mass.: Harvard University Press, 1918.

Hart, H. L. A. *The Concept of Law*. Oxford: Oxford University Press, 1961.

Hayek, Friedrich. *The Road to Serfdom*. Chicago: University of Chicago Press, 1944.

Head, Francis Bond. *Rough Notes Taken During Some Rapid Journeys Across the Pampas and Among the Andes*. London: n.p., 1826.

Heckscher, Eli F. *Mercantilism*. 2 vols. London: George, Allan & Unwin, 1955.

Heras, Carlos. "Introducción." *Reforma constitucional de 1860: Textos y documentos fundamentales*. La Plata: Universidad Nacional de La Plata, 1961.

Herrero, Fabián. "Buenos Aires, año 1816: Una tendencia confederacionista." *Boletín del Instituto de Historia Argentina y Americana 'Dr. Emilio Ravignani.'* 12 (2nd sem. 1995): 7–32.

Hirschman, Albert O. *Exit, Voice, Loyalty: Responses to Decline in Firms, Organizations and States*. Cambridge, Mass.: Harvard University Press, 1970.

————. *The Passions and the Interests: Political Arguments for Capitalism Before Its Triumph*. Cambridge, Mass.: Harvard University Press, 1977.

Hobbes, Thomas. *Leviathan*. London: Penguin, 1968.

Hobsbawm, E. J. "The Making of a 'Bourgeois Revolution.'" *Social Research* 56:1 (Spring 1989): 5–32.

Hont, Istvan, and Michael Ignatieff. "Needs and Justice in the *Wealth of Nations*." In Istvan Hont and Michael Ignatieff, eds., *Wealth and Virtue: The Shaping of Political Economy in the Scottish Enlightenment*, pp. 1–44. Cambridge: Cambridge University Press, 1983.

Horwitz, Morton J. *The Transformation of American Law, 1780–1860*. Cambridge, Mass.: Harvard University Press, 1977.

Huergo, Palemon. *Cuestiones políticas y económicas*. Buenos Aires: n.p., 1855.

Humphreys, R. A., ed. *British Consular Reports on the Trade and Politics of Latin America, 1824–26*. London: Royal Historical Society, 1940.

Ibarra de Roncoroni, Graciela. "Un aspecto del comercio salteño (1778–1811)." *Anuario del Instituto de Investigaciones Históricas* 8 (1965): 313–23.

Infesta, María Elena. "La enfiteusis en Buenos Aires (1820–1850)." In Marta Bonaudo and Alfredo Pucciarelli, eds., *La problemática agraria: Nuevas aproximaciones*, vol. 1, pp. 93-120. Buenos Aires: Centro Editor de América Latina, 1994.

————. "Usufructo y apropriacion de tierras públicas: Buenos Aires, 1820–1850." Ph.D. diss., Universidad de la Plata, 1991.

Infesta, María Elena, and Marta E. Valencia. "Tierras, premios y donaciones: Buenos Aires, 1830–1860." *Annuario del IEHS* 2 (1987): 177–213.

Ingenieros, José. *La evolución de las ideas argentinas*. 2 vols. Buenos Aires: El Ateneo, 1951 [1918].

Jacobsen, Nils. *Mirages of Transition: The Peruvian Altiplano, 1780–1930*. Berkeley: University of California Press, 1993.

Jefferson, Thomas. *Notes on the State of Virginia*. New York: Norton, 1982.

John, Michael. *Politics and the Law in Late Nineteenth-Century Germany*. Oxford: Oxford University Press, 1989.

Johnson, Lyman. "Distribution of Wealth in Nineteenth-Century Buenos Aires Province." In K. J. Andrien and Lyman Johnson, eds., *The Political Economy of Spanish America in the Age of Revolution. 1750–1850*, pp. 197–213. Alburquerque: University of New Mexico Press, 1994.

———. "The Military as Catalyst of Change in Late Colonial Buenos Aires." In Mark D. Szuchman and Jonathan C. Brown, eds., *Revolution and Restoration: The Rearrangement of Power in Argentina, 1776–1860*, pp. 27–53. Lincoln: University of Nebraska Press, 1994.

Jones, Charles A. *International Business in the Nineteenth Century: The Rise and Fall of a Cosmopolitan Bourgeoisie*. Brighton, Sussex: Wheatsheaf Press, 1987.

———. "British Financial Institutions in Argentina, 1860–1914." Ph.D. diss., University of Cambridge, 1973.

Jones, H. S. *The French State in Question: Public Law and Political Argument in the Third Republic*. Cambridge: Cambridge University Press, 1993.

Jones, Kristine L. "Indian-Creole Negotiations in the Southern Frontier." In Mark D. Szuchman and Jonathan C. Brown, eds., *Revolution and Restoration: The Rearrangement of Power in Argentina, 1776–1860*, pp. 103–23. Lincoln: University of Nebraska Press, 1994.

Kagan, Richard L. *Lawsuits and Litigants in Castile, 1500–1700*. Chapel Hill: University of North Carolina Press, 1981.

Katznelson, Ira. *Liberalism's Crooked Circle*. Princeton: Princeton University Press, 1996.

Kautsky, John. *The Politics of Aristocratic Empires*. Chapel Hill: University of North Carolina Press, 1982.

Kelley, Donald. *Historians and the Law in Postrevolutionary France*. Princeton: Princeton University Press, 1990.

Kemp, Arthur. *The Legal Qualities of Money*. New York: Pageant Press, 1956.

Kennedy, Duncan. *Sexy Dressing etc.* Cambridge, Mass.: Harvard University Press, 1993.

Kindleberger, Charles P. *Manias, Panics and Crashes: A History of Financial Crises*. New York: Basic Books, 1978.

Klein, Herbert S. "Structure and Profitability of Royal Finance in the Viceroyalty of the Río de la Plata in 1790." *Hispanic American Historical Review* 53 (1973): 440–69.

Kronman, Anthony T. "Contract Law and the State of Nature." *Journal of Law, Economics and Organization* 1:1 (Fall 1985): 5–32.

Kuethe, Allan J., and Lowell Blaidsell. "French Influence and the Origins of the Bourbon Colonial Reorganization." *Hispanic American Historical Review* 71:3 (Aug. 1991): 579–607.

Lamas, Andrés. *Estudio histórico y científico del Banco de la Provincia de Buenos Aires*. Buenos Aires: Establecimiento Tipográfico de "El Nacional," 1886.

———. *La legislación agraria de Bernardino Rivadavia*. Buenos Aires: n.p., 1933.

Langley, Lester D. *The Americas in the Age of Revolution, 1750–1850*. New Haven: Yale University Press, 1996.

Larson, Brooke. "Caciques, Class Structure and the Colonial State in Bolivia." *Nova Americana* 2 (1979): 197–235.

Lavardén, Manuel José de. *Nuevo aspecto del comercio en el Río de la Plata*. Buenos Aires: Editorial Raigal, 1955 [1801].

Lerner, Ralph. "Commerce and Character: The Anglo-American as New Model Man." *William and Mary Quarterly* 36:1 (Jan. 1979): 3–26.

Lettieri, Alberto Rodolfo. *Vicente Fidel López: La construcción histórico-política de u liberalismo conservador*. Buenos Aires: Editorial. Biblos, 1995.

Levaggi, Abelardo. "Espíritu del constitucionalismo argentino de la primera mitad del siglo XIX." *Revista de Historia del Derecho Ricardo Levene* 9 (1981): 239–301.

———. "La interpretación del derecho en la Argentina en el siglo XIX." *Revista de Historia del Derecho* 7 (1980): 23–121.

Levene, Ricardo. "El 5 y 6 de 1811 y sus consecuencias nacionales." In Levene, comp., *Historia*, vol 5:2, pp. 343–69.

———. *La anarquía de 1820 en Buenos Aires*. Buenos Aires: El Ateneo, 1933.

———. "Asonado del 1° enero de 1809." In Levene, comp., *Historia*, vol 5:1., pp. 469–88.

———. "El Congreso General de las Provincias y la Conferencia del 18 de diciembre." In Levene, comp., *Historia*, vol. 5:2, pp. 291–324.

———. "El derecho patrio argentino y la organización del poder judicial (1810–1820)." In Levene, comp., *Historia*, vol. 7, pp. 375–438.

———. "Funciones económicas de las instituciones virreinales." In Levene, comp., *Historia*, vol. 4, pp. 291–305.

———. "Intentos de Independencia en el Virreinato del Plata (1781–1809)." In Levene, comp., *Historia*, vol. 1, pp. 423–69.

———. *Investigaciones acerca de la historia económica del Virreinato del Río de la Plata*. La Plata: Facultad de Humanidades, 1927.

———. "Las Juntas Provinciales creadas por el Reglamento de 10 de Febrero de 1811 y los orígenes del federalismo." In Levene, comp., *Historia*, vol. 5:2, pp. 325–41.

———. "La obra orgánica de la revolución." In Levene, comp., *Historia*, vol. 5:2, pp. 243–89.

———. *El pensamiento vivo de Moreno*. Buenos Aires: Losada, 1942.

———. *El proceso histórica de Lavalle a Rosas*. La Plata: Archio Histórico de la Provincia de Buenos Aires, 1950.

———. "Significación histórica de la obra económica de Manuel Belgrano y Mariano Moreno." In Levene, comp., *Historia*, vol. 5:1, pp. 489–520.

———. "Los sucesos de Mayo." In Levene, comp., *Historia*, vol. 5:1, pp. 11–40.

———. *Vida y escritos de Victorián de Villaba*. Buenos Aires: Facultad de Filosofía y Letras, 1946.

————, comp. *Historia de la Nación Argentina*, vols. 1, 4–6 (1941), and 7 (1949). Buenos Aires: El Ateneo, 1941–49.

Levi, Margaret. *Of Rule and Revenue*. Berkeley: University of California Press, 1988.

Libecap, Gary D. *Contracting for Property Rights*. Cambridge: Cambridge University Press, 1989.

————. "Property Rights in Economic History: Implications for Research." *Explorations in Economic History* 23:3 (July 1986): 227–52.

Lilla, Mark. *G. B. Vico: The Making of An Anti-Modern*. Cambridge, Mass.: Harvard University Press, 1993.

Liss, Peggy K. *Atlantic Empires: The Networks of Trade and Revolution, 1713–1826*. Baltimore: Johns Hopkins University Press, 1983.

Livingston, James. *Origins of the Federal Reserve System: Money, Class, and Corporate Capitalism, 1890–1913*. Ithaca: Cornell University Press, 1986.

López Rosas, José Rafael. *Historia constitucional argentina*. 3rd ed. Buenos Aires: Editorial Astrea, 1986.

López, Vicente Fidel. "Autobiografía." *La Biblioteca* 1 (1896): 325–55.

Lynch, John. *Argentine Dictator: Juan Manuel de Rosas, 1829–1852*. Oxford: Oxford University Press, 1981.

————. *The Caudillos of Spanish America*. Oxford: Oxford University Press, 1992.

————. *Spanish Colonial Administration, 1782–1810: The Intendent System in the Viceroyalty of the Río de la Plata*. London: Athlone Press, 1958.

Mabragaña, H. *Los Mensajes*, vols. 1–3. Buenos Aires: Comisión Nacional del Centenario, 1910.

Machiavelli, Niccolò. *The Prince*. London: Penguin, 1961.

Machina, Mark J. "Choice Under Uncertainty: Problems Solved and Unsolved." *Journal of Economic Perspectives* 1:1 (Summer 1987): 121–54.

MacKinnon, Commander Lauchland Bellingham. *Steam Warfare in the Paraná: A Narrative of Operations by the Combined Squadrons of England and France, in a Foreign Passage up That River*. 2 vols. London: Charles Ollier, n.d.

Macneil, Ian. "Relational Contract: What We Do and Do Not Know." *Wisconsin Law Review* 3 (1985): 483–505.

Macpherson, C. B. *The Life and Times of Liberal Democracy*. Oxford: Oxford University Press, 1977.

Madison, James. *The Federalist Papers*. New York: Penguin, 1961.

Maeder, Ernesto J. A. *Historia económica de Corrientes en el período virreinal, 1776–1810*. Buenos Aires: Academia Nacional de la Historia, 1981.

Magnusson, Lars. *Mercantilism: The Shaping of an Economic Language*. New York: Routledge, 1994.

Maier, Charles. "Political Economy and History." In Maier, *The Search for Stability: Explorations in Historical Political Economy*, pp. 1–16. Cambridge: Cambridge University Press, 1987.

Malagarriga, Carlos C. *Código de Comercio según la doctrina y la jurisprudencia*. Buenos Aires: J. Lajouane, 1917.

Mandrini, Raúl. "Las transformaciones de la economía indígena bonaerense (c. 1600–1820)." In Raul Mandrini and Andrea Reguera, comps., *Huellas en la tierra: Indios, agricultores y hacendados en la pampa bonaerense*, pp. 45–74. Tandil: Instituto de Estudios Historico-Sociales, 1993.

Manning, William R., ed. *Diplomatic Correspondence of the United States: Inter-American Affairs, 1831–60*, vol. 1. Washington, D.C.: Carnegie Endowment for International Peace, 1932.

March, James G., and Johan P. Olsen. "The New Institutionalism: Organization Factors in Political Life." *American Political Science Review* 78:3 (Sept. 1984): 734–49.

Marichal, Carlos. *A Century of Debt Crisis in Latin America: From Independence to the Great Depression, 1820–1930*. Princeton: Princeton University Press, 1989.

Mariluz Urquijo, José M. *Estado e industria, 1810–1860*. Buenos Aires: Ed. Macchi, 1969.

———. *El régimen de la tierra en el derecho indiano*. Buenos Aires: Editorial Perrot, 1968.

———. "Las sociedades anónimas de Buenos Aires antes del Código de Comercio." *Revista del Instituto de Historia del Derecho Ricardo Levene* 16 (1965): 39–48.

Marshall, T. H. "Citizenship and Social Class." In Marshall, *Class, Citizenship and Social Development*. Chicago: University of Chicago Press, 1964.

Martiré, Eduardo. "La reforma de 1889 al Código de Comercio." *Revista del Colegio de Abogados de Buenos Aires* 49:3 (Dec. 1989): 16–25.

Marx, Karl. *Grundisse: Introduction to the Critique of Political Economy*. New York: Vintage Books, 1973.

Maxwell, Kenneth J. "Hegemonies Old and New: The Ibero-Atlantic in the Long Eighteenth-Century." In Jeremy Adelman, ed., *Colonial Legacies*, forthcoming.

Mayer, Jorge M. *Agüero o el dogmatismo constitucional*. Buenos Aires: Academia Naconal de Derecho y Ciencias Sociales, 1981.

———. *Alberdi y su tiempo*. 2 vols. Buenos Aires: Academia Nacional de Derecho y Ciencias Sociales de Buenos Aires, 1973.

Mayo, Carlos A. *Estancia y sociedad en la Pampa, 1740–1820*. Buenos Aires: Editorial Biblos, 1995.

———. "Estancia y peonaje en la región pampeana en la segunda mitad del siglo XVIII." *Desarrollo Económico* 92:23 (Jan.–May 1984): 609–16.

———. "Estructura agraria, revolución de independencia y caudillismo en el Río de la Plata, 1750–1820." *Anuario del IEHS*, forthcoming.

———. "Landed but Not Powerful: The Colonial Estancieros of Buenos Aires (1750–1810)." *Hispanic American Historical Review* 71:4 (Nov. 1991): 761–79.

Mayo, Carlos, and Amalia Latrubesse. *Terratenientes, soldados y cautivos: La Frontera (1736–1815)*. Mar del Plata: Universidad Nacional de Mar del Plata, 1993.

McCann, Michael W. "Resurrection and Reform: Perspectives on Property in the American Constitutional Tradition." *Politics and Society* 13:2 (1984): 143–76.

McCann, William. *Two Thousand Miles' Ride Through the Argentine Provinces*. 2 vols. London: Elder & Co., 1953.

McCoy, Drew. *The Last of the Fathers: James Madison and the Republican Legacy.* Cambridge: Cambridge University Press, 1989.

McFarlane, Anthony. "Rebellions in Late Colonial Spanish America: A Comparative Perspective." *Bulletin of Latin American Research* 14:3 (Sept. 1995): 313–38.

Méndez Calzada, Luis. *La función judicial en las primeras épocas de la independencia.* Buenos Aires: Editorial Losada, 1944.

Mendoza, Gunnar. "La Universidad de San Francisco Xavier." *Presencia,* Aug. 6, 1975, 915–31.

Mensajes de los Gobernadores de la Provincia de Buenos Aires, 1822–1849. 2 vols. La Plata: Archivo Histórico de la Provincia de Buenos Aires, 1976.

Mensch, Elizabeth V. "The Colonial Origins of Liberal Property Rights." *Buffalo Law Review* 31 (1981): 635–735.

Merediz, Rodolfo. "Comercio de frutos del pais entre Buenos Aires y mercados europeos entre 1815 y 1820." *Trabajos y Comunicaciones* 16 (1966): 136–52.

Merryman, John Henry. *The Civil Law Tradition: An Introduction to the Legal Systems of Western Europe and Latin America.* Stanford: Stanford University Press, 1969.

Michelet, Jules. *Oeuvres choisies de Vico, contenant ses memoires, ecrits par lui-meme, la science nouvelle, les opuscules, lettres, etc.* 2 vols. Paris: Libraire Classique de L'Hachette, 1835.

Mitre, Bartolomé. *Historia de Belgrano y la independencia argentina.* 4th ed., 2 vols. Buenos Aires: Felix Lajouane, 1887.

Molinari, Diego Luis. *La representación de los hacendados de Mariano Moreno: Su ninguna influencia en la vida económica del pais y en los sucesos de Mayo de 1810.* Buenos Aires: Facultad de Ciencias Económicas, 1939.

Monsma, Karl M. "Ranchers, Rural People, and the State in Post-Colonial Argentina." Ph.D. diss., University of Michigan, 1992.

Monteagudo, Bernardo. *Escritos políticos.* Buenos Aires: L. J. Rossa, n.d.

Montoya, Alfredo J. *La ganadería y la industria de salazon de carnes en el período 1810–1862.* Buenos Aires: Editorial El Coloquio, 1971.

————. *Historia de los saladores argentinos.* Buenos Aires: Editorial Raigal, 1956.

Moreno, Mariano. *Escritos.* 2 vols. Buenos Aires: Ediciones Estrada, 1943.

————. *Escritos políticos y económicos.* Buenos Aires: Cultura Argentina, 1915.

Morgan, Edmund S. *Inventing the People: The Rise of Popular Sovereignty in England and America.* New York: W. W. Norton, 1988.

Moutoukias, Zacarías. *Contrabando y control colonial en el siglo XVII: Buenos Aires, el Atlántico y el espacio peruano.* Buenos Aires: CEAL, 1988.

————. "El crecimiento en una economía colonial del antiguo régimen: Reformismo y sector externo en el Río de la Plata (1760–1796)." *Arquivos do Centro Cultural Caluste Gulbenkian* 34 (1995): 771–813.

————. "Resaux personnels et autorité coloniale: Les négociants de Buenos Aires au XVIII siecle." *Annales, Economies, Sociétés, Civilisations* 4–5 (July–Oct. 1992): 889–915.

Murrin, John. "A Roof Without Walls: The Dilemma of American National

Identity." In Richard Beeman, Stephen Botein, and Edward C. Carter, II, eds., *Beyond Confederation: Origins of the Constitution and American National Identity*, pp. 333–48. Chapel Hill: University of North Carolina Press, 1987.

Myers, Jorge. *Orden y virtud: El discurso republicano en el régimen rosista*. Quilmes: Universidad Nacional de Quilmes, 1995.

———. "Revoluciones inacabadas: Hacia una noción de 'revolución' en el imaginario histórico de la nueva generación argentina: Alberdi y Echeverría, 1837–1850." In Noemí Goldman, ed., *Imagen y recepción de la Revolución Francesa en la Argentina*, pp. 247–63. Buenos Aires: Gel, 1990.

———. "Una genealogía para el parricidio: Juan María Gutiérrez y la construcción de una tradición literaria." *Entrepasados* 3:4–5 (fines 1993): 65–88.

Neal, Larry. *The Rise of Financial Capitalism: International Capital Markets in the Age of Reason*. Cambridge: Cambridge University Press, 1990.

Nedelsky, Jennifer. *Private Property and the Limits of American Constitutionalism: The Madisonian Framework and Its Legacy*. Chicago: University of Chicago Press, 1990.

Nettels, Curtis. "England and the Spanish-American Trade, 1680–1715." *Journal of Modern History* 3 (Mar. 1931): 1–31.

Nicolau, Juan Carlos. *Dorrego Gobernador: Economía y finanzas (1826–1827)*. Buenos Aires: Editorial Sadret, 1977.

———. *Industria argentina y aduana, 1835–1854*. Buenos Aires: Editorial Devenir, 1975.

———. "Movimiento marítimo exterior del puerto de Buenos Aires (1810–1854)." *Nuestra Historia* 12 (1973): 351–61.

———. *La reforma económico-financiera en la Provincia de Buenos Aires (1821–1825)*. Buenos Aires: Fundación del Banco de la Provincia de Buenos Aires, 1988.

———. *Rosas y García: La economía bonaerense (1829–1835)*. Buenos Aires: Editorial Sadret, 1980.

Nino, Carlos S. *Un país al margen de la ley*. Buenos Aires: Emecé, 1992.

North, Douglass C. *Institutions, Institutional Change and Economic Performance*. Cambridge: Cambridge University Press, 1990.

———. *Structure and Change in Economic History*. New York: Norton, 1981.

———. "A Theory of Institutional Change and the Economic History of the Western World." In Michael Hechter, ed., *The Microfoundations of Macrosociology*, pp. 190–215. Philadelphia: Temple University Press, 1983.

North, Douglass C., and Barry R. Weingast. "Constitutions and Commitment: The Evolution of Institutions Governing Public Choice in Seventeenth-Century England." *Journal of Economic History* 49:4 (Dec. 1989): 803–32.

Nussbaum, Arthur. *Money in the Law*. Chicago: Foundation Press, 1939.

O'Brien, Patrick K. "International Trade and the Development of the Third World Since the Industral Revolution." *Journal of World History* 8:1 (1997): 76–97.

———. "The Political Economy of British Taxation, 1660–1815." *Economic History Review* 41:1 (Feb. 1988): 1–32.

O'Phelan Godoy, Scarlett, and David Cahill. "Forging Their Own History: Indian Insurgency in the Southern Peruvian Sierra, 1815." *Bulletin of Latin American Research* 11:2 (May 1992): 127–67.

Oddone, Jacinto. *La burguesía terrateniente argentina.* 3rd ed. Buenos Aires: Ediciones Populares Argentinas, 1956.

Orgáz, Raúl. *Alberdi y el historicismo.* Córdoba: Imprenta Argentina, 1977.

Ornstein, Leopoldo R. "La Expedición Libertadora al Paraguay." In Levene, comp., *Historia,* vol. 5:2, pp. 189–211.

Ots Capdequí, J. M. *España en América: El régimen de tierras en la época colonial.* Mexico City: Fondo de Cultura Económica, 1959.

Padilla, Alberto. *La Constitución de Estados Unidos como precedente argentino.* Buenos Aires: Jesus Menendez, 1921.

———. *Lecciones sobre la Constitución.* Buenos Aires: Editorial Perrot, 1961.

Pagden, Anthony. "Identity Formation in Spanish America." In Nicholas Canny and Anthony Pagden, eds., *Colonial Identity in the Atlantic World, 1500–1800,* pp. 51–93. Princeton: Princeton University Press, 1987.

———. *Lords of All the World: Ideologies of Empire in Spain, Britain and France, c. 1500–c. 1800.* New Haven: Yale University Press, 1995.

———. *Spanish Imperialism and the Political Imagination: Studies in European and Spanish-American Social and Political Theory, 1513–1830.* New Haven: Yale University Press, 1990.

Palcos, Alberto. "Prólogo." In Esteban Echeverría, *Dogma Socialista.* Edición de Alberto Placos, pp. vii–xcvi. La Plata: Universidad Nacional de La Plata, 1940.

———. *Rivadavia: Ejecutor del pensamiento de Mayo.* 2 vols. La Plata: Universidad Nacional de la Plata, 1960.

Palmer, R. R. *The Age of Democratic Revolution: A Political History of Europe and America, 1760–1800.* 2 vols. Princeton: Princeton University Press, 1959.

Parish, Woodbine. *Buenos Ayres and the Provinces of the Rio de la Plata: From Their Discovery and Conquest by the Spanish to the Establishment of Their Political Independence.* 2nd ed. London: J. Murray, 1852.

Parker, David. "Sovereignty, Absolutism and the Function of the Law in Seventeenth-Century France." *Past and Present* 122 (Feb. 1989): 36–74.

Parry, J. H. *The Spanish Seaborn Empire.* Los Angeles: University of California Press, 1990.

Pasqualí, Patricia S. "La expansión artiguista, 1813–1815." *Res Gesta* 22 (July–Dec. 1987): 149–72.

Pastore, Mario. "Trade Contraction and Economic Decline: The Paraguayan Economy Under Francia, 1810–1840." *Journal of Latin American Studies* 26:3 (Oct. 1994): 539–96.

Peña, Milciades. *El paraíso terrateniente.* Buenos Aires: Ediciones Fichas, 1969.

Peña, Roberto I. "Los derechos naturales del hombre en la ideología del siglo XVIII rioplatense." *Cuadernos de historia* 2 (1992): 11–31.

Pestalardo, Agustín. *Historia de la enseñanza de las ciencias jurídicas y sociales en la Universidad de Buenos Aires.* Buenos Aires: Imprenra Alsina, 1914.

Piccirilli, Ricardo. *Rivadavia y su tiempo.* 2 vols. Buenos Aires: Peuser, 1943.

Piglia, Ricardo. "Sarmiento the Writer." In Tulio Halperín Donghi, Iván Jaksic, Gwen Kirkpatrick, and Francine Masiello, eds., *Sarmiento: Author of a Nation*, pp. 127–44. Berkeley: University of California Press, 1994.

Pirenne, Henri. *Economic and Social History of Medieval Europe*. New York: Harcourt Brace, 1937.

Pocock, J. G. A. *The Machiavellian Moment: Florentine Political Thought and the Atlantic Republic Tradition*. Princeton: Princeton University Press, 1975.

———. *Virtue, Commerce, and History: Essays on Political Thought and History, Chiefly in the Eighteenth Century*. Cambridge: Cambridge University Press, 1985.

Polanyi, Karl. *The Great Transformation: The Political and Economic Origins of Our Time*. Boston: Beacon Press, 1957.

Posadas, Gervasio Antonio. "Autobiografía." In *Biblioteca de Mayo*, vol. 2, pp. 1410–60. Buenos Aires: Senado de la Nación, 1960.

Prebisch, Raúl. "Anotaciones sobre nuestro medio circulante." *Revista de Ciencias Económicas* 9:3 (Oct. 1921): 190–205.

———. "Desde el primer Banco Nacional hasta la crisis de la Oficina de cambios." *Revista de Ciencias Económicas* 9:4 (Nov. 1921): 283–307.

Province of Buenos Aires. *Informe de la Comisión de Cuentas año de 1856*. Buenos Aires: n.p., 1858.

———. *Memoria sobre la organización de la Oficina de Crédito Público de la Provincia de Buenos Aires*. Buenos Aires: n.p., 1882.

Przeworski, Adam. *Capitalism and Social Democracy*. Cambridge: Cambridge University Press, 1985.

———. *Democracy and the Market: Political and Economic Reforms in Eastern Europe and Latin America*. New York: Cambridge University Press, 1991.

Punta, Ana Inés. "Los intercambios comerciales de Córdoba con el puerto de Buenos Aires en la segunda mitad del siglo XVIII." *Anuario del IEHS* 9 (1994): 35–60.

Quintero Ramos, Angel M. *A History of Money and Banking in Argentina*. Rio Piedras: University of Puerto Rico, 1965.

Quiroga de la Rosa, Manuel. *Tesis sobre la naturaleza filosófica del derecho*. Buenos Aires: n.p., 1837.

Ragin, Charles C. *The Comparative Method: Moving Beyond Qualitative and Quantitative Strategies*. Berkeley: University of California Press, 1987.

Rama, Angel. *The Lettered City*. Durham: Duke University Press, 1996.

Ratto, Silvia. "Conflictos y armonias en la frontera bonaerense, 1834–1840." *Entrepasados* 6:11 (fines 1996): 21–34.

Ravignani, Emilio. "El Congreso Nacional de 1824–1827." In Levene, comp., *Historia*, vol. 7, pp. 18–27.

———. "El Congreso Nacional de 1824–1827, la Convención Nacional de 1828–1829. Incontitución y régimen de pactos." In Levene, comp., *Historia*, vol. 7, pp. 185–94.

———. "Las finanzas argentinas desde 1810 á 1829." Ph.D. diss., Universidad de Buenos Aires, 1911.

———. *Historia constitucional de la República Argentina*, vol. 1. Buenos Aires: n.p., 1930.

———. "El Virreinato del Río de la Plata (1776–1810)." In Levene, comp., *Historia*, vol. 4, pp. 11–189.

————, ed. *Asambleas constituyentes argentinas seguidas de los textos constitucionales legislativos y pactos interprovinciales que organizaron políticamente la Nación.* 7 vols. Buenos Aires: Facultad de Filosofía y Letras, 1937.

Ravignani, Emilio, and Humberto Mandelli. "La gestión económico-financiera de la Liga del Norte contra Rosas." *Boletín del Instituto de Historia Argentina y Americana* 25 (1941): 192–202.

Reber, Vera Blinn. *British Mercantile Houses in Buenos Aires, 1810–1880.* Cambridge, Mass.: Harvard University Press, 1979.

Reddy, William R. *Money and Liberty in Modern Europe.* New York: Cambridge University Press, 1987.

Reeder, John. "Economía e ilustración en España: Traducciones y traductores, 1717–1800." *Moneda y Crédito* 147 (Dec. 1978): 47–70.

Regalsky, Andrés. "Banking, Trade and the Rise of Capitalism in Argentina, 1850–1930." In Alice Teichova, Ginette Kurgan–van Hentenryk and Dieter Zeigler, eds., *Banking, Trade and Industry: Europe, America and Asia from the Thirteenth to the Twentieth Century,* pp. 359–77. Cambridge: Cambridge University Press, 1997.

Rene-Moreno, Gabriel. *Ultimos días coloniales en el Alto Perú.* La Paz: Editorial Juventud, 1970.

Riesman, Janet A. "Money, Credit, and Federalist Political Economy." In Richard Beeman, Stephen Botein, and Edward C. Carter, II, eds., *Beyond Confederation: Origins of the Constitution and American National Identity,* pp. 128–61. Chapel Hill: University of North Carolina Press, 1987.

Rípodas Ardanaz, Daisy. "La biblioteca de Mariano Izquierdo." *Revista de Historia del Derecho* 12 (1984): 303–36.

————. *La biblioteca porteña del Obispo Azamor y Ramirez, 1788–1796.* Buenos Aires: CONICET, 1994.

————. *Bibliotecas privadas de funcionarios de la real Audiencia de Charcas.* Caracas: Academia Nacional de Historia, 1975.

Rivarola, Rodolfo. "Del régimen federativo al unitario." In Rivarola, *Ensayos Historicos.* Buenos Aires: Ed. Coni, 1941 [1908].

Rivera, Andrés. *La revolución es un sueño eterno.* Buenos Aires: Alfaguara, 1993.

Robertson, J. P., and W. P. Robertson. *Letters on South America; comprising Travels on the Banks of the Paraná and Rio de la Plata.* London: J. Murray, 1843.

Rock, David. *Argentina, 1516–1984.* Berkeley: University of California Press, 1985.

Rodríguez, Martín. "Memoria autobiográfica." In *Biblioteca de Mayo,* vol. 2, pp. 1507–20.

Rogers, James Steven. *The Early History of the Law of Bills and Notes: A Study of the Origins of Anglo-American Commercial Law.* Cambridge: Cambridge University Press, 1995.

Romano, Silvia. "Finanzas públicas de la provincia de Córdoba, 1830–1855." *Boletín del Instituto de Historia Argentina y Americana 'Dr. Emilio Ravignani.'* 6 (2nd sem. 1992): 99–147.

Romero Cabrera, Liliana Betty. *José Miguel de Tagle: Un comerciante americano de los siglos XVIII y XIX.* Córdoba: Universidad Nacional de Córdoba, 1973.

Romero, José Luis. *A History of Argentine Political Thought*. Stanford: Stanford University Press, 1963.

Root, Hilton. *The Foundations of Privilege: Political Foundations of Markets in Old Regime France and England*. Berkeley: University of California Press, 1994.

Roover, Raymond de. *Business, Banking and Economic Thought in Late Medieval and Early Modern Europe*. Chicago: University of Chicago Press, 1974.

Rosa, José María. *La Reforma Monetaria en la República Argentina*. Buenos Aires: n.p., 1909.

Rose, Carol M. *Property and Persuasion: Essays on the History, Theory and Rhetoric of Ownership*. Boulder, Colo.: Westview, 1994.

Rottjer, Enrique. "La Guerra del Brasil: Las operaciones terrestres." In Levene, comp., *Historia*, vol. 7, pp. 209–35.

Roxborough, Ian. "Unity and Diversity in Latin American History." *Journal of Latin American History* 16:1 (May, 1984): 1–26.

Ruíz Moreno, Isidoro J. *La lucha por la Constitución (1820–1853)*. Buenos Aires: Editorial Astrea, 1976.

Ryan, Alan. *Property and Political Theory*. Oxford: Blackwell, 1984.

Sabato, Hilda. *Agrarian Capitalism and the World Market: Buenos Aires in the Pastoral Age, 1840–1890*. Albuquerque: University of New Mexico Press, 1990.

———. "Citizenship, Political Participation and the Formation of the Public Sphere in Buenos Aires, 1850s–1880s." *Past and Present* 136 (Aug. 1992): 139–63.

Sabato, Hilda, and Elías Palti. "¿Quién votaba en Buenos Aires? Práctica y teoría del sufragio, 1850–1880." *Desarrollo Económico* 119:30 (Oct.–Dec. 1990): 395–424.

Sabato, Hilda, and Luis Alberto Romero. *Los trabajadores de Buenos Aires: La experiencia del mercado, 1850–1880*. Buenos Aires: Sudamericana, 1992.

Sábato, Jorge. *La clase dominante en la argentina moderna: Formación y características*. Buenos Aires: Gel, 1988.

Sabor, Josefa Emilia. *Pedro de Angelis y los orígenes de la bibliografía argentina*. Buenos Aires: Solar-Hachette, 1995.

Saguier, Eduardo R. "El mercado del cuero y su rol como fuente alternativa de empleo." *Revista de Historia Económica* 9:1 (Winter 1991): 103–26.

Sahlins, Marshall. *Islands of History*. Chicago: University of Chicago Press, 1985.

Sala de Touron, Lucía, Nelson de la Torre, and Julio C. Rodríguez. *Artigas y su revolución agraria, 1811–1820*. México: Siglo XXI, 1978.

———. *Estructura económico-social de la colonia*. Montevideo: Ediciones Pueblos Unidos, 1967.

Saldías, Adolfo. *Como surgió Urquiza*. Buenos Aires: Plus Ultra, 1973.

———. *Historia de la Confederación Argentina*. 3 vols. Buenos Aires: Ediciones Clio, 1975.

———. *Por qué se produjo el bloqueo anglofrancés*. Buenos Aires: Plus Ultra, 1974.

Salvatore, Ricardo. "The Breakdown of Social Discipline in the Banda Oriental and the Littoral, 1790–1820." In Mark D. Szuchman and Jonathan C. Brown, eds., *Revolution and Restoration: The Rearrangement of Power in Argentina, 1776–1860*, pp. 74–102. Lincoln: University of Nebraska Press, 1994.

———. "Fiestas federales: Representaciones de la república en el Buenos Aires rosista." *Entrepasados* 6:11 (fines 1996): 45–68.

Sampay, Arturo Enrique. *Las ideas políticas de Juan Manuel Rosas*. Buenos Aires: Juárez Ediciones, 1972.

———, comp. *Las constituciones de la Argentina (1810/1872)*. Buenos Aires: Eudeba, 1975.

Sánchez Albornoz, Nicolás. "Extracción de mulas de Jujuy al Perú." *Estudios de Historia Social* 1 (1965): 107–20.

———. "La saca de mulas de Salta al Perú, 1778–1809." *Anuario del Instituto de Investigaciones Históricas* 8 (1965): 261–312.

Santos Muñoz, Pablo. *Años de lucha (1841–1845): Urquiza y la política del litoral rioplatense*. Buenos Aires: Ediciones Cabargón, 1973.

Sarlo Sabajanes, Beatriz. *Juan María Gutiérrez: Historiador y crítico de nuestra literatura*. Buenos Aires: Editorial Escuela, 1967.

Sarmiento, Domingo F. *Argirópolis*. Buenos Aires: Editorial Tor, 1938.

———. *Campaña en el Ejercito Grande*. Buenos Aires: Eudeba, 1962.

———. *Las ciento y una*. Buenos Aires: Cultura Argentina, 1916.

———. *Comentarios de la Constitución de la Confederación Argentina*. Santiago de Chile: Belin, 1853.

———. *Life in the Argentine Republic in the Days of the Tyrants, or Civilization and Barbarism*. New York: Hafner, 1971.

———. *Obras completas*. 53 vols. Buenos Aires: La Facultad, 1913.

———. *El Pacto de San Nicolás*. Valparaíso: n.p., 1852.

Sarratea, Mariano E. de. *Observaciones con motivo de los artículos suscritos por J.B.A. en El Mercurio de Valparaiso*. Buenos Aires: n.p. 1854.

Sarría, Gustavo. "Las asambleas constituyentes argentinas y los antecedentes del derecho constitucional anglo-norteamericano, 1818–1860." *Cuadernos de Historia* 2 (1992): 95–100.

Sastre, Marcos. "Inauguración." In *Antecedentes de la Asociación de Mayo, 1837–1937: Homenaje Consejo Deliberante de la Ciudad de Buenos Aires en el centenario de su fundación*. Buenos Aires: Consejo Deliberante, 1939.

Sazbón, José. "La representación de la historia en *Facundo*." *16 Anuario: Segunda Epoca* (Rosario, 1993–94): 32–42.

Scobie, James. *La lucha para la consolidación de la nacionalidad argentina, 1852–1862*. Buenos Aires: Solar-Hachette, 1964.

———. "Monetary Development in Argentina, 1852–1865." *Inter-American Economic Affairs* 8:2 (Autumn 1954): 54–83.

Sebreli, Juan José. *La saga de los Anchorena*. Buenos Aires: Sudamericana, 1985.

Seckinger, Ron. *The Brazilian Monarchy and the South American Republics, 1822–1831*. Baton Rouge: Lousiana State University Press, 1984.

Segreti, Carlos. *Moneda y política en la primera mitad del siglo XIX*. Tucumán: Fundación Banco Comercial del Norte, 1975.

Serulnikov, Sergio. "Disputed Images of Colonialism: Spanish Rule and Indian Subversion in Northen Potosí, 1777–1780." *Hispanic American Historical Review* 76:2 (May 1996): 189–226.

Sewell, Jr., William H. *A Rhetoric of Bourgeois Revolution: The Abbé Sieyes and "What Is the Third Estate?"* Durham: Duke University Press, 1994.

————. *Work and Revolution in France: The Language of Labour from the Old Regime to 1848.* Cambridge: Cambridge University Press, 1980.

Shumway, Nicolas. *The Invention of Argentina.* Berkeley: University of California Press, 1991.

Sklar, Martin. *The Corporate Reconstruction of American Capitalism, 1890–1916.* Cambridge: Cambridge University Press, 1988.

Smith, Adam. *An Inquiry into the Nature and Causes of the Wealth of Nations.* Chicago: University of Chicago Press, 1976 [1776].

Smith, Robert Sidney. *The Spanish Guild Merchant: A History of the Consulado, 1520–1700.* Durham: Duke University Press, 1940.

Smith, Roger. "Political Jurisprudence: The 'New Institutionalism' and the Future of Public Law." *American Poltical Science Review* 82:1 (Mar. 1988): 84–108.

Smith, Rogers M. *Liberalism and American Constitutional Law.* Cambridge, Mass.: Harvard University Press, 1990.

Socolow, Susan Migden. *The Bureaucrats of Buenos Aires, 1769–1810: Amor al Real Servicio.* Durham: Duke University Press, 1987.

————. "Marriage, Birth, and Inheritance: The Merchants of Eighteenth-Century Buenos Aires." *Hispanic American Historical Review* 60:3 (Aug. 1980): 388–405.

————. *The Merchants of Buenos Aires, 1778–1810: Family and Commerce.* Cambridge: Cambridge University Press, 1978.

Somers, Mararet R. "The 'Misteries' of Property: Relationality, Rural-Industrialization, and Community in Chartist Narratives of Political Rights." In John Brewer and Susan Staves, eds., *Early Modern Conceptions of Property*, pp. 62–92. London, New York: Routledge, 1996.

Sommer, Doris. *Foundational Fictions: The National Romances of Latin America.* Berkeley: University of California Press, 1991.

Spalding, Karen. "Hacienda-Village Relations in Andean Society to 1830." *Latin American Perspectives* 11:1 (Spring 1975): 107–21.

Stedman-Jones, Gareth. "Society and Politics at the Beginning of the World Economy." *Cambridge Journal of Economics* 1 (Mar. 1977): 77–92.

Stein, Stanley J. "'Un raudal de oro y plata que corría sin cesar de España a Francia': Política mercantil española y el comercio con Francia en la época de Carlos III." *Actas del Congreso Internacional sobre Carlos III y la Ilustración.* 3 vols. Madrid: Ministerio de Cultura, 1989.

Stein, Stanley J., and Barbara H. Stein. *The Colonial Heritage of Latin America: Economic Dependence in Historical Perspective.* New York: Oxford University Press, 1970.

————. "Concepts and Realities of Spanish Economic Growth, 1759–1789." *Historia Ibéria* 1 (1972): 103–19.

Stern, Steve J. "The Variety and Ambiguity of Native American Intervention in European Colonial Markets." In Brooke Larson and Olivia Harris, eds., *Ethnicity, Markets, and Migration in the Andes: At the Crossroads of History and Anthropology*, pp. 73–100. Durham: Duke University Press, 1995.

Stigler, George J. "Law or Economics?" *Journal of Law and Economics* 30:2 (Oct. 1992): 455–68.

Stoetzer, Carlos O. "Raices intelectuales de la Constitución Argentina de 1853." *Jahrbuch fur Geschichte vin Staat, Wirtschaft und Gesellschaft Latinamerikas* 22 (1985): 295–339.

Stone, Lawrence. "Introduction." In Lawrence Stone, ed., *An Imperial State at War: Britain from 1689–1815*, pp. 1–20. London: Routledge, 1994.

Street, John. *Artigas and the Emancipation of Uruguay*. Cambridge: Cambridge University Press, 1959.

————. *Gran Bretaña y la independencia del Río de la Plata*. Buenos Aires: Paidós, 1967.

————. "Lord Strangford and the Río de la Plata." *Hispanic American Historical Review* 33:4 (Nov. 1954): 479–510.

Sushka, Marie Elizabeth, and Brian W. Barrett. "Banking Structure and the National Capital Market, 1869–1914." *Journal of Economic History* 44:2 (June 1984): 463–77.

Swanson, Donald, and Andrew Trout. "Alexander Hamilton, Conversion and Debt Reduction." *Explorations in Economic History* 29:4 (Oct. 1992): 417–92.

Szuchman, Mark D. *Order, Family and Community in Buenos Aires, 1810–1860*. Stanford: Stanford University Press, 1988.

Tandeter, Enrique. *Coercion and Market: Silver Mining in Colonial Potosí, 1692–1826*. Albuquerque: University of New Mexico Press, 1993.

————. "Crisis in Upper Peru, 1800–1805." *Hispanic American Historical Review* 71:1 (Feb. 1991): 35–71.

————. "Forced and Free Labor in Late Colonial Potosí." *Past and Present* 93 (Nov. 1981): 98–136.

Tandeter, Enrique, Vilma Milletich, and Robert Schmit. "Flujos mercantiles en el Potosí colonial tardío." *Anuario del IEHS* 9 (1994): 97–126.

Tau Anzoátegui, Victor. *Causismo y sistema: Indagación histórica sobre el espíritu del Derecho Indiano*. Buenos Aires: Instituto de Investigaciones de Historia del Derecho, 1992.

————. *La codificación en la argentina (1810–1870)*. Buenos Aires: Facultad de Derecho y Ciencias Sociales, 1977.

————. "La costumbre en el derecho argentino del siglo XIX." *Revista de Historia del Derecho* 4 (1976): 231–303.

————. *Formación del estado federal argentino (1820–1852)*. Buenos Aires: Editorial Perrot, 1965.

————. *Las ideas jurídicas en la argentina (siglos XIX–XX)*. Buenos Aires: Editorial Perrot, 1987.

————. "Los orígenes de la jurisprudencia de los Tribunales en la Argentina." *Revista de Historia del Derecho* 6 (1978): 324–29.

Tau Anzoátegui, Victor, and Eduardo Martire. *Manual de historia de la instituciones argentinas*. Buenos Aires: La Ley, 1981.

TePaske, John J. "The Fiscal Structure of Upper Peru and the Financing of Empire." In Karen Spalding, ed., *Essays in the Political, Economic and Social History of Colonial Latin America*, pp. 69–83. Newark: University of Delaware Latin American Studies Program, 1982.

———. "New World Silver, Castile and the Philippines, 1590–1800." In J. F. Richards, ed., *Precious Metals in the Later Medieval and Early Modern Worlds*, pp. 425–45. Durham: Carolina Academic Press, 1983.

———. "Spanish America." *The International History Review* 6:4 (Nov. 1984): 511–18.

Ternavasio, Marcela. "Nuevo régimen representativo y expansión de la frontera política: Las elecciones en el estado de Buenos Aires, 1820–1840." In Antonio Annino, ed., *Historia de las elecciones en Iberamérica, siglo XIX: De la formación del espacio político nacional*, pp. 65–105. Buenos Aires: Fondo de Cultura Económica, 1995.

Thelan, Kathleen, and Sven Steinmo. "Historical Institutionalism in Comparative Politics." In Sven Steinmo, Kathleen Thelan, and Frank Longstreth, eds., *Structuring Politics: Historical Institutionalism in Comparative Analysis*, pp. 1–32. Cambridge: Cambridge University Press, 1992.

Thompson, I. A. A. "The Rule of Law in Early Modern Castile." *European History Quarterly* 15:2 (Apr. 1984): 221–34.

Tilly, Charles. *European Revolutions, 1492–1992*. Oxford: Blackwell, 1993.

———. *From Mobilization to Revolution*. Reading, Mass.: Addison-Wesley, 1978.

———. "War Making and State Making as Organized Crime." In Peter B. Evans, Dietrich Rueschemeyer, and Theda Skocpol, eds., *Bringing the State Back In*, pp. 169–91. Cambridge: Cambridge University Press, 1985.

Tjarks, Germán O. E. *El Consulado de Buenos Aires y sus proyecciones en la historia del Río de la Plata*. 2 vols. Buenos Aires: Facultad de Filosofía y Letras, 1962.

———. "Panorama del comercio interno del virreinato del Río de la Plata en sus postrimerías." *Humanidades* 36 (1960): 15–72.

Tjarks, Germán O. E., and Alicia Vidaurreta de Tjarks. *El comercio ingles y el contrabando: Nuevos aspectos en el estudio económica en el Río de la Plata (1807–1810)*. Buenos Aires: n.p., 1962.

Tocqueville, Alexis de. *Democracy in America*. 2 vols. New York: Random House, 1945.

Treves, Renato. "Vico y Alberdi: Notas para la historia de la filosofía jurídica en la Argentina." In *Vico y Herder: Ensayos conmemorativos*. Buenos Aires: Facultad de Filosofía y Letras, 1948.

Trueba, Eduardo. "La jurisdicción marítima en la carrera de Indias durante el siglo XVI." *Anuario de Estudios Americanos* 39 (1982): 93–131.

Unger, Roberto Mangabeira. *The Critical Legal Studies Movement*. Cambridge, Mass.: Harvard University Press, 1983.

———. *What Should Legal Analysis Become?* London: Verso, 1996.

Van Caenegem, R. C. *An Historical Introduction to Private Law*. Cambridge: Cambridge University Press, 1992.

Vandervelde, Kenneth J. "The New Property of the Nineteenth Century: The Development of the Modern Concept of Property." *Buffalo Law Review* 29 (1980): 325–67.

Van Kleffens, E. N. *Hispanic Laws Until the End of the Middle Ages*. Edinburgh: University of Edinburgh Press, 1968.

Vásquez, Aníbal S. *Causas económicas del pronunciamiento de Urquiza contra Rosas*. Paraná: Editorial Nueva Impresora, 1956.

Veitch, John M. "Repudiations and Confiscations by the Medieval State." *Journal of Economic History* 46:1 (Mar. 1986): 31–36.

Vélez Sarsfield, Dalmacio. *Dictamenes en la asesoria del Gobierno del Estado de Buenos Aires*. Buenos Aires: Facultad de Derecho y Ciencias Sociales, 1982.

———. *Escritos jurídicos*. Buenos Aires: Abeledo-Perrot, 1971.

Véliz, Claudio. *The New World of the Gothic Fox: Culture and Economy in English and Spanish America*. Berkeley: University of California Press, 1994.

Venturi, Franco. *Italy and the Enlightenment*. London: Longman, 1972.

Vieytes, Juan Hipólito. *Antecedentes económicos de la revolución de Mayo*. Buenos Aires: Editorial Raigal, 1956.

Vilar, Pierre. *A History of Gold and Money*. London: Verso, 1976.

Villaba, Victorián de. "Apuntes para una reforma de España, sin trastorno del Gobierno Monarquico ni la Religión" (1797). In Ricardo Levene, *V˙ ˹ y escritos de Victorián de Villava*. Buenos Aires: Facultad de Filosofía ⌐etras: lxxix–cxx.

Villalobos, Sergio R. *Comercio y contrabando en el Río de la Plata y Chile*. Buenos Aires: Eudeba, 1986.

Viner, Jacob. "Power Versus Plenty as Objectives of Foreign Policy in the Seventeenth and Eighteenth Centuries." In D. C. Coleman, ed., *Revisions in Mercantilism*, pp. 61–91. London: Methuen, 1964.

Waldron, Jeremy. *The Right to Private Property*. Oxford: Clarendon Press, 1988.

Walker, Geoffrey J. *Spanish Politics and Imperial Trade, 1700–1789*. Bloomington: Indiana University Press, 1979.

Watson, Alan. *Sources of Law, Legal Change, Ambiguity*. Philadelphia: University of Pennsylvania Press, 1985.

Webster, C. K., ed. *Britain and the Independence of Latin America, 1812–1830: Select Documents from the Foreign Office Archives*. Oxford: Oxford University Press, 1938.

Weinberg, Félix. "Introducción." In Weinberg, ed., *El Salón Literario de 1837*, pp. 9–114. Buenos Aires: Hachette, 1977.

Weiss, Ignacio. *Los antecedentes europeos de Pedro de Angelis*. Buenos Aires: El Ateneo, 1944.

———. "Pedro de Angelis y la difusión de la obra de Juan Bautista Vico." In *Vico y Herder: Ensayos conmemorativos*. Buenos Aires: Facultad de Filosofía y Letras, 1948.

Whigham, Thomas. "Cattle Raising in the Argentine Northwest: Corrientes, c. 1750–1870." *Journal of Latin American Studies* 20:2 (Nov. 1988): 313–34.

———. *The Politics of River Trade: Tradition and Development in the Upper Plata, 1780–1870*. Albuquerque: University of New Mexico Press, 1991.

―――. "Trade and Conflict on the Rivers: Corrientes, 1780–1840." In Mark D. Szuchman and Jonathan C. Brown, eds., *Revolution and Restoration: The Rearrangement of Power in Argentina, 1776–1860*, pp. 150–76. Lincoln: University of Nebraska Press, 1994.

White, Eugene Nelson. "The Political Economy of Banking Regulation, 1864–1933." *Journal of Economic History* 42:1 (Mar. 1982): 33–40.

Whitman, James Q. *The Legacy of Roman Law in the German Romantic Era*. Princeton: Princeton University Press, 1990.

Williams, Judith B. "The Establishment of British Commerce with Argentina." *Hispanic American Historical Review* 15:1 (Feb. 1934): 43–64.

Williamson, Oliver E. *The Economic Institutions of Capitalism: Firms, Markets, Relational Contracting*. New York: The Free Press, 1985.

Williford, Miriam. *Jeremy Bentham on Spanish America*. Baton Rouge: Louisiana State University Press, 1980.

Wolf, Eric R., and Edward C. Hansen. "*Caudillo* Politics: A Structural Analysis." *Comparative Studies in Society and History* 9:2 (Jan. 1967): 168–79.

Wolin, Sheldon S. *The Presence of the Past: Essays on the State and the Constitution*. Baltimore: The Johns Hopkins University Press, 1989.

Wood, Gordon S. *The Creation of the American Republic, 1776–1787*. New York: W. W. Norton, 1972.

Wortman, Richard S. *The Development of Russian Legal Consciousness*. Chicago: University of Chicago Press, 1976.

Zaefferer de Goyeneche, Ana. *La navegación mercante en el Río de la Plata*. Buenos Aires: Emecé, 1987.

Zelizer, Viviana. "Making Multiple Moneys." In Richard Swedberg, ed., *Explorations in Economic Sociology*, pp. 193–212. New York: Russell Sage Foundation, 1993.

―――. *The Social Meaning of Money*. New York: Basic Books, 1994.

Zorraquín Becú, Ricardo. *La organización judicial argentina en el período hispánico*. Buenos Aires: Editorial Perrot, 1981.

Zorrilla, Rubén H. "Estructura social y caudillismo en la Argentina (1810–1870)." *Nova Americana* 2 (1979): 135–67.

Index

In this index an "f" after a number indicates a separate reference on the next page, and an "ff" indicates separate references on the next two pages. A continuous discussion over two or more pages is indicated by a span of page numbers, e.g., "57–59." *Passim* is used for a cluster of references in close but not consecutive sequence.

12, 215–16, 221–22; colonial, 47–48;
104–5; and state, 54–55; agrarian, 58–
60, 64–65, 69–70; market-driven, 121,
289; of hinterlands, 126–27. *See also*
Finance, financing
Education: legal, 167–68
Elections, 80, 82, 115–17, 290
Elío, Francisco, 79, 85, 87
Elites, 7, 21, 39, 82, 116–17, 128f, 292
Enfiteusis, 100
Enfranchisement, 204–5
Enlightenment, 50–51, 62f, 68, 71f,
301n1; and Buenos Aires, 52–53; and
Spain, 53–54; Neapolitan, 55–56;
monarchy and, 56–57; freedom and,
81–82; revolution and, 284f
Ensenada, Marquis of, 23
Entre Ríos, 87f, 91, 120, 127, 133, 188,
282
Esperon, Santiago, 1
Estates, *estancieros*, 35–40 *passim*, 232;
building of, 128–29; fragmentation
of, 129–30
Esteves Saguí, Miguel, 240
Europe, 260, 263, 272
Evolución de las ideas argentinas, La (In-
genieros), 50
Exchange rate: stabilizing, 259–60
Exchange standard, 270–71
Exile, 181, 185
Export economy, 2, 44–45, 122ff

Facio, Domingo, 242
Facundo (Sarmiento), 185ff, 213
Famatina, 101
Families, 39, 131
Federales, 174, 182
Federalism, federalists, 11, 87f, 111,
127, 139, 202, 207, 220, 304–5n42,
306n77, 319n32; riparian, 120, 125,
132–35 *passim*; Sarmiento on, 187f
Federalists, U.S., 106
Federal League, 88
Federal Pact (1831), 207
Ferdinand, 23
Ferdinand VII, 77, 84
Ferré, Pedro, 118, 127
Figueredo, Santiago, 167
Filangeri, Gaetano, 55
Finance, financing, 12, 283, 308n9;
revolution, 93–95; public, 99–101;

state, 101–3; liquidity of, 102–4; warfare, 112, 267–68; interior, 126–27;
under Rosas, 135–39; of merchants,
228–29; ministries of, 239–40; government, 258–67 *passim*, 328n83; reform of, 265–66, 270–71; stabilization
of, 269–75; Confederation, 276–77
Finance Ministry, 275
First Junta: organization of, 81, 83; battles of, 84–85; factionalism in, 88–89
First Triumvirate, 89f
Fiscal system: Bourbon reforms and,
25–27; post-colonial, 91–92; trade
goods and, 92–93, 96; militias and,
93–94
Flores, Venancio, General, 272
Foodstuffs, 31f
Ford, Guillermo, 152
Foro, El (newspaper), 245
*Fragmento preliminar al estudio del dere-
cho* (Alberdi), 179–80
Fragueiro, Antonio, 269
Fragueiro, Mariano, 197, 218, 234, 237,
250–51; *Cuestiones argentinas*, 236;
Organización del crédito, 236, 312n76;
government finance and, 262–63
France, 22, 124f, 146, 170, 172; trade
goods, 28–29; war with, 40, 168; and
revolutions, 52–53; and Spain, 75–79
passim; and Littoral wars, 133–38 *pas-
sim*
Freedom, 62, 81–82
Freeholds, 128–29
Free trade, 30–31, 54–55, 59, 111, 281;
Buenos Aires and, 121–23, 224
French Restoration, 175
French Revolution, 79–80
Frontier, 34–35, 127–29, 130
Fuerte Azul, 129

Gaceta Mercantil (newspaper), 117, 196
Gache, Mariano, 231
Galiani, Ferdinando, 55
Gálvez, José de, 30, 50, 61
García, Manuel José, 92, 100, 102
Gari, Paulino, 167
Garibaldi, Guiseppe, 135
Gauchos, 66, 186
General Administration of Finance and
Credit, 263
Generation of 1837, 167, 172

Library of Congress Cataloging-in-Publication Data

Adelman, Jeremy
    Republic of capital : Buenos Aires and the legal
transformation of the Atlantic world / Jeremy Adelman.
        p.   cm.
    Includes bibliographical references and index.
    ISBN 0-8047-3379-1 (cloth : alk. paper)
    1. Buenos Aires (Argentina)—Economic conditions—
19th century.   2. Buenos Aires (Argentina)—Commerce—
History—19th century.   3. Property—Argentina—History—
19th century.   4. Constitutional history—Argentina.
5. Argentina—Politics and government—1776–1810.
6. Argentina—Politics and government—1810–1817.
7. Argentina—Politics and government—1817–1860.
I. Title.
HC178.B9A34   1999
320.982'12—dc21   98-48249
                                                              CIP

This book is printed on acid-free, recycled paper.

Original printing 1999
Last figure below indicates year of this printing:
08   07   06   05   04   03   02   01   00   99